LORDS OF THE SALT ROAD

OSPREY
PUBLISHING

To the people of Orkney and Shetland,
the heart of the old Norse earldom.

ANGUS KONSTAM

LORDS OF THE SALT ROAD

THE NORSE EARLS OF ORKNEY AND THE VIKING WORLD

OSPREY PUBLISHING
Bloomsbury Publishing Plc
Kemp House, Chawley Park, Cumnor Hill, Oxford OX2 9PH, UK
Bloomsbury Publishing Ireland Limited,
29 Earlsfort Terrace, Dublin 2, D02 AY28, Ireland
Bloomsbury Publishing Inc.
1359 Broadway, 12th Floor, New York, NY 10018, USA
E-mail: info@ospreypublishing.com
www.ospreypublishing.com

OSPREY is a trademark of Osprey Publishing Ltd

First published in Great Britain in 2026

A catalogue record for this book is available from the British Library.

ISBN: HB 9781472874733; eBook 9781472874757; ePDF 9781472874702;
XML 9781472874719; Audio 9781472874726

26 27 28 29 30   10 9 8 7 6 5 4 3 2 1

Plate section image credits and captions are given in full in the
List of Illustrations and Maps (pp. 7–9).

Divider: Whalebone plaque. (MichaelMaggs, Wikimedia Commons, CC BY-SA 4.0,
https://creativecommons.org/licenses/by-sa/4.0)

Acknowledgements: Dragon carving by Nigel Konstam. (Author's collection)

Maps by www.bounford.com
Index by Fionbar Lyons
Typeset by Lumina Datamatics Ltd
Printed and bound in Great Britain by Clays Ltd, Elcograf S.p.A.

Osprey Publishing supports the Woodland Trust, the UK's leading woodland conservation charity.

To find out more about our authors and books visit www.ospreypublishing.com.
Here you will find extracts, author interviews, details of forthcoming events and the
option to sign up for our newsletter.

For product safety related questions contact productsafety@bloomsbury.com

CONTENTS

LIST OF ILLUSTRATIONS AND MAPS

PLATE SECTION ILLUSTRATIONS

The *Sea Stallion*, a Danish-built replica longship, pictured while visiting Orkney on its maiden voyage to Dublin in 2007. It is based on the mid-11th-century 'Skudelev 2' wreck, whose remains are displayed at Roskilde, Denmark – *Sea Stallion*'s home port. (© Charles Tait)

Duncansby Head marked the north-east corner of Caithness. Beyond the lighthouse is the often treacherous Pentland Firth, with the southern coast of Orkney visible just over six miles to the north. (© Charles Tait)

The Dornoch Firth and the River Oykel which ran eastwards from it marked the southern border of the earldom. So, this viewpoint on Struie Hill, looking west, is on what was the Scottish side of the firth. (© Charles Tait)

This dragon was carved into the interior wall of the Neolithic chambered tomb of Maeshowe in Orkney. The carving was done by Norsemen, possibly even the warriors who waited out a blizzard there during 'The War of the Three Earls'. (© Charles Tait)

This whalebone 'Dragon plaque' formed part of the funerary objects discovered during the excavation in 1991 of the Norse boat burial site at Scar in Sanday, in Orkney's North Isles. It dates from the early years of the Orkney earldom. (© Charles Tait)

The small tidal island of the Brough of Birsay, on the north-west tip of the Orkney mainland. Birsay village, on the shore to the right, was where the earls maintained their residence, and where Earl Thorfinn built his Christ Church. (© Charles Tait)

The excavation of the Norse settlement at Quoygrew in Westray, in the North Isles of Orkney. This shows the main farm building, in what was an extensive complex, which was in use from the 10th to the 13th century. (© Charles Tait)

7

In 1136, Earl Paul Hákonsson was hunting otters on the Orkney
    island of Rousay when he was attacked and kidnapped by Svein
    Ásleifarson. The hall of his host Sigurd of Westness lay just
    behind these trees overlooking Rousay's southern shore.
    (© Charles Tait)

These Norse runes are graffiti, carved inside the Neolithic tomb of
    Maeshowe in Orkney. Their wording suggests they were carved
    by 'mound-breakers' in early 1153. Runes were the usual form
    of Norse writing, before the adoption of the Roman alphabet.
    (© Charles Tait)

The tidal island of the Brough of Birsay is now uninhabited, but it
    was once a Pictish fortress. Later it became a prestigious Norse
    settlement, the ruins of which can be seen here, dominated by
    the remains of a 12th-century church. (© Charles Tait)

The harbourfront of Kirkwall, the main town of Orkney. The
    Orkney earls based themselves here from the 12th century –
    an ideal location for their administration, and for seaborne
    trade and communications with both Shetland and Norway.
    (© Charles Tait)

In 1919, workmen in St Magnus Cathedral unearthed a wooden box
    containing human remains. Analysis suggests this skull is that of
    Earl Magnus, or St Magnus, which bears the axe blows that killed
    him in 1117. The remains were reinterred. (© Charles Tait)

These wooden bas-relief carvings from St Magnus Cathedral
    represent the three figures responsible for its building. From
    left to right, these show its architect Kol Kalason, his son Earl
    Rognvald (later St Rognvald) and William 'the Old', Bishop of
    Orkney. (© Charles Tait)

This ruined 12th-century church of St Magnus on the small island
    of Egilsay was reputedly built on the spot where Earl Magnus
    Erlendsson was murdered at the hands of his cousin, Earl
    Hákon, in 1117. (© Charles Tait)

The magnificent Norse-built St Magnus Cathedral in Kirkwall
    was built to serve as the resting place of the remains of Earl
    Magnus, or St Magnus. Work on the cathedral began in 1137,
    during the reign of Earl Rognvald Kali. (© Charles Tait)

Every January, the Shetlanders celebrate 'Up Helly Aa', a fire festival which in theory celebrates the islands' Norse heritage. A parade through the streets of Lerwick culminates in the celebratory burning of a replica Norse longship. (© Charles Tait)

In the 12th century, the small island of Gairsay in Orkney was the home of the Viking adventurer Svein Ásleifarson. He reputedly maintained Orkney's largest 'drinking-hall' there, on the site now occupied by the island's only homestead. (© Charles Tait)

MAPS

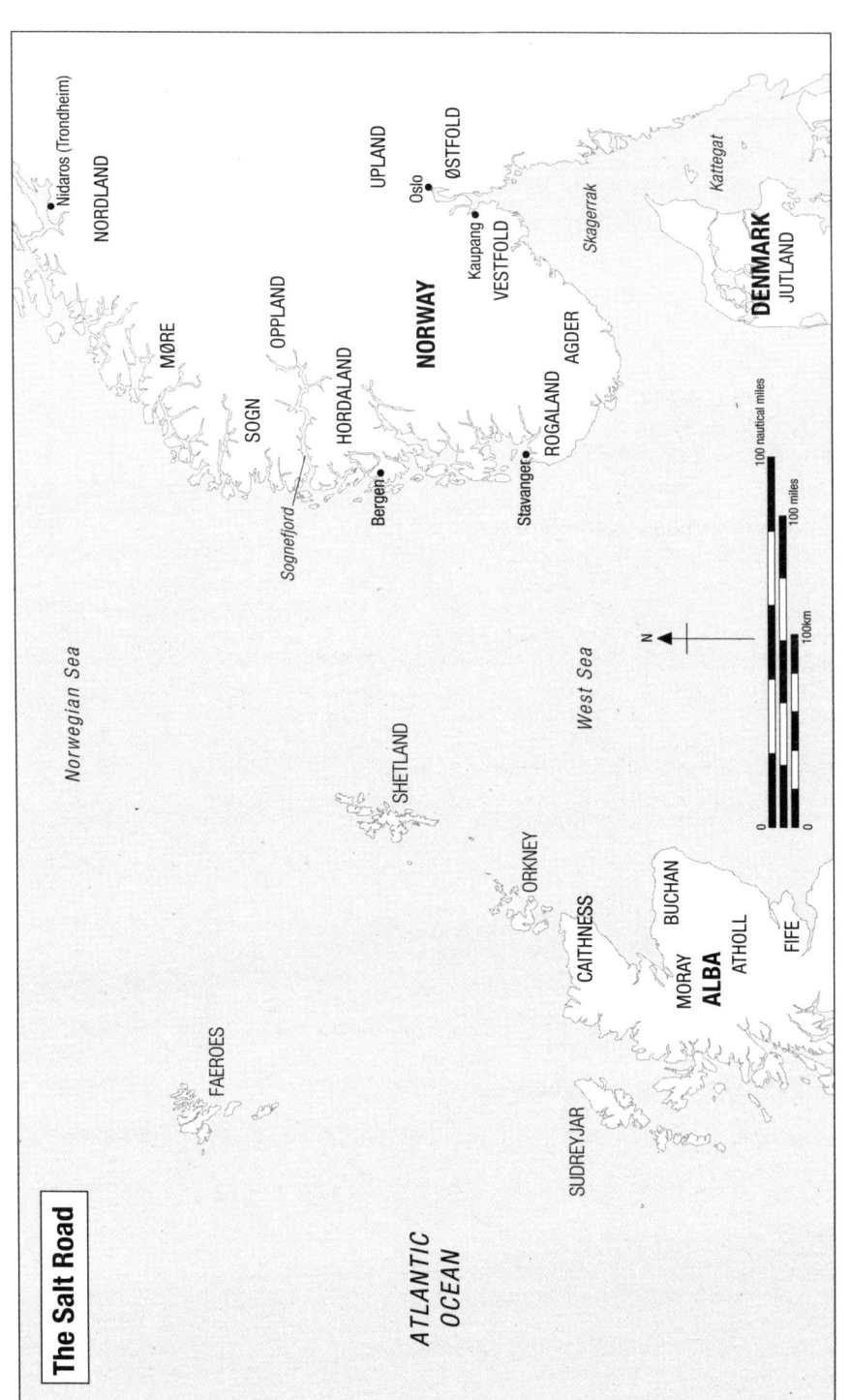

The Salt Road

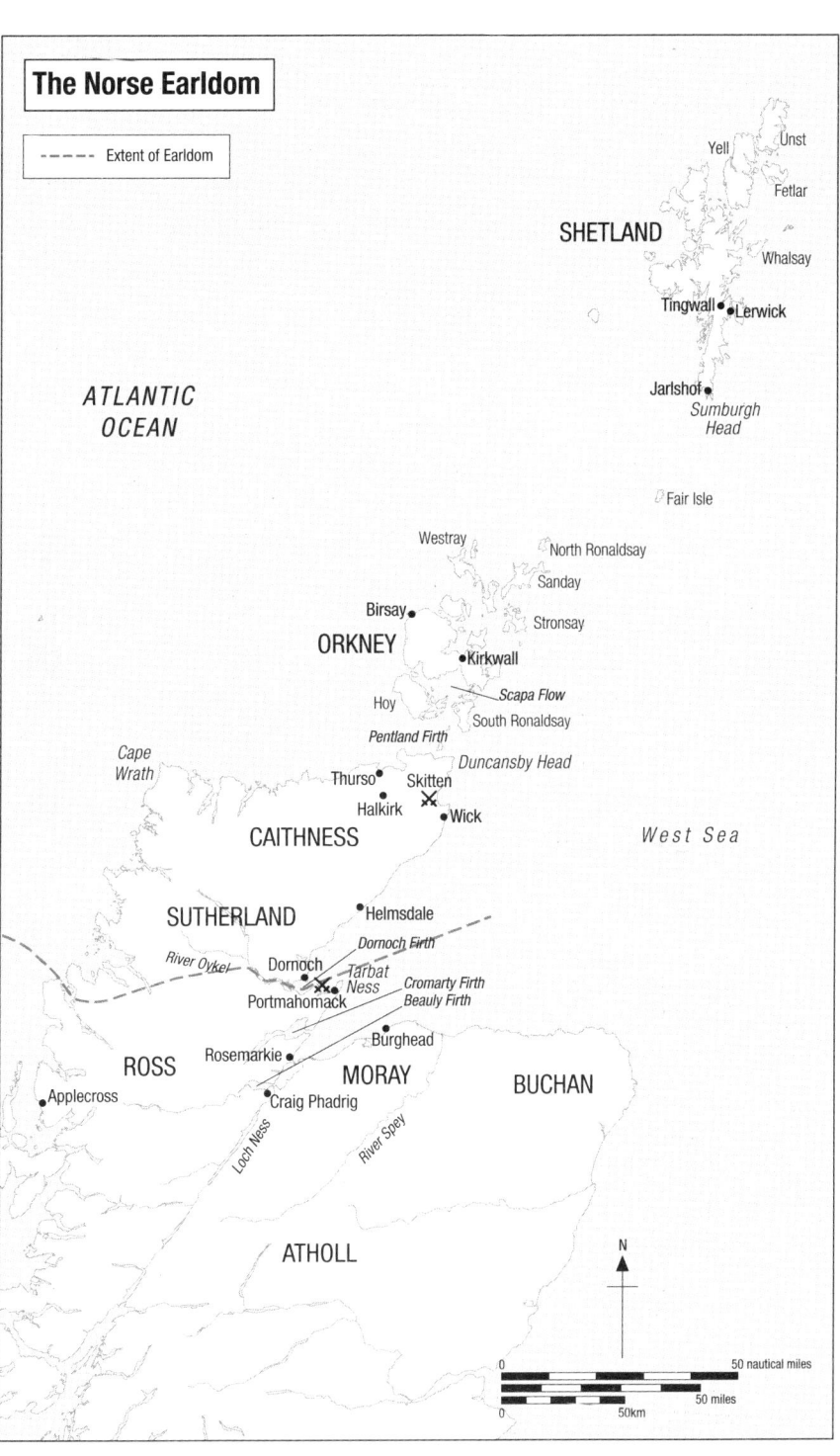

The Norse Earldom

- - - - - Extent of Earldom

ATLANTIC
OCEAN

SHETLAND

Yell
Unst
Fetlar
Whalsay
Tingwall • Lerwick

Jarlshof •
Sumburgh
Head

◦ Fair Isle

Westray
North Ronaldsay
Sanday
Birsay •
ORKNEY
Stronsay
• Kirkwall

Hoy
Scapa Flow
South Ronaldsay

Pentland Firth

Cape
Wrath
Duncansby Head
Thurso •
Skitten
Halkirk •
• Wick

West Sea

CAITHNESS

SUTHERLAND
• Helmsdale

Dornoch Firth
River Oykel
Dornoch
Tarbat
Ness
Cromarty Firth
Portmahomack
Beauly Firth

Burghead •

Rosemarkie •
ROSS
MORAY
BUCHAN

• Applecross
Craig Phadrig

Loch Ness
River Spey

ATHOLL

N

0   50 nautical miles
0   50km
50 miles

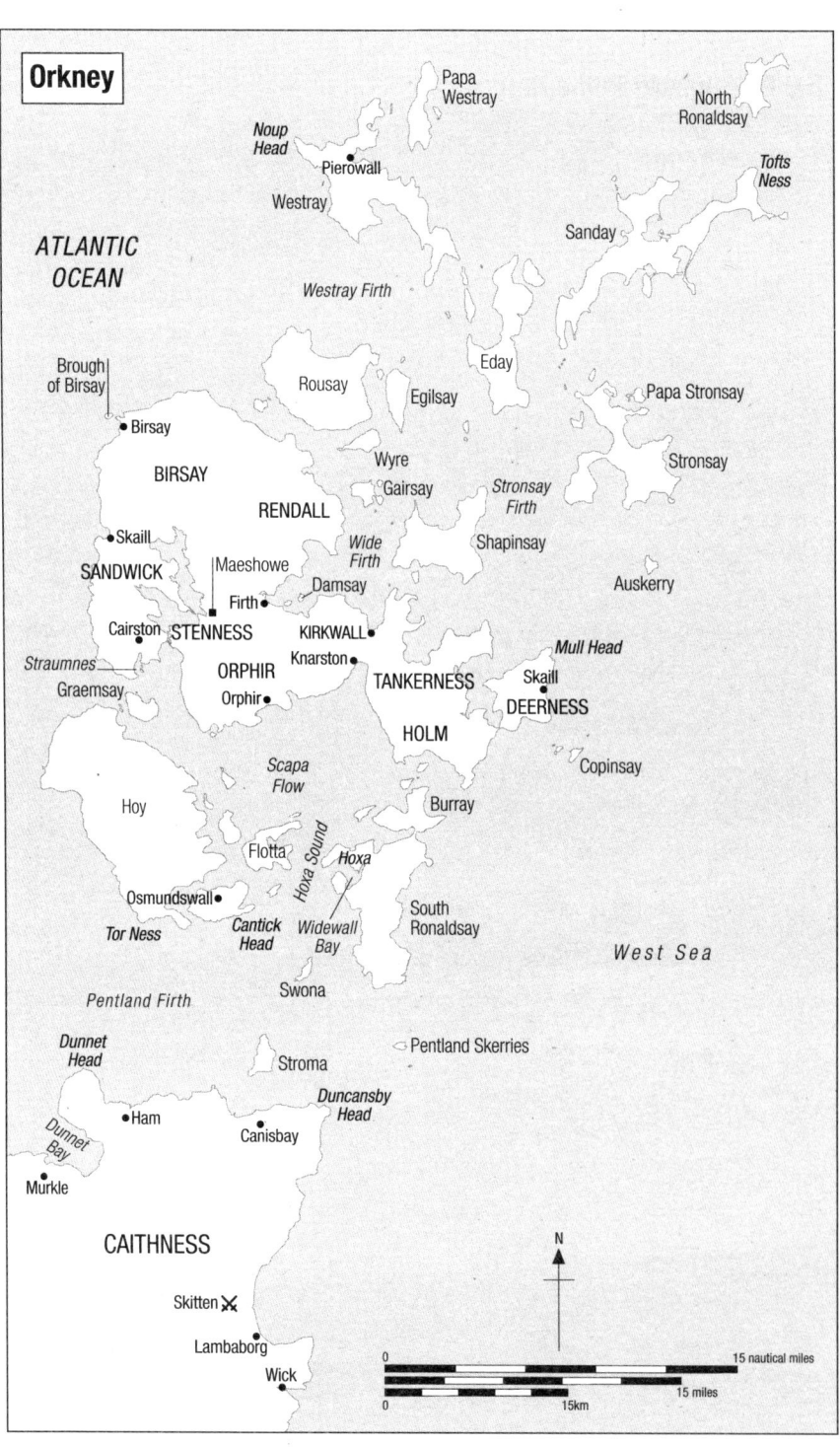

The British Isles in the Norse Era

- - - - - Extent of Earldom

SHETLAND

ORKNEY

CAITHNESS   *West Sea*

SUDREYJAR

ATLANTIC
OCEAN

MORAY   BUCHAN

Skye

ALBA   ●Dunnottar

Dunkeld
●

Mull   St. Andrews
Iona ●   ●

Dumbarton
●
✖Largs   LOTHIAN   ●Lindisfarne
STRATHCLYDE   Bamburgh
●

Derry
●   Stainmore
ULAID   ●
✖
Armagh   Isle   NORTHUMBRIA
●   of Man

CONNACHT   Jorvik ●✖Stamford Bridge
(York)
MEATH ✖Clontarf Anglesey   **ENGLAND**
IRELAND Dublin●   ●Lincoln   *The Wash*
✖Menai Strait Nottingham
LEINSTER   *Irish*   ●   Norwich
Sea   GWYNEDD   ●
●Leicester   EAST
MUNSTER   ●Wexford   MERCIA   ANGLIA

London
WESSEX   ●
Winchester Canterbury●
●   KENT

N
▲   Exeter
●

English Channel

SCILLY
ISLANDS

0   200 nautical miles

200 miles

0   200km

DRAMATIS PERSONAE

THE EARLS OF ORKNEY

Sigurd (Sigurðr) I Eysteinsson, 'the Powerful': Brother of Rognvald Eysteinsson, Earl of Møre, reigned *c. 888–c. 892*

Guthrom (Guthormr) Sigurdsson: Son of Earl Sigurd I, reigned *c. 892–893*

Hallad (Hallaðr) Rognvaldsson: Nephew of Earl Sigurd I, reigned *c. 893–c. 895*

Einar (Einarr) I Rognvaldsson, 'Turf-Einar': Nephew of Earl Sigurd I, reigned *c. 895–910*

Arnkell Einarrsson: Son of Earl Einar I, reigned 910–*c. 954, joint rule with Erlend I and Thorfinn I*

Erlend (Erlendr) I Einarrsson: Son of Earl Einar I, reigned 910–*c. 954, joint rule with Arnkell and Thorfinn I*

Thorfinn (Thorfinnr) I Einarsson, 'Skullsplitter': Son of Earl Einar I, reigned 910–963, *joint rule with Arnkell (910–c. 954) and Erlend I (910–c. 954)*

Arnfinn (Arnfinnr) Thorfinnsson: Son of Earl Thorfinn I, reigned 963–*c. 965*

Hávard (Hávarðr) Thorfinnsson, 'Harvest-blessed': Son of Earl Thorfinn I, reigned *c. 965–c. 972*

Ljót (Ljótr) Thorfinnsson: Son of Earl Thorfinn I, reigned *c. 972–c. 980*

Hlodvir (Hlǫðvir) Thorfinnsson: Son of Earl Thorfinn I, reigned *c. 980–991*

Sigurd (Sigurðr) II Hlodvirsson, 'the Stout': Son of Earl Hlodvir, reigned 991–1014

Sumarladi (Sumarliði) Sigurdsson: Son of Earl Sigurd II, reigned 1014–1016, *joint rule with Brúsi and Einar II*

Brúsi Sigurdsson: Son of Earl Sigurd (II), reigned 1014–1031, *joint rule with Sumarladi (1014–1016), Einar II (1014–1026) and Thorfinn II (1025–1031)*

Einar (Einarr) II Sigurdsson, 'Crooked-mouth': Son of Earl Sigurd II, reigned 1014–1026, *joint rule with Sumarladi (1014–1016), Brúsi (1014–1026) and Thorfinn II (1025–1026)*

Thorfinn (Thorfinnr) Sigurdsson II, 'the Mighty': Son of Earl Sigurd II, reigned *c.* 1025–1064, *joint rule with Einar II (1025–1026), Brúsi (1025–1031) and Rognvald I (1036–1046)*

Rognvald (Rognvaldr) I Brúsason: Son of Earl Brúsi, reigned *c.* 1036–1046, *joint rule with Thorfinn II*

Paul (Páll) I Thorfinnsson: Son of Earl Thorfinn II, reigned 1064–1098, *joint rule with Erlend II*

Erlend (Erlendr) II Thorfinnsson: Son of Earl Thorfinn II, reigned 1064–1098, *joint rule with Paul I*

Sigurd (Sigurðr) III Magnusson, 'Jerusalem-farer': Son of King Magnus 'Bare-legged' of Norway, reigned 1098–1103

Hákon Paulsson: Son of Earl Paul I, reigned 1104–1123, *joint rule with Magnus I (1106–1117)*

Magnus (Magnús) I Erlendsson, St Magnus: Son of Earl Erlend II, reigned 1106–1117, *joint rule with Hákon*

Harald (Haraldr) I Hákonsson, 'Smooth-talking': Son of Earl Hákon, reigned 1123–1130, *joint rule with Paul II (1123–1126)*

Paul (Páll) II Hákonsson, 'the Speechless': Son of Earl Hákon, reigned 1123–1126, *joint rule with Harald I*

Rognvald (Rognvaldr) II Kali Kolsson, St Rognvald: Son of Kol Kalason and grandson of Earl Erlend II, reigned 1136–1054, *joint rule with Harald II (1138–1054) and Erlend III (1151–1154)*

Harald (Haraldr) II Maddadarson, 'the Old': Grandson of Earl Hákon, reigned 1138–1206, *joint rule with Rognvald II (1138–1054), Erlend III (1151–1154) and Harald III (1191–1198)*

Erlend (Erlendr) III Haraldsson: Son of Harald Hákonsson, reigned 1151–1154, *joint rule with Rognvald II and Harald II*

Harald (Haraldr) III Eiríksson, 'the Young': Grandson of Earl Rognvald II, reigned 1191–1198, *joint rule with Harald II*

David Haraldsson: Son of Earl Harald II, reigned 1206–1214, *joint rule with Jón*

Jón Haraldsson: Son of Earl Harald II, reigned 1206–1231, *joint rule with David (1206–1214)*

Magnus (Magnús) II (poss.) Gillechristsson: Grandson of Earl Rognvald II, reigned 1231–1239

Gilbert, son of Matilda (father unknown): Grandson of Earl Jón, reigned 1239–1256

Magnus (Magnús) III Gilbertsson: Son of Earl Gilbert, reigned 1256–1273

Note: After the death of Earl Jón, the details of the lineage of the subsequent earls are unclear, and what sparse information there exists is contradictory. Magnus II was possibly the son of Earl Gille Christ of Angus, who it is thought may have married Ingibiorg Eiríksdóttir of Caithness, the daughter of Ingirid Rognvaldsdóttir and her husband Eirík 'Staybrailer'. There may have been two Gilberts, but this is unclear, and fairly unlikely. With luck, more research into these 'Shadow Earls' will help fill in the gaps.

THE KINGS OF NORWAY

* Absentee rule (a Danish king, who had others rule a conquered Norway for them)

** Uncrowned ruler, acting as regent for the absentee king

Harald (Haraldr) I Halfdansson, 'Finehair': Son of King Halfdan 'the Black' of Vestfold, reigned *c.* 872–932

Eirík (Eiríkr) I Haraldsson, 'Bloodaxe': Son of King Harald I, reigned *c.* 932–934

Hákon I Haraldsson, 'the Good': Son of King Harald I, reigned *c.* 934–961

* Harald (Haraldr), 'Bluetooth' (King of Denmark): Son of King Gorm 'the Old' of Denmark, reigned 961–*c.* 985, *ruled through a vassal king, Harald II 'Greycloak'*

Harald (Haraldr) II Eiríksson, 'Greycloak': Son of King Eirík I, reigned 961–971, *vassal king of King Harald 'Bluetooth' of Denmark*

** Hákon Sigurdsson, 'Hákon Jarl' or 'the Bad' (Earl of Lade): Son of Sigurd Hákonsson, Earl of Lade, reigned 971–995, *ruled as regent for the Danish crown*

Oláf (Óláfr) I Tryggvason: Son of King Tryggvy of Viken, reigned 995–1000

* **Svein (Sveinn) Haraldsson, 'Forkbeard' (King of Denmark):** Son of King Harald 'Bluetooth' of Denmark, reigned 1000–1013, *ruled through regents, the Earls of Lade*

** **Eirík (Eiríkr) Hákonsson (Earl of Lade):** Son of Hákon Sigurdsson, Earl of Lade, reigned 1000–1015, *joint rule with Svein as regents for the Danish crown*

** **Svein (Sveinn) Hákonsson (Earl of Lade):** Son of Hákon Sigurdsson, Earl of Lade, reigned 1000–1015, *joint rule with Eirík as regents for the Danish crown*

Oláf (Óláfr) II Haraldsson, St Oláf: Son of King Gudrød of Vestfold, reigned 1015–1028

* **Knút (Knútr) Sveinsson, 'the Great' (King of England from 1016 and Denmark from 1018):** Son of King Svein 'Forkbeard' of Denmark, reigned 1028–1035, *ruled through regents, the Earls of Lade*

** **Hákon Eiríksson (Earl of Lade):** Son of Eirík Hákonsson, Earl of Lade, reigned 1028–1029, *ruled as regent for the Danish crown*

** **Svein (Sveinn) Knútsson (Earl of Lade):** Son of King Knút 'the Great', reigned 1029–1035, *ruled as regent for the Danish crown*

Magnus (Magnús) I Oláfsson, 'the Good': Son of King Olaf II, reigned 1035–1047, *joint rule with Harald II (1046–1047)*

Harald (Haraldr) II Sigurdsson, 'Hardrada': Son of King Sigurd of Vestfold, reigned 1046–1066, *joint rule with Magnus I (1046–1047)*

Magnus (Magnús) II Haraldsson: Son of King Harald II, reigned 1066–1069, *joint rule with Oláf III (1067–1069)*

Oláf (Óláfr) III Haraldsson, 'the Peaceful': Son of King Harald II, reigned 1067–1093, *joint rule with Magnus II (1067–1069)*

Hákon II Magnusson, *Hákon Toresfostre*: Son of King Magnus II, reigned 1093–1095, *joint rule with Magnus III*

Magnus (Magnús) III Oláfsson, 'Bare-legged': Son of King Olaf III, reigned 1093–1103, *joint rule with Hákon II (1093–1095)*

Oláf (Óláfr) IV Magnusson: Son of King Magnus III, reigned 1103–1115, *joint rule with Eystein I and Sigurd I*

Eystein (Eysteinn) I Magnusson: Son of King Magnus III, reigned 1103–1123, *joint rule with Oláf IV (1103–1115) and Sigurd I (1103–1123)*

Sigurd (Sigurðr) I Magnusson, 'Jerusalem-farer': Son of King Magnus III, reigned 1103–1130, *joint rule with Oláf IV (1103–1115) and Eystein I (1103–1123)*

Magnus (Magnús) IV Sigurdsson, 'the Blind': Son of King Sigurd I, reigned 1130–1135 and 1137–1139, *joint rule with Harald IV (1130–1135) and rival king to Sigurd II (1137–1139)*

Harald (Haraldr) IV Magnusson, *Harald Gille*: Son of King Magnus III, reigned 1130–1136, *joint rule with Magnus IV (1130–1135)*

Sigurd (Sigurðr) II Haraldsson, *Sigurd Munn*: Son of King Harald IV, reigned 1136–1155, *joint rule with Inge I (1136–1155), Eystein II (1142–1155) and Magnus V (1142–1145)*

Inge (Ingi) I Haraldsson, 'the Hunchback': Son of King Harald IV, reigned 1136–1161, *joint rule with Sigurd II (1136–1155), Eystein II (1142–1157), Magnus V (1142–1145) and Hákon II (1157–1161)*

Eystein (Eysteinn) II Haraldsson: Son of King Harald IV, reigned 1142–1157, *joint rule with Sigurd II (1142–1155), Inge I (1142–1157) and Magnus V (1142–1145)*

Magnus (Magnús) V Haraldsson: Son of King Sigurd II, reigned 1142–1145, *joint rule with Sigurd II, Inge I and Eystein II*

Hákon II Sigurdsson, 'the Broad-shouldered': Son of King Sigurd II, reigned 1157–1162, *joint rule with Inge I (1157–1161) and Magnus VI (1161–1162)*

Magnus V Erlingsson: Son of Earl Erling 'the Lopsided' and grandson of King Sigurd I, reigned 1161–1184, *joint rule with Hákon II (1161–1162)*

Sverre (Sverrir) Sigurdsson: Falsely claimed to be son of King Sigurd II, reigned 1184–1202

Hákon III Sverresson: Son of King Sverre, reigned 1202–1204

Guttorm (Guttormr) Sigurdsson: Infant grandson of King Sverre, reigned 1204

Inge (Ingi) II Bárdsson: Grandson of King Sigurd II, reigned 1204–1217

Hákon IV Hákonsson, 'the Old': Son of King Hákon III, reigned 1217–1263

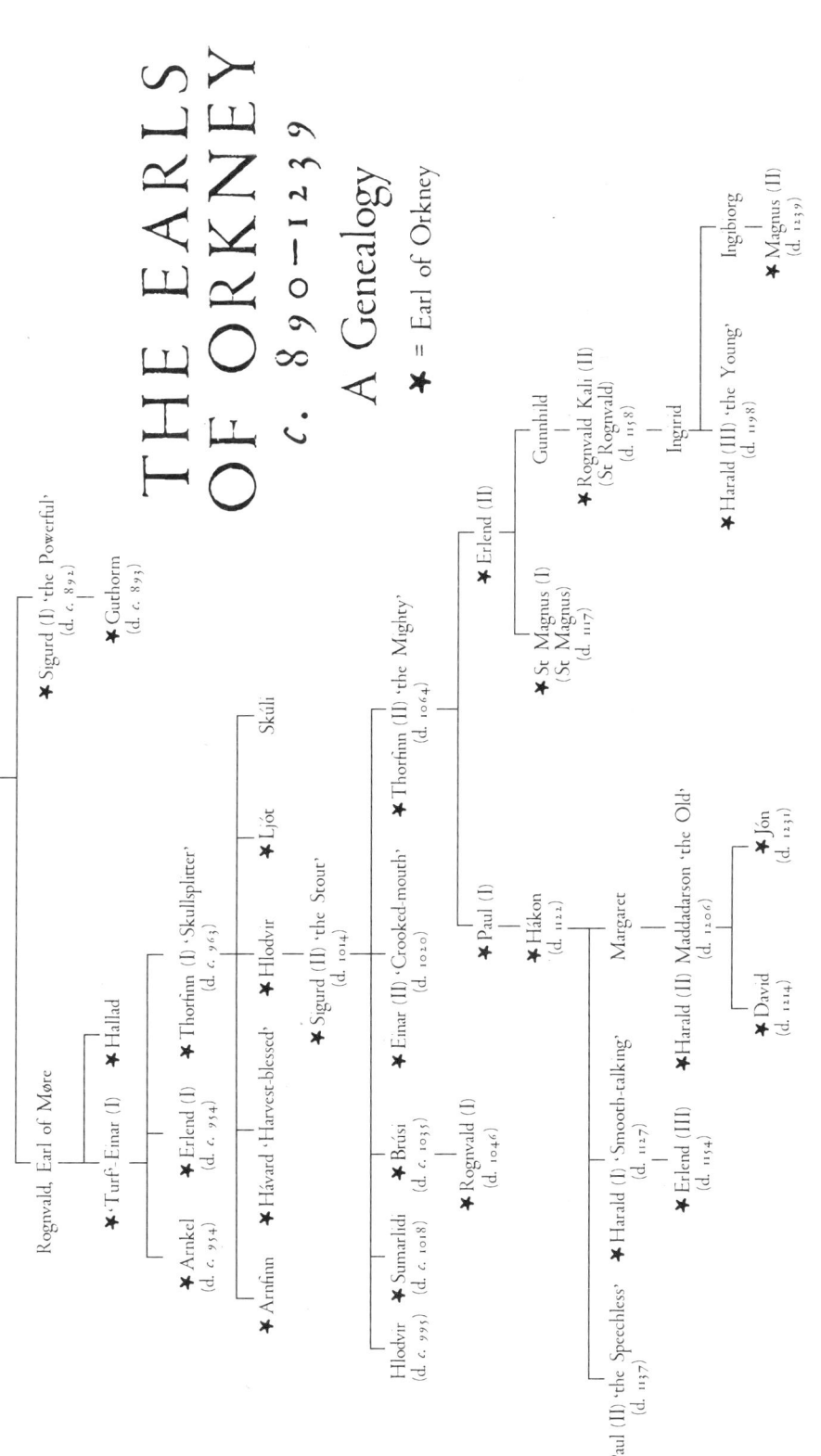

THE EARLS
OF ORKNEY
c. 890–1239
A Genealogy

★ = Earl of Orkney

Magnus (II) was followed by the descendants of Jón: Gilbert (d. 1256) and Magnus (III) (d. 1273)

ACKNOWLEDGEMENTS

In the mid-12th century, Norsemen carved a dragon on the stonework of the Neolithic tomb of Maeshowe in Orkney. After visiting the tomb in 1972, the author's late uncle, the sculptor Nigel Konstam, carved this version of it onto a stone, while sitting on the beach at Skaill.

I'm incredibly grateful to all the people who've helped me in this absorbing project. The book would have been much the poorer without your help. Writing is a solitary business, and only by begging the help of others, especially those steeped in Norse history and myth, could I have delved so deeply into this world.

I'd like to thank the staff of the Orkney Library and Archive, the Orkney Museum, the National Museum of Scotland, The National Library of Scotland, the National Records of Scotland, Shetland Museum and Archives, the Caithness Archive Centre and the Manx

Museum. In all these places, the staff were both incredibly helpful and extremely knowledgeable.

I'd also like to single out three individuals, all experts in their field: Dr Siobhan Cook-Miller, Dr Ragnhild Ljosland and Tom Muir. You all played a key part in keeping me on the right track, thanks to your immense knowledge of your subject. Similarly Catriona Matheson, with her deep knowledge of Anglo-Saxon England, was also of great help.

Fortuitously, Judith Jesch's new translation of *The Saga of the Earls of Orkney* (or *The Orkneyinga Saga*) was published just as this book was being edited. So, thanks to her work, and the kindness of Hugh Andrew at Birlinn, her publisher, we were able to draw on this, the first translation of this fragmentary saga in half a century, and one which represents a huge step forward in Norse studies.

Then there's the staff of Osprey Publishing, part of Bloomsbury Publishing. I've worked with them for years, but they were hugely encouraging with *Lords of the Salt Road*. In particular, I'd like to thank my friend and publisher Marcus Cowper for being the catalyst for this project and seeing it through to the finish. The same applies to my gifted literary agent Andrew Lownie, the staunchest defender of authors one could ask for.

I'd also like to single out David Nicholl, who once posed for the cover of the Haynes Manual of the *Viking Warrior*, and who supported my efforts with tea and biscuits.

Finally, I'd be remiss if I didn't mention the inspiration for my interest in the Norse world, the late 'Willie' Thomson, Rector of Kirkwall Grammar School, and a man who knew how to draw out the best in people.

PREFACE

When I was little, my aunt and uncle visited us in Orkney and gave me a plastic Viking helmet. As I recall, it came with a plastic shield and cudgel. I don't remember much about those, but I really liked the helmet and wore it whenever I could. It was a real thing of its time, complete with plastic horns. I even wore it when my neighbour Archie, a Shetlander, told me stories about the Norse earls who'd ruled Orkney and Shetland, rulers who'd set out on Viking raids, and who'd conquered places far afield.

In Papdale Primary School – what people in the United States would call an elementary school – I was reintroduced to these Vikings. There, we were divided into school houses. I was in 'Erlend', while the others were called 'Einar' and 'Sweyn'. It turned out two of these names were Norse earls of Orkney, while Sweyn was a local Viking adventurer called Svein. The teachers told us about them, and took us on trips to places which featured in Orkney's rich Norse history, like the magnificent St Magnus Cathedral, and the neighbouring bishops' and earls' palaces. It was only later, when as a 12-year-old I moved to the 'big school', that a wonderful history teacher, Miss Mitchell, taught us more about these characters, and a lot else besides.

That really opened my eyes to Orkney's rich historical tapestry. It also sowed the seeds of my fascination with the past. Looking back, I was very fortunate to grow up in such a magical place as Orkney. I'm not an Orcadian – we came here when I was a toddler – but I grew to love the place. Six decades later, after travelling the world, I still do. Orkney is full of history, from the neolithic village of Skara Brae to the remnants of two World Wars. It was little wonder I became a historian. Later, when the Royal Navy paid me through university, they didn't really care what I studied. So, I opted for medieval history, with a spot of archaeology thrown in. It gave me a grounding in a historical period that I've rarely written about … until now.

This book came about through a conversation with a publisher, who was looking for a book that offered a 'new angle' on the Viking world. It took me a nanosecond to come up with his perfect solution – a history of the Norse earls of Orkney. If anyone encapsulated this colourful and turbulent era it was them. It was only when I was about to start work that I realised quite what a task this would be. I'd spent most of the past three decades writing about maritime history. This then, for me, was uncharted territory.

Fortunately, someone had done the job before. The *Earls' Saga*, also known as the *Orkneyinga Saga*, was written by an anonymous Icelandic author in the 13th century, and it tells the same tale – the amazingly colourful story of the Norse earls of Orkney. The saga, then, was my starting point, although the tale it tells had to be bolstered by other contemporary sources.

The aim was to breathe life into the world these Norse earls inhabited, and to set them in their proper place as the guardians of the Salt Road. Incidentally, the title *Lords of the Salt Road* was suggested by the publisher, when he learned the phrase had been used to refer to the North Sea, the conduit for Viking raiding and Norse settlement between Norway and the island clusters of Orkney and Shetland. It seemed a perfect way to sum up the Norse earls of Orkney, who controlled the crossroads of this hugely important maritime pathway.

In writing this, it struck me that while the saga is well-known in Orkney and Shetland, and among medieval historians, this colourful tale filled with murder, betrayal and revenge, Viking raids and pitched battles, plus poetry and love isn't so familiar to others. This book, then, is an attempt to bring this Norse world to a wider audience. Over the years I've written history books which are underpinned by solid research, but which wear their scholarship lightly. While the story of the Norse earls has been superbly covered in academic works, as well as by those which concentrate on the superb storytelling of the sagas, I felt there's a need for this amazing tale to be told again, in a way that's both readable and accessible. This is the result. I hope you enjoy this journey into the very heart of the Viking world.

Angus Konstam
Herston, Orkney, 2026

INTRODUCTION

T HE STORY OF THE Norse earls of Orkney began in the last years
of the 9th century, when the Norwegian king, Harald 'Finehair',
supposedly created the earldom. At the time, the earldom consisted
of the two island groups of Orkney and Shetland. Over the years, the
earldom expanded to incorporate a large chunk of Northern Scotland,
as well as the Western Isles, called the *Suðreyjar* (or Sudreyjar), the
'southern isles' to the Norsemen. At its greatest extent, the earldom
stretched as far south as the Isle of Man, some 475 miles from the
northernmost tip of Shetland.

This sprawling and powerful Norse earldom of Orkney existed
for almost four centuries. Its wealth and much of its fame rested on
its geography. Orkney and Shetland lay on the western side of the
'West Sea', the Norse name for what we now call the North Sea. The
islands lay at the crossroads of the 'Salt Road' – the sea route between
Norway and the British Isles. From Orkney, Viking raiders could cruise
down the west coast, towards Ireland, Wales and Cornwall, or down the
eastern side, towards the rich hinterland of Scotland and Anglo-Saxon
England. Norse settlers, following in their footsteps, could carve out
settlements within the expanding earldom, or go further afield, north
to the Faeroes or Iceland, or south to the burgeoning Scandinavian
kingdom centred around Jorvik – now York.

The Orkney earldom served as a base for Viking raiders until well
into the 12th century. This is over two centuries after the supposed
end of the 'Viking Age' in 1066. Thanks to geography, the earldom
also punched well above its weight in its influence over the countries
emerging to the south, England, Ireland, Scotland and Wales. The
earls of Orkney fought and sometimes died there, in military ventures
which centred around the struggle to maintain Norse control in the
face of the growing power of these increasingly unified kingdoms. The
earls also had trouble from Norway, where a similar growth of royal
power threatened the earls' control of their own destinies.

The earldom of Orkney, then, was a great prize, and inevitably this led to a succession of internal struggles between the earls and rival claimants to their land and power. Frequently, the earldom was shared between brothers or cousins, a situation which could lead to jealousy, rivalry, and ultimately to betrayal, murder or civil war. The history of the Norse earldom is littered with violence, where earls or claimants to power try to burn their rivals to death through arson, fight each other on land or sea, or deal with their opponents through assassination, poisoning or grisly execution. Few died in their beds. There are acts of love and compassion too, and through these we can see something of the real nature of these lords of the Salt Road.

The tale is also one where Norse culture and belief shines through the violence. It was a time when the old Norse gods were being replaced by new Christian beliefs. One earl was forcibly converted at sword point but then died in battle beneath the raven banner of Odin. His successors, though, embraced the new religion, and used it to strengthen their own position as rulers of a large seaborne fiefdom – a kingdom in all but name. These Norse earls of Orkney were often men of culture, who encouraged the arts, wrote poetry and built churches, palaces and even a beautiful cathedral. In their world, being a warrior and a poet were not mutually exclusive.

The result is that this all makes for an incredible story. It's one that was first told by an anonymous Icelandic author around 800 years ago, to entertain the elite of medieval Scandinavia. It became known as the *Earls' Saga*, the *Orkneyinga Saga* or *The Saga of the Earls of Orkney*. Of course, as few people speak Old Norse, most of what we make of these Norse sagas is down to the way they're translated.

Fortunately, I was able to draw on a new version, *The Saga of the Earls of Orkney*, translated by Judith Jesch, which was published while this book was being edited. This is not only a great work of scholarship, but this translation, which will become the standard version of the saga, retains far more of the flavour of the Norse original than earlier translations did. Drawing on Judith Jesch's work really brings the world of these Norse earls to life. For the sake of brevity, though, when I mention the saga I'll usually refer to it as the *'Earls' Saga'*. This is merely shorthand for Professor Jesch's translation.

This great saga, though, doesn't tell the whole story. It was written for its target audience, the upper strata of Norse society – kings, nobles, bishops and wealthy landowners who had the time and money to hire courtly *skalds* (poets) to recite the sagas to them, or to afford a treasured copy they could read for themselves. For many years the most popular name for the work was the *Orkneyinga Saga* – the saga of the Orcadians – the people of Orkney. They, however, are barely mentioned in it. Instead, the saga is about the nobles who ruled over them, and the way these great lords carved their own path in the Viking world.

Although recognised as being historically accurate, at least for the most part, the saga has occasional lapses, and sometimes it omits important events entirely. So it needs to be compared with other sagas and contemporary documents in order to let us see the bigger picture. These include Irish annals and Anglo-Saxon or Scottish chronicles, as well as other Norse sagas. This gives us the chance to set the events happening in and around the earldom in a wider context. For example, in the mid-11th century, the brothers Paul and Erlend Thorfinnson shared the earldom between them, and by all accounts they ruled it well. However, they soon became embroiled in the bid by Harald 'Hardrada', king of Norway, to conquer England in 1066. This means that you really need to understand the way the Norman Conquest of England unfolded, so you can place the role of the two earls in this bigger canvas. Unlike King Harald, they made it home alive, but there would be no Bayeux Tapestry to celebrate their achievements.

So, may I present *Lords of the Salt Road*, the story of the Norse earls of Orkney, who at one time ruled almost a quarter of Britain. My aim has been to capture something of the flavour of these fascinating events, and to set them in their proper context, at the heart of the Norse world. Over the course of this book, you'll see this world change from the era of Viking raiding and plunder to a new age, which saw the building of powerful British and Scandinavian kingdoms. The earldom of Orkney eventually found itself caught between two of them. This historical tale probably isn't new to the Orcadians and Shetlanders who were brought up with these stories, but many other readers will find this is a part of the Viking past they hadn't known much about. I hope you find this historical tale as enjoyable and fascinating as I do. If you do, then I've achieved my goal: to present the story of these larger-than-life lords of the Salt Road to a fresh audience.

PART ONE
THE COMING OF THE NORSEMEN

ONE

Harald 'Finehair'

I F YOU WANT TO know about the Norse earls of Orkney, you should really start with *The Saga of the Earls of Orkney*. It's often popularly known as *The Orkneyinga Saga*, or sometimes simply the *Earls' Saga* (or *Jarls' Saga*). Unfortunately, its reliability can be questionable in places. It can also be very stylised in the way the sagas often are, and it only tells us a fraction of what we really want to know. It leaves out a lot of the background, and it often doesn't give us the detail which we need to understand the whole story. So, we're left with a lot of unanswered questions. Still, no other saga specifically tells the story of the earldom of Orkney, or describes the lives of these powerful Norse nobles who guarded the 'Salt Road'. This is surprising, as once upon a time these earls ruled over almost a third of what's now Scotland.

The lack of detail, though, can be frustrating. For instance, the saga claims that the earldom was created by the Norwegian king Haraldr the Fine-haired (or Harald 'Finehair'), but it doesn't say when that happened. We're left to work that out from other sources. It also doesn't tell us anything about who lived in Orkney and Shetland at the time, or why King Harald needed an earl to rule the islands on his behalf. However, as a starting point it's hard to beat. Here's what the saga says about the way the earldom was founded:

One summer, Haraldr the Fine-haired went west across the sea to control Vikings, as he had become tired of their hostilities, when they harried in Norway in the summers, and were in Shetland and the Orkneys during the winters. He subjugated Shetland and the Orkneys and the Hebrides; he went all the way west to the Isle of Man and laid waste the Manx settlements. He had many battles there, and acquired land further west than any king of Norway, since then. Ívarr, son of Rǫgnvaldr, fell in one of the battles. And when

King Haraldr sailed east, then he gave Earl Rǫgnvaldr Shetland and the Orkneys in compensation for his son.[1]

This is the standard version of the founding of the Orkney earldom. It describes its creation by King Harald, and its gift to his right-hand man Rognvaldr (or Rognvald) Eysteinsson, the earl of Møre. This was in recognition of the death of the Norwegian nobleman's son in the king's service. The trouble is that this story doesn't quite ring true. In the saga, King Harald crossed the North Sea – which was called the 'West Sea' by the Norse. When he reached the islands of Orkney and Shetland on its western fringe, he subdued the troublesome Vikings there. Then he sailed around the west coast of Scotland, conquering everything in his path. He went as far as the Isle of Man, 350 miles south of Orkney, before he was done. Strangely, this expedition wasn't mentioned in any Scottish or Irish annals. It only appears in the sagas. This alone is enough to make us doubt *The Saga of the Earls of Orkney*'s version of events. Still, *Heimskringla*, the saga recording the lives of the Scandinavian kings, tells a similar story, and it even adds a little more detail:

> King Harald heard that the Vikings, who were in the West Sea [our North Sea] in winter, plundered far and wide in the middle part of Norway. Therefore, every summer, he made an expedition to search the isles and out-skerries on the [Norwegian] coast. Wheresoever the Vikings heard of him they all took flight, and most of them out into the open ocean. At last the king grew weary of this work, and therefore one summer he sailed his fleet right across the West Sea. First, he came to Hjatland [Shetland] and he slew all the Vikings who couldn't save themselves by flight. Then, King Harald sailed southwards to Orkneyjar [Orkney] and cleared them of the Vikings.[2]

It went on to say he conquered the Sudreys – the 'southern islands' of the Hebrides – before ending his expedition by conquering the Isle of Man. This raises more questions. Who were these Vikings – a term which specifically meant sea robbers and raiders – and why had they been attacking the Norwegian coast? Why did they base themselves on the far side of the West Sea? Why did Harald 'Finehair' conquer the Sudreys?

Above all, when did this happen? Although a range of likely dates have been proposed over the years, one thing is clear. The expedition was launched after Harald became the king of Norway. Norwegian tradition claimed this happened in AD 872, but most historians now agree he united Norway later, around AD 885. That means the expedition across the West Sea took place a few years after that, around AD 890. This is the timeline we'll work with – using *c.* AD 890 as the rough foundation date for the Orkney earldom.

That, of course, is if the expedition happened like the sagas claim. It's been pointed out that the whole story of the expedition closely resembles another later one, made through the same waters in 1098 by another Norwegian king, Magnus 'Bare-legged'.[3] There's a good possibility the saga writer merged the two expeditions into one. Others have come to question if King Harald was even involved in it. There's a theory that he stayed in Norway, and the whole expedition was led by Earl Rognvald himself, or by others in his family. It's claimed the saga's version might be covering up what was a private venture, conducted with or without royal support.[4]

Another point is that Harald's expedition across the West Sea would have taken much longer than the quick, whirlwind operation that the saga suggests. After all, the start of the account mentioned that King Harald had ships patrolling his coastline every summer, hunting down Vikings who'd crossed the West Sea to raid his shores. If that limited pirate-hunting operation in home waters took a whole season, this much larger expedition across the West Sea could have taken two or three years to complete. That made it very likely that the king would have remained in Orkney over the winter, between each campaigning season.[5]

As for why he campaigned against the Scots, in *Heimskringla* there's a piece of skaldic verse by King Harald's own court *skald* ('poet') Torbjørn 'Hornklofi'. It celebrates Harald's campaign against the Scots, and the sacking of the Isle of Man:

> The wise, the noble King, great whose hand so freely scatters gold,
> Led many a northern shield to war, against the town upon the shore,
> The wolves soon gathered on the sand, of that sea shore,
> For Harald's hand the Scottish army drove away, and on the coast
>   left wolves a-prey.[6]

It still doesn't explain why Harald was fighting the Scots, but it seems he defeated them and then plundered their coastline. Irish or

Scottish annals, though, don't mention any of this. Instead, they speak about Viking attacks on the Picts along the east coast of Scotland, which began in AD 866 and continued for two decades.[7] In the late 9th century, Scotland was a patchwork of various kingdoms, peoples, rulers and alliances. It was simpler at the start of the century, around AD 800, when the Highlands and the north-east of Scotland were ruled by the Picts. Their territory extended north to Orkney and Shetland, and west to include the Inner Hebrides and the Isle of Skye. In the south-east the Gaelic-speaking Scots of Dál Riata ruled Argyll, and the nearby islands from Mull to Arran.[8]

The following century was one of war and conquest, where the Scots extended their borders at the expense of the Picts. By the time King Harald 'Finehair' supposedly led his expedition down the west coast of Scotland in the late 9th century, everything from Skye down to Galloway was part of Alba, the recently united kingdom of the Scots. These then were the people Harald 'Finehair' fought during his expedition, after he dealt with the troublesome Vikings. Although there's no local account of Harald's Norse foray, *Heimskringla* mentions the killing of 'many Vikings who formerly had had men-at-arms under them' when Harald swept through the Sudreys. 'Men-at-arms' is a poor Victorian translation for Norse warriors, possibly even a hearthguard, a personal retinue of seasoned fighters.[9]

This suggests some of the Norsemen being targeted by King Harald's punitive expedition were important Norse leaders rather than mere 'Vikings'. That term meant sea robbers, rather than Norse noblemen who'd sought sanctuary on the far side of the West Sea. They'd probably moved there to avoid exactly this sort of heavy-handed retribution that Harald 'Finehair' meted out. The reason they were there in the first place is revealed in *Eyrbyggja Saga*, written in 13th-century Iceland. Although it dealt with feuding in Iceland, it contains a passage which sheds more light on all this: 'Just about that time King Harald Fine-Hair was forcing his way to power in Norway. During the campaign many men of high standing abandoned their estates in Norway, some emigrating east, some west over the North [West] Sea. Others used to winter in the Hebrides or in Orkney, then spend the summer raiding in Harald's kingdom, causing plenty of damage.'[10]

These so-called 'Vikings' were really the losers in a civil war, noblemen in exile from Norway and men who'd opposed King Harald.

They'd fled west, taking their families, retainers and followers with them. To understand what they were doing there, we need to go back a couple of decades, to see why they thought that King Harald 'Finehair' was such a threat.

———

If it wasn't for *Heimskringla*, we wouldn't know very much about Harald at all, even if it was written almost four centuries after the event. Still, it chronicles the histories of Scandinavian kings, and it starts with *Harald 'Fairhair's' Saga*. Until a few decades ago this account of King Harald was largely taken at face value. Then, historians began questioning much of what *Heimskringla* had to say, and the debate over its accuracy has continued ever since.

Today, the most widespread view is that King Harald was a regional ruler or sub-king who ruled Vestlandet, or 'West Norway'. There, the district of Sogn around the Sognefjord has historical associations with both Harald and his semi-legendary father, Hálfdan the Black. During the 19th-century revival of Norwegian nationalism, Harald was portrayed as 'The father of Norway', the country's first true king, who unified Norway and set it on its path to nationhood. This may well be true, but this path started in one small petty kingdom and expanded from there through conquest. It might be more accurate to say Harald unified much of Norway, and was then able to extend his rule to embrace the islands at the far side of the West Sea.[11]

According to *Heimskringla*, Harald, when he was just ten years old, became the ruler of the small Norse kingdom of Vestfold. Thanks to two regents, his mother Ragnhild and his uncle Guthorm, the ruling family maintained control of Vestfold until Harald came of age.[12]

When Harald was old enough to rule himself, he wooed Gyda, the daughter of the king of Hordaland, on Norway's western coast. She told him, though, that she would only marry a king who ruled all of Norway, not just a tiny part of it. So, as the saga claims, Harald vowed not to cut or comb his hair until he'd subdued the whole country.

What followed, according to the sagas, was a long and brutal war of conquest, as King Harald began subduing his fellow rulers in southern Norway, one after the other. If we agree with the mainstream view that Harald won control of Norway in a sea battle fought around AD 880, give or take, then we have some sort of rough timeline for this war.

King Harald of Vestfold began his war of conquest around AD 874 by striking north, marching into Oppland, where Lillehammer now stands. Then, he continued through the mountains towards the Trondheimsfjord. After subduing the Trøndelag region, he marched north to Namsos and Namdalen, where the local ruler King Hrollaug swore allegiance to Harald. In return he was made an earl (or 'jarl' in Norse), and allowed to keep his lands. These became the northern buffer zone of Harald's rapidly expanding kingdom. Harald established his base at Nidaros, now Trondheim, on the southern side of the Trondheimsfjord. He built his feasting hall there at Lade, just outside Nidaros itself. Next, he ordered a fleet of longships to be built, to help him conquer the small coastal kingdoms to the south.

In the spring of AD 875 the fighting resumed, and Harald added the regions of Møre and Romsdal to his tally, after slaying the local rulers in a battle fought near Ålesund. So far everything had gone Harald's way, but he couldn't campaign and govern his newly won territories at the same time. So, he appointed earls to rule his conquered lands for him. In Trøndelag, Hákon Grjotgardson ruled the region as the earl of Lade, while further south Rognvald Eysteinson became the earl of Møre. Harald considered these earls to be his most trusted subordinates.[13]

In AD 876, in a hard-fought sea battle, Harald defeated the local kings of Nordmøre and Romsdal. This was fought off Solskjel Island, at the southern entrance to the Trondheimsfjord. This gave King Harald control of a 30-mile swathe of the rugged coastline bordering the fjord. Next, King Vemund of Firdafylke, who ruled the shores of the Førdefjord, a little to the south, was burned to death in his feasting hall. Harald took his lands, too. This meant that Harald now ruled most of central and southern Norway, apart from the small kingdoms in the south-west of the country: Hordaland, Rogaland and Telemark. By now, having achieved so much, Harald was in no mood to stop.[14]

However, Harald was distracted by a crisis in Vestfold. King Eiríkr (or Eirík) of Sweden had taken advantage of this war in Norway to invade Harald's lands around the Oslofjord. So King Harald led his fleet there, and while securing his old kingdom, he couldn't bring the

Swedish king to battle. Inevitably, the remaining kings in southern Norway saw an alliance with the Swedes as the best way to preserve their little kingdoms. They formed a coalition to oppose King Harald and asked Eirík of Sweden for help.

King Harald, King Eirík and the kings of this coalition were all prepared to gamble everything on one decisive battle. Harald had spent the previous winter in Nidaros. In the spring of AD 880, when he learned that the coalition was gathering a fleet, Harald sailed south to confront it. Eirík of Sweden also headed west to join his Norwegian allies, but he left it too late, and Harald got there first. Harald's fleet came upon the enemy assembling off Jæren on the low-lying sand coast of Rogaland, a dozen miles south of the town of Stavanger. Harald feigned a withdrawal, hoping the coalition fleet would pursue him. It did. Harald planned to draw them into his chosen spot for the coming sea fight – the sheltered waters of the narrow Hafrsfjord, just south of Stavanger.

What little we know about the battle itself comes from Harald's *skald* Þórbjǫrn (or Torbjørn) 'Hornfloki'. Harald's enemies 'came from the eastward, eager for fighting, with gaping figureheads and graving ship prows', as King Eirík of Hordaland, who led the coalition's Norwegian allies, pursued King Harald's fleet north. They found Harald's ships waiting for them in the sheltered waters of the Hafrsfjord. Sea battles of the time were nothing like what we might expect, with neat lines of warships and carefully executed manoeuvres. Instead they were fought like land battles, with longships often tied together to form fighting platforms, and warriors deciding the issue in ferocious and bloody hand-to-hand combat. Axe, spear, sword and shield decided the day.

Here's how Torbjørn described it:

The berserkers bellowed as the battle opened – the wolfcoats shrieked loud and shook their weapons. Their strength would they try, but he [King Harald] taught them to flee. The Lord of the Eastmen, who at Útstein dwelleth [King Eric], the steeds of the Nokkvi [longships] he steered out, when started the battle.

Then boomed the bucklers [shields] ere a blow felled 'Haklang' ['Long chin' – possibly King Ólaf 'the White' of Dublin]. The thick-necked aethling [King Kjotve of Agder] behind the isle took shelter. He grew loath, against 'Lufá' ['mop of hair', the nickname for King

Harald] to hold the land of his fathers. [His warriors] hid under benches, and let their buttocks stick up, they who were wounded thrust their heads keelwards [surrendered].[15]

Heimskringla provides more detail:

A great battle began, which was both hard and long; but at last King Harald gained the day. There King Eirík [of Hordaland] fell, and King Sulke [of Rogaland], with his brother Earl Sote. Thor Haklang, who was a great berserk, had laid his ship against King Harald's, and there was above all measure a desperate attack, until Thor Haklang fell, and his whole ship was cleared of men. Then King Kjotve fled to a little isle outside, on which there was a good place of strength. Thereafter all his men fled, some to their ships, some up to the land; and the latter ran southwards over the country of Jadar.[16]

The battle marked the unification of Norway, or rather its Central and Southern portions. King Eric of Hordaland was slain in the battle, and the victor King Harald claimed his grieving daughter Gyda as his wife. She, after all, had provided the incentive for Harald's trail of slaughter. Then, according to *Heimskringla*, Harald had fulfilled the vow he made to himself all those years ago, and finally cut his long and unruly hair. Now Harald 'Mop-hair' truly become King Harald 'Finehair', the ruler of a unified Norway.

This, though, wasn't quite the end of the story. Many of the survivors of the battle fled Norway or resettled in parts of the country in the north, beyond King Harald's reach. As *Heimskringla* put it: 'Some, and they were a great multitude, fled out of the country, and thereby great districts were peopled. Jämtland and Hälsingland [both Swedish provinces] were peopled then, although some Norwegians had already set up their habitation there.' The saga added that Iceland and the Faeroe Islands were also 'discovered and peopled'. Others, the saga tells us, headed across the West Sea to Orkney, Shetland and the Hebrides. Norse settlers had already established themselves there, but rather than merely settling down and farming, these exiles were out for revenge.[17] So, many of them turned Viking, and continued the war by raiding King Harald's coasts.

At some point a few years after his victory at the Battle of Hafrsfjord, King Harald 'Finehair' supposedly sailed across the West Sea, at the head of a powerful fleet of longships. His warriors subdued Orkney and Shetland, and then, from this secure base, Harald dealt with the Norwegian exiles in the Hebrides. Afterwards, the saga tells how King Harald then gave Orkney and Shetland to Earl Rognvald of Møre, as compensation for the death of his son Ivar, killed in battle during the fighting in the Hebrides. That, then, marked the foundation of the earldom of Orkney – a reward to the king's right-hand man for lives lost and services rendered. From that point, from *c.* AD 890 on, the Orkney earls – the Lords of the Salt Road – began carving out their own powerful realm, based off the top of the British Isles.

TWO

Origin Myths

A T SCHOOL IN ORKNEY, my headmaster was William P. L. Thomson, a man of almost saintly bearing, with the patience and good grace to match. Still, you sometimes got the idea that 'Willie' had half a mind on other far more important things. Sure enough, it was only later I learned he wasn't just a headmaster – he was also a first-rate historian.

Over the years William (or 'Willie') Thomson wrote a lot about Orkney's past, from its Pictish and Norse origins to the modern age, with the blossoming of farming, two World Wars and the coming of the oil boom. It was in 1987, at the launch of his book *The History of Orkney*, that he spoke to me about the Icelandic saga of the Orkney earls.[1]

'Most people can't get into it', he said. 'The first bit is all about gods and giants, water, wind and fire. That all sounds like nonsense to the modern reader. Most people get bored by it and give up. I usually tell people to ignore it. Instead they should start four chapters in, with Harald Finehair's expedition to Orkney, and the coming of the Vikings. It's much more readable.' I took his word for it, and was soon hooked by the tale. It was only later that I turned back to the origin part of the *Earls'* or *Orkneyinga Saga*, and wondered what it all meant. You too can miss out this chapter, and it won't alter the historical tale at all. If you persevere though, you'll understand more of the mindset of the Norse earls who ruled over the Salt Road.

In recent years fantastic worlds full of giants, elves, dragons and fairies have become highly popular, as has the notion of such creatures rubbing shoulders with humanity. While the chronicler of these tales never read or watched *Game of Thrones* or *Lord of the Rings*, he and those like him – the revered saga-writers of Iceland – were all thoroughly versed in Norse mythology and folklore. So too were the people who first read their works. For them, anchoring the lineage of the earls of Orkney in this realm of gods and monsters was perfectly acceptable. It was in tune with the Norsemen's view of their own beginnings. Today, with the benefit of science and logic, we can say that giants and trolls never walked the earth, while belief in the old Norse gods has faded away and been consigned to the realm of mythology. What is still a bit strange is that the *Earls' Saga – The Saga of the Earls of Orkney* – was written at a time when these old gods had been replaced by a single new one, which had come to dominate religious belief in the Norse world. Why, then, did the saga still root itself in the beliefs of the old ways?

The answer of course is to provide a mythical foundation to the earldom which stretched back into the mists of time – all the way to the very creation of the Norse world itself. When the *Earls' Saga* was written around 1200, Christianity had taken firm hold across the old Norse world. Elements of the older religion still lingered though, at least in terms of mythology, stories and superstitions, passed down from one generation to the next. In other words, devout Christian or not, most people of the Norse world knew all about the tales of the old gods, and the world they inhabited. The author who wrote the *Earls' Saga* was no fool. By basing the lineage of the Orkney earls firmly in this mythical past, he gave them something priceless. He gave them an unquestionable mythological pedigree.[2]

This was why the opening three chapters of the saga – William Thomson's first part about 'gods and giants, water, wind and fire' – is sometimes called the Fundinn Noregr or 'Foundation of Norway' story. In essence it is an origin myth – one the medieval readership of the *Earls' Saga* would have no trouble following. It showed that rather than being mere distant mortal offspring of a god, the earls of Orkney were the descendants of giants who ruled Scandinavia long before the Norse gods were even established. This meant that not only were the earls one step above other mortals, but they could trace their ancestry back to a Nordic world that existed long before the kingdom of Norway was ever created.

Essentially, this origin myth began like this: 'There was a king whose name was Fornjótr. He ruled over the land called Finnland, or Kvenland. It lies to the east of the sea-gulf that leads towards Gandvík; we call that Helsingjabotn.'[3] Ancient Kvenland, or Karelia, was in the far Arctic north of Scandinavia, between North Cape, the northernmost tip of Norway, eastwards to the modern Russian port of Archangel. It was a forbidding wilderness of snow-covered mountains and rocky plateaus, and vast expanses of Arctic tundra, interspersed with frozen lakes. It was little wonder that the old Norse imagined this was an impossibly remote land inhabited by giants. In the eyes of the Norsemen, it was further north than you could possibly go.

King Fornjótr (or Fornjót) was a giant, a *jötunn*, which in Norse terms weren't gods and weren't mortals. Instead the *jötnar* – in the word's plural form – existed in the boundary region between the worlds of gods and men. The term could encompass both giants and trolls, but some *jötnar* weren't necessarily overly huge or markedly ugly. They were also set apart from the dwarves and elves who inhabited the fringes of the Norse realm. Fornjót and his offspring were meant to be a ruling family of giants. Sure enough, our Fornjót makes an appearance in the *Prose Edda*, Snorri Sturlasson's great saga of Norse mythology, which deals with the creation of the Norse world and its gods, and their relations with the *jötnar*. Of course, Fornjót was a legendary figure rather than a real one, but he and his descendants held a special place in the origin myth of Norway. His name too is made up – an amalgam of *forn-jótr* (meaning the original *jötunn*) and *for-njótr* (which means the first owner). So, Fornjót was at the root of the family tree that would eventually include the first Norse earls of Orkney.[4]

In *The Saga of the Earls of Orkney*, Fornjót was described as a ruler of Finland and Kvenland. Then, in the 14th-century *Flateyjárbok* or 'Book of Flatey', it rather surprisingly claims he was also the ruler of Gotland and Jutland. This Baltic realm doesn't sit so well with the story that followed, as in Norse mythology the land of the giants was firmly placed on the outer fringes of their known world. In the *Prose Edda*, the giants lived in Utgard or 'the Outer Lands', a perfect name for Fornjót's ice-covered wilderness at the northernmost end of the Norse world.[5]

After introducing Fornjót, the *Earls' Saga* follows by providing us with the first of two genealogical lists, each spanning five generations. These are a bit like the long, dreary Biblical passages linked by the word 'begat'. In this case, though, the first of these is enlivened by the rather unusual names chosen for the 'begotten'. It claims that Fornjót had three sons, called Ægir (or Hlér), Kári and Logi. These were names associated with natural elements, Ægir representing the sea, Kári the cold north wind, and Logi meaning fire. These three mythical sons then were the personification of sea, wind and fire. Incidentally, according to Norse mythology Ægir was married to a goddess, Rán, who also represented the sea, and the couple hosted the Norse gods in their feasting hall in Asgard, the home of the gods. For good measure the nine daughters of Ægir and Rán personified the waves, while their son Snær represented snow.

It seems that a giant naming his *jötnar* offspring after sea, wind and fire might have been a strange choice, but it set a pattern for future generations of this royal family of giants. This genealogical sequence continues by saying that Kári the wind giant had a son whom he called Frosti or Jökul, representing the frost. In his turn Frosti had a son called Snær 'the Old', the same name as Ægir's son – his mythical first cousin once removed. The sequence then continued when Snær had a son of his own, whom he named Þorri (or Thorri), who was associated with thunder. The *Flateyjárbok* describes Thorri as a king of Finland and Kvenland, just like his great-great-grandfather Fornjót. Significantly, it also claims that, like his ancestor, Thorri ruled over the Baltic island of Gotland.[6]

This is important to our origin story, as usually the land of the giants was firmly based in the icy northern Arctic periphery of Scandinavia beyond the realm of mortals. Gotland was mentioned before as being part of Fornjót's realm. So, the story is starting to edge into the known world. If we take the southern reaches of the land ruled by Thorri as the Gulf of Bothnia between modern-day Finland and Sweden, that places us on the edge of the Baltic Sea. In Norse times this was a bustling maritime thoroughfare. That meant it was very much on the Scandinavian map. From this point on, the origin story of the earls of Orkney is firmly set in a real geographical landscape – one any saga-reader would know, and many actually lived in.

King Thorri, the successor to Fornjót's kingdom, had three children: two boys called Nórr and Górr, and a daughter, Gói, a name which, like her grandfather Snær, was associated with snow. According to *The Saga of the Earls of Orkney*, Thorri was a devout ruler, and he held an annual midwinter sacrificial feast in honour of the gods. One year, after the feast was over, Thorri and his family discovered that Gói was missing. Despite all their best efforts, they couldn't find any trace of her. This changes the whole track of the story. Until now it has been little more than a mythical family tree. Now, though, it becomes both a quest and a land grab: 'three winters later, the brothers swore an oath that they would search for her'. Their arrangement was for Nórr to scour the mainland, and Górr used his ships to search all the islands and outlying skerries. Each had a strong force of men. Górr searched the Gulf of Bothnia and the Baltic Sea, before working his way west past Gotland and on to Denmark.

For his part Nórr waited until the snows came, so he and his men could travel using skis. Then he set off westwards from Kvenland, to pass through the land of the Lapps. Although the Lapps threatened to fight Nórr, the saga claims they were put off by his 'power and magic'. So they left Nórr and his warriors well alone. Eventually Nórr and his followers climbed the mountainous spine between modern-day Norway and Sweden. From its crest Nórr followed the rivers as they flowed west to the shores of what is now the Norwegian Sea.

Nórr then turned south, crossing the Trondheimsfjord to reach the region known as Møre, where one day Earl Rognvald would rule his earldom. During Nórr's journey through Norway he claimed lordship of all the people and lands he passed through. According to the saga, anyone who opposed him was soon forced to submit, thanks again to the *jötunn*'s magical powers. Those who proved immune to it were easily defeated by Nórr and his followers. Meanwhile, finding no trace of his sister, Górr sailed west through the Skagerrak, and continued on up the coast of what is now Norway. Eventually, on the shores of the Sognefjord, some 60 miles north of the modern city of Bergen, the two brothers were reunited.

Górr hadn't been conquering territory because during his voyage the lands he'd passed through were in the hands of either his father or his kinsmen, the descendants of Ægir, the sea god. Now, though, he wanted his own share of this new and prosperous-looking land. So the two brothers made a deal. From that point on Nórr would rule the land he'd claimed, which he named 'Norway' after himself. Górr would rule the islands and skerries off the coast of his brother's kingdom. A dividing line between the kingdoms was established. Any channel between islands and the coast where a vessel could sail without grounding its steering oar would be the border between the brothers' new kingdoms. While all this sounds as if Nórr got the better part of the deal, a quick glance at the map of Norway shows just how many hundreds of islands there were, which effectively made this a far more even split.

The other thing that came out of the brothers' reunion was the news that neither of them had managed to find any trace of their sister. So, they both resumed the search. In the end it was Nórr who tracked Gói down. It seems that during Thorri's midwinter feast, Gói had been snatched away by King Hrolfr from Berg, who ruled the Hedmark region to the east of the Sognefjord. Hrolfr was a *jötunn* too, the son of the giant Sðadi (or Svadi), who lived in the Dovre Mountains, a little further to the north. So, gathering his men, Nórr and his warriors marched east into the mountains to track down Hrolfr, confront him and claim back Gói. When they met, Hrolfr challenged Nórr to single combat, but in the duel that followed both men fought each other to a standstill. In the end they agreed to make a deal.[7]

It turned out that Gói, who loved Hrolfr, was in no hurry to be rescued. So, it was agreed she'd stay with King Hrolfr in Hedmark. In return her brother Nórr agreed to marry Hrolfr's sister. So, what could have been a bloodbath turned into a peaceful union of two *jötnar* houses. Nórr then returned to his new kingdom of Norway and ruled it for the rest of his days. The kingdom then passed peaceably to his sons, and then on to their descendants. Somehow, along the way, these semi-mythical *jötunn*, the rulers of the kingdom of Norway, evolved into mortals, albeit ones who claimed an ancestry that began in the land of giants at the edge of the known world.

Meanwhile Górr and his descendants ruled over their share of Norway – its islands and skerries. Given their sea-dominated realm, they came to be known as Sea Kings. That made them a bit like their kinsman Ægir and his descendants, who were based further south, in the lands bordering the Kattegat, between Denmark and Sweden.

Eventually, King Górr had two sons, who were called Heiti and Beiti. They were more warlike than their father, and according to the saga they frequently raided the lands of their cousins, the sons of Nórr. Nobody really won in these near-constant raids and skirmishes, although no doubt the plunder helped fill the coffers of the Sea Kings.[8]

On one occasion, the saga tells how on a raiding expedition up the Trondheimsfjord, Beiti plundered the shores of the fjord as far as it went. He then anchored his ships there, off the village of Beitstad, some 50 miles north-east of Trondheim. He remembered the agreement between his father and uncle, that Górr could lay claim to anywhere he could reach where a boat could sail without grounding its steering oar.

So, with his father Górr seated at the helm, Beiti had one of his boats hauled across country, through the fertile valley of Namdalseid, then on to the Namsenfjord, some 20 miles from where they'd started. As a result, Górr and his sons claimed a sizeable chunk of the Trøndelag region, which had been to port of their boat during its cross-country portage from the Trondheimfjord to the Namsenfjord.[9]

The saga probably included this tale to show how clever the Sea Kings were, using their initiative and inventiveness to expand their kingdom. In fact, though, both the Norwegian kingdom and the realm of the Sea Kings were in decline. With each generation, the lands ruled by Górr and Nórr were divided between the male descendants and so became increasingly small. As *The Saga of the Earls of Orkney* put it: 'And so the territories became smaller as the kings became more numerous and in this way they were broken up into provinces'. This, though, also served as a useful literary bridge by the saga writer, as it marked a transition from the realm of pure myth to one where myth and historical reality were intertwined.[10]

This transition continues in the second genealogical list of the origin myth. This was really the most important part of the whole tale, hidden in an otherwise innocuous, dull-sounding passage. It says that 'Heiti, the son of Górr, was the father of Sveiði the sea-king, the Sea King Sveiði, father of Hálfdan the Old, father of Ívarr an earl of the people of Oppland, father of Eystein Rattle, father of Earl Rǫgnvaldr the Powerful and the Clever-in-advice.'[11] That of course made Earl Rognvald the great-great-grandson of Sveiði, the last-named Sea King. This made him the distant kin of Górr, the original Sea King.

If we apply the rule that a generation spans about 25 years, then it suggests Rognvald was alive a century and a half after Górr first carved out his Sea Kingdom. A century and a half further back, Rognvald's lineage reached King Fornjót. This timeline of course was nonsense, but it served its purpose. It provided a direct link with an older Scandinavia, a larger than life one where first giants and then Sea Kings inhabited the same world as the saga readers. It also showed that Rognvald was no ordinary man. Twelve generations before, his ancestor had been a king of the giants.

This is all very well, but what earthly use was a lineage like that? The simple answer was one-upmanship. In *Heimskringla* the Norwegian kings have their own origin myth. It claims that Odin the all-father, head of the Æsir – the Norse pantheon of gods – was their ancestor. Odin and the Æsir left their realm of Asgard in 'Asia' and travelled northwards into Scandinavia. Once there, the people worshipped them as gods.[12]

In the surviving fragments of the *Skjöldunga Saga* ('The Saga of the Scyldings') it says that once he arrived in Scandinavia, Odin divided the land, giving Sweden to his son Yngvi (also known as Frey) and Denmark to his son Skjöldr.[13] Later kings of the Swedish Yngling or the Danish Skjöldjung dynasties proudly laid claim to this lineage that stretched back to Odin himself. In *Heimskringla*, the early Norse kings claimed they too were the descendants of Odin, while their successors preferred to link themselves to the god Frey, the twin brother of the goddess Freya. This seemed a better fit for a king, as Odin could be violent and unpredictable, while his son Frey was seen as a more just and kindly god of peace and prosperity.[14]

This was all very well, if you still believed in the old gods. By the time *The Saga of the Earls of Orkney* was written, though, Scandinavia was largely Christian, and claiming you were a descendant of Odin held less appeal. Still, lineage was important to the people of the Norse world. It marked a person's place in the pecking order of the time. Social status was often underpinned by this form of inventive mythical pedigree.

For Earl Rognvald of Møre, his ancestral link with the old Sea King gave him a claim to royal status. His older descendants and their links to the natural elements – wind, sea, fire, frost and snow – had a supernatural quality, which might suggest Rognvald could somehow harness these himself. These natural elements were all rooted in northern Scandinavia, and its often-harsh environment. Then, by going all the way back through the mists of time to the giant Fornjót, the first of the *jötunn*, Rognvald was claiming an ancestry that was as old as Scandinavia itself – older even than the Norse gods themselves.[15]

As if that wasn't enough, there was another strand to this ancestral line. *The Saga of the Earls of Orkney* said that Rognvald was the son of Eysteinn 'Rattle' (or 'the Noisy'), a minor king in western Norway, and the grandson of Ívarr of the Uplands, which meant the Swedish region of Uppland, a little above modern Stockholm. It then went on to say his great-grandfather was Hálfdan the Old. He was a legendary Danish king of the Skjöldjung dynasty and represented the point where Rognvald's lineage moved from myth to semi-historical reality.

It was another link to royal status, and it proved that royal blood ran through Earl Rognvald's veins.

Essentially, with his own 'origin myth', Earl Rognvald was making a powerful political statement. The earldom of Orkney was a dynastic one, so any future earls who were descendants of Rognvald shared the same family tree. They might be mere noblemen, but they had royal blood and could trace their roots back to an older Norse world. In Norse mythology the gods and the giants had been rivals. So, as a descendant of both, Rognvald was a man with a foot in both ancestral camps. As pedigrees go, this was quite impressive.

In the end, my old headmaster had a point. All this 'origin myth' doesn't make a whole lot of sense to modern readers of the *Earls' Saga*. You can easily bypass it and plunge straight into the main storyline. If you do, though, you'd miss a very important point – one that spoke volumes about how the Orkney earls saw themselves. Although their earldom was created by a Norwegian king, and each new earl had to pay lip service to these kings being their rulers, the whole 'origin myth' demonstrates that they really saw themselves as every bit the equal of their monarch, or even slightly superior. As a result, while it suited them, the earls of Orkney would do what the king ordered. When it didn't, and without asking permission from him, they would force their own path. After all, the descendants of gods and giants, water, wind and fire couldn't be expected to have it any other way.

THREE

Land and People

W HEN THE EARLDOM OF ORKNEY was presented to Rognvald, Earl of Møre, on a platter, there's no evidence that he'd ever set foot on the islands before. So, to him the islands of Orkneyjar (Orkney) and Hjatland (Shetland) might well have been nothing more than strange, uncharted islands on the far side of the West Sea. The same went for the Sudreys, where his son Ivar died fighting for Harald 'Finehair'. Like any visitor to Orkney, though, he might well have been captivated by the place. The soft features of the landscape, the bare rolling hills, the sandy beaches and the rich farmland would all have come as a pleasant surprise. Today, visitors often describe Orkney as a magical place, with beautiful, captivating views at every turn. Native Orcadians, though, will patiently explain that winters there are slightly more challenging.

Shetland too possesses a singular beauty, albeit one of a more rugged form than the more verdant archipelago 50 miles to the south. Shetland's long thin coastline is broken by numerous inlets or geos, reminiscent of the Norwegian fjords less than 200 miles to the east, but without the trees and mountains around their shores. The land itself is more barren, and it lacks the rich soil of its southern island neighbour. There's some truth in the adage that a typical Orcadian is a farmer with a boat, while the Shetlander is a fisherman with a croft. The waters around both archipelagos are rich in fish, although Shetland has easier access to bountiful offshore fishing grounds.

The two archipelagos vary considerably in appearance and in geography. Both have a main island, called simply the 'mainland' or *meginland* in Norse, although the Orkney one was also called Hrossey. Each archipelago has numerous smaller islands clustered around it. Shetland is just under 75 miles long from its northernmost tip on the island of Unst (or 'Ornyst') to the southernmost point of the mainland at Sumburgh (or 'Svinborg'). At its widest point, it's only 20 miles across, and in parts of the south this drops to just over two miles. Halfway down the east coast is Lerwick (or 'Leirvik'), the main town. While parts of Shetland are fertile, the bulk of the land is rough and heather clad. The general appearance, then, is vaguely reminiscent of the west of Scotland, only with a more rugged, frontier-like quality to it.

Orkney is slightly smaller, but its low hills have a more rounded appearance. Here, the archipelago is just over 50 miles long, from the northern tip of North Ronaldsay (or 'Rinasey') to the southern end of South Ronaldsay (or 'Rognvaldsey'). Unlike Shetland, though, its axis is east to west, like a figure of eight lying on its side. The narrow waist between the two loops divides the East Mainland from the larger West Mainland. In this mile and a half-wide gap between the two lies the main town of Kirkwall ('Kirkjuvág'), now dominated by its magnificent Norse cathedral. The rest of the archipelago is split between the North Isles and South Isles, the latter encircling the large natural harbour of Scapa Flow, which served the Royal Navy well in two World Wars. In Orkney, the land is more fertile than in Shetland. Even in Norse times the rich black soil was a farmer's delight.

Both island groups have a lot of similarities, and as many differences, but even today the islanders share common bonds. The local Orcadians and the Shetlanders are a hardy, resilient people, and in both places there's a strong sense of community, and a deep love of their island home. Today, tests have shown that in these archipelagos the native islanders display a high level of Norse DNA. Shetland, of course, has 'Up Helly Aa', a festival that celebrates the island's Norse past. These islanders are clearly proud of their Nordic ancestry, and on 17 March, in both Kirkwall and Lerwick, they mark Norwegian Constitution Day with a parade. Both communities share a bond in their Norse heritage.

Today ferries link Orkney and Shetland to the Scottish mainland, as do regular scheduled flights. Even then, though, an islander landing in Aberdeen or in Caithness is still a long way from the seats of power in Edinburgh or London. This all adds to a sense of remoteness, accentuated by maps that stick the islands in a box at the top-right corner of the British Isles. A thousand years ago, though, the islands were at the centre of things rather than on its northern fringe.

Imagine the islands before the coming of modern roads, railways and air travel. Any journey from London or Edinburgh to Orkney would take several weeks by land, on roads that were often impassable in winter. It was much quicker by sea, with the passage taking days rather than weeks. From London, Orkney is 560 nautical miles away, while Shetland a hundred miles further north. If you look east to Norway though, Orkney is just 260 miles from Stavanger, while Shetland is 200 miles from Bergen. Even distant Trondheim, 350 miles from Shetland, is half the distance the island is from London. So, connections with Norway were always relatively easy, even before the invention of the aircraft. Back then, as in the Viking Age, the sea was the artery for trade, travel and news, and it linked the islands to Norway far more easily than it did to the seats of power in the British Isles.[1]

If you were a Viking raider with a crew eager for plunder, in fair weather you could easily cross the West Sea to Orkney. While Danish raiders and settlers tended to make landfall on the coast of England, the Norse found it easier to sail west to Orkney or Shetland and make their landfall there. From Orkney, you had the option of raiding down the eastern coast of the British Isles, or down the west. Inevitably then, the islands became a Viking haven. This also made them well-suited to Norse colonisation, and ultimately to Norse rule.

Orkney and Shetland were occupied long before the coming of the Norsemen. Unfortunately, the sagas say almost nothing about the people who lived there. In fact, the *Earls' Saga* doesn't even give them a mention. It was almost as if there was no 'first contact' at all, and the first Norsemen stepped ashore on a desert island. Of all these Scandinavian accounts, only the 12th-century *Historia Norvegiae* comes close to the historical truth. Even that, though, is pure invention: 'These islands were first inhabited by the Picts (*Peti*) and the *Papae*. Of these, one race, the Picts, little exceeded pygmies in stature. They did marvels, in the morning and the evening, in building [walled] towns, but at midday they entirely lost their strength, and lurked through fear in little underground houses.'[2]

It seems that the indigenous inhabitants of these islands had been turned into a mythical people, not unlike the elves, dwarves and sprites that are sprinkled throughout Norse mythology. However, there's no doubt people lived in Orkney and Shetland before the coming of the Norsemen. After all, the Neolithic village of Skara Brae in Orkney was built around 3300 BC, some four millennia before the arrival of the first Scandinavians. The great Neolithic complex at the Ness of Brodgar, a few miles further inland, dates from roughly the same period, as do many of Orkney's other Neolithic sites, such as its standing stone circles like the Ring of Brodgar, and burial mounds like nearby Maeshowe. Later, the so-called 'Broch Period' of the Iron Age created the large circular drystone towers called brochs which can be found in both archipelagos. The most impressive of these can still be seen at Mousa in Shetland and Gurness in Orkney. Although built for defence, they were also designed for show, and so probably acted as regional seats of power.

Up to a century ago it was suggested that these had all been abandoned, and that the first Norsemen found the islands completely empty. Archaeology, though, has proved this wrong. Dating now suggests that some of these old Iron Age buildings, including Mousa and Gurness, were still in use around the time the Norsemen first appeared. In fact, the islands were still inhabited by the very descendants of the people who built the imposing brochs. These were the supposed 'pygmy people' described in the *Historia Norvegiae*. Traces of the pre-Norse inhabitants can still be found in the islands in the remains of their buildings, in the carved stone markers with curious-looking symbols on them, and in placenames. These same people also inhabited Scotland's eastern side as far south as the Forth bridges.

Nobody really knows what these people called themselves. The Romans used the term *Picti*, which means 'the painted ones'. Presumably this referred to their wearing of body paint or tattoos.[3] These people, though, weren't exotic at all. They were simply the Celtic-speaking descendants of the Iron Age tribes who lived in that part of what we now call Scotland. In other words, these were the same people the Romans had been fighting beyond the wall for centuries.[4]

They left no written record, save for Latin copies of lists of kings, but throughout what was once Pictish land they have left behind their enigmatic stone carvings – not just mysterious symbols but also images of themselves, their boats and horses, as well as of wild animals. On the Brough of Birsay, a tidal island off the Atlantic coast of Orkney, a Pictish symbol stone found there depicts three well-dressed warriors. Could this be a long-forgotten Pictish king of Orkney, and his leading warriors? Unfortunately, any such interpretation would be mere speculation. Still, in Orkney and Shetland Pictish-age dwellings have been excavated, and these, together with other scientific or scholarly disciplines, reveal traces of the Pictish people who lived in the archipelagos all those centuries ago.

The Greek explorer Pytheas claimed to have circumnavigated Britain in the 4th century BC. He mentioned the islands known as the 'Orchades', the earliest version of the name 'Orkney'. Then, on Ptolmey's map of Scotland created in the late 1st century AD, it was made clear that these islands were occupied by the same Celtic people who lived on the Scottish mainland.[5] The 8th-century Anglo-Saxon scholar Bede described Orkney as part of the realm of the Picts, and the 8th-century Welsh monk Nennius recorded that the Picts ruled these islands, as well as the lands to the south. This all points to Orkney being part of the Pictish kingdom before the coming of the Norsemen in the 9th century.

The remnants of Pictish placenames in Orkney and Shetland support this. Even the Pentland Firth, the water dividing Orkney from the Scottish mainland, was called the Pictland Firth by the Norse. Then there are those enigmatic Pictish symbol stones, like the one found at the Brough of Birsay. William Thomson summed it all up quite neatly when he said, 'It seems likely that the historical Picts were the direct descendants of the broch-builders, and that the roots of Pictish Orkney extend back into the early Iron Age.'[6]

Thanks to archaeology we know how these people lived and what they ate, while a study of placenames helps us understand where they settled. Incidentally, we can also prove they weren't pygmies! Fortunately, there's also a handful of intriguing written references, which help shed some more light on these early islanders. One of these describes the Christian missionary Columba's visit to the court of the Pictish High King Bridei around AD 561. It probably took place in Craig Phadrig, a hillfort near modern-day Inverness. When Columba arrived, he found the Pictish *regulus* (the 'sub-king') from Orkney was there, and that Bridei was holding Orcadians hostage to ensure the islanders' good behaviour. This suggests Orkney was part of Bridei's Pictish realm, although their loyalty to the king warranted the holding of hostages.[7]

Then, a century later, in AD 682, the Irish Annals record that 'The Orcades were wiped out by Brudhei'. This was another King Bridei, who it seems led a destructive punitive expedition against his own subjects, the Picts of Orkney. 'Willie' Thomson thought that this might have been linked to the war further south, which three years later led to Bridei's victory over the Northumbrians at the Battle of Nechtansmere in AD 685.[8] It all suggests that Pictish Orkney was the loser in a devastating power struggle. The Pictish *regulus* in Orkney had backed the wrong horse, siding with the Northumbrian King Ecgfrith rather than with his own high king. The clue is the 12th-century historian William of Malmesbury's claim that half a century earlier, King Edwin of Northumbria 'had an influence which extended as far north as Orkney'. As a result, in the late 7th century, the Pictish sub-kingdom was 'wiped out'.[9]

It seems the Pictish sub-kings of Orkney had a rebellious streak, and in AD 682 they paid the price for it. It certainly raises an interesting possibility. Pictish Orkney may have been 'wiped out' by a Pictish royal army less than a century before the arrival of the first Norsemen. This might explain why apparently there was no organised Pictish resistance against these Norse incomers. Put simply, the leaderless Picts didn't put up a fight.

For decades, academics, archaeologists, linguists and others have tried to answer a crucial question. How did the Norsemen and the Picts in these islands interact with each other? There is clear evidence that Harald 'Finehair's' expedition didn't bring the first Norsemen to Orkney and Shetland. The whole point of the venture was to clear the islands of the Norse Vikings who'd been raiding the Norwegian coast. Most probably these Vikings were Norwegian exiles and rebels, fleeing from King Harald. Many of them would have been on the losing side of the Battle of Hafrsfjord. These were Viking raiders who looted and plundered not for a living, but as a way of seeking revenge.[10]

Becoming an exile often means you take your belongings with you. In the case of Norse noblemen this would include their families, possessions, money, ships and followers. They would have settled in Orkney, Shetland and the Sudreyjar and once there they'd have lived alongside the indigenous islanders. Many would have established farms there, to ensure their long-term survival. The rich farmlands of Orkney must have come as a pleasant surprise to incomers from the Norwegian fjords. It also helped that these exiles weren't the first Norse settlers to establish themselves on the far side of the Salt Road.

Historical and archaeological evidence suggests that Norse raiders and settlers arrived in Orkney and Shetland several decades before the founding of the earldom. This of course had a lot to do with the start of Viking raids on the British Isles. The *Anglo-Saxon Chronicle* entry for AD 793 recorded several ominous portents which included the appearance of fire-breathing dragons. Then, 'Not long after, on the sixth day before the ides of January in the same year, the harrowing inroads of heathen men made lamentable havoc in the church of God in Holy-island, by rapine and slaughter.'[11]

Not to be outdone, the Northumbrian cleric Alcuin of York, writing from the safety of the Emperor Charlemagne's court in Aachen, claimed, 'Never before has such terror appeared in Britain. Behold the church of St Cuthbert [Lindisfarne Monastery], splattered with the blood of God's priests, robbed of its ornaments.'[12] So, AD 793 is often taken as the start of what's often called 'The Viking Age'. It marked the beginning of more than a century of Viking raids around the British Isles, carried out by both Norsemen and Danes.

A year later in AD 794 it was the turn of the monastery of Iona, on a small island off the west coast of Scotland. That same year, raids were carried out on the northern coast of Ireland. Other raids followed, in increasing size and quantity, so that by the mid-9th century Viking raids were commonplace around the shores of the British Isles. Undoubtedly these raiders would struggle to carry out such far-reaching voyages from Norway. It made more sense to use the Orkney, Shetland or the Sudreyjar as a forward base.

So we can assume that when either Harald 'Finehair' or the earlier wave of exiles arrived in the islands, they'd have found Norse settlements already established there, serving as bases for Viking raids. These Norsemen had probably established themselves in Orkney and Shetland for the best part of a century before the earldom of Orkney was created. 'Willie' Thomson coined a shorthand for this, when he labelled it the 'pre-earldom time'. The question, though, remains of what happened at the moment of 'first contact' between Norseman and Pict.[13]

In the past, there have been two schools of thought. The original view was the 'War' one, which draws on the description of raids on Lindisfarne, Iona and elsewhere to emphasise the rapacity of Viking raids. If these Vikings needed an island base for their operations, then they'd simply have seized it. This would have made them conquerors rather than mere settlers. The 'Peace' stance draws on the evidence that the Picts of Orkney weren't driven off or wiped out, but instead they co-existed with these early Norsemen.

The excavation of the 9th-century Norse dwelling at Buckquoy in Orkney revealed an interesting overlap between Norse and Pictish influences. This suggests a non-violent integration. A lengthy transition could have taken place, where the development of agriculture and trade played an important part in the development of the archipelagos. Here the emphasis was on integration rather than conflict. The suggestion that there was a reasonably peaceful integration of the newcomers is also reflected in the placenames in Orkney and Shetland. The majority are Norse, but older Pictish placenames also remain alongside them. It all points to integration rather than extermination.[14]

In fact, you can see elements of this at work in the islands today, where an increasing number of incomers from elsewhere in Britain have established themselves. For the most part this is a relatively frictionless integration, although tensions sometimes exist. Here, though, the process of assimilation is helped when these incomers willingly absorb something of the culture and tradition of the islands, and their children are raised there, together with local youngsters. Perhaps it was a similar process in the 9th century.

In truth, the most likely way this integration happened in the 'pre-earldom' time might have been a mixture of both schools. The first Vikings to arrive in Orkney may have seen it as a place to loot and plunder and might well have seized land to create their own settlements. If organised Pictish government was 'wiped out' in AD 682, then this would have been relatively easy. Then, over time, the emphasis would have turned from raiding to the establishment of farms, trading centres, harbours and communities. Certainly, this process would have been well under way by the time the earldom was first created.

Possibly fresh evidence will come to light, but for now the best guess is that generally, the integration of the Norse and the Picts was probably a relatively peaceable one, or rather it was by the early 9th century. What was still lacking in Orkney and Shetland, though, seems to be any form of government. For better or worse, that would come with the establishment of the earldom of Orkney. It was created almost at a whim, by a Norwegian king who needed to bring order to what he saw as a troublesome Viking lair on the far side of the West Sea. Now, all the earls of Møre had to do was to bring order to the islands, and to shape this new earldom into their own secure and lucrative fiefdom.

FOUR

The Earldom

A S WE'VE SEEN, it says in the *Earls' Saga* that after completing his expedition, King Harald 'Finehair' decided what to do with the islands he'd conquered: 'On his way back to Norway, King Harald gave Earl Rognvald Shetland and Orkney in compensation for his son'. If this happened the way the saga claims, then it created a problem for Rognvald. He was already the earl of Møre, with extensive lands back in Norway. He was also the king's right-hand man, so he really needed to remain close to Harald. He'd little use for a backwater on the wrong side of the West Sea. Being awarded the earldom was an honour, but it wasn't worth moving so far away from the royal seat of power in Nidaros.

So, the saga explained what he did: 'Earl Rǫgnvaldr gave his brother Sigurðr both lands; he was King Haraldr's forecastle-man'. The two brothers parted company when the royal fleet returned to Nidaros and 'When he went east, the king gave Sigurðr the rank of earl, and Sigurðr stayed behind in the west.' So, Sigurðr (or Sigurd) became the first earl of Orkney, whose lands encompassed the archipelagos of Orkney and Shetland, on the western side of the West Sea. Rognvald didn't even tour the earldom before he handed it over to his younger sibling. This is the *Earls' Saga* version of how the earldom came into being. It might, though, have happened very differently.[1]

The need for Norway to control the islands on the far side of the West Sea was clear. Whoever held Orkney and Shetland controlled 'The Salt Road', the main route across the West Sea from Norway to the British Isles. The islands served as a strategic Norwegian base astride the Salt Road. Throughout the 'pre-earldom' these islands had been used by Norse exiles and Viking raiders, most of whom had come there from south-west Norway. Surviving Viking hoards of coins, silver and jewellery testify to a long-standing link between the two regions.

Some of these were evidently plundered in the same raid, and once divided, they landed up in both Orkney and south-eastern Norway. For Harald, the islands, together with the Sudreys, were now evolving into a haven for the Norse exiles who opposed him. That meant they posed a threat. Controlling Orkney and Shetland was vital to both the prosperity of Norway and the security of Harald's throne.[2]

With so much to do in Norway, King Harald couldn't govern Orkney directly. He needed a reliable lieutenant – someone he could trust and a warrior with the martial skills needed to deal with these Vikings and exiles. After his victory at Hafrsfjord in *c.* 880, there was probably nobody more suitable than Earl Rognvald of Møre. The question is, did Harald lead the expedition himself, or did he leave the task to Rognvald? After all, an absence of two or three years was a long time for a king who'd only just united his kingdom – one which was still exposed to attacks from enemies, both foreign and domestic.

There's also a possibility Rognvald undertook the expedition on his own initiative – a case of taking first and asking permission later. Rognvald was probably powerful enough to undertake this empire-building venture on his own. According to the *Historia Norvegiae*, Rognvald might well have organised and carried out the whole thing. In doing so he gained a secure power base and trading centre on the far side of the West Sea, which he and his successors could control. According to this version, Harald 'Finehair' played no part in the expedition. Instead, the expedition was a sort of colonial land-grab by Earl Rognvald and his family.[3]

The *Historia Norvegiae* says: 'In the days of Harald "Fairhair", king of Norway, certain Vikings, of the family of the most vigorous prince Rognvald, set out with a great fleet, and crossed the Solundic [West] ... and subdued the islands for themselves. And, being provided there of safe winter havens, they went in summer, working tyranny upon the English and the Scots, and sometimes also on the Irish.'[4]

If this is true, it suggests that the whole story about the foundation of the earldom given in *The Saga of the Earls of Orkney* was a lie. Rognvald or rather his family had established themselves in the islands well before Harald's expedition supposedly reached the islands. Either this conquest took place with the king's blessing, or it was a *fait accompli* in which Harald 'Finehair' took no part, but officially recognised it after the event by creating the earldom.[5]

Interestingly, this paragraph in *Historia Norvegiae* makes no direct mention of Earl Rognvald. It was 'certain Vikings' from his family who conquered the islands. One can read that as suggesting the whole expedition wasn't spearheaded by either Harald 'Finehair' or Earl Rognvald. The most likely candidate then, would be Rognvald's brother Sigurd Eysteinsson.

To muddy the waters, an Irish annal mentioned that in AD 860, two younger sons of Albdan, king of Norway, drove out the eldest son, Ragnall son of Albdan, for fear he would seize the kingship of Norway after their father died. So, Ragnall fled to Orkney. Unfortunately, no Norwegian character called Ragnall Albdansson can be traced, and although it's been suggested that this might be an early and mis-named reference to Rognvald Eysteinsson, this is unlikely, as the earl of Møre was consistently loyal to King Harald. More likely is that it referred to a 'pre-earldom' Viking leader, who used Orkney as a base decades before the earldom was established.[6]

Still, my old headmaster summed up the whole problem of Rognvald, Sigurd, King Harald and the foundation of the earldom when he said that 'The whole episode is so embedded in the Orkney consciousness that, whatever its faults, it will always remain the "real" story of the coming of the Norwegians.' He then added sagely: 'For that reason, it is best to start with what the saga has to say, without for the moment worrying overmuch about its accuracy.'[7]

Of course, neither Rognvald or his brother Sigurd were really called an 'earl'. The Norse word was *jarl*, but for the sake of clarity we'll use the better-known English equivalent. The term *jarl* has roots which predate the Norse era. Earlier Germanic cultures used a similar word, *ierl*, which like the later Danish *jærl* was midway between the Norse *jarl* and the Anglo-Saxon *eorl*. In all these cultures, the word meant a nobleman, one of society's elite, and a leader of warriors. In the Norse Eddic poem *Rígsmál*, jarls are portrayed as: 'the idle aristocrat ... whose sole occupations are raiding, hunting and swimming'. This description, though, never really applied to the Norse earls of Orkney.[8]

In Norse society the rank of *jarl* was often achieved through martial endeavours, but at first it was also considered a dynastic title, much like the modern English equivalent 'earl' today. It was usual for the title to be awarded by a king. So, a powerful warrior or war leader could acquire the title as a reward for their military service, as happened to Rognvald Eysteinsson and the earldom of Møre. Just as possibly, a *jarl* could be stripped of his title when he fell out of favour with his king. In the case of the Orkney earldom, though, the title was passed from one brother to the next, which underlines that it was very much considered a dynastic title.

Rognvald's brother Sigurd Eysteinnson, the forecastleman on the royal longship, was described as a *hǫfdingi*, which equates to a chief, or a leader of warriors. This was a lesser form of noble, akin to a feudal baron. Presumably, despite the claim in the *Earls' Saga* that Rognvald was the son of the Eysteinn 'Rattle', one of the minor kings of western Norway, Rognvald hadn't inherited his father's throne, but he was a leading warrior. So he was probably a *hǫfdingi* like his brother, until his elevation to the earl of Møre. Still, whatever the background of the Eysteinsson brothers, they had now reached the pinnacle of Norse society. Both were earls, one of Møre and the other of Orkney. That meant they were true Norse aristocrats, second only to the kings of Norway.

The aim of their 'origin myth' was to underpin the earls' right to substantial autonomy from the Norwegian crown. Of course, Earl Sigurd already had that thanks to geography. On the far side of the West Sea, he was beyond easy reach of the Norwegian king, and so he and his successors were usually left alone to rule without interference. In any case, Norwegian rulers usually had bigger worries than scrutinising the way the Orkney earls operated.

For the most part, then, Earl Sigurd and his descendants were free to govern their lands as they liked. If they paid their dues to the Norwegian king, and didn't cause too much trouble, they would be left alone. It was a good arrangement for Harald 'Finehair' and his successors. The earldom of Orkney was a strategic nodal point, midway between Norway and the Viking hunting grounds around the British Isles. By controlling the islands, the earls could control future Viking raids or the king could use them to support his own military campaigns. In other words, controlling the islands strengthened Norway's military hand.

In fact it was Earl Sigurd rather than the Norwegian king who'd take advantage of this to expand his earldom further into the lands of the Picts and Scots. This, though, could only be achieved with a sizeable force of ships and warriors. The earls of Orkney could galvanise Vikings in the two archipelagos into a larger force – a free source of effective Norse warriors which could be harnessed to further the earls' own military ambitions.

In the 9th and 10th centuries the most powerful earldoms in Norway were those of Lade and Møre. These two earls supplied the bulk of warriors for the royal army, and the *Ladejarler* ('earls of Lade') were often seen as Norwegian 'kingmakers'. This made them dangerous, though, and from the reign of King Ólaf Haraldsson in the late 10th century, attempts were made to increase royal authority. This of course was achieved at the expense of the power of the two earldoms. So, after the death of Earl Hákon of Lade in a shipwreck off Orkney in *c.* 1030, the Lade earls weren't replaced, and their lands were taken by the crown. The Orkney earldom was lucky, in that it wasn't seen as a threat to royal rule, and so was usually left alone.[9]

By giving the earldom to a royal son, the threat to the crown was reduced. This was done elsewhere in Norway, until virtually all the earls were of royal blood, apart from the ones in Orkney. Then, under Ólaf's successor King Magnus 'the Good', hereditary succession was abolished. When an earl died, it was up to the king to choose his replacement. Under Magnus, an earl was seen as much as an administrator as a warrior. The exception once again was the earldom of Orkney, which remained a dynastic title throughout the Norse period. By then, only the king's sons and the earls of Orkney had the right to use the title of earl. This made the Orkney earldom unique.[10]

However, the Norwegian kings increasingly demanded that the Orkney earls swear an oath of fealty to the crown, in return for being allowed to continue holding their title. This threat from the crown was why their 'origin story' was so important. It underlined their claim that they had every bit as much royal blood in their veins as any of these princes and kings. This may help explain why the Norse earldom of Orkney survived for over 600 years. This, though, was set against another less impressive trend. From the early 11th century, the tendency was for sons or brothers to share the earldom. This of course created room for friction, and led to some of the most murderous confrontations in the earldom's already blood-soaked history.[11]

It seems peculiar that the term 'earl' was still used throughout this period, when the earls of Orkney ruled what really amounted to a kingdom. After all, in both the Sudreys and the Isle of Man, Norse rulers were called kings. In Orkney, though, the earls appeared content with their seemingly lesser title. The *Historia Norvegiae* tells us that although the rulers of the Sudreys and the Isle of Man were *reguli* ('sub-kings'), both earls and sub-kings were considered equals, under the overlordship of the Norwegian king. In Norse high society, what title you held was irrelevant, if you held power and knew your rightful place in the pecking order.[12]

What, then, was the benefit of being a Norse earl? The earls of Orkney were always largely autonomous, despite their supposed fealty to the Norwegian crown. They were empowered to gather *skatt* ('tax') from their people and raise troops and maintain longships. They also needed to maintain records, as well as a treasury and storehouses to hold *skatt* and produce given to them in lieu of silver. This meant they had to establish their own administrative system and have the men to run it.

So, Earl Sigurd's priority was to create this administration, find room for it to work, and to house both its records and its income. First, Sigurd's administrators had to tour the islands, and see exactly who was there and what land they held. The earl needed to know where the landed wealth was in his territory, and who had the money to pay in silver coin, and who could only provide payment in kind. The accuracy of this census was probably limited at first but became increasingly reliable over time. Records from the late 13th century onwards reveal that by then the earldom's administrative powers had become both thorough and well organised.[13]

This wasn't an easy task, given that for much of the year, sea communications between Orkney and Shetland were subject to the often-capricious weather conditions. Gales could come from any direction and turn an easy voyage into one of nightmares. The same was true when crossing the notorious Pentland Firth, between Orkney and Caithness, the northernmost part of the British mainland. Here, fast currents, strange tidal rips, rocks, skerries and cliffs all made the passage dangerous, especially in an open boat.

Each of the two archipelagos was made up of a large island called the 'mainland', and numerous smaller islands of various sizes. Not all of these islands were inhabited, but it made the task of the earls' agents all the harder. It would have taken several years to survey the islands, to make a census of the population, to evaluate both the quality of the land, and to work out who owned what. The arable parts of Orkney, Shetland and the Sudreyjar were largely made up of dispersed farms, which merely added to the difficulty of keeping track of land ownership. Still, once compiled, this information then formed the basis of governance in the earldom.

This land was divided into small taxation districts called *urislands*, which were then used to levy a *skatt* on the population there, either in money or sometimes in animals, crops or other forms of produce. In Norway these were known as *ouncelands*. All these parcels of land equated to the equivalent worth of an ounce of silver. Later, from the 12th century on, a smaller land unit, the *pennyland*, was used. This equated to a coin, a silver penny rather than a weight of metal, and it appears that in Orkney an *ounceland* was divided into 18 *pennylands*. Effectively, though, each of these smaller units was roughly the equivalent of a single family-run farm.[14]

This provided the basis of land taxation. In addition, money could also be raised through a wealth tax. The *Earls' Saga* shows how Orkney remained a base used by Viking raiders well into the reign of Earl Harald Maddadarson, who ruled the earldom in the late 12th century. The main point, in terms of revenue for the earls of Orkney, is that plunder kept being brought into the islands from Viking raids for over a hundred years after what historians usually deem the end of the Viking Age in the mid-11th century.[15]

For the earls, plunder almost certainly meant income. A sizeable number of Viking silver hoards have been found in Orkney and Shetland, which confirm Viking plunder was a recognised source of income in the Norse earldom. In the Norse world, payment for services, such as to the retainers of the earls or prominent landowners, was made using silver. It all suggested a currency based on weight of silver, which tied in neatly to the *ouncelands* and *pennylands* used in land tax.[16]

This would probably have been gathered by the earl's *skatt* collectors from Viking raiders or their financial backers in the form of a wealth tax. In other words, the earls profited from Viking raids, which may explain why Vikings were perfectly welcome in their lands as late as the 12th century. One of the most famous of them, Svein Ásleifarson, raided twice a year, his voyages timed to coincide with slack periods in the annual farming cycle. The rest of the year he raised crops to feed his animals through the winter and made his money as a peaceable farmer. Almost certainly the earls benefited from both of his profit-making activities, as they did from dozens of others.[17]

Whatever it was called and our lack of knowledge about how it was gathered doesn't really alter the basic fact. The earl taxed the people in his earldom, and used it to maintain his halls and storehouses, his 'hearthguard' of seasoned warriors and his fleet of longships. In this semi-feudal system, it paid to be the man at the top.

Of course, some of this revenue was sent east across the West Sea to the Norwegian king. In the Sudreyjar, the nature of taxation changed over time. There, at times the Norwegian king retained the right to gather taxes himself, rather than administer them through the earls of Orkney. It didn't help when, in the late 10th century, the king appointed a rival Norwegian family, the earls of Lade, to administer the Hebrides on the king's behalf. Meanwhile, in the earldom's lands on mainland Scotland, a similar arrangement was in place with the Scottish crown. There, a share of the earldom's *skatt* was sent south to the Scottish court rather than to the Norwegian one.

So, from some time in the late 9th century, the earldom of Orkney was firmly established, with the earl ruling over the people of Orkney and Shetland regardless of whether they were native Picts or Norse settlers. In terms of the Norse world, the fertile lands of Orkney and the abundant fishing waters around Shetland would have made the earldom a relatively wealthy place. Then, the earl's treasure was boosted by income from Viking raids, and from trade. The result was that he was able to maintain his own bodyguard of seasoned warriors and a sizeable fleet of longships. The earl could also draw on a population of farmers and Viking raiders who knew perfectly well how to handle themselves in a fight. It was little wonder that as soon as Earl Sigurd was securely established as the first earl of Orkney, he set about using these ships and men to expand his island earldom.

PART TWO
CARVING OUT A KINGDOM

FIVE

Earl Sigurd 'the Mighty'

A s THE *EARL'S SAGA* EXPLAINS, the first true Orkney *jarl* was Sigurd Eysteinsson, the younger brother of Rognvald, Earl of Møre. Both brothers were close to the Norwegian king Harald 'Finehair', but when Harald sailed back to Norway, Earl Sigurd was the one who was left behind to rule the islands. Unfortunately, despite the importance of Earl Sigurd in the history of the earldom, the *Earls' Saga* says very little about him. Instead, it mainly concentrates on his somewhat bizarre death, several years later, around AD 892.[1]

What singled out Earl Sigurd's reign and earned him the Norse epithet *Ríki* ('the Mighty') was his dramatic expansion of the earldom from Orkney to the mainland of Pictland, which was evolving into part of Alba. To make this happen, Sigurd needed ships, men and money. It took time to raise funds for a large expedition, although some of the family's money – or even the brothers' share of plunder from King Harald's expedition – might have been set aside to fund Sigurd. In any case, if we work back from the probable date of Earl Sigurd's death, we can assume this great venture began around the late spring or early summer of AD 889 or 890. If many of his warriors were *bondi* (yeomen), raised from within the earldom, then like Viking raiders, the campaigning season would be planned to take place between the spring planting and the autumn harvest.

At least Caithness wasn't far away. From the author's home in the Orkney island of South Ronaldsay, the low, purple-coloured coast of Caithness is clearly visible, ten miles away to the south. At Burwick at the southern end of the island, the Pentland Firth is just six miles across. Today, daily ferries ply from one side to the other, but in the days of oar and sail, crossing this treacherous waterway was a dangerous undertaking. Undoubtedly Sigurd would have used local fishermen or mariners as pilots, and chose his moment to make the crossing. While waiting, Orkney provided good anchorages for his ships, such as Long Hope in the island of Hoy (off the modern village of Longhope), or Widewall Bay, a few miles away across Hoxa Sound, in South Ronaldsay.

Once again, *The Saga of the Earls of Orkney* tells us very little about Earl Sigurd's great expedition. It says: 'Earl Sigurðr became a great chieftain. He joined up with Þorsteinn the Red, son of Ólafr "the White" and Auðr the Deep-minded, and they conquered all of Caithness, and much of the rest of Scotland.'[2]

The campaign was a great success. The earl had planned carefully, and sought out a powerful ally, so he could strike Caithness and the lands to the south from two directions. This shows that Sigurd was both well-connected and a man who understood strategy. It was an ambitious and aggressive venture, which involved the conquest of the Pictish lands in Caithness, and then their settlement by the growing number of Norse settlers arriving in Orkney. This was as much about a land grab as it was about power and prestige. By expanding into Caithness, Earl Sigurd could expand his landholdings while also reducing the risk of another warlord seizing what he must have considered a prize that was there for the taking.

Another motivation was plunder. Maintaining a powerful fleet and bodyguard of warriors was expensive, and for this venture Sigurd undoubtedly boosted his small standing force by raising the men of Orkney to fight alongside him, under his banner. Plunder meant the earl could reward his men with their own share, while also filling his own coffers. Although there were no rich Christian monasteries in Caithness, he would have heard of the monastic sites further south in eastern Ross, and probably hoped they would provide some of the plunder every Norse warlord craved.

This campaign would bring Earl Sigurd's Norse warriors into contact with the Celtic-speaking people on the mainland. This began with a clash – the first of many – and then the mingling of two cultures. It was a process that would continue for centuries. In Sigurd's time, these first Norse settlers would essentially be frontiersmen. They would face the daunting challenge of establishing themselves and building a community in what had only recently been foreign soil. However, they did so under the protection of the earldom's warriors. Gradually, over the centuries, the flow ebbed, and in 1098 Caithness became part of the Scottish kingdom, albeit one which was still ruled by the earls of Orkney. This continued until the mid-14th century, when Caithness became firmly part of a unified kingdom of Scotland. Today, the Norse presence there can be traced in a county peppered with Norse placenames.

At the end of the 9th century, though, Caithness was part of the Pictish realm, as well as part of a gradually evolving Alba. It had once been the kingdom of Cat, one of seven such provinces of Pictish sub-kings on the Scottish mainland north of the Firth of Forth. The people there followed a different religion from the Norsemen, as thanks to Celtic missionaries, Christianity had become established in Caithness.[3]

This wasn't the only difference. The Norsemen were used to the Norwegian landscape of the fjords, or the rolling lush farmland of Orkney. Caithness was more of a wilderness, with most of the land being the flat 'flow country' of peaty moorland and bog. Without trees, it presents a somewhat dismal appearance, its featureless vista broken only by a handful of lochs and small rivers. At its southern end, though, the land becomes hillier and ultimately rises to form part of a more traditional mountainous Highland landscape.

The coastline of Caithness is fringed with cliffs, but these are broken by stretches of sandy beaches and small sheltered havens. The best farmland is found near the coast before the land gives way to the flow country, which was largely unsuited to agriculture. Inevitably, these coastal areas were where the Norse settlers wanted to establish themselves, and this is reflected by the Norse placenames found in abundance there. The indigenous Celts seem to have been driven inland, to eke out what living they could in the bleak flow country. Caithness then, under Norse rule, would have a fertile, productive coastal fringe, farmed by Norsemen, and a hinterland where a sparse population of resentful Celts presented the earls with a potential source of trouble.

The religious division was just as important. Any invasion by heathens risked provoking the enmity of all Picts and Scots, with the potential chance of facing a large and vengeful enemy army fighting in the name of their religion. To do this, the Pictish king Giric ('Gregory' in English) would have had to muster troops and then march north through rugged country, interspersed with rivers and large inlets (known as 'firths'). By contrast, all Earl Sigurd had to do was to cross the Pentland Firth and land in one of the nearby beaches or havens, such as modern-day Thurso Bay or Dunnet Bay on the north coast, or Sinclair's Bay or Wick Bay in the east.

To reduce the risk of the Pictish king coming to the rescue of their lands in Caithness, Sigurd came up with a plan to prevent the Picts from sending an army north to confront him. The key to it was another powerful Norse warrior, albeit with Irish blood, Þorsteinn (or Thorstein) 'the Red'.

Thorstein played a crucial part in Earl Sigurd's plans, but the *Earls' Saga* tells us very little about him. All it gives is his background – that he was the son of King Ólaf 'the White' of Dublin and the grandson of Ketill 'Flatnose'. Fortunately, other sagas shed more light on Thorkell's family, but they also wildly contradict each other. The Icelandic *Laxdæla Saga* claims that his grandfather Ketill 'Flatnose' came from Romsdal in western Norway, close to Møre, the earldom given to Rognvald Eysteinsson by Harald 'Finehair'.

According to another Icelandic work, the *Eyrbyggja Saga*, King Harald placed Ketill 'Flatnose' in command of an expedition across the Western Sea, to root out the troublesome Vikings in Orkney, Shetland and the Hebrides, who were raiding the Norwegian coast. This sounds suspiciously like the description of the royal expedition that featured prominently in the *Earls' Saga*. It claims Ketill took his family with him on the expedition and was successful in subduing the Vikings in the Hebrides. He then sent the bulk of the fleet home, telling Harald that he planned to rule the islands for himself. Once established, he ruled them and formed his own alliances with neighbouring Gaelic rulers. A peeved Harald responded by seizing Ketill's Norwegian lands in Romsdal.[4]

However, the *Laxdæla Saga* tells a different story. Here, Ketill 'Flatnose' was a powerful *hersir* ('chieftain') in Romsdal, who lived there with his wife Yngvild and his five children. In this version, he fled Norway to escape from Harald 'Finehair'. When his lands were threatened with annexation, Ketill called the people together and told them that 'It seems to me that there are two choices left us, either to fly the land or to be slaughtered each in his own seat'.[5] They opted to leave. So while some made for Iceland, led by two of Ketill's sons, Ketill led the rest of his family and followers across the Western Sea, and, bypassing Orkney and Shetland, they landed in the Hebrides. There the locals were welcoming: 'They offered him [Ketill] there such station as he would like to take, and Ketill and his company of kinsfolk settled down there.'[6]

This places him among the first of the exiles who sought safety from Harald 'Finehair' on the far side of the Western Sea. Both sagas agree, though, that once there, Ketill made himself master of the Hebrides. Yet another saga, the *Landnámabók* ('the Book of Settlements'), repeats the version of events that Ketill was part of King Harald's expedition, but returned with the king. He was then sent back to the Hebrides when Harald learned that Vikings were re-establishing themselves there. This time, Ketill subdued them completely, and ruled the lands on behalf of King Harald.[7] Ketill eventually died in the Hebrides at some point around AD 880, and as no sons took over his lands, the islands reverted to local Gaelic rule.

The various saga versions of Ketill's story are at odds, though, and almost certainly got much of it wrong. After all, if Ketill's grandson Thorstein 'the Red' was a war leader in *c.* AD 889–890, then this means his grandfather, two generations further back, was active around AD 840, which predates King Harald's expedition by at least four decades. The possibility is that Ketill 'Flatnose' carved out his realm in the Hebrides well before Harald's expedition across the Western Sea and the foundation of the earldom of Orkney. This makes it more likely he was either a Viking warlord himself, or he was an exile, fleeing some other unrecorded threat in Norway.

Our focus, though, is not so much on Ketill 'Flatnose' as his daughter Auðr (or Aud) 'the Deep-Minded'. She married the Hiberno-Norse king Ólaf 'the White' (known as Amláib in the Irish annals), who together with his brother Ímar took control of Dublin in AD 853 and ruled it jointly with him. The pair were the first Norse kings of Dublin.[8] The Irish, though, preferred the title 'Kings of the Foreigners'. Ólaf and Aud had two sons, one of whom has been tentatively identified as Thorstein (or Oistin). He was almost certainly the Thorstein 'the Red' who formed the alliance with Earl Sigurd.

The last mention of King Ólaf 'the White' in the Irish annals is in AD 871.[9] They claimed he sailed off 'to wage war on the Lochlanns, and to aid his father Goffridh [Guthfrith in Norse] for the Lochlanns had made war against him...' The Lochlanns (Irish Gaelic for the 'Norsemen') could suggest that King Ólaf 'the White' and his father, probably the King Guthfrith who ruled Vestfold in this period, set off to campaign in Norway, or fought against the Vikings infesting the Hebrides, Orkney and Shetland. Interestingly, Torbjørn Hornfloki, the *skald* of King Harald 'Finehair', may have mentioned Ólaf in his poem about the Battle of Hafrsfjord: 'Then boomed the bucklers ere a blow felled Haklang'. It has been proposed that Haklang ('Long Chin'), was a reference to Ólaf 'the White'. Another Scottish annal has Ólaf (Amláib) dying in battle against the Pictish King Causantín (or Constantine) in AD 874.[10]

As for Thorstein, his career had been very successful even before his alliance with Earl Sigurd. After his father's death in the early 870s, Thorstein and his mother Aud abandoned Dublin for the Hebrides and joined Ketill 'Flatnose' there. Thorstein, then probably in his 20s, had developed into an accomplished warrior and had married, taking 'Thurid daughter of Eyvind' as his wife. Before long, though, he soon began claiming land for himself. As the *Laxdæla Saga* put it: 'forthwith [he] betook himself to warring, and harried Scotland far and wide, and was always victorious. Later on he made peace with the Scots and got for his own one-half of Scotland.'[11] This might have been an exaggeration, even if you include the Hebrides, which were still ruled by his grandfather. Still, it suggests Thorstein had been busy carving out his own fiefdom in Argyll and among the islands of the Inner Hebrides.

This put him in an ideal position to form an alliance with Earl Sigurd. After all, he was already poised at the western end of the Great Glen, the geological fault line that cuts diagonally across Scotland. It stretches in a straight line beginning in the west at the end of the long fjord-like Loch Linnhe, where Fort William now stands. It then runs up to Inverness, 62 miles away to the north-east, on the shores of the Moray Firth, an inlet of the North Sea. To the Norse, though, the Moray Firth was the Breidafjordr ('Broad Fjord'), an inlet of the West Sea.[12]

Today the Great Glen is best known for incorporating Loch Ness, 23 miles long and 750 feet deep, ending in a river which flows into the Moray Firth. On its march to join Sigurd, Thorstein's small army would have had to pass along its shores. According to Adomnán of Iona, it was there, in AD 565, that St Columba had a dramatic encounter with the 'water beast' living in its depths. It was driven off, it was claimed, by the monk's words, and by his making the sign of the cross.[13] Thorstein's advance would then eventually take him to the mouth of the River Ness, where Inverness stands today.

This was near to where the old Pictish kings maintained their hilltop stronghold at Craig Phadrig, the probable site where King

Bridei met the saint shortly after his encounter with the 'water beast'. From there, or at least nearby, Thorstein could effectively guard Earl Sigurd's back, preventing any Pictish army from interfering with Sigurd's invasion. So, after landing in Caithness, most probably in the late spring of AD 889 or 890, Sigurd's men broke any Pictish resistance and secured control of the region. Once this was done, probably around mid-summer, Earl Sigurd would march the bulk of his small army south into the neighbouring Pictish region of Ross. This was part of the Pictish sub-kingdom of Fidach, which incorporated Moray to the south-east and Ros ('Ross') to the north-west. In the middle of Fidach, waiting for Sigurd, sat Thorstein and his army.[14]

The campaign went well, and on his way south, Sigurd undoubtedly sacked the Celtic monastic sites at Portmahomack on the Dornoch Firth and Rosemarkie on the 'Black Isle', between the Dornoch and Moray firths. Excavations have revealed signs that Portmahomack was razed at some point in the late 9th century.[15] No doubt Sigurd's fleet would have accompanied his army as it moved down the coast, allowing Sigurd to cross the various inlets which barred the route south. The two Norse leaders were finally able to join forces around modern-day Inverness towards the end of the campaigning season. Then, ships in the Beauly Firth would probably have taken Sigurd's *bondi* home to bring in the harvest, while the two Norse commanders planned their next move.

Presumably Sigurd or Thorstein also had a small squadron of longships working its way along the western coast of Caithness and Ross. The saga claimed that Sigurd conquered the coast there as far south as the southern portion of Argyll. This was also part of Alba, land that had been part of the kingdom of the Dál Riadan Scots before the unification of Picts and Scots some four decades earlier. The lack of response to all this by the Pictish king Giric is surprising. A look into the Scottish annals of the time, though, goes some way towards explaining why.

In the mid-9th century, the Dál Riadan Scots king Cínaed mac Ailpin (or 'Kenneth MacAlpin' in English) invaded the kingdom of the Picts, and by AD 843 he'd conquered it. He was already king of Dál Riada, but from that point on he adopted the title King of the Picts.[16] This gained him the epithet of 'The Conqueror', and today Kenneth MacAlpin is seen as the founder of the unified country of Alba, a country which would eventually become Scotland. On his death in AD 858, he was first succeeded by his brother, and then by his own sons. However, in AD 878 the smooth succession went awry when his son Áed died. He was then succeeded as King of the Picts by Giric mac Dúngail. The Scottish annals have little to say about him, but it was claimed that he killed Áed and seized his throne.[17]

It was also possible he ruled jointly with Eochaid, the king of Strathclyde, a territory which was based around Dumbarton on the River Clyde. The two kings were probably related, but exactly how is unknown. In the late 880s, though, Strathclyde was at war with the neighbouring Anglo-Saxon kingdom of Northumberland. So, it was left to Giric to deal with Sigurd and Thorstein. Suddenly, in AD 889, both Eochaid and Giric vanish from the records. This was roughly when Sigurd launched his invasion. It was clearly a time of Viking raids, but there's also a claim that Giric and possibly Eochaid were slain at the Pictish hillfort of Dundurn in what is now Perthshire.[18]

For Earl Sigurd, the timing couldn't have been better. The likelihood is that Giric had been killed by his successor Domnall ('Donald' in English), the son of Constantine I and the grandson of Kenneth MacAlpin.[19] When Donald gained the throne in AD 889, the kingdom had clearly undergone some sort of dynastic upheaval, or possibly a civil war. It would take him time to exert control over the kingdom. Meanwhile it was under external threat from the Northumbrians, from Viking raiders, and from Earl Sigurd. As a result, as a contemporary Scottish chronicle put it, 'The Northmen wasted Pictland at this time'.[20]

So, Domnall was unable to deal with Sigurd and Thorstein. Instead, he left it to his *mormaer* in Moray to sort out the problem.[21] Meanwhile, the two Norse leaders had been strengthening their foothold in the north. At this point *The Saga of the Earls of Orkney* says of Sigurd that 'There he had a fortification built in the southern part of Moray'.[22] Nowadays Moray extends from the North Sea coast southwards into Speyside and the Highlands. In the 9th century, though, it also incorporated the land around the Moray Firth. So it could mean somewhere there, like the old hilltop fort at Craig Phadrig.

More likely though, by Moray the writer meant the Moray Firth, where any fort built by Sigurd could be easily supplied and reinforced from the sea. Professor Barbara Crawford and others have suggested that Sigurd's fort could have been at Burghead, a coastal headland

30 miles north-east of Inverness.[23] It was the ideal location, as there was a Pictish fortress there already. Today, after walking through Burghead's ordered streets you emerge at the tip of the promontory amid the remains of earthen banks – all that remains of what was probably the most significant Pictish fortress in Moray.

A promontory fort may have been built there during the Iron Age, but it was the Picts who enlarged it into a substantial fortress around the 6th to 7th centuries. The fort, along with the church within its walls, appears to have been destroyed in the 9th or 10th century. This might have been the work of Earl Sigurd, or of later Norse attackers. The possibility remains that the earl captured it, then used it as his own forward base, deep in the heart of enemy territory.[24] It was probable that the events which followed, which saw a major reversal of Norse fortunes, took place in subsequent campaigning seasons. For the moment, though, Earl Sigurd had achieved all he'd set out to do, and more.

He'd captured Caithness, which then stretched south to its boundary with Ross at the Dornoch Firth, then inland to the west by way of the Kyle of Sutherland and the River Oykel. He also held Ross, or rather the coastal parts of it, including both shores of the Cromarty Firth and the Moray Firth, with the 'Black Isle' in between them. Then, thanks to Thorstein 'the Red', the Norse war leaders controlled the Great Glen. This was especially important to them as it allowed the movement of ships along it, using existing lochs and rivers, with just two portage points where boats were dragged overland. This cut out the risks inherent in a much longer sea voyage around Cape Wrath, to ensure safe sea communications around Scotland. At that point neither of the victorious Norse war leaders realised just how badly things could go wrong.[25]

SIX

A Tooth and an Eye

S IGURD EYSTEINSSON 'THE MIGHTY' would have considered
himself a lucky man. He'd conquered a large swathe of northern
Scotland, and thanks to his ally Thorstein Ólafsson 'the Red' he also
controlled a direct route to the west coast of Alba. There seemed
little to prevent him from pushing outwards from this secure base and
conquering the rich Pictish province of Moray. Without the main Scots
army appearing with King Donald at its head, the way forward seemed
clear. All that stood in his way was the army of the *mormaer* ('earl')
of Moray, a Pictish nobleman called Melbrikta Tooth ('Máel Brigte'
to the Scots). No doubt his Picto-Scots warriors were no match for
Sigurd's own Norsemen. It would be even sweeter, though, if victory
over Mormaer Máel Brigte of Moray could be achieved quickly, and at
no cost. So, Earl Sigurd hatched a plan which would virtually guarantee
this easy and relatively bloodless result.

He sent a message to the *mormaer*, suggesting that the two men
should meet and negotiate some form of beneficial settlement. Finally,
a venue was arranged, most probably somewhere near the shores of the
Moray Firth. It was agreed that both Earl Sigurd and Mormaer Máel
Brigte would attend in person, with a bodyguard of just 40 mounted
warriors. The Pictish earl agreed to this, and *The Saga of the Earls of
Orkney* explains what happened next: 'They would get together and
settle their issue at a nominated place with forty men each.' However,
'And when the appointed day came, Sigurðr thought the Scots were
unreliable'. So, the wily Sigurd had 80 men mounted on the 40 horses.
It was a nice touch that the saga claimed the reason Sigurd broke his
word was that he didn't trust the Scots! By the time Máel Brigte saw
what his foes were doing it was too late to escape. Instead, he turned
to his men and gave them a short speech: 'I see two men's legs on each
side of a horse, and the men must be twice as many as the mounts. Let

us steel our spirits now and make sure that each has taken out one man before we die.'[1]

This rallying call to his men to sell their lives dearly might have helped steel them before their last battle, but it wasn't enough. Sigurd had another ruse, which helped the skilled tactician stack the odds even more. He dismounted each of the second riders, and led the remaining 40 mounted warriors forward, riding as hard as they could to break the Scots' ranks. Then, while the two well-matched sides were locked in fierce hand-to-hand combat, the remaining body of dismounted warriors outflanked the Scottish line and fell on them from behind. It was a decisive blow. As the saga put it, 'the battle there was hard and it was not long before Melbrikta fell along with his retinue'.[2]

Earl Sigurd had got his way. With its *mormaer* dead, the province of Moray lay open to him. First, though, he and his men relished the moment. Sigurd ordered his men to lop off the heads of the slain enemy, and tie these to their saddle pommels. Then they returned to their camp to celebrate their victory. Naturally Earl Sigurd selected the head of his Scots counterpart, the *mormaer* Máel Brigte, who'd been nicknamed 'tooth' or even 'the buck-toothed'. The Scots nobleman's epithet, it seems, reflected his large tooth, which protruded from his mouth. No doubt this grisly trophy would form the centrepiece of the evening's victory celebrations. However, according to the saga, as they rode off and Earl Sigurd's horse picked up speed, the head swung around as it hung from the earl's pommel, and the tooth grazed Sigurd's leg. It was only a scratch, and he thought little of it.

After the victory celebration, and over the days that followed, Earl Sigurd began to feel unwell, with sweating, shivering and light-headedness setting in. It was sepsis. The *Earls' Saga* claims that: 'The wound began to swell and ache, and it was this that led to the death of Sigurd the powerful.'[3] It couldn't have been an easy death. Soon, septic shock would have set in, with the earl unable to stand up, and becoming sleepy and confused. Eventually, he would die. Victory in his campaign had been snatched away by what was a senseless accident. Earl Sigurd Eysteinsson 'the Mighty', conqueror of Caithness, Ross and Moray, had been ignominiously felled by a misshapen tooth.

However, the real cause for the sudden death of Earl Sigurd mightn't have been due to the tooth after all. The story drew on two commonly used themes of the period, the decapitation of enemies and their display as trophies. Whether it happened as the saga describes or not, it probably served as a moral comment on the smug, self-assured hubris of Earl Sigurd.[4]

In fact, it wasn't just Earl Sigurd who didn't live to see the end of this dramatic Norse expansion into northern Alba. The death of his ally had left Thorstein 'the Red' in a difficult position. Without Sigurd's army, which was bound to return to Orkney, he lacked the men he needed to hold on to his conquests around the Great Glen and the Moray Firth. For the same reason, he couldn't continue the campaign on into Moray. Even withdrawing to the west coast by way of the Great Glen posed problems, as it exposed him to a flank attack by the Scots. So, he struck a deal.

According to the *Læxdala Saga*, a temporary truce was agreed with the Scots, and Thorstein and his men marched north into Caithness. It's possible that Thorstein was holding the region on behalf of the Orkney earldom until a new earl could join him. It seems, though, the Scots didn't keep the peace with Thorstein for very long. Instead, as the saga claims, they 'treacherously murdered him'. Unfortunately, the saga doesn't provide any details, but as no Scottish annals mention a campaign there, it is more likely Thorstein was killed either through treachery and murder, or during a local uprising.[5]

The saga adds an interesting sidenote. It seems Thorstein's mother Aud 'the Deep-Minded' was living with her son in Caithness at the time of his death. With her father Ketill 'Flatnose' now dead, together with her husband Ólaf 'the White' and her son Thorstein 'the Red', Aud decided it was time to leave. So she secretly had a boat built, embarked what remaining kinsfolk and servants she had, and sailed to the Faeroes. First, though, she arranged the marriage of Thorstein's daughter Groa to a Caithness nobleman, Duncan of Duncansby. In the Faeroes, she married off Thorstein's second daughter Olof. Finally, she continued on to Iceland, where the rest of her family had settled. These two marriages would have a bearing on the future course of the Orkney earldom.[6]

As for the late Earl Sigurd, his body was taken north across the Moray Firth and the inlet beyond it, the Dornoch Firth. The funerary longship would have put ashore on the north bank of the firth, which at the time marked the southern boundary of Caithness. Further inland, the firth became the River Oykel, which the Norse settlers of Caithness called Ekkjal. There, about three miles west of the modern town of Dornoch, a great burial mound was built on the Ekkjalsbakki ('banks of the Oykel'). Unfortunately, there's no trace of it today, although Cyder Hall farm there was formerly called 'Sydera'. In the 13th century, it was called a word derived from the Norse 'Sigurdarhaugr' (Sigurd's howe). Both *'haugr'* and *'howe'* in Old Norse mean a burial mound. Today, a small patch of nearby woodland is still called Sydera Wood. That means that Earl Sigurd 'the Mighty', the first earl of Orkney, was almost certainly buried a stone's throw from the place where a modern causeway crosses the Dornoch Firth, carrying a major road, the A9, south from Caithness to Inverness.[7]

There, when it was first erected, Earl Sigurd's great howe would have been seen for miles overlooking the waters of the Dornoch Firth, especially when viewed from Struie Hill in Ross, on the firth's southern shore. It would have served as a prominent marker between the lands of the earls of Orkney in Caithness, and the lands ruled by the Scots. Although the fighting between the two peoples – Norse and Scots – would continue throughout the existence of the Norse earldom, Sigurd's howe served as a boundary marker between the two people, as well as a statement of Norse ownership. After Sigurd's death, the Norse settlement of Caithness would continue apace, until the ownership of the land and its people there was unquestioned. In the end, Earl Sigurd had his way.

Unfortunately, there is no record of where the other great Norse adventurer of the story, Thorstein 'the Red', was interred further to the north in Caithness. So, unless an archaeological breakthrough is made, his burial place remains unknown. His death also marked the end of his family's foray into the mainland of Scotland. It seemed that the Hebridean lands ruled by his grandfather Ketill 'Flatnose' were lost soon after his death, much as those of Thorstein's father were around Dublin. Other Norse or Gaelic-Norse warlords would eventually surface, but for the moment it offered a welcome reprieve to Donald II of the Picts and Scots.

This of course still left the problem of the earldom of Orkney. Now his brother Sigurd was dead, Rognvald Eysteinsson, Earl of Møre had the authority to assume control of the earldom himself, or to appoint one of his family to take it over. After considering the problem, he chose his nephew Guthormr (or Guthrum), Earl Sigurd's son, who duly took up the earldom. We know virtually nothing about Orkney's second earl, but it seems Guthrum Sigurdsson lacked the robust stamina of his late father. The *Earls' Saga* says that he died within a year. Earl Guthrum had no heir, so once again his uncle Earl Rognvald faced the task of selecting a replacement.[8]

Lacking any more of Sigurd's offspring to take up the earldom, Rognvald turned to his own family. His wife Ragnhildr (or Ragnhild) had given him three sons: Ívarr (or Ivar), who the saga says was killed during Harald 'Finehair's' expedition to the Hebrides, Þóorrir (or Thorir) 'the Silent' and Hrólfr (or Rolf) who was nicknamed Walking-Hrólfr, or 'Rolf the Walker'. The earl of Møre also had at least three illegitimate sons, called Halladr (or Hallad), Hrollaugr (or Hrollaug) and Einarr (or Einar).[9]

At the time, the earldom was under threat from an unexpected source. King Harald 'Finehair' had several sons, and many of them had been appointed to rule the kingdom's earldoms. These had taken to feuding among themselves, which led to instability in Norway. The possibility that they might cause trouble within Møre encouraged Rognvald to keep his heir Thorir close by. His second legitimate son Rolf was highly suitable, and according to *Heimskringla* he was so large and strong that no horse could carry him – hence his epithet Rolf 'the Walker'. However, the saga claims that on his way back from a summer raid, he stopped at Viken on the Oslofjord and looted some cattle. As a result, 'The king assembled a *Thing* (parliament), and had Rolf declared an outlaw over all Norway.'[10]

Rolf Rognvaldsson went into exile and eventually landed in Valland (the former Western Roman Empire). There, according to *Heimskringla*, 'He plundered, and subdued for himself a great earldom, which he peopled with Northmen, from which that land is called Normandy.' His 10th-century Frankish biographer Dudo of St Quentin altered his name to the less Nordic 'Rollo', the first ruler of Normandy, and the forebear of Duke William of Normandy, who conquered the English throne in 1066. Although historians question Rollo's origins, most agree that he was one of the principal leaders of the Viking Siege of Paris in AD 885–886, and by AD 918 he appears indelibly on the historical record of Normandy.[11]

As a result, Earl Rognald had no option but to turn to his illegitimate sons. The earl had at least three of these, but probably more, born to a variety of women. The eldest of these, Halladr (or Hallad) Rognvaldsson was duly picked to take charge of the Orkney earldom. He did as he was bid, but it soon became clear that Hallad lacked the abilities of either his father or his uncle Sigurd. *The Saga of the Earls of Orkney* records that: 'And when Halladr came west, he established himself in [the Orkney] Mainland…' However, all wasn't well in the earldom, as Vikings had recently taken to raiding in Orkney – something they wouldn't dare if Sigurd 'the Mighty' had still been alive. The saga recorded that Vikings had even begun basing themselves in the archipelago.[12]

Presumably Earl Hallad tried to deal with them. After all, he'd the nucleus of his uncle's army at his disposal, and his fleet. It's possible, though, that his cousin Earl Guthrum had disbanded much of it, and Hallad was no man of action. Whatever the reason, Hallad proved an abject failure when it came to protecting his earldom and its people. The saga finished its account with a damning verdict on his reign: 'And when the householders complained to Earl Halladr about their losses, he thought it difficult to right their wrongs and he grew tired of the honour.' So he gave up the earldom, and went back to Norway as a common landholder or squire. This, the saga claims, 'was considered to be very humiliating', both for Hallad himself and for the earldom.[13]

After the failure of Hallad, Earl Rognvald found himself running out of options – and sons. So, Rognvald finally turned to his two other illegitimate sons Hrollaug and Einar. According to *Heimskringla*, like their brother Hallad, they were older than Rognvald's legitimate offspring. This, though, was no real bar to their suitability to take on the challenge of the Orkney earldom. *The Saga of the Earls of Orkney* claims that when Hrollaug asked if he should go, his father Earl Rognvald replied that he wasn't destined for the earldom. Instead, he would go to Iceland and make a name for himself there. So that left Einar.[14]

On the face of it, Einar was singularly unsuitable. He was described as 'a large and ugly man', who'd already lost an eye. The *Earls' Saga*, though, added that Einar was 'one-eyed, and yet keen-sighted'. He was Earl Rognvald's least-favourite son, the unwanted offspring of one of his concubines, a serving woman. When Einar stepped forward, he offered a solution that would benefit both the father and the son. The saga recorded the frosty conversation between the imposing father and his unloved bastard son. After Hrollaug was dismissed, the earl's youngest son Einar came forward and offered his father a deal; 'Do you want me to go to the islands? I will promise you that which you will think me most helpful, that I will never come back to your sight. There is also little that is good for me here to part from, and it is unlikely my flourishing will be any less than here.'[15]

Earl Rognvald weighed up his son's offer, then made his decision. 'You are no chieftain material because of your mother, who is slave-born in all her kin. But it is true that I would like it best if you go away sooner and came back later.' With that, Rognvald sought royal assent from King Harald 'Finehair', and soon Einar was given the title of earl of Orkney. Of course, Einar couldn't go empty-handed. Rognvald gave Einar a fully-equipped longship of 20 rowing benches, which meant it would have been manned by up to 40–50 Norse warriors. No doubt Rognvald gave his youngest son funds too, and possibly even a few clerics and administrators. With that, Earl Einar set off to claim his earldom.[16]

Like his half-brother Rolf (or 'Rollo'), Einar was essentially cast off by his father, the earl of Møre. After that initial gift of men and resources, he was forced to make his own way. Rollo, though, was a famed warrior, and a highly successful Viking leader. All the ugly, one-eyed Einar had going for him was his newly granted title, and his wits. His biggest problem was the Vikings who had plagued the earldom since the death of Earl Sigurd 'the Mighty'. Two of them, Danish Viking leaders called Þórir (Thorir) 'Treebeard' and Kálfr (Kalf) 'Scurvy', had established themselves in Orkney. Clearly Einar had to defeat these Vikings before he could claim his earldom.[17]

The fact they were Danish is an interesting little snippet, but one with potentially serious consequences. Normally, Danish Vikings raided the coast of Anglo-Saxon England and had been operating there since AD 787. A century later they carved out their own kingdom, the Danelaw. It was created during the campaigns of what the Anglo-Saxons called 'The Great Heathen Army'. This large Danish host was led by the brothers Hálfdan and Ivar 'the Boneless'. It was claimed they were both the sons of the legendary Viking leader Ragnar Lothbrok. From AD 865 to 878 this powerful Danish army campaigned across much of central and southern England before a settlement with the English was agreed. The Danes' claim to the Danelaw was recognised in return for a lasting peace. For Danes to come so far north as Orkney, though, was a sign that news of the weakness of the Orkney earldom had reached both Denmark and the Danelaw, its new English colony.

It was harvest time when Einar crossed the West Sea, possibly around the autumn of *c.* AD 894. Einar was intelligent, and so rather than confront his enemies in Orkney head-on, he began by shaping a course for Shetland. After making landfall there the Shetlanders rallied to him, and he swiftly gained control of the archipelago. In the process he would either have killed or driven off any Vikings there, or more likely he forced them to swear allegiance to him. As a result, he gathered a force large enough to take on his Danish opponents with some chance of success.

Heimskringla describes the clash that followed, as does the *Earls' Saga*, but neither provide us with much detail. It seems that Einar sailed from Shetland, with his reinforcements aboard, and passing Fair Isle, the midpoint between the two archipelagos, he reached the sheltered waters of Orkney. There, he and his men sighted two longships approaching. It was Thorir 'Treebeard' and Kalf 'Scurvy', coming out to meet him. Einar didn't hesitate, but headed towards them, and in the ensuing seaborne battle he and his men emerged victorious. Both the Viking leaders were killed, and so Einar was able to land in Orkney and claim his earldom.

The battle was remembered in a couplet, recorded slightly differently in the two sagas. In the *Earls' Saga*, 'Turf "Einar" gave "Treebeard" to the trolls, killed Kalf "Scurvy".' The version in *Heimskringla* runs: 'Then gave he Treskeg ("Treebeard") to the trolls, Turf-Einar slew Skurva ("Skurvy")'. The name the sagas give, Turf-Einar, reflects the misleading story given in *The Saga of the Earls of Orkney* that 'He was the first man to dig peat for fuel, firewood being very scarce on the islands'. Slabs of dried peat (called 'turf' in Norse), cut from the moorlands of the north of Scotland, is still sometimes used as a solid fuel there today, giving off a wonderfully distinctive earthy smell as it burns in the grate.[18]

Earl 'Turf' Einar proved to be a good earl, and if he'd been left in peace the earldom would have flourished under his rule. Instead, though, dark deeds in Norway soon cast their shadow over it. King Harald 'Finehair' continued to rule his kingdom, but the simmering feud between several of his many sons led to violence. At its root was the jockeying for position and power among them, as their father hadn't named an heir. His wife Gyda, who'd first spurred her suitor on to become king of all Norway, had died, while before that, Harald had been married to Åsa, the daughter of Hákon, Earl of Lade. Hákon, together with Earl Rognvald of Møre, had been one of King Harald's staunchest allies.

At some point he'd also married a beautiful Sámi woman, Snæfríð (or Snaefrid) who gave him four sons, Sigurd, Hálfdan, Guðrøðr (or Gudrod) and Rognvald. The king had probably sired more illegitimate offspring, but the sagas don't agree how many of these there were. As King Harald grew older, his sons, who ruled their own provinces, considered who would gain the throne when their father died. They had all been feuding for some time, but the four sons of Snæfrith were regarded as being particularly unruly. According to *Heimskringla*, after the death of their mother they'd been fostered by a *skald*, Thjodolf of Hvinir, from the southern tip of Norway. These youths 'came early to strength and manhood'. Eventually, two of them, Hálfdan 'High-leg' and Gudrod 'Light', hatched a plan to expand their power at the expense of their father's old ally, Earl Rognvald.[19]

In the spring of *c.* AD 895 or thereabouts, the two brothers led a powerful body of men into Møre and crept up to Earl Rognvald's home near Ålesund. After surrounding the house without being spotted, they barred its doors and set fire to it. The wooden building blazed fiercely, and Earl Rognvald and 60 of his family, retainers and servants were burned alive. Whatever Hálfdan and Gudrod hoped to gain from this is unclear, other than getting rid of a potential enemy and temporarily seizing his lands. Rognvald, known by then as Earl Rognvald 'the Wise', had been a loyal friend of Harald 'Finehair', and so the news of his death infuriated the king.

As *The Saga of the Earls of Orkney* records, 'King Harald flew into a rage and had his men arrest his sons. Hálfdan took ship to Orkney and escaped, but Gudrod gave himself up to his father. In compensation for the death of his loyal supporter Earl Rognvald, King Harald immediately approved Thorir's succession to the earldom. He also presented the new earl with his daughter Álof's hand in marriage'. Somewhat mollified, Thorir, now the Earl of Møre, was convinced not to seek revenge on his father's killers. Back in Orkney, his half-brother 'Turf' Einar, Earl of Orkney hadn't heard of his father's death before the murderer himself appeared in Orkney. Unable to take one earldom from Earl Rognvald, Hálfdan 'High-leg' now planned on seizing another from the murdered earl's son.[20]

SEVEN

Trouble on the Salt Road

'TURF' EINAR WAS TAKEN completely by surprise. Not long after his murder of Einar's father, Hálfdan 'High-leg' arrived in Orkney at the head of a strong force of warriors. For once, the adage that 'bad news travels fast' didn't seem to work. 'Einar probably hadn't even heard of the murder before his father's killer arrived. The *Earls' Saga* lays out the bare bones of what happened: 'Hálfdan "High-leg" arrived in the Orkneys, and as soon as it was common knowledge that a son of King Haraldr had arrived, they became full of fear. Some joined Hálfdan but Earl Einarr fled the islands up to Scotland. Hálfdan subjugated the islands and became king over them.'[1]

So 'Turf' Einar quit Orkney, and sought refuge in Caithness. No doubt he took some of his longships with him, along with a small hearthguard of warriors. These would act as the nucleus of a force he planned to raise in Caithness. Meanwhile, the prince Hálfdan 'High-leg' ruled Orkney, and it seems most of the islanders accepted this *fait accompli*. Einar, though, wasn't planning to give up so easily. The saga explained that later in the year, Einar returned to confront Hálfdan. *Heimskringla* adds a little more detail, saying it was harvest time when Einar made his move, probably after gathering intelligence of Hálfdan's whereabouts in Orkney. *Heimskringla* says Einar's return to Orkney went unnoticed, which suggests he took Hálfdan unawares.[2]

The two rivals met at sea off the small Orkney island of Rinansey (North Ronaldsay), the northernmost island in the archipelago. According to both sagas it was a fierce, hard-fought sea battle, but in the end, as darkness fell, after the battle turned against him, Hálfdan jumped overboard and vanished into the darkness. Afterwards, according to *Heimskringla*, 'Einar and his men lay all night without tents, and when it was light in the morning, they searched the whole island, and killed every man they could lay hold of.'[3] So far there was no sign of Hálfdan 'High-leg'. Then Einar spotted something. '"I don't know what's bobbing up and down out there," said Earl Einar. "It's either a man or a bird. Let's go and find out."' It turned out to be the wounded Hálfdan, trying to hide from Einar's search parties. He was seized and taken before Earl Einar.

If Hálfdan 'High-leg' expected mercy on account of his royal status, then he was out of luck. 'Turf' Einar wasn't in a forgiving mood. For him this was all about revenge – avenging the gruesome murder of his father, Earl Rognvald. According to the *Earls' Saga*, Einar had spent the evening composing verses. They emphasised his right to seek revenge while also teasing his more placid brothers, particularly the 'ale-swilling' Thorir Rognvaldsson 'the Silent', Earl of Møre, who hadn't raised a finger to avenge his murdered father.

> I don't see spears flying from Hrólfr's hand or Hrollaigr's to the enemy crowd;
> we would avenge our father. Yet, while we wage battle, Earl Þórir sits silent, in Møre this evening over his vessel-stream.[4]

'Turf' Einar had hate in his heart, and regardless of his prisoner's royal status, he planned to make his father's murderer pay the ultimate price. So he had his men take a firm hold of Hálfdan, and there, held face down on the grass of North Ronaldsay, the prince became the victim of the ritual known as the 'Blood Eagle'.

'Einarr had an eagle cut on his back with a sword and all the ribs cut from his spine and the lungs pulled out there and gave him to Oðinn for his victory.'[5]

While this grisly execution was taking place, 'Turf' Einar, an amateur *skald*, composed a celebratory verse:

> Many a fellow is seen broad-bearded with the sheep.
> While I'm in the island at the king's young son's fall.
> Magnates say the courageous ruler is dangerous to me,
> I've cut a notch in Haraldr's shield, but shall not fear that.[6]

Heimskringla tells a similar story. 'Earl Einar went up to Hálfdan, and cut a blood eagle upon his back, by striking his sword through his back into his belly, dividing his ribs from the backbone down to his loins, and tearing out his lungs; and so Hálfdan was killed.' Afterwards, in this version, Einar sang his verse, which went like this:

> For Ragnvald's death my sword is red,
> Of vengeance it cannot be said,
> That Einar's share is left unsped.[7]

This was one of only two blood eagle rituals recorded in the sagas. The other was the death of another royal figure, the Anglo-Saxon king Ælle of Northumbria, supposedly carried out by the sons of Ragnar Lothbrok in retaliation for the murder of their father. There, 'Ivar, he who held court at York, had an eagle hacked in Ella's back.'[8] In both instances, a sharp blade or special edged tool was used to cut open the victim's back, exposing the spine. Then, the ribs would be severed from it, allowing the lungs to be pulled through the gap, then spread out across the dying victim's shoulders. This ritual killing, the 'blood eagle', is generally seen as a human sacrifice to the god Odin.

To the Norse, this story would have been immediately recognised as linking the one-eyed Einar and the one-eyed god Odin, who was incidentally also the Norse god of poetry. In the saga, Einar was playing the part of Odin, with the blood-eagle seen as a vengeful sacrifice to himself! Some historians doubt whether this ever happened. They suggest that the gory details were the result of a misreading of the original Norse texts by translators and their enthusiasm to present a gory version of events. Medical experts have also pointed out that even if the victim had survived the initial cutting open, they would die almost immediately after the first ribs were severed.[9]

Still, both *The Saga of the Earls of Orkney* and *Heimskringla* made a point of explaining what happened on North Ronaldsay that autumn. Moreover, 'Turf' Einar didn't seem the kind of man to shirk from extracting as much suffering as he could from his father's murderer. Somehow, given the circumstances, the saga accounts ring true. Afterwards, the saga claimed that 'Turf' Einar came out with another few lines of skaldic verse, considering the likely vengeance Einar could expect from King Harald 'Finehair':

> I'll always be glad since spears of battle-eager men bit the king's
> young son;

it's good to do bold deeds.
I don't deny the wound-falcon's gladdener thinks it's a boast;
there the grey corpse-gnawer flew past islets at the wounded.[10]

However brutal the execution was, and with his one eye on the arrival of a vengeful Norwegian king, Earl Einar had a burial mound built on North Ronaldsay. The mangled remains of Hálfdan 'High-leg', prince of Norway were then laid to rest inside it. No trace of such a burial mound has been found on the island, which is less than three square miles in size. However, the remains of Norse settlements have been discovered, and perhaps the ploughed-over remains of the grave of Hálfdan is nearby, waiting to be discovered. At the interment, 'Turf' Einar came out with another stanza of skaldic verse. This time he composed it to justify his actions, and to emphasise that the blood feud with Hálfdan's royal family was now at an end – at least from his side.

I consider Rǫgnvaldr's death avenged for my fourth part;
the Norns arranged that right; the people's prop's now fallen.
Keen lads, do throw stones at High-leg, because we have won
   the victory;
I choose a hard tax for him.[11]

Back in Norway, King Harald had mourned the death of his friend Earl Rognvald, but he'd also encouraged Earl Thorir to stay his hand, and not publicly demand vengeance on behalf of his murdered father. One of the two murderers, Gudrod, had been sent east into exile. So, the only loose end had been Hálfdan 'High-leg'.

News of Earl Einar's retribution must have come as a shock to the Norwegian king. Still, he was a pragmatic ruler. The *Earls' Saga* records: 'And when this news was known in Norway, then his brothers became very displeased, and pledged to travel to the Orkneys and avenge him, but King Haraldr caused this to be postponed'.[12] This restraint on the part of King Harald saved the life of 'Turf' Einar, and probably preserved his earldom too. Still, some form of accounting was needed. Earl Einar had heard of the threats on his life made by King Harald's sons, and he even wrote another stanza about them:

Many men, not of low birth and of various kin, are eager for my life
    based on the true tidings.
Any yet they do not know until they have felled me,
    whose lot is to go beneath the sole-thorns of the eagle.[13]

Inevitably though it was King Harald himself who crossed the West
Sea again, at the head of a fleet of longships. Fearing being blood-
eagled himself, Earl Einar fled to Caithness for the second time in as
many years. Harald stayed in Orkney and made no attempt to pursue
Einar. True to form, the earl in exile even composed a skaldic stanza
which summed up the volatile situation.

Many a bearded man must roam, an exile from his house and home,
For cow or horse; but Hálfdan's gore is red on Rinansey's wild shore.
A nobler deed – on Harald's shield, the arm of one who ne'er will yield,
Has left a scar. Let peasants dread the vengeance of the Norsemen's head:
I reck not of his wrath, but sing, 'Do thy worst! – I defy thee, king!'[14]

Despite Einar's bombast, neither side really wanted more bloodshed.
So envoys were sent, and eventually a dialogue was established. A
deal was arranged where the king and the earl could be reconciled,
albeit at a price. The saga explains the arrangement: 'King Haraldr
imposed a tax on the islands and ordered them to pay sixty marks
of gold.'[15]

Essentially it was *wergild* ('blood money'), a fine on Einar for his
killing of a prince. At the time there was no mint in Norway, so coins
tended to be ones taken in Viking raids. Almost all of these were silver
though – gold coinage was a real rarity, and so was of great value.
This meant that the total cost of the blood payment was substantial –
around a third of a million British pounds or half a million US dollars
in today's money. In the reign of King Harald and Earl Einar, such a
payment would probably have emptied the earldom's treasury, if it had
been paid in its entirety by the earl.[16]

However, King Harald demanded it from the people of the earldom,
rather than from the earl himself. That meant the Orkney farmers
would bear the repayment of the blood money, rather than Einar. The
cost for Orkney's population would be cripplingly high. This was
probably an attempt by King Harald to weaken the earldom and sow

unrest. However, the saga explained that instead, Einar offered to pay the whole sum out of his pocket, on the condition that he should hold all of the properties in the earldom. In return, the original owners would pay the earl rent. In other words, the earl would effectively own the land in Orkney, and the population would be his tenants until the blood money reparations were repaid.

The Orkney farmers reluctantly approved the terms. 'The householders agreed to that because the wealthy ones thought they would be able to redeem their ancestral lands and the poor ones did not have the money.' This meant that under Norse odal law (known as udal in the Norse earldom), the earl would own the hereditary rights to the land, at least until the blood money was paid off. So, Earl Einar paid the whole blood money payment to King Harald out of his own coffers, but the people of Orkney – the udal-paying farmers – would be bound to him for generations to come. The blood money reparation payment would continue to be levied on the people of the earldom for another hundred years – until the remaining sum was 'written off' by Earl Sigurd 'the Stout'.[17]

After the reparations were arranged, the king and his powerful subject shook hands and parted in peace. Both the Orkney earl and his people might be considerably poorer, but at least peace could return to the islands, and its farmers and raiders could continue with their lives. As for 'Turf' Einar, *The Saga of the Earls of Orkney* had nothing more to add about him, largely because during the last years of his rule the islands were left alone by the tide of greater events.

All it recorded was that 'Earl Einarr ruled over the Orkneys during a long life, and died of an illness.' For a man of his lowly background to rise to rule an earldom was extremely unusual. It seems, though, that after the tumult caused by Hálfdan 'High-leg' had faded away, he proved to be one of the better rulers of Orkney and Shetland. In the late 9th century, for any ruler to die peaceably in their bed was a rarity and spoke volumes about Einar's ability to govern his earldom.[18]

Before we leave Earl Einar, it's worth taking a moment to mention his aspirations as a poet. After all, they're quoted extensively above, where they're taken from both *The Saga of the Earls of Orkney* and *Heimskringla*. It isn't surprising they're repeated, as Snorri Sturlasson drew extensively on the *Earls' Saga* when he was writing *Heimskringla*. These snippets of skaldic poetry reveal a little about Einar himself. They show a proud man, and a capable one, who felt himself superior to his elder brothers, as he acted after his father's murder while they didn't. This is surprising, given his humble and illegitimate roots. They also reveal a belief that the Norse gods were on his side, and that he was somehow predestined for greatness. Ugly and one-eyed though he was, 'Turf' Einar wasn't a man to be trifled with.[19]

Earl Einar died around AD 920, although the date is open to debate. He left behind three sons, called Arnkel, Erlendr (or Erlend) and Þorfinnr (or Thorfinn), as well as an older daughter named Þordís (or Thordis). She was born in Einar's youth, before he took up the earldom, and she was raised by her grandfather, Earl Rognvald, and was eventually married off to a Norwegian nobleman, Thorgeir 'the Clumsy'.[20]

'Turf' Einar was extremely important in the story of the Orkney earls. His origins – the illegitimate son of a slave and an earl – show someone capable of rising high in Norse society. Not only did he become an earl, he was also the real founder of the dynasty which would rule Orkney for centuries. He, then, as much as his father Earl Rognvald, was the person for whom the whole fantastical mythical origins story was aimed at. His roots, and those of his descendants, were anchored by the mythical links to Sea Kings, giants, gods and the natural elements of Norway. That was all part of the process of legitimising the rule of Earl Einar and his descendants.

His 'rags to riches' story also formed part of the aura the saga created for Einar and his descendants. The *Earls' Saga* emphasised Einar's skills as a warrior, a poet and a ruler willing to risk everything for his family's name. They were all the attributes that a good Norse earl should have. In a way, he was setting the standard in the saga, for his descendants to emulate. If they wanted to be worthy rulers, they should follow Earl Einar's example. Einar Rognvaldsson, the one-eyed earl of Orkney, warrior, *skald*, peat-cutter and avenger, would be a hard act to follow.[21]

When their father Einar died, his sons decided to share the earldom between them. So, from *c.* AD 920 on, there were three Einarsson earls of Orkney: Earl Arnkel, Earl Erlend and Earl Thorfinn 'Skullsplitter'. Clearly this was an arrangement which could potentially bring problems. It seems, though, that the three sons of 'Turf' Einar got on well, and so the earldom prospered, with more settlers arriving, good harvests and an increase in trade with both Norway and the mainland of Scotland. One of the trades was in timber, something that was extremely scarce in Orkney, Shetland and Caithness, but plentiful in both Norway and the rest of Scotland. In return, Orkney provided bountiful harvests of grain and cattle, while the Shetlanders were able to trade in dried fish.

Then there was raiding, and as we've already seen, Orkney and Shetland were ideally placed for this, especially for raids into Ireland, as well as the British mainland. It seems that as a young man Thorfinn Einarsson first made a name for himself in these Viking raids. The late 9th and early 10th centuries were a time of considerable upheaval in the British Isles, and already Viking raiding was giving way to larger-scale conquest. In AD 870–871, Norse raiders captured Dumbarton Rock, the imposing stronghold of the Britons of Strathclyde which dominated the Firth of Clyde. This was only the most prominent of many Norse incursions into Alba. As a result, for much of the next century the country's western seaboard would be under Norse control. As internal power struggles in Alba continued, Norse and Norse-Irish rulers and warlords supported either Pictish-Scots kings or their rival claimants, in return for financial reward or political gain. It was a heady time to be a Norseman.[22]

In Ireland, the Norse had founded Dublin in AD 841, and their hold over this enclave ended in AD 902 when the city fell to the Irish. In AD 919, though, Dublin was recaptured and remained in Scandinavian hands for another three generations. During this time Norse-Irish fortunes waxed and waned, but it wasn't until the end of the 10th century that the Irish cause triumphed once again. Even then, the Norse-Irish rulers wouldn't go easily, and it wasn't until 1014 that they were finally evicted from Ireland. This followed in the wake of a decisive battle which would see an earl of Orkney die beneath his bloodstained magical banner.[23]

At around the same time as the Norse city of Dublin was founded, the Danelaw emerged as a substantial Danish kingdom on English soil. In AD 866, when the Danes captured York, the city was renamed Jórvik and became the capital of the Danelaw. As a result, England became a divided land, with the Anglo-Saxon king Alfred controlling Wessex and part of Mercia. This left the Danish king Guthrum to rule virtually everything else. Edward of Wessex succeeded his father Alfred in AD 899, but it was another 11 years before he was strong enough to make his move. From AD 910 on, he gradually recaptured Mercia and drove the Danes back almost to the gates of Jórvik. The city was finally captured in AD 927, when Edward's son Æthelstan became the king of a united England. The Danes weren't done though. They would return – this time dragging the earls of Orkney into the struggle to reclaim their lost lands.[24]

Throughout most of this the earldom of Orkney had largely been a bystander, apart from its own campaign of conquest on the Scottish mainland. Inevitably, though, it would become drawn into these wars and would pay the price. It was surprising because it involved the death of the man who'd agreed to the earldom's very creation. The trouble began following the death of King Harald 'Finehair'. Yet again, the dating of this is a matter of debate, but in roughly AD 930, the ageing king shared his Norwegian crown with one of his sons, Eiríkr (or Eirík) Haraldsson, who went by the epithet 'Bloodaxe'.

His mother was Ragnhild Eiríksdóttir, daughter of King Eirík of Jutland. King Harald 'Finehair' had left all of his previous wives for Ragnhild, but she died after in AD 897, after only three years as queen. In that time she only had one son, Eirík, named after her Danish father. As a youth Eirík had been King Harald's favourite son, thanks to the king's love for Ragnhild. When he grew to manhood Eirík had quickly made a name for himself as a Viking and was undoubtedly a powerful and ambitious warrior. Three years later, when King Harald died in his bed, Eirík undoubtedly expected to succeed him as ruler of Norway.[25]

During the latter years of his reign Harald had lived at Avaldsnes, two dozen miles north of the site of his great victory at Hafrsfjord. He was buried in a great mound nearby, at Haugesund. Before this mound was even built, his son Eirík was busily making sure he'd be his father's only possible successor. This of course meant killing his siblings. The *Earls' Saga* skips over most of the mayhem that followed King Harald's death, saying only that after King Harald died, his son Eirík 'Bloodaxe' ruled over Norway. Then, King Harald's younger son Hákon took over the reins of power and Eirík was forced to flee the country. This, though, was a very sanitised version of events. In fact, the numerous sons of King Harald had been vying for power for years. After assuming his shared crown, Eirík moved quickly to deal with his sibling rivals, killing his half-brothers Ólaf and Sigrod in battle, and then two more half-brothers, Rognvald and Bjørn. It was by killing his siblings that Eirík gained the gruesome epithet of 'Bloodaxe'.[26]

After that, King Eirík ruled his father's kingdom, and some degree of calm descended. However, trouble was brewing. In England another half-brother, the teenage Hákon, had been fostered by the English king Æthelstan and so had been beyond the brother-killer Eirík's reach. However, in AD 933, and with the English king's backing, Hákon and a few supporters sailed to Trondheim in a bid to seize Norway from his half-brother. When he landed there, he was welcomed by Earl Sigurd Hákonsson of Lade, at the head of his hearthguard. What followed was essentially a bloodless coup, as Hákon's followers grew steadily as increasing numbers of Norwegians joined his cause. As a result, he was able to raise a sizeable army, and a fleet. Similarly, King Eirík's support steadily ebbed away, until eventually he realised that he'd no hope of holding on to his kingdom.

So, in the spring of AD 934, Eirík fled Norway, accompanied by his family and what few supporters and warriors remained. It was inevitable that he would head across the West Sea to Orkney. While he probably didn't expect to win back his lost throne, he could at least rally whatever support he could find there. Then he might possibly be able to carve out a new kingdom to rule somewhere else. As a result, the peace of the Orkney earldom was about to be shattered.[27]

EIGHT

Eirík 'Bloodaxe' and His Brood

I T WAS A PATTERN of sorts. For a century, beginning in AD 954, the earls of Orkney took part in three major 'headline-grabbing' foreign ventures. All of them would end in outright disaster. It may be significant that these were all roughly two generations apart, in AD 954, 1014 and 1066. It was almost as if it took that long for the lessons to be forgotten and for a new generation to arrive, eager to repeat the mistakes of the past. In between, the earldom itself was riven by spates of civil war, dynastic murder and periodic acts of invasion, destruction and revenge. This grim cycle all began with the arrival of Eirík 'Bloodaxe'.

However, it took two decades for Eirík's troublesome influence to make itself felt. After fleeing Norway in AD 934, the exiled King Eirík sailed across the West Sea to Orkney, where he recruited more men. He was accompanied by his wife Gunnhildr (or Gunnhild) and his numerous children. Eirík then solicited the help of the sons of 'Turf' Einar, who now jointly ruled the earldom.[1] Earl Einar's sons Arnkel and Erlend ruled the earldom together. At the time their younger brother Thorfinn was still too young to share power with them.

Eirík then spent the best part of two decades playing the role of a Viking, raiding England, Scotland and Ireland.[2] *Heimskringla* went on to claim that in *c.* 936 King Æthelstan, the first king of a united England, then granted Eirík the fiefdom of Northumberland – or rather the southern part of it around Jórvik. This was the rump of the Danelaw, now reduced to something the size of a small English county. In return, Eirík and his family agreed to convert to Christianity, and were all duly baptised. This, though, was the same Anglo-Saxon king who'd fostered the young Hákon Haraldsson, the young man who'd just ousted his half-brother Eirík 'Bloodaxe' from the Norwegian throne.

It would seem unlikely Æthelstan would so openly help the rival of his young Norwegian protégé.[3] It is more likely that *Heimskringla* is confusing its timeline and such an offer was never made.

Anyway, the question of who ruled Scandinavian York wasn't straightforward. Æthelstan captured Jórvik from the Norse-Irish king Gofraid in AD 936, and for the next three years he ruled it himself. The following year, Aethelstan consolidated his hold on all of England following his victory at the Battle of Brunanburh. He'd fought and decisively beaten a coalition that included Gofraid's son Ólaf, King Constantine II of Alba and King Owain of Strathclyde. That one battle made any need for a client king redundant, as it ensured Æthelstan's unchallenged supremacy over the whole country, including Jórvik.[4]

Two years later, though, Æthelstan was dead. Almost immediately, the people of Jórvik turned on their Anglo-Saxon overlords, and invited King Ólaf Guthfrithson of Dublin to rule Northumberland. He'd been on the losing side at Brunanburh. For the next few years England was ruled by Æthelstan's half-brother Edmund, who recaptured Jórvik from Ólaf in AD 944, two years before the Anglo-Saxon king was killed at the hand of an assassin. That same year, AD 946, Jórvik's people rejected Anglo-Saxon rule again, and invited Eirík 'Bloodaxe' to be their new ruler. This was probably the offer *Heimskringla* had mentioned but had got the date wrong by a decade. Meanwhile, another of Æthelstan's half-brothers, Eadred, became the next king of England, and he immediately marched north to try to restore order.[5]

That's when Eirík 'Bloodaxe' arrived to claim his kingdom, accompanied by his family. This had been arranged by Wulfstan, the Archbishop of York, but the cleric's attempt to play kingmaker came unstuck the following year, when he was captured by King Eadred and sent into exile. By this point the people of Jórvik had become fed up with Eirík, and for the second time in his life his support ebbed away. As King Eadred's army approached Jórvik, Eirík fled into exile once more. This time, though, he intended to return and reclaim his lost kingdom. Although its timeline appears slightly muddled, the *Earls' Saga* records Eirík 'Bloodaxe' then sailing north to Orkney to beg for the support of the three earls.[6]

An alternative version has Eirík driven from York in AD 954 by a coup staged by Oswulf of Bamburgh. This was when Eirík realised he would struggle to beat King Eadred's Anglo-Saxon host, and so he sent to Orkney for reinforcements. That's when the two earls joined him, together with Norse supporters from the Hebrides. This is at odds with the sagas, but however it happened doesn't really alter the result. King Eirík convinced the earls of Orkney to help him reclaim Jórvik. Earls Arknel and Erlend Einarsson gathered what was probably a sizeable detachment of men and longships, and these joined Eirík's own fleet. Their younger brother Earl Thorfinn 'Skullsplitter' would remain behind to rule the earldom in their absence.[7]

Both *Heimskringla* and *The Saga of the Earls of Orkney* follow Eirík 'Bloodaxe's' movements in AD 954. It was a circuitous voyage. He sailed to the Hebrides to raise more troops. Then, ever the Viking, he raided the coasts of Ireland and Strathclyde to boost his coffers. Only after that did he sail south to England, probably making his landfall somewhere on the north-eastern coast of Morecambe Bay. Then he advanced on Jórvik. The *Earls' Saga* claims that 'The king that Játmundr [Edmund] had sent to rule that land was called Óláfr.' This was probably Earl Oswulf of Bamburgh, who governed all of Northumbria, including York, in King Eadred's name.[8]

Eirík was told that he had the support of the inhabitants of Jórvik. However, according to the saga Eirík was brought to battle by Oswulf before he reached the city: 'since Eiríkr had a large number of people, he advanced from his ships. Óláfr also gathered a large crowd and advanced towards him.' From this it sounds as if Oswulf had called out the Northumbrian *fyrd* – the levy – to boost his already large force. It is likely that Eirík's scouts had told him of Oswulf's approach, and he realised he was outnumbered. So, Eirík tried to retire to his ships, but Oswulf caught up with him in the Pennines, and the Norse army was forced to stand and fight.[9]

The saga continues: 'There was a great battle, and many of the English were killed first during the day, but whenever one was killed, three came in their place'. That was when everything started to unravel. 'After midday the Norwegians began to fall and at the last King Eiríkr was killed and six kings with him. One of these was called Guthormr. Also killed were Earls Arnkell and Erlendr, the sons of Turf-Einarr.'[10]

The six kings were minor rulers from the Hebrides, and the most significant casualties, apart from Eirík Haraldsson 'Bloodaxe', former king of Norway, were the two earls of Orkney, who were slain on the battlefield. The site of the battle has been tentatively identified as Stainmore in the Pennines, where an old Roman road, now the A66, ran through a gap in the hills. It appears that Eirík and his men were heading towards Cumbria and his fleet when they were overwhelmed by their Anglo-Saxon pursuers. The survivors who managed to escape brought word of the disaster to Earl Thorfinn in Orkney. So, from AD 954 on, the sole remaining son of 'Turf' Einar was left to rule the earldom alone.

Unfortunately, this wasn't quite the end of the story. Even from beyond the grave on a windswept hillside in the Pennines, Eirík 'Bloodaxe' could still cause trouble. He left behind him a wife and a variety of offspring of various ages. His Danish-born wife was Gunnhild Gormsdóttir, who was described in *Heimskringla* as 'the most beautiful of women – clever, with much knowledge, and lively'. Mind you, it also described her as 'a very false person, and very cruel in disposition.' She must have been in her forties when her husband died and left her with eight children to raise, the eldest of which were teenagers when their father was cut down.[11]

When word reached her that Eirík was killed, Queen Gunnhild was in Northumbria, and according to *Heimskringla* she took command of her husband's fleet – which undoubtedly included the longships of the slain Orkney earls. After embarking her children and household staff, their baggage, her husband's treasury, and the remnants of his defeated army, she fled north to Orkney. *Heimskringla* helpfully listed her eight offspring, who suddenly arrived in Orkney. She had seven sons, Gamle being the oldest, then Guthorm, Harald, Erling, Ragnfrød, Gudrod and Sigurd. She also had a single daughter called Ragnhild. All these youngsters were meant to have shared their parents' good looks. Of the boys, Gamle and Guthorm might still have been teenagers, but they were already skilled warriors. It was when Queen Gunnhild and her family arrived in Orkney, in the remnants of her husband's fleet, that Thorfinn would have first learned that his two brothers were dead.[12]

Despite mourning his brothers and forced to deal with the issues that arose from that, Thorfinn would have extended every courtesy to his royal guests. What he didn't expect was a coup. With remarkable brevity the *Earls' Saga* described it in just five words: 'Gunnhildr's sons subjugated the islands.' It seems that Thorfinn was either deposed or else he was forced to cede control of the earldom to the queen and her thuggish sons Gamle and Guthorm. In *Heimskringla*, it claimed that the sons 'committed great excesses in Orkney.' It's likely that with the survivors of the Northumbrian expedition backing the queen, and with the best of the earldom's warriors lying dead in the Pennines, Thorfinn was in no position to resist even if he'd wanted to.[13]

While their mother Gunnhild ruled Orkney, her eldest sons spent their summers leading Viking raids, preying on Anglo-Saxons and Scots alike, and probably Norwegians too. In between, the brothers over-wintered in Orkney, celebrating their exploits in the unfortunate Thorfinn Einarsson's own feasting hall. Later, the 10th-century Icelandic *skald* Glúmr Geirason composed a verse celebrating their Viking exploits:

The hero who knows well to ride, the sea-horse o'er the foaming tide,
He who in boyhood wild rode o'er the seaman's horse to Skanea's shore,
And showed the Danes his galley's bow, right nobly scours the ocean now.

On Scotland's coast he lights the brand of flaming war; with conquering hand,
Drives many a Scottish warrior tall, To the bright seats in Odin's hall.
The fire-spark, by the fiend of war fanned to a flame, soon spreads afar.
Crowds trembling fly, the southern foes fall thick beneath the hero's blows:
The hero's blade drips red with gore, Staining the green sward on the shore.[14]

Fortunately for Thorfinn 'Skullsplitter', this royal sojourn in Orkney didn't last long. Events in Norway created an opportunity which Queen Gunnhild felt she could exploit. Since his seizure of the Norwegian crown from Eirík 'Bloodaxe' in AD 934, King Hákon 'the Good' had ably consolidated his position in the country. He devoted a lot of his energies to spreading the rule of law throughout his kingdom and he developed a reputation as a fair law-maker. He was also a good organiser, transforming Norway's defences by building a standing fleet, and improving the country's military organisation and its coastal defences. Although he soon rejected the Christianity instilled in him by his foster-father Æthelstan, he did nothing to prevent the religion from gaining ground in Norway. By all accounts he ruled the country well, with the help of Earl Sigurd of Lade in the north, and his two nephews in the east. The real danger, though, was Denmark.[15]

Within a year of Queen Gunnhild's arrival in Orkney, King Haraldr Bláton (Harald 'Bluetooth') of Denmark embarked on a war with Norway. The conniving Gunnhild, who had family ties to the Danish crown, immediately threw in her lot with her Danish kin. So she and her family left Orkney in *c.* AD 956, much to Earl Thorfinn's relief. Before she left, though, she left behind what amounted to a ticking time bomb.

Her daughter Ragnhildr Eiríksdóttir (or Ragnhild Eiríksdaughter) was married off to Arnfinnr (or Arnfinn), the eldest son of Thorfinn 'Skullsplitter'. No doubt Thorfinn felt this was a small price to pay to regain control of his earldom. After Earl Thorfinn's death, though, the true cost of this marriage would prove to be incredibly high. At the time, nobody knew that the beautiful Ragnhild Eiríksdaughter was the ultimate *femme fatale* of the Viking world.[16]

Queen Gunnhild joined King Harald 'Bluetooth' at his court at Roskilde, to the west of modern Copenhagen, where they were warmly welcomed. Harald gave Gunnhild and her sons a Danish estate, which provided them with an income. He also took the teenage Harald Eiríksson as his foster-son, raising him at the Danish court. Harald 'Bluetooth' intended to use Eirík's sons as a weapon, harnessing their hatred for King Hákon of Norway to his own advantage. Eirík 'Bloodaxe's' eldest sons, although still inexperienced, were demonstrating they'd inherited something of their father's abilities – and his flaws.

According to *Heimskringla*, in *c.* AD 956, King Harald sent a Danish fleet to raid Rogaland in south-west Norway. Gamle and Guthorm, the two eldest sons of Eirík 'Bloodaxe', were placed in charge of the venture. King Hákon eventually brought the Danes to battle near Avaldsnes (called Ogvaldsnes in the saga), where Hákon often lived and had his court. It was a hard-fought battle, but Hákon emerged victorious, and 'Guthorm fell, and his standard was cut down'. Afterwards, the battlefield was known locally as 'Blood Heights'.[17]

The war would drag on, and Harald 'Bluetooth' continued to use the sons of Eirík 'Bloodaxe' to spearhead this war by proxy. Two years later, in *c.* AD 958, they tried again, this time landing at the southern tip of Norway, near Kristiansand. Once more, King Hákon intercepted the Danes, and in the bloody battle which followed he soundly defeated them, and they fled back to their longships. During the pursuit, Gamle Eiríksson was drowned as he tried to reach the longships. Back in Orkney, Earl Thorfinn would have been grimly satisfied that both of his tormentors – Queen Gunnhild's eldest sons – were now dead, thanks to the Norwegian king.[18]

Then, in AD 961, Harald 'Greycloak', the third son of Eirík 'Bloodaxe' – the one who'd been raised in Harald 'Bluetooth's' court – led another Danish expedition against Norway. This was the largest one yet. If everything went to plan, it would end the war in a single stroke. The objective was nothing short of regime change – the killing of King Hákon 'the Good', and his replacement by Harald, the foster-son of King Harald 'Bluetooth'. If the enterprise succeeded, and Harald 'Greycloak' could seize the Norwegian throne, then he would almost certainly become a puppet ruler, who owed his allegiance to the Danish king.

For this daring venture Harald, now the eldest survivor of the Eiríksson brothers, was joined by his younger siblings Erling and Sigurd 'Sleva'. Also in the expedition were two of their uncles, brothers of Queen Gunnhild – Eyvind 'Skreyja' and Alf 'Askman'. The Danish fleet sailed to Hordaland on the west coast of Norway, midway between Bergen and Stavanger. There they landed on the island of Stord on the southern side of the Selbjørdsfjord. King Hákon maintained a hall there, beside the small township of Fitjar. He was holding court in Fitjar at the time, and once the Danish learned this, they'd planned the venture to catch him unawares. Although the Danish landing went undetected, the alarm was raised as the Danes approached Fitjar, and King Hákon had just enough time to prepare for the coming battle.[19]

Most probably the king only had his hearthguard with him, as the sagas say he was heavily outnumbered. *Heimskringla* claims the odds were six to one. When the two shield walls met 'there was a hard combat, and much bloodshed.' King Hákon was in the thick of the fight, wearing a gold-decorated helmet, and so he was very conspicuous. Gunnhild's two brothers tried to hack down the Norwegian king but they both died in the attempt. One of them, Eyvind 'Skreyja', was cleaved in two by King Hákon's sword 'Kvernbit'. This was a turning point in the battle, as Harald's bodyguard broke the enemy shieldwall: 'Fear overcame the army of Eirík's sons, and the men began to flee.' Everything was going King Hákon's way. Suddenly, seemingly out of nowhere, an arrow struck him in the shoulder.

Heimskringla claimed it was shot by one of Queen Gunnhild's pages, a youth named Krisping. It seemed harmless at the time, and King Hákon's men chased the Danes back to their ships. It was a slaughter, but somehow a handful of them escaped, including Harald 'Greycloak'. As his men pursued the Danes, the king's wound was inspected. Whatever the healers tried, it wouldn't stop bleeding. By nightfall it was clear King Hákon was dying from loss of blood. With his council around him, he gave his incredible final declaration. A message should be sent to Eirík's sons, saying one of them should rule Norway after his death. Hákon had no son to succeed him, so he was trying to avoid further conflict. He died lying on a hillside overlooking the sea.[20]

So ended the life of Hákon 'the Good', one of Norway's better kings. At his request the king was placed in a burial mound, Håkonshaugen in the village of Seim, 12 miles north of Bergen, where the king had another estate. According to the sagas his death was mourned throughout Norway. To help him on his way, the *skald* Eyvind 'Skaldaspiller' ('the Plagiarist') composed a poem, which included the lines:

> In Odin's hall, an empty place stands for the king of Yngv's
> [Yngling] race,
> 'Go my Valkyries', Odin said, 'Go forth my angels of the dead,
> Gonul and Skogul, to the plain, drenched with the battle's bloody rain,
> And to the dying Hákon tell, here in Valhalla shall he dwell.'[21]

Later that year Harald 'Greycloak', son of Eirík 'Bloodaxe', duly became king of Norway and ruled the country with the help of his surviving brothers. His authority beyond the western coast of Norway was limited, though, as many there were reluctant to accept him as their ruler, as they had recently waged war against him and were reluctant to be ruled by the son of a king whom they'd already ejected from the throne.[22] So he spent much of his reign attempting to increase his power, either by force or persuasion, but without any real success. He also tried to reduce his dependence on King Harald 'Bluetooth' of

Denmark, who treated King Harald 'Greycloak' as a vassal king. In the end, Harald's attempts to throw off Danish dominance finally led to his murder in AD 970.[23]

His killer Hákon, Earl of Lade, had every right to hate King Harald 'Greycloak'. Eight years before, in AD 962, and within a year of his coming to power, King Harald had callously burned Hákon's father to death in his hall. It was all part of Harald 'Greycloak's' bid to extend his royal power throughout Western Norway, which included the Lade earldom, which encompassed the Trondheimsfjord. In retaliation, Earl Hákon masterminded the murder of Harald 'Greycloak' when King Harald had been on a diplomatic trip to Denmark. Afterwards, Earl Hákon's grabbing of the throne didn't end Norway's troubles, as a civil war then erupted between Earl Hákon and King Harald's remaining brothers. After that, Norway was ruled directly by King Harald 'Bluetooth', although he quickly installed the compliant Hákon, Earl of Lade as his new vassal ruler.

After the last of the Eiríksson brothers finally fled Norway, King Hákon continued to rule the country as the puppet of the Danish king. Most of the sagas, though, refuse to acknowledge his royal status, and so he was normally called 'Jarl Hákon'. What all this bloodshed and treachery in Norway meant for the earldom of Orkney was that, while all this was going on, they were left well alone. In theory the earls owed their position to the Norwegian crown, so they would have to seek official recognition of their position as earls of Orkney from a succession of Norwegian rulers. In practice, though, this probably didn't happen. After all, the earls had much more to worry about than their formal recognition by a Norwegian king on the far end of the Salt Road.[24]

In Orkney, while all this had been playing out, Earl Thorfinn 'Skullsplitter' had been able to rule his earldom without interference. It seems that 'Turf' Einar's last remaining son proved to be a good, strong ruler, as well as a first-rate warrior. Unusually for this period, in c. AD 963 he died peacefully in his bed. A burial mound was raised for him, which was reputedly at the base of the small peninsula of Hoxa in the Orkney island of Rognvaldsey (now South Ronaldsay). Incidentally, the mound – alas, the remains of a broch rather than a burial howe – is visible from this writer's study window, across Widewall Bay. Earl Thorfinn's real grave still remains to be found.

Earl Thorfinn 'Skullsplitter' left behind five sons. In order of age, they were called Arnfinn, Hávarðr (or Hávard), Hloðvir (or Hlodvir), Ljótr (or Ljót) and Skúli. As the eldest of them, it was Arnfinn who'd succeeded his father as the earl. Unfortunately, a few years earlier, Eirík 'Bloodaxe's widow, Queen Gunnhild, had sown an evil seed which would lead to the slaughter of most of Thorfinn's sons. The word 'evil' though, doesn't begin to cover it.[25] The catalyst began when Queen Gunnhild convinced Thorfinn to let her daughter Ragnhild marry his eldest son Arnfinn. The novelist Eric Linklater said of her that she 'infected her lovers with bloody intention, and was the death of four notable men, and an unknown number of their anonymous followers.' In the process, she almost brought the earldom of Orkney to its knees.[26]

PART THREE

GLORY, GOD
AND GOLD

The Phoenix from the Ashes

THE RULE OF THE earldom by Thorfinn's sons was of one of the most needlessly grisly periods in its history. This all came about thanks to Ragnhild, the daughter of King Eirík 'Bloodaxe' and his wife Queen Gunnhild. It began in AD 976 with the death of Earl Thorfinn 'Skullsplitter'. The eldest of the earl's five sons was Arnfinn Thorfinnsson, so he inherited his father's title. By then he'd married Ragnhild. Everything went well for several years. It was only around AD 979 that the killing spree began. It started dramatically when, according to the saga, Ragnhild masterminded the assassination of Arnfinn while he was visiting Murkle in Caithness, a cluster of Norse farms a few miles east of Thurso.[1]

Afterwards she must have played the part of the bereft, helpless widow to perfection. After the 'crocodile tears' she married Arnfinn's younger brother Hávrðr 'inn arsæli' (Hávard 'Harvest-blessed'). After Hávard Thorfinnsson inherited the earldom he proved to be a popular, efficient ruler. He earned his unusual nickname due to his enthusiasm for agriculture, which may have led to the period of bountiful harvests enjoyed in the earldom. As the saga put it, 'Hávarðr took the earldom and was a good chieftain and blessed in his harvests.'[2]

However, Earl Hávard's sister had a grown-up son called Einarr (or Einar) 'Butty'. He was a successful Viking, and the saga said of him that 'He was a great chieftain and had a large troop and spent the summers raiding.' Einar, the new earl's nephew, would soon be drawn into his aunt's deadly web.[3]

It seems that Ragnhild eventually grew tired of Hávard, probably due to his preoccupation with farming rather than with her. So, during a feast in Hávard's hall she had a quiet word with Einar. She told him he'd make a far better earl than his uncle. Einar begged her to stop such talk, but Ragnhild was persuasive, and eventually she convinced him to lead a rebellion. The saga claims that one day, a Norse seer pleaded with Einar to stay at home that day: 'Do not do this deed today but rather tomorrow, or there will be a long history of kin-killing in your kin'. Einar, though, blinkered by Ragnhild's praise, had already made up his mind. So, he ignored the seer. Instead, he gathered his many followers and marched on Stenness, an area in the West Mainland of Orkney where Earl Hávard was staying at the time. Einar's rebels confronted the earl's men, and a hard battle took place there, at a spot later called 'Hávard's field'. During the fight, Earl Hávard was slain by Einar and his rebel band.[4]

After killing the earl, Einar tried to claim the earldom for himself. He'd hoped to marry Ragnhild too, so perhaps she'd offered her hand by way of encouragement. The widespread outcry over Einar's killing, though, made Ragnhild realise that linking herself to her nephew Einar 'Butty' would prove disastrous. So she distanced herself from him and spurned any request for marriage.

It seems that Ljót, the third of the Thorfinnsson brothers, was reluctant to avenge the slaying of Hávard. So Ragnhild, playing the part of the distraught widow again, approached Einarr (or Einar) 'Hard-jaws', the son of another of Thorfinn's daughters. She encouraged him to arm himself and avenge the killing of his uncle. By then Einar 'Butty' was trying to play the part of the earl in Orkney, albeit without any authority or the support of the remaining Thorfinnsson brothers, Hlodvir, Ljót and Skúli.[5]

So Einar 'Hard-jaws' chose his moment and murdered Einar 'Butty'. It seems the seer's prophecy was coming true. One after another, the family of Thorfinn 'Skullsplitter' were being whittled down. At that point Ragnhild abandoned Einar 'Hard-jaws' and threw in her lot with Ljót Thorfinnsson. So, for the third time she married one of the Thorfinnsson brothers. Then, with her encouragement, Ljót claimed the earldom for himself. This of course, meant civil war, as Einar 'Hard-jaws' was now trying to claim the earldom too. Einar began gathering warriors. When Ljót learned of this, he launched a raid and captured Einar before he could make his move. Einar 'Hard-jaws' was quietly put to the sword, leaving Earl Ljót Thorfinnsson the undisputed ruler of the earldom.

For a while, Earl Ljót and his new wife Ragnhild lived in peace, and the troubled earldom slowly began to recover from all the bloodletting. Trade began to prosper, and the earldom soon began to benefit from improved contacts with the Scots. At the time, Alba was ruled by King Kenneth II, who was too busy dealing with England to worry about his northern borders. So he left the defence of these to his local *mormaers*.[6]

In *c.* AD 978 Earl Ljot's brother Skúli Thorfinnsson quietly left Orkney, and visited Kenneth's court, where he had a meeting with the king. As a result, Skúli was rewarded with the Scots title of 'Mormaer of Caithness'. The Scots had never recognised the Norse seizure of Caithness and Suðrland (or Sutherland), as the southern lands of the earldom came to be known.[7] This was Kenneth's bid to reclaim these lost lands. Any *mormaer* who ruled Caithness owed fealty to Kenneth, even though these lands were still part of the earldom of Orkney. It seems that Skúli Thorfinnsson planned to rule Caithness in his own name, rather than as a part of his brother's Orkney earldom.

Once in Caithness, and with Kenneth's help, Skúli began raising an army. Skúli planned to use this force to seize his brother's earldom, so he gathered a fleet and transported it to Orkney. However, 'Ljótr gathered a troop and went to meet Skúli, and had more men'. The site of their clash wasn't recorded. It seemed that Ljót then tried to reason with his brother, but 'Skúli wanted nothing more than to fight. There was a hard fight there and Ljótr was victorious, while Skúli fled over to Ness [Caithness]'.[8]

Having driven off his brother, Earl Ljót went to Caithness to regain control of it in case Skúli returned. Sure enough, in *c.* 980 Skúli marched north 'with a great army which the king of Scots had got for him and Earl Magbjóðr [Macbeth], and they encountered Ljótr in the "Dales" in Caithness, and there was a great battle there, and the Scots were very keen on themselves at the beginning of the battle'.[9] It seemed Ljót's warriors, though, were better trained, and their shieldwall held. The Scots began to tire after failing to push the Norse back. The saga claims Ljót fought like a hero, encouraging his men to keep up the pressure. It continues: 'And when it had been like this for a while, then the Scots' formation broke up and after that they fled.' Skúli was killed as the Scots army fled. It is thought the battle site, the Dales of Caithness, is at Moss of Wester, beside the disused wartime airfield of RAF Skitten, midway between John o'Groats and Wick.[10]

After burying his brother, Ljót remained in Caithness, as he expected the Scots to seek revenge. Sure enough, the *mormaer*

Macbeth marched north at the head of a fresh Scottish force. The two sides met near the same spot at Skitten. The saga explained what followed: 'Earl Ljótr did not have a troop with him, and yet Ljótr attacked so fiercely that the Scots gave way, and there was a short battle, before those who accepted life fled, but the majority were wounded.' It's suspicious that two battles were fought in such quick succession and on the same battlefield. As there are no Scottish records which mention these two battles, it's quite possible there was only one of them, fought near Skitten between Earl Ljót and an allied army under Macbeth and Skúli.[11]

According to the *Earls' Saga*, after the battle Earl Ljót felt this threat had been dealt with, and so he returned to Orkney. He'd saved Caithness, but his men had suffered heavy casualties, and he'd been badly wounded himself. His injury proved fatal. Earl Ljót Thorfinnsson died in Orkney in *c.* 980, shortly after his return from Caithness. The saga says he'd been a good and popular earl and had ruled wisely. Despite the fratricide and fighting, Earl Ljót had provided a much-needed period of stability to the earldom. This time, though, the death of Ljót and Skúli Thorfinnsson couldn't be laid at the door of the earl's troublesome wife. As for the thrice-widowed Ragnhild herself, she quietly faded from the records, and the likelihood is that she died at some point during the decade-long reign of Earl Ljót's successor.[12]

Earl Ljót was succeeded by his last remaining brother, Hlodvir Thorfinnsson. Little is known about him, although the saga claims that he 'was a great ruler'. At some point he married Eðnu (or Eithnie), the daughter of an Irish sub-king, Kjarval (Cerball) of Osraige, a province in what is now Kilkenny.[13] The couple had at least three children. Of the two girls, Hvarflod was married to Gille, a powerful chieftain from the Hebrides, while her unnamed sister married Hávard, Earl Hlodvir's steward or deputy in Caithness. The son was called Sigurðr (or Sigurd) Hlodvisson. As for Sigurd's father, Earl Hlodvir avoided the grim fate of his older siblings, largely by not becoming ensnared by Ragnhild. So, he eventually died of natural causes in *c.* AD 991.[14]

Earl Hlodvir, the last of the sons of Thorfinn 'Skullsplitter', was reputedly buried in a mound at 'Ham' (Huna) on the northern coast of Caithness, between John o'Groats and Gills Bay, from where a daily ferry now sails to Orkney.[15] He was succeeded by his son Sigurd Hlodvisson, who went by the nickname Sigurd 'the Stout'. Strangely, Sigurd isn't mentioned much in the *Earls' Saga*, save for an account of his war-banner and his dramatic death in battle. This is surprising for such a skilled leader, who ruled for two decades and successfully expanded the earldom. It does though say, 'He was a great chieftain with a great territory'.[16]

When Sigurd succeeded his father to the earldom he had a marked advantage over his predecessors. He was an only son, and so there were no male siblings to lay rival claims to his title. So it remained undivided, much as it had been in the time of his grandfather Thorfinn 'Skullsplitter'. Crucially, this meant there was no scope for the bitter feuding that had led to the deaths of his uncles.[17]

From the start, Earl Sigurd followed a policy of expansion, much as his relative the first Earl Sigurd had. Unlike 'Sigurd the Mighty', though, whose campaigning was limited to the far north of Scotland, Sigurd 'the Stout' was a great deal more ambitious. According to *Njal's Saga*, 'The Earl [Sigurd the Stout] owned these lands in Scotland: Ross, Moray, Sutherland and Argyll.'[18] This was a bold claim, but as placename evidence suggests, there was little in the way of Norse settlement beyond Sutherland, the 'southern lands' to the Norse. In the late 10th century the traditional border between the Scottish province of Moray and the Norse earldom of Orkney was the River Oykel and the Dornoch Firth. Ross, though, the region to the south of Sutherland bordering the Cromarty Firth and the Moray Firth, was probably a form of 'debatable land', claimed by both sides.[19]

'Argyll' encompassed much of the former Scots kingdom of Dál Riata (or 'Dalr' in Norse), on the western coast of Scotland and the Inner Hebrides. This was the territory conquered by Sigurd 'the Mighty' and Thorstein 'the Red' a century before. Four generations later, they were still under the rule of the Orkney earls. Here, Sigurd was greatly helped by an alliance with his future brother-in-law Gille, the Norse-Gael Hebridean chieftain who married Sigurd's sister Hvarflod in AD 980. Gille became a secondary earl, acting as the governor of the region for Earl Sigurd. While other Norsemen ruled the northern part of the Sudreyjar for the Norwegian earls of Lade, Gille ruled the southern part from his island base on Colonsay.[20]

For three years, starting in AD 986, Sigurd and Gille waged war against the kingdom of Man. It was a time of trouble in the Irish Sea, with Viking raids and rival kings and warlords rampaging there seemingly at will. Much of the problem lay with the Norse-Gael king of the Isle of Man, Gudrod (or Godfrey) Haraldsson. He was the nephew of King Ólaf Sigtrygsson 'the Red' of Dublin, who'd previously had a hand in the struggle for Jórvik. King Godfrey and his brother Maccus had carried out Viking raids all around the Irish Sea. So Sigurd's expansion south from Argyll brought him into direct contact with this redoubtable Viking ruler.

In AD 987, Sigurd attacked the Isle of Man, and depending on who you believe, his invasion force was either driven off with heavy losses, or 'They [the Norse] were victorious, and killed Dungal, the king's son, and took much booty.'[21] Njal's Saga said that afterwards, Sigurd sailed to Coll to meet Gille, so presumably Sigurd had attempted a sudden surprise attack without involving his Hebridean ally. Perhaps both outcomes were right: Sigurd invaded the Isle of Man and plundered it, but was then forced to withdraw. Gudrod's son was killed while resisting this attack. Two years later, though, in AD 989, Sigurd returned, and together with Gille he successfully stormed and captured the island.

Irish annals claim that King Godfrey was killed by the men of Dál Riata. They probably meant Gille's Hebridean contingent of Sigurd's invasion force. Afterwards, Sigurd left Gille to rule the Isle of Man, and he returned home to Orkney. After that, with Gille's assistance, Sigurd would continue to hold the entire west coast of Britain as far as the Isle of Man until his death a quarter of a century later.[22] After conquering the Isle of Man, Sigurd turned his attention to the Scottish mainland. He already held Caithness and Sutherland there. According to the Earls' Saga, though, he had a major rival. 'It was one summer that Finnleikr, earl of the Scots, challenged Sigurðr to battle at Skitten Mire on a named day, and Sigurðr went to take advice from his mother; she had magical powers. The earl said to her that the difference in numbers would be no less than seven to one.' His challenger was Finláech (or Finlay) mac Ruaidri, the Scots mormaer of Moray, who ruled the lands beyond the southern border of Sigurd's earldom.[23]

Before this pre-arranged battle took place, Sigurd had to raise more men, as his army had been depleted during the campaigns in the west. So, he turned to Orkney and Shetland to find more warriors. In order to do this he decided to return the udal rights to the people of his earldom. These had been taken away from them three generations earlier by Sigurd's great-grandfather Earl 'Turf' Einar to cover the blood money owed to the Norwegian King Harald 'Finehair', after making a 'blood eagle' of his son. Now, Sigurd waived what remained of the communal debt, and returned ownership of their land to the earldom's landowners. This undoubtedly increased his stock and encouraged the landowners to support him by releasing their own tenants for military service. This in turn helped Earl Sigurd raise the men he needed for the coming battle.[24]

Earl Sigurd Hlodvirsson also found another way to give himself an edge in the coming fight. He called upon his Irish-born mother Eithnie, the widow of Earl Hlodvir, who had a reputation for witchcraft. 'So, he visited her – a visit she'd already foreseen – and he told her about the coming battle, adding that the odds would be heavily stacked against him. She answers, "If I had known that you intended to live forever, I would have brought you up for a long time in my wool-basket."' That was fair enough, but she relented and offered him a more supernatural, magical solution.

She handed him a beautifully made war banner, with the words, 'Take this banner which I have made with all my cunning, and I expect that victory will go to the one before whom it is borne'. Inevitably, though, as was the way with the supernatural, there was a catch. She added, 'and death to the one who bears it.' Sigurd was angered by this grim caveat, but he still took his mother's gift away with him. After all, it was a battle-winner.[25]

It was a stunningly crafted piece of work. As the saga put it: 'The banner was made with great skill and outstanding handicraft; a picture of a raven was worked into it, and when the wind blew the banner, then it was as if the raven was spreading its wings.' Despite the likely odds, as Mormaer Finlay of Moray was reputedly raising a large army, if it worked this magical raven banner might give Sigurd a chance of victory. Clearly the motif of the raven, a common one in Scandinavia, was a reference to the god Odin who used ravens as his spies and messengers. The caveat about the standard bearer was also significant, though, as it represented, in effect, a sacrifice to Odin.[26]

Taking his new banner with him, Sigurd gathered his army and set off for Skitten in Caithness. This was a deliberate choice of battleground for Mormaer Finlay. It was the same one where Sigurd's uncle Earl Ljót had vanquished a former *mormaer* of Moray a generation earlier. So, defeating the Norse earl there would be a sweet revenge for the Scots. The *Earls' Saga* tells us what happened when Sigurd and Finlay finally met: 'And when the battle was engaged, then Earl Sigurðr's standard-bearer was shot to death. The earl asked another man to bear the banner and when the fight had been on for a while, he fell. Three of the earl's standard-bearers fell, but he had the victory'.[27]

It's a wonderful story, and Earl Sigurd's magical raven banner became embedded in the whole rich folklore of the Viking Age and was emblematic of the era. There are a few problems with the account, though. The battle isn't mentioned anywhere other than in the *Earl's Saga*. Also, Finlay, *mormaer* of Moray wasn't killed along with his men at Skitten, but he outlived Earl Sigurd, and died during an uprising in Moray in 1020. The *Annals of Ulster* add that in 1020 Finlay was killed by rivals, who wanted to claim Moray for themselves.[28]

―――――――――

Whether Sigurd's raven banner existed or not, its mention in the sagas reflects Sigurd's return to the old gods after a brief and enforced flirtation with Christianity. The enforced conversion of the earldom of Orkney to Christianity came about following a fraught encounter between Earl Sigurd and Ólafr (or Ólaf) Tryggvason, a Viking warlord who would soon be the new Norwegian king.[29]

Ólaf would have been about 40 when the two men met. He was the son of a king of Viken on the eastern side of the Oslofjord, and possibly a great-grandson of Harald 'Finehair'. It was this tenuous connection that formed the basis of his later claim to the Norwegian throne. His life is recorded in several sagas, most of which contradict each other, or leave big gaps in his story. However, in AD 995, when he met Earl Sigurd, he was a Viking leader, who'd spent part of his youth in Kyiv and Novgorod before trying his hand at being a Viking in the Baltic.[30]

During his travels Ólaf married Geira, daughter of a king of Wendland in northern Germany. He soon proved his worth as a warrior fighting for the king's ally the Holy Roman Emperor during a campaign against King Harald 'Bluetooth' of Denmark. When Geira died in AD 984, the grief-stricken Ólaf resumed his Viking raiding. This included attacks on the Hebrides and the Isle of Man, which possibly led to him crossing paths with Earl Sigurd and his brother-in-law Gille. Then, around AD 988, Ólaf married again, this time to Gyda, the sister of Ólafr (or Ólaf) Sigtryggsson, king of Dublin.[31]

By AD 994 Ólaf was in southern England, blazing a swathe of destruction in what is now England's Home Counties, slaughtering, plundering and burning as he went. This rampage only ended when King Ethelred agreed to pay Ólaf a hefty *Danegeld*, protection money, to leave them alone. This was paid in Andover in Hampshire, and to seal the deal Ólaf agreed to be baptised.[32] The *Danegeld* was also paid on the agreement that Ólaf would quit England. He duly honoured the agreement and returned to Gyda in Ireland.[33]

After a spell in Dublin, Ólaf learned that Earl Hákon Sigurdsson, the acting ruler of Norway, was unpopular, particularly with the Norwegian nobles. So, Ólaf saw an opportunity to claim the throne for himself. In early AD 995 he set off for Norway with five longships crewed by hard-bitten warriors from his Viking warband. Ólaf Tryggvason, though, was no longer a mere Viking warlord. His conversion to Christianity had changed him. Although brought up in the old Norse religion, he'd encountered Christianity throughout his life, especially during his travels around the Baltic and the British Isles. After AD 994, it seems he embraced it with a missionary zeal. As a result, he felt that everyone else should follow his example.

When he finally gained the Norwegian throne, Ólaf set about forcibly converting his new subjects to Christianity. This is where his dramatic intervention in the Orkney earldom marked a major turning point in its history. Ólaf Tryggvason was a man with a mission. He planned to oust Earl Hákon and turn Norway into a Christian country. He wasn't Norway's first Christian ruler though – Hákon 'the Good' or 'Aðalsteinsfóstri' ('Æthelstan's foster-son') had tried it before him, in the mid-10th century. More recently, the Danish king Harald 'Bluetooth' had encouraged the spread of Christianity in Norway, much as he'd done in Denmark.

King Harald, though, ruled Norway at a remove, relying on his Norwegian ally Earl Hákon Sigurdsson to govern on his behalf. In

Norwegian history books, he is usually referred to as 'Jarl Hákon'. This was the man Ólaf Tryggvason was now on his way to fight. Once on the Norwegian throne, Ólaf had no intention of begging his new subjects to reject the Norse gods and accept Christianity. He planned to convert the Norwegian people by force. On his way there, he seized the unexpected chance to test his skills of religious conversion on Earl Sigurd 'the Stout'.[34]

TEN

Earl Sigurd 'the Stout'

A CCORDING TO THE *EARLS' SAGA*, the coming of Christianity to Orkney was all down to the tide. The Pentland Firth between Orkney and Caithness is some 20 miles long and six to eight miles wide. It can look placid enough, but it has a fierce tide running through it – one of the strongest in the British Isles. It runs at around 10 knots one way from east to west, and then, after a short period of slack water, it does the same in the other direction. There are other hazards too: deadly rocks, especially the Pentland Skerries at its eastern end, two small islands funnelling the tides in the middle section, and then a full exposure to Atlantic gales at its western end. Even today it causes problems for ships passing through this busy waterway. In vessels reliant on wind and oars, passage through it was much more fraught.

In AD 995, during his voyage from Ireland to Norway, Viking adventurer Ólaf Tryggvason planned to pass through the Pentland Firth to reach the West Sea beyond it. He was on his way to start a rising in Norway and his five longships were crammed with the hardened veterans of his Viking raids. Halfway through, finding the tide turning against him, he veered north into Hoxa Sound. His plan was to wait somewhere for the tide to change, so that it helped rather than hindered him. There are two main anchorages there where a longship can wait out the tide. To the west is what's now called Widewall Bay in the island of Rognvaldsey (South Ronaldsay), close to where Earl Thorfinn 'Skullsplitter' was supposedly buried. To the east is the island of Háey (Hoy). At Hoy's southern end there was another snug anchorage at Osmundswall.

According to the *Earls' Saga*, this was where he encountered Earl Sigurd. The earl had three longships with him and was lying off Osmundswall while preparing to go on one of his seasonal Viking raids. It must have come as a real shock to see five powerful, heavily manned longships enter the haven, and then drop anchor close by. Ólaf hailed the earl, and invited Sigurd aboard his *drakkar*, his dragon-prowed flagship. There, he made him an offer Sigurd couldn't refuse.

'It is my wish that you should have yourself baptised along with all the people who serve you, or you shall die here immediately, and I will afterwards go across all the islands with fire and sword'. In other words, Sigurd would be executed, while Orkney and Shetland would suffer the same utter devastation that the south of England had the year before. Sigurd 'the Stout' didn't really have a choice. The saga continues: 'And when the earl saw what situation he was in, he put the matter in Óláfr's hands. He [Óláfr] then had him [Sigurðr] baptised'.[1]

After leaving Orkney, Ólaf headed across the West Sea to Norway where his five longships entered the Trondheimsfjord. There, they came across Jarl Hákon's son Erlendr (or Erlend), with three longships. Outnumbered, Erlend's ships turned away and beached off the fjord's southern shore. Erlend and his men jumped into the water, but Ólaf, manning the tiller of his *drakkar*, unshipped it and smashed the swimming Erlend over the head, crushing his skull. The youth vanished beneath the cold waters of the fjord. With Erlend dealt with, Ólaf landed near Nidaros (now Trondheim), where the locals welcomed him as their leader. It turned out that the people of Trøndelag – the area around the fjord – had rebelled against Jarl Hákon, and that a day or two earlier the earl had been in Melhus, 20 miles to the south. The rebels had been massing near there, and it seems that as Hákon lacked a military escort, when he encountered them there he fled south to the valley of the ice-covered River Gaula. The rebels duly pursued him.[2]

There, near the hamlet of Rognes, Hákon hid in a hole in the snow-covered ground, next to a pig farm. The earl's slave, Tormod Kark, covered it over with a screen of planks and snow. Hákon hid there, waiting for the rebels to give up and go home. Instead, Ólaf and his men arrived and searched for the elusive earl. Eventually, after missing Hákon's hiding place, they gave up the search and went back to Melhus and a warming fire. That night, once Hákon fell asleep, his slave slit his throat. After cutting off Hákon's head, Tormod took it to Ólaf, clearly hoping for a big reward. Ólaf, though, wasn't going to reward a slave who'd brutally killed his master. Instead, he had Tormod Kark beheaded. The slave's head was then stuck on a pole and displayed overlooking the Trondheimsfjord as a warning to others.

Shortly after, at a *Thing* (Parliament) held in Nidaros, Ólaf Tryggvason became the new king of Norway.[3]

This regime change left Earl Sigurd 'the Stout' in an awkward position. His new king was evidently a religious zealot, who'd forced him at swordpoint to become a Christian. He'd also made the earl swear to force the rest of his subjects to abandon the Old Norse religion too. Normally, an earl of Orkney would ignore this kind of demand – or at least would have as soon as the king sailed away. However, before he left, Ólaf took Sigurd's son Hlǫðvir (or Hlodvir) 'Hundi' as a hostage to make sure the earl would do as he'd been told. The youth was Sigurd's eldest son, and therefore his heir. So, at least for the moment, Sigurd reluctantly did what he was told, and paid lip service to the new religion.[4]

The *Earls' Saga* suggests that Orkney's conversion to Christianity was the direct result of this encounter in AD 995. It claimed that after the forced baptism of Earl Sigurd, 'Then all the islands were Christianised'. This, though, probably wasn't the case. Archaeological evidence suggests that during the 10th century Christianity had gained ground in the earldom. While 9th-century Norse burials there were identifiably made according to the Old Norse religion, an increasing number in the 10th century were Christian burials.[5]

By the time Ólaf and Sigurd met at Osmundswall, it was likely that Christian beliefs had taken a firm hold in the earldom. Of course, the Picts had been Christian, and the *papae* – the Early Celtic Christian monks, missionaries and hermits – had already established themselves in Orkney and Shetland. In the islands their religious sites are preserved in placenames, such as the small islands of Papa Stronsay and Papa Westray, or Papdale, an area in Orkney's main town of Kirkwall.[6]

Unlike King Ólaf Tryggvason, who continued his forcible baptisms across Norway, Earl Sigurd was no born-again follower of 'the martyred god'. He had been brought up following the Old Norse religion, as had all the earls before him. His mother followed the old ways, as demonstrated by her sewing of Sigurd's raven banner, the bird associated with Odin. So, he probably took a pragmatic view of religion, and would happily pay public fealty to Christianity while privately retaining his belief in the old gods. Sigurd's loyalty to King Ólaf and his religion was largely tied to the fate of his kidnapped son.[7]

The *Earls' Saga* said of the hostage that: 'The king had him baptised with the name Hlóðvir'. It then added that after his arrival in Norway,

Hlodvir 'Hundi' only 'lived a short time', adding that 'after that Earl Sigurðr showed King Óláfr no subservience.' So, it seems once the news of the youth's death reached Orkney, a grieving Sigurd reacted by throwing off his allegiance to King Óláf. He also abandoned his newly adopted religion and returned to openly following the old ways. Although the saga never admitted to Sigurd's religious retreat from his enforced conversion, it made much of Sigurd's 'heathen' raven banner which the earl carried until his death.

Sigurd's campaigns down Britain's western coast had secured control over a large swathe of territory from the Hebrides down to the Isle of Man. On the Scottish mainland, the Orkney earldom included most of Argyll. Still, there had been no progress in pushing his earldom's southern border beyond Sutherland and Ross. The various battles with *mormaers* of Moray in Caithness suggested that the Scots were aggressively challenging Norse control of their enclave on the Scottish mainland.

After breaking his allegiance to King Óláf of Norway, it was clear Earl Sigurd could use an ally he could call on in time of need. Sigurd's father Earl Hlodvir had married Eithnie, the daughter of an Irish king, and Sigurd's own campaigning off the west coast suggested this might be the direction his diplomatic endeavours might take. Somewhat surprisingly, though, he turned to the kingdom of Alba instead. We know little about what diplomatic moves led to the forging of an alliance with the Scots. All the *Earls' Saga* says is that 'Earl Sigurðr then went to marry the daughter of Melkólme, king of Scots'. Unfortunately there's no corresponding Scottish mention of this important strategic union.[8]

The phrasing suggests this was the daughter of Malcolm II, King of Scots. Malcolm won the throne in 1005, having killed his predecessor King Kenneth III in a battle fought beside Loch Monzievard, in western Perthshire. Little is known of Malcolm, apart from his clashes with his English neighbours. He lacked sons, though, and so he strengthened his position by marrying off his daughters. The saga claims one of these was married to Earl Sigurd, and 'Willie' Thomson suggests her name might have been Plantula. Another daughter called Donula might have been married to Sigurd's rival, Finlay, *mormaer* of Moray.[9]

It's also possible that the saga got it wrong, and Earl Sigurd was wed to a daughter of Malcolm Máel Brigte, a nobleman from Moray. In 1020 this Malcolm killed Finlay and so became the *mormaer* of Moray. In some chronicles, this title is given as 'King of Scotland'. That's where the confusion arises. Either Malcolm II or Malcolm of Moray could have been the father of the bride, but the weight of evidence suggests the Moray noble was the more likely. In either case, this alliance would have helped to stabilise the earl of Orkney's southern border. This in turn would allow Sigurd to devote his considerable energies elsewhere.[10]

For a while, Earl Sigurd's energy was satisfied by leading Viking raids. In *Thorstein Sidu-Hallsson's Saga*, written in the 13th century, the exploits of this Icelandic noble are recounted. He was related to Earl Sigurd and spent a winter as a guest at the earl's court. Then he went raiding with his host: 'That summer, Earl Sigurd harried across a wide area throughout Scotland, and no one could challenge Thorstein with regard to either valour or temperament.' Clearly the Icelandic guest was enjoying himself. It continues: 'The Vikings pillaged and burned over a wide area in the British Isles. Late in the autumn, the earl went home to the Orkney Islands, and rested there for three months, and then gave his friends handsome gifts.'[11]

Unfortunately, the saga doesn't say when these Viking raids took place, but they probably happened during the first decade of the 11th century. One of these 'handsome gifts' might have gone to an Icelandic *skald* called Gunnlaug 'Serpent-Tongue'. The late 13th-century Icelandic *Saga of Gunnlaug 'Serpent-Tongue'* deals with the love of two Icelandic *skalds* for the same woman. In the saga, Gunnlaug toured various courts, including Earl Sigurd's hall in Orkney. His lively performance there earned him an axe, decorated with fine silver inlay. It seems, then, that Earl Sigurd had a routine. He went off campaigning or leading Viking raids from the spring to the autumn. Then he stayed in Orkney over the winter, where he extended largesse to his followers, and acted as a patron to visiting artists.[12]

———

Inevitably, given Earl Sigurd's interest in the Sudreyjar, the earl would be tempted to resume his campaigning there. In the early 11th century, the earldom of Orkney encompassed Orkney and Shetland as well as much of the north of Scotland, extending as far south as the Moray Firth, opposite modern-day Inverness. On Scotland's west coast his lands extended further south to encompass the western end of the Great Glen. This included the string of islands there, from Skye down to Jura. Thanks to the stewardship of Earl Gille of Colonsay, Sigurd ruled all the Sudreyjar, including both the Inner and Outer Hebrides. The presence of Norse settlements throughout the Sudreyjar is reflected in the surviving placenames, which show just how far south the earldom of Orkney's reach extended.

Further to the south, Sigurd and Gille controlled the Kintyre peninsula and the Isle of Arran in the Firth of Clyde. This is affirmed by placename evidence, which include names which are Norse in character, as well as the more common Gaelic ones. Then, some 75 miles further south, there was the Isle of Man. There it seems Earl Sigurd maintained overlordship, but allowed others to rule there in return for the paying of a tribute to boost the earl's coffers.[13]

This, though, wasn't just about territory. Trade was important too. Sigurd already controlled both ends of the Great Glen, but now, thanks to his alliance with the Scots, he had safe access down its length. This gave him a useful trade route from one side of Scotland to the other. This allowed the earldom to enjoy the benefits of trade in the region, and commodities such as timber, fish and grain. From the Mull of Kintyre, which Sigurd controlled, it was less than 12 miles to the north-eastern tip of Ireland. Sigurd was also familiar with Ireland, having raided extensively there, and his earldom also had trading links there. So the political situation in Ireland and access to its markets were of considerable interest to him.

In AD 997, Brian Boru, the Irish king of Munster, formed an alliance with Máel Sechnaill, king of Mide, and also the High King of Ireland. They split Ireland between them, with Brian Boru controlling the southern half of the island. In between the two was the Hiberno-Norse kingdom of Dublin. The two Irish kings declared war on King Sigtrygg 'Silkbeard' of Dublin, and in late AD 999 Brian Boru defeated the Dubliners, together with their allies from Leinster. As a result, Dublin was sacked, and its defences damaged. King Sigtrygg went into exile, but eventually he returned and regained his small kingdom. This time, though, he had to swear fealty to Brian Boru. Then Brian Boru launched a diplomatic and military campaign against Máel Sechnaill, and by 1002 Brian had gained the titular High Kingship.[14]

King Sigtrygg 'Silkbeard' then, was a vassal of the Irish High King. Clearly the Norse king resented this arrangement, and so in 1012 he allied himself with others who resented Brian's overlordship, including Máel Sechnaill, and the fighting resumed. It went badly, though, and the following year Brian Boru arrived outside Dublin and laid siege to the Norse city until the coming of winter. So Sigtrygg spent the winter seeking help from other Irish or Norse rulers. Inevitably, one of these was Earl Sigurd 'the Stout', the most powerful Norse ruler in the British Isles. When Sigtrygg arrived in Orkney, cap in hand, Sigurd was willing to help him. Although there's no record of it, he might well have been eyeing up the chance to expand his earldom into Ireland or at least benefit from favourable trading deals.[15]

So, in early 1014, Earl Sigurd sailed south from Orkney to go to the aid of the king of Dublin. He was accompanied by a sizeable Norse army, recruited from the veteran Viking raiders based in the earldom, who boosted Earl Sigurd's own hearthguard and followers. He also collected men from the Hebrides and the Isle of Man before reaching Dublin. Earl Gille remained in the Sudreyjar to maintain order. Similarly, Sigurd's steward Hárek stayed in Orkney to look after the earldom in his absence.

Sigurd landed in Dublin around the Norse festival of Sigrblot, which marks the coming of spring. The Christians in Sigurd's force equated it to Palm Sunday, a week before Easter. By then Brian Boru's army had arrived outside Dublin. The High King was accompanied by his warrior son Murchad and his old rival Máel Sechnaill, who'd made his peace and joined Brian's army. In the battle, though, both ageing Irish kings remained in reserve, and it was Murchad mac Brian who led the forces of the Irish High King. It seems King Sigtrygg remained in Dublin, watching the battle from its walls, together with his wife Sláine, Brian Boru's daughter. She would watch her brother, uncles and nephew take on her husband's warriors.[16]

Before the battle, *Njal's Saga* tells of a whole host of supernatural events – one night a rain of boiling blood fell on the Norse longships, and the next evening swords and axes magically leaped into the air and fought each other. On the third night it was the turn of flocks of ravens, who attacked the Norsemen in their boats with claws and beaks made from iron. Each time, one man aboard each of the longships was killed.

Inevitably this caused alarm in the Norse fleet, and Ospak, a Viking leader from the Isle of Man, defected, along with his followers.[17]

Early on the morning of Good Friday, 23 April 1014, the two sides gave battle. The chosen ground lay to the north of Dublin, between the city and the main Irish camp, beyond the small River Tolka. The Norse contingent crossed the river by a bridge, not far from where Croke Park stadium stands today, and the two shieldwalls deployed for battle a little to the north-east, in a field which is now a pleasant tree-lined park. The battle is recounted in several Irish annals, including the *Annals of Ulster*, but from the Norse standpoint the best account is in *Njal's Saga*.[18]

With King Sigtrygg remaining in Dublin, it was left to his brother Máel Mórda to lead the Dublin contingent. Earl Sigurd led his own men, while Bróðir (or Brodir), a Norse chieftain from the Isle of Man, commanded the Manx warriors. An Irish account claims that the battle opened with a duel between two warriors, who simultaneously killed each other. That done, the shieldwalls advanced, and battle was joined. 'The ranks went at each other. The fighting was very fierce. Brodir went through the enemy force and killed everyone who was in his way, and no steel could bite him.' Brodir, though, was hit three times by Brian Boru's brother Ulf 'Hraeda' ('the Quarrelsome'), and in the end his nerve went and he fled into the woods. In an Irish annal, though, it claims it was Brian's son Murchad who took on the 'foreign Vikings'.[19]

Njal's Saga continues: 'Earl Sigurd had a hard fight with Kerthjalfad [Brian Boru's son]. Kerthjalfad came on so fiercely that he killed everybody in his way. He cut his way through Earl Sigurd's ranks right up to the banner and killed the banner-bearer. The earl then found another man to carry the banner. The battle became fierce again. Kerthjalfad dealt this man a death blow, and those around him, one after the other.' Once again, the curse of the magical raven banner was coming true. Standing around Earl Sigurd were some of his most trusted warriors, the Icelander Þorsteinn (or Thorstein) Hallsson, Ámundi 'the White' and Hrafn 'the Red'. Running out of other options, and in the teeth of this spirited Irish assault, Sigurd called on them to pick up the fallen banner.

Earl Sigurd asked Thorstein Hallson to carry the banner. Thorstein was ready to take it. Then, Ámundi 'the White' said, 'Don't carry the banner! Everybody who does gets killed!' 'Hrafn the Red', said the earl – 'you carry the banner'. 'Carry that devil of yours yourself!', answered Hrafn. So, Earl Sigurd was left with no other option.

'Then it's best that the beggar and his bag go together', and he took the banner off the pole, and stuck it between his clothes. A little later, Ámundi 'the White' was killed. Then the earl was pierced through by a spear.[20]

Here the saga and the Irish accounts differ slightly. The likelihood is that in this same fierce hand-to-hand fracas around Sigurd's banner, Brian Boru's son Murchad was killed, possibly after delivering the spear-thrust that killed Earl Sigurd. Not long after, the Dublin Norsemen broke and fled back towards woodland or to the Norse longships. With their earl dead, the Orkneymen did the same. *Njal's Saga* claimed that Thorstein Hallsson was spared as he was an Icelander, while Hrafn 'the Red' was being dragged under while escaping across the river, but was eventually freed from the 'underwater demons' lurking there. Many, though, didn't make it to safety. With the rising tide making it impossible to reach the longships, many were cut down in the shallows of Dublin Bay.

The luck of the Irish, though, wasn't completely with the victors. According to Irish annals, in the chaos that followed the end of the battle the Viking Brodir reached the Irish camp and found the High King's tent. Inside it King Brian Boru was praying, presumably giving thanks for his victory. He was killed as he knelt there. *Njal's Saga*, though, has him cut down on the battlefield: 'He [Brodir] ran out of the woods and cut his way through the shield wall, and swung at the king. The boy Tadk brought his arm up against it, but the blow cut off the arm, and the king's head too.'[21] Brodir was caught, and Ulf 'the Quarrelsome' cut Brodir open and unravelled his intestines, ensuring a slow and agonising death for the Viking. Also cut down in the final stages of the battle was Murchad's son Toirdelbech, thus playing havoc with the High King's line of succession.

A handful of weary survivors of the Battle of Clontarf eventually returned to Orkney, bringing news of the defeat. Many, though, had heard the news already, or rather a grim harbinger of it. *Njal's Saga* claimed that the earl's steward Hárek, left behind in Orkney, saw Sigurd and his men returning, and he went out to meet them.

Watchers saw them meet, and then everyone continued walking on until they disappeared behind a hill. Neither Hárek nor Earl Sigurd's ghost army were ever seen again. In Colonsay, Earl Gille was visited by a messenger in a dream, who told him what happened a week before Hrafn 'the Red' appeared in the flesh to tell him the bad tidings.

Then, in Caithness, 12 women were seen, spinning and singing. They were Valkyries, spinning intestines on a loom made from spears, swords and arrows, and their chanting was them directing the course of the battle. When they finished, they tore up their entrail-spun cloth, split into two groups and rode away, half to the north, and the rest to the south. It was clear that Odin's gatherers of dead warriors would be kept busy after the battle, escorting the fallen Norse heroes to Valhalla. Among them, no doubt, was Sigurd 'the Stout', Earl of Orkney, still clutching his magical raven banner to his blood-soaked body.[22]

ELEVEN

The Rise of Earl Thorfinn

T HE STORY OF THE Norse earls of Orkney is littered with sibling rivalry. Norse noblemen were raised to be proud and ambitious, especially if they had a chance of succeeding to their family's title. What followed the bloody death of Earl Sigurd was one of the most violent of these collisions between siblings, and one of the longest-lasting. Essentially, it spanned half a century and involved two generations before it played itself out. At its heart was a youngest brother whose greed for power was boundless. The result was that under Earl Thorfinn Sigurdsson 'the Mighty', the earldom of Orkney became a true force to be reckoned with. Under this great Norse warrior, the earldom was never larger nor more powerful.

It was a real achievement for a boy who was the runt of the litter. In *Njal's Saga*, it claims that Earl Sigurd 'the Stout' was enticed to take part in the Dublin adventure when King Sigtrygg 'Silkbeard' offered Sigurd the hand of his mother Kormlod in return. In fact, it seems that Sigurd was a true family man, and loyal to his Scottish-born wife, the 'daughter of a King of Scots'.[1] Given the timeframe, it was likely Sigurd was married before this, but no record of an earlier union survives. Sigurd's eldest son Hlodvir had died while being held hostage by King Ólaf of Norway. However, when Sigurd was killed on the battlefield of Clontarf, he still had four more sons to succeed him.

In order of age, they were called Sumarliði (or Sumarlidi), Brúsi, Einarr (Einar) and Þorfinnr (Thorfinn). Thorfinn was only five when his father died, but his three elder brothers were all in their late teens or early twenties. Thorfinn, being the youngest, was left out in the cold, and his three elder siblings agreed to divide up the earldom between them. This division into thirds would end in disaster, but at the start everything worked well. For his part Thorfinn was shipped off to Scotland, probably accompanied by his widowed mother.

Thorfinn was supposedly raised at the court of King Malcom II of Scotland, far from the islands of his birth. Meanwhile his three older brothers ruled the earldom.[2]

The author of the *Earls' Saga*, though, might have made a mistake. If Thorfinn's mother was the daughter of the *mormaer* of Moray rather than the king of Scotland, then she would have taken her son to her relatives there. So the boy would have been raised by Malcolm, the *mormaer* of Moray. Afterwards, the saga's author might well have confused the two Malcolms. This second version makes more sense, given the events that played out later in Thorfinn's reign.[3]

In either case, as a youth, Thorfinn would have been taught all the skills of a young ruler: the arts of diplomacy and court politics, the abilities of the warrior and the patience of the huntsman. After this, the *Earls' Saga* then claims that 'The king of the Scots then gave his daughter's son Þorffinr Caithness and Sutherland, and the rank of earl, and appointed people to govern with him.'[4] In other words, the Scots still regarded the part of the earldom of Orkney on the Scottish mainland as part of their kingdom. Thorfinn's father Sigurd had walked this line, with the Scottish king on one side and the Norwegian one on the other. It was one that Thorfinn had to walk too. It seems, though, that the three older brothers who ruled the earldom were content to allow this arrangement, and accepted that their youngest brother would rule the earldom's lands south of the Pentland Firth.[5]

In Orkney and Shetland the brothers Sumarlidi, Brúsi and Einar continued to rule their sprawling earldom. On Sigurd's death it's likely that Earl Gille continued to hold the Hebrides, Argyll and the other lands off Britain's western coast on behalf of the Orkney earls. The Isle of Man was already semi-independent, and Gille exacted tribute from it, on behalf of the earldom. From 1030 on, that island kingdom was ruled by Ólaf Sigtryggsson, the son of the deposed king of Dublin. It was clear, though, that after Sigurd the Orkney earldom's influence had contracted, and now only really extended as far as the southernmost tip of Argyll.[6]

Within a few years, Earl Sumarlidi – the oldest of the four brothers – died of some undisclosed illness. The *Earls' Saga* paints an interesting picture of the two elder Sigurdsson brothers who remained. 'The brothers Einarr and Brúsi were different in temperament. Einarr was a stubborn and ambitious man, aggressive and a great warrior. Brúsi was an even-tempered person, composed, modest and well-spoken'. Until then each of the three older brothers had held a third of the earldom, apart from Caithness and Sutherland, which remained Thorfinn's preserve. Now, in around 1018, Thorfinn, although still a child, tried to claim the third of the earldom which had been ruled by Sumarlidi.

The kind and easy-going Brúsi thought it was fair that Thorfinn should have more of a stake and said he was content with his own third share of the earldom. In other words, he was happy to turn Sumarlidi's third over to his youngest brother. Einar's response, though, was a firm and emphatic no. He backed this up with the convincing argument that his younger brother controlled his lands on the Scottish mainland, which already equated to roughly a third of the whole earldom. So, once again, Thorfinn was left out. Of course, he'd be far from destitute. Although he was still a child, he had stewards gathering taxes on his behalf across roughly 3,000 square miles of northern Scotland.[7]

Earl Einar then took Sumarlidi's third of the earldom, so that he now controlled two-thirds of it. Unlike his grasping younger brother, Brúsi, although the eldest of the three, was quite content with his own third. Einar, though, was greedy, and even though he ruled two-thirds of the earldom, he still increased the taxes on his people. He needed the money to fund men and longships to conduct Viking raids. As the *Earls' Saga* put it, 'The great warrior Earl Einarr in the Orkneys, son of Earl Sigurðr, was not thought to be a man of equity.' In other words, he cared less about his people than he did his band of Viking followers.[8]

Einar and his warriors went raiding every summer, but often the plunder he brought home wasn't enough to keep his earldom going. So, he boosted his income by levying heavy taxes on his subjects. This caused a lot of resentment, as these were much heavier than in Brúsi's third of the earldom. When the farmers and landholders complained, Einar refused to listen. It was hardly surprising his people nicknamed him Einar 'Crooked-mouth'. In essence, Earl Einar was a bully, and his taxes led to suffering and shortages across what otherwise would have been a fertile, prosperous community. By contrast, in the part of the land which Brúsi had, there were good harvests and an easy life for the householders; for that reason he was popular.[9]

At some point before 1020, when Thorfinn was still about ten, Einar 'Crooked-mouth' called a *Thing* or assembly at Dingieshowe, a narrow sandy peninsula on the eastern side of Orkney's East Mainland. This probably happened on the howe or mound there, which gave the area its name. The local farmers planned to use the *Thing* to air their grievances, and they asked Ámundi, a farmer from nearby Deerness, to make their views known to the earl. When Ámundi wasn't willing to speak, the farmers convinced his son Þorkell (or Thorkell) to address Earl Einar instead.

The saga recalls what happened. 'And when the earl held an assembly, then Þorkell spoke on behalf of the householders, described the people's need, and asked the earl to spare the men.' Surprisingly, Einar agreed to slim down the size of his next Viking raid from six ships to three. However, he ordered Thorkell not to make any more requests from him. The farmers, of course, were delighted.[10]

Earl Einar 'Crooked-mouth' went on his raid, and the farmers were left alone until the following harvest. Then, Einar called another *Thing*, and announced he'd impose the levy he'd held back on the previous year. Once again, Thorkell spoke up for the farmers, but the earl wasn't in the mood for listening. As the saga puts it, 'The earl answered angrily and said that the lot of the householders would get much worse as a result of his speech. He made himself so furious and angry that he said that he [Thorkell] would not both be in one piece at the assembly the following spring'.

Wisely, Thorkell's father Ámundi told his son he had to leave Orkney for his own safety. So Thorkell fled to Caithness, where he met the young Thorfinn. The two quickly formed a bond, and the exiled farmer's son soon became a surrogate father to the boy. Eventually, he became known as Thorkell 'Fosterer'.[11]

When Thorfinn came of age, around 1025, he wrote to Einar, claiming what he saw as his rightful third of the earldom. Unfortunately, 'Einarr was disinclined to diminish himself in this way'. So, with Thorkell 'Fosterer's' help, the teenager began raising warriors to claim his share by force if he had to. When he learned of this, Einar did the same. So, when Thorfinn and his followers landed in Orkney, Einar's army set off to meet him. Surprisingly, though, so did Brúsi, but he was there to mediate rather than to start a war. In the end, Thorfinn got his way and was given his third without having to fight for it. It was just as well, as Einar probably had the more experienced warriors at his back, men honed through regular Viking raiding.[12]

Earls Brúsi and Einar agreed to unite the remaining two-thirds of the earldom, with Einar acting as its head of state. It went unsaid, but presumably the more diplomatic Brúsi would manage the earldom's economy. Another decision, obviously dictated by Einar, was that when either of the two older brothers died, the surviving sibling would rule the whole two-thirds slice of the earldom. Although Einar had no sons to succeed him, Brúsi had one called Rǫgnvaldr (or Rognvald), who would then lose any claim to his inheritance if his father died before his uncle Einar. Still, for the sake of peaceful relations the easy-going Earl Brúsi agreed to the arrangement.

For the next few years, the three brothers co-existed peaceably enough. Thorfinn remained in Caithness with Thorkell 'Fosterer', and had stewards manage his lands in Orkney and Shetland. Brúsi remained in Orkney, looking after his lands and raising his son Rognvald, while Einar spent most of his summers plundering his way around the Irish Sea before returning home to Orkney for the winter.[13]

Like his father Sigurd, Einar 'Crooked-mouth' favoured raiding around the Irish Sea. In one raid, though, he suffered a major setback when he went ashore at Lough Larne in Ulster. There, the Vikings were opposed by a local Irish king who inflicted a crushing defeat on Einar's raiders, thanks in part to a band of Viking allies led by a warrior called Eyvindr (or Eyvind) 'Aurochs-horn'. After that, Einar exhibited more caution in picking his targets.[14]

In theory, the earls of Orkney owed their position to the king of Norway. In practice, as it was a dynastic succession, this rarely happened. Still, in the summer of 1020 Thorfinn was invited to Norway to meet the new Norwegian ruler, King Ólaf II 'the Holy', who'd gained the throne five years before. It seems the king was well aware of the tensions in the earldom. It was also clear Ólaf had a dislike of Earl Einar, as a few years before he'd killed Eyvind 'Aurochs-horn', who'd been a loyal follower of the Norwegian king.

For Einar this was an act of revenge, as Eyvind had fought alongside Einar's Irish opponent at Lough Lorne. So when Eyvind and his Viking band were stormbound in Osmundswall in Hoy, Earl Einar captured them and killed Eyvind before letting most of his men go free. King Ólaf took this murder of his follower as a personal slight. After his death, Ólaf would be canonised, becoming Saint Ólaf, but in life, despite his supposed sanctity, he was a man who could bear grudges. The king was also a shrewd and manipulative political operator. So, Einar had unwittingly crossed the wrong man.[15]

In the autumn of 1020 Thorfinn sailed to Orkney to open fresh negotiations with his brothers. As he saw it, Caithness was his by right, as it had been granted to him by the Scottish crown. His third of the earldom, then, should be a third of the rest of it. When the two earls began arguing over their share of the earldom, Einar gathered his men and was squaring up for a confrontation. Once again, Brúsi played the part of peacemaker, and the two brothers backed down. Still, beneath the surface, tensions between Thorfinn and Einar remained at boiling point.

Afterwards, Thorfinn returned to Caithness and left Thorkell to manage his lands in Orkney in his stead. As a demonstration of peace and reconciliation, it was agreed that Thorkell 'Fosterer' and Earl Einar would take turns in throwing a feast for each other. It was Thorkell who hosted first, in his family hall at Skaill in Deerness. It was scheduled to take place around Álfablót in late October, the Norse equivalent of Halloween, which was held once the harvests were in and before winter firmed its grip on the islands. As was the Norse custom, the feasting and celebrations would last for a few days.[16]

Thorkell's great hall was large, with a door at each end, and a great fireplace. In front of it a huge banquet had been laid out for the earl and his followers, and for Thorkell and his leading men. The saga says of Einar 'Crooked-mouth' that 'And when the earl was there at the feast, the entertainment was lavish. The earl was not cheerful.' Still, nothing untoward happened until the feasting wound to a close and it was time for Earl Einar to leave. The arrangement was that Thorkell would accompany Einar across Orkney to the earl's own hall in the West Mainland. Thorkell, though, didn't trust Einar, so he sent out men to scout the route. It was just as well. The saga's account continues: 'And when they came back, they told Þorkell that they found three ambushes of armed men, "and we think it is true to say to you that treachery is behind it."'[17]

So Thorkell made some excuse to delay their departure while he gathered his most loyal men and sketched out his plan. Meanwhile Einar was growing impatient, but 'Þorkell said he had much to do; he kept going out and in'. Einar was itching to leave, but nevertheless he stayed where he was, sitting on a bench and warming himself by the great fire. That's when Thorkell made his move. 'Then Þorkell went in by another door and with him a man who is named Hallvarðr; he was an Icelander, from an East Fjords family; he closed the door. Þorkell went further into the hall between the fire and where the earl was sitting.' As he approached the earl, Thorkell kept an axe hidden behind his back. Then, when 'The earl asked "Are you ready now?" Þorkell answers "I am". Then Þorkell struck the earl on the head.'[18]

The earl was killed outright, and his body fell forward into the fire. Several of the earl's followers were standing frozen in the room, still dumbstruck by what they'd just witnessed. Teasingly, Thorkell's accomplice Hallvarðr (or Hallvard) scolded them for not helping pull their earl out of the fire before he used the curve of his axe to do the job himself. Hallvard hooked the back of the dead earl's neck with it, and dragged the blood-splattered body clear of the flames. With that, Thorkell and Hallvard made a swift exit before the horrified earl's men could react. Outside, Thorkell's fully armed warriors were waiting for them, to protect the pair from the earl's men. The earl's bodyguard, though, didn't seek bloody revenge. Instead, as the saga puts it, they followed Thorkell outside, and 'The earl's men grabbed him, and he [the earl] was by then dead, but all of them failed to take revenge.' So Thorkell was spared any immediate retribution, and he and his followers were able to escape. Just to make sure, Thorkell had a longship ready and immediately put to sea, bound for Norway. It says a lot about the lack of popularity of Einar 'Crooked-mouth' that even his most loyal followers weren't prepared to avenge his death.

As the earl's men took Einar's body home by sea, Thorkell risked the worsening weather to cross the West Sea and explain his actions to King Ólaf. The Norwegian king, probably swayed by his dislike of Einar, absolved Thorkell of the murder. Thorkell stayed there for the winter until the furore died down, and he returned home in the spring of 1021. Then he explained himself to Brúsi and Thorfinn. After Einar's burial, Earl Brúsi took over the two-thirds share of the earldom, following the terms of the agreement reached between him and Einar. This of course meant that Brúsi's son Rognvald, now almost ten, would inherit the earldom when his father died.[19]

This, though, didn't suit Thorfinn, who was too greedy to let the arrangement stand. So, over the course of several meetings between the brothers, he repeatedly insisted on having an equal share of the earldom – each brother getting half. Brúsi wasn't grasping like his younger brother, but he clearly wanted to maintain the arrangement for the benefit of his son. However, he wasn't in a particularly strong position. Thorfinn had more ships and men at his back if it came to a fight, and he could also call on the backing of the Scots. So Brúsi set off across the West Sea to visit King Ólaf in Nidaros to ask for his intervention. This, though, turned out to be a big mistake.

King Ólaf II had foreseen all this, and relished the meeting. During his dealings with the Orkney earls, the future saint showed little sign of any holy virtue. When Brúsi met Ólaf, the king resurrected the old claim that the Orkney earls were the vassals of the Norwegian king, and so he alone had the right to appoint an earl of Orkney. As Ólaf put it, 'Now I will give you this option, that you can become my man; I will then grant you the tenure of the islands.' In the end, Brúsi had to comply, and swore an oath of fealty to King Ólaf. After that, though, not only did Brúsi leave without Ólaf's guarantee of backing, but he also lost his two-thirds claim to the earldom too, as Ólaf held Einar's portion back while he decided what to do with it. It seems that Earl Brúsi had been completely blindsided by the Norwegian king.[20]

At that point Earl Thorfinn made the voyage to Norway too, to make sure his part of the earldom was secure. Again, King Ólaf demanded that Thorfinn swear fealty to him in return for his title. Thorfinn was reluctant, as he'd already sworn fealty to King Malcolm for his lands in Caithness and Sutherland. King Ólaf was blunt: 'If you, Earl, do not wish to become my man, the other option is for me to put the man I want in charge of the Orkneys. And, I want you to swear an oath not to claim the lands of the person I put in charge and leave them in peace from you.' This unexpected demand was a real body blow to the ambitious young earl.

Thorfinn begged for time to consider this, claiming, "'All my advisers are at home" he says, "and my age still makes me a child.'" King Ólaf, though, was having none of this. However, Thorkell 'Fosterer' sent an urgent message to Thorfinn, warning him that he shouldn't leave Norway without reaching a settlement. After all, Thorfinn didn't really have a choice. So he duly took the knee and swore his oath to the Norwegian king. Only then, with the sworn fealty of both Orkney earls under his belt, did Ólaf deliver his decision. The two Sigurdsson brothers would retain the earldom, but only as vassals of the crown. Each would have a third of the earldom. Einar's third would be kept by King Ólaf himself. His invented excuse was that it was restitution for Einar's killing of his friend Eyvind.[21]

It was clearly meant as a humiliation. What had been established as a dynastic earldom had, in a moment, been turned into one which owed everything to the king of Norway. For Ólaf, it was a brilliant political coup. Later, the *skald* Óttar 'the Black' composed a verse celebrating King Ólaf's diplomatic triumph over the Orkney earls. It praised how Ólaf had managed to force the allegiance of the Orkney earls not through war but purely through his ability to enforce his will.

> Noble – hold with moderation the realm of good kings of nations,
> Shetlanders are acknowledged to be your subjects,
> No prince, terror-swift, came on earth who,
> Sooner than you, seized the westward isles into his power.[22]

King Ólaf, though, wasn't quite finished. Almost as an afterthought, after further talks with Earl Brúsi once a humiliated Thorfinn had sailed off, Ólaf offered a sweetener. The king returned Einar's third of the earldom to Brúsi in return for the promise to govern and tax it on Ólaf's behalf. This meant Brúsi now controlled two-thirds of the earldom again, and Thorfinn had one-third. This was another diplomatic masterstroke. King Ólaf would be saved the trouble and expense of appointing stewards to govern his portion of the Orkney earldom while also winning back the support of the elder of the two Orkney earls. Perhaps he also made a vague offer of military support in case Thorfinn caused any more trouble to Brúsi.

Even this offer, portrayed as a concession, came at a price. Ólaf also needed to guarantee that the two earls wouldn't forget their oaths.

The standard way of doing that was to take a hostage, much as the earlier King Ólaf had done with Earl Sigurd's son. Thorfinn was still a teenager and had no offspring, but Brúsi did. So Brúsi was forced to hand over his ten-year-old son Rognvald Brúsason to the Norwegian king. The boy, who was said to be tall for his age with long, golden hair, would now become the king's foster-son and grow up in the Norwegian court.[23]

A deflated Earl Brúsi returned home to join his younger brother in ruling their earldom. Any sign that either of them was stepping out of line could lead to Rognvald's death. In fact, Rognvald did well out of the arrangement. The youngster was raised by his foster-father in the ways of the court, much as Thorfinn had been in Scotland. In return, Rognvald would remain loyal to his foster-father, even when Ólaf's power crumbled. In a few years, Rognvald Brúsason would return to challenge his uncle Thorfinn for control of the Orkney earldom. For the moment, though, he remained in Norway, a latent threat to the young Earl Thorfinn.

There was still one loose end. During their stay in Norway, King Ólaf had raised the outstanding matter of Thorkell's murder of Einar 'Crooked-mouth'. While the king had no love for Einar, it was clear that Thorkell should atone for his crime or risk being dubbed an outlaw, free for any man to kill. Ólaf, though, refused to adjudicate. Instead, he left justice in the hands of the two Sigurdssons. Before Thorfinn left Norway, Thorkell came to him and threw himself on the mercy of his foster-son. The saga recounted the moment. 'And when he was fully ready, then it happened one day, when the earl was drinking on his ship, that Þorkell Ámundason came to him suddenly and laid his head on his knees and told him to do with it whatever he wanted.' Earl Thorfinn immediately forgave his foster-father. Back in Orkney, Earl Brúsi would do the same.[24]

After the earls returned home, Thorfinn remained in Caithness and relied on Thorkell 'Fosterer' to act as his steward in Orkney, while others did the same for both earls in Shetland, the Sudreyjar and Argyll. Although it seems that neither earl went on Viking raids as Einar had done, the earldom itself wasn't immune from Viking attacks. This was largely due to the growing volatility around the shores of the West Sea. The trouble began following the death of the Danish king Sveinn (also Svein or Sweyn) 'Forkbeard' several years before in 1014.

At the time, Sweyn ruled a Nordic empire encompassing Denmark, Norway and a large part of England.[25]

In 1015, five years before his first meeting with Earl Thorfinn, Ólaf Haraldsson became King Ólaf II of Norway. Meanwhile in Denmark, Sweyn's son Harald ruled the country. He died after just four years on the throne, and was succeeded in 1018 by another of Sweyn's sons, Knut, a name usually Anglicised to 'Canute'. Since 1016 Knut 'the Great' had sat on the throne of England, and now with Denmark too he posed a major threat to Ólaf's Norway. All this change led to growing unrest and an increase in the number of Viking raids. Orkney and Shetland began to suffer from them, but Earl Brúsi seemed unable to defend the joint earldom. Thorfinn, the junior partner, protected his own lands, but did little to help his brother protect his. The saga claims that Norwegian and Danish Vikings raided Orkney, and although it doesn't mention it, the same probably happened in the earldom's possessions in the west of Scotland.[26]

Brúsi criticised Thorfinn for not doing more to protect the two northern archipelagos. So Thorfinn made his brother an offer: 'Brúsi could have one-third of the earldom, and Thorfinn would have the other two-thirds'.[27] In return Thorfinn would have sole charge of the defence of the whole of the earldom. Unlike his younger brother, Earl Brúsi was no warrior, and so he had little choice but to agree.[28]

So Thorfinn gained the majority-share of the Orkney earldom. With that, he quickly cleared the islands of the Vikings and ensured they were so well protected that the raiders would be unlikely to try their luck again. Still, it was a difficult time – one where the troubles in the earldom were just a byproduct of the upheavals and regime changes taking place across the West Sea in Norway, and beyond the earldom's borders in Denmark and England. At least now, though, the earldom of Orkney had an earl in majority control who was more than capable of fighting his corner.

TWELVE

The Prince of the Salt Road

A FTER THORFINN DEALT WITH the Viking raiders, the two remaining Sigurdsson brothers got along well, without any real sign of conflict. For the moment, the earldom enjoyed a rare spell of peace, and its people prospered. Still, the political upheavals that bedevilled the Norse world continued. Although the Norwegian king Ólaf still claimed his share of the earldom's revenues, he left the two brothers to govern without interference.

He had, after all, much bigger problems to deal with. Shortly before his meeting with the two Orkney earls, King Ólaf had married Astrid, the daughter of King Ólaf of Sweden. Undoubtedly Brúsi and Thorfinn would have met this beautiful new queen when they visited Ólaf's court. In theory this marriage to a Swedish princess gave the Norwegian king a useful ally against King Knut. In 1027, though, the Norwegians and Swedes were defeated by the Danes in a naval battle at Helgeå in southern Sweden. This left Knut the dominant ruler in Scandinavia. Knut then followed up his victory with an offensive. The following year Knut appeared in Agder in southern Norway, at the head of a large, well-manned fleet. He then worked his way around the coast, forcing the Norwegians to swear allegiance to him. By the time he reached Nidaros in 1029, he'd effectively become the new king of Norway.[1]

Ólaf II was forced to flee to the lands of the Kyivan Rus, taking the young Rognvald Brúsason with him. This of course neatly solved a problem for the Orkney earls. Their oath had been sworn to Ólaf, so this meant the end of their enforced fealty. Both Brúsi and Thorfinn, however, took great care to keep out of the way of his far more powerful successor King Knut, now the ruler of a sprawling Scandinavian empire that encompassed Denmark, England and Norway.

By 1030, Earl Thorfinn was 21 years old, and a fully-grown man. In the *Earls' Saga* he is described as 'a very tall and strong man, ugly, dark-haired, with sharp features and a big nose, and quite bushy eyebrows.' He was forceful, he'd already demonstrated his abilities as a leader of men and he was both a courageous warrior and a skilled tactician. His greed and occasional ruthlessness were equally evident. At 15 he'd led raiding expeditions and had fought in battle. Even at that age, his own *jarlaskáld* ('earl's poet') Árnor Thordarsson was composing verses about him:

> The ruler reddened sword-edges, in the gale of helmets;
> Huginn's foot-reddener set out before he was fifteen.
> Under the cloud-hall, there's no younger battle-bold man than
>   Einarr's brother,
> Who's declared himself ready to defend the land, and to attack.[2]

Although Thorfinn had largely broken ties with the Norwegian crown, he still benefited from Scottish support. By then Thorfinn was the dominant partner in the earldom, as Brúsi left politics and war to his sibling. For the past year Norway had been ruled on King Knut's behalf by Hákon Eiríksson, the earl of Lade. As well as holding extensive lands in Norway, the earls of Lade had also ruled the northernmost part of the Hebrides since 1016. They'd been granted to the Lade earls by King Ólaf II following the death of Earl Sigurd 'the Stout', and so represented both lost territory and lost income to the earls of Orkney. In 1029, Earl Hákon of Lade was drowned in a shipwreck in the Pentland Firth, while returning from a visit there. So Thorfinn planned to fill this void and take control of the Norwegian earldom's lands in the Sudreyjar.

Then, without warning, the two earls faced a potentially serious threat from Norway, which put Thorfinn's plans on hold. Seizing the opportunity and helped by the kings of the Rus and the Swedes, King Ólaf staged a comeback. Accompanied by a force of loyal warriors, which included Rognvald Brúsason, Ólaf travelled from Kyiv to Sweden, and from there he crossed the mountains into Norway. On reaching Trøndelag he unfurled his banner and began raising troops. Word of his arrival spread and a large opposing army was raised there which was loyal to Knut. It was led by an assortment of local landowners, but the main one was Kálfr (or Kálf) Árnason from Trøndelag. On 29 July 1030, the two armies clashed at Stiklestad, just over 40 miles to the north-east of Nidaros.[3]

According to *St Ólaf's Saga*, King Ólaf led his men forward with shouts of 'Forward, Forward, Christ-Men – Cross-Men – King's Men!' The *skald* Sigvat wrote:

> Thundered the ground beneath their tread, as, iron-clad, thick-tramping, sped
> The warriors, in row and rank, past Stiklestad's sweet grassy bank.
> The clank of steel, the bowstrings' twang, the sounds of battle, loudly rang,
> And bowmen hurried on advancing, their bright helms in the sunshine glancing.[4]

Ólaf tried to break through the enemy ranks, probably after forming a 'swine-snout' or wedge of his best warriors. 'Then the bonde-army [farmer army] pushed on from all quarters. They who stood in front hewed down with their swords; they who stood next thrust with their spears; and they who stood hindmost shot arrows, cast spears, or threw stones, hand-axes, or sharp stakes. Soon there was a great fall of men in the battle. Many were down on both sides.'[5] The battle continued throughout the day, but gradually numbers began to tell, and Ólaf's ranks began to thin. Ólaf himself, standing beneath his banner, was easy to spot, and ultimately he paid the price.

He was wounded twice in the fighting that followed. Finally, having fought his way through to him, Kálf Árnason and a small knot of his kinsfolk surrounded the king. Ólaf fought with desperate determination, but in the end a spear-thrust pierced his chest. Then Kálf Árnason finished Ólaf off by a sword cut to the throat. After King Ólaf fell, most of the warriors who formed his wedge were also cut down. A counter-attack led by one of Ólaf's captains, Dag Hringsson, was too late to save the king, but the fighting continued until darkness fell. Only then did the survivors of Ólaf's army flee the blood-soaked field.

With his death, the Orkney earls were spared any further constitutional threat to their earldom. Afterwards, Ólaf was canonised and eventually became Norway's patron saint. His name would even be given to Kirkwall's first proper church. While he was a devout Christian, his methods of 'spreading the faith' had been as overbearing as those of his namesake and distant kinsman King Ólaf Tryggvason three decades earlier. Still, as a Norse warrior king, Ólaf II, or St Ólaf as he became, had been an inspiring figure.

During the battle, King Ólaf's 15-year-old half-brother Harald Sigurdsson had fought alongside him. The youngster would eventually become the famed Harald 'Hardrada', king of Norway and one of the main figures in the two-pronged invasion of England in 1066. In 1030, though, his time had yet to come. Harald had been badly wounded in the fight and left for dead. However, he was found by another young warrior in Ólaf's army, Rognvald Brúsason. The son of Earl Brúsi of Orkney dragged Harald to safety in a nearby wood, and the two teenage warriors hid there until they could make their escape. Rognvald was four years older than Harald at the time, and the two became firm friends. The youths then escaped to Novgorod, where they decided what to do next. Both would eventually turn up in Orkney and would play their own part in the life-tapestry being woven for the Orkney earls.[6]

At this point Earl Thorfinn had been feeling secure, with a two-thirds stake in the Orkney earldom and complete control of Caithness and Sutherland on the Scottish mainland. Then, in 1032, almost out of the blue, a new threat appeared – the most serious Thorfinn would ever have to face. It came from a ruler the *Earls' Saga* calls 'Karl Hundason'. This was an insult rather than a name, as in Old Norse it meant 'peasant son of a dog'. In Gaelic, this ruler, the new *mormaer* of Moray, was called Macbethad mac Findláech. In its English form, his name was Macbeth. What followed was a short but bloody war fought between Thorfinn and Macbeth.

Their rivalry can be traced back to the time when the five-year-old Thorfinn was taken south to live with his grandfather King Malcolm. As we've seen, historians are uncertain whether this meant Malcolm of Scotland or Malcolm, *mormaer* of Moray. Frankly, though, it didn't really matter as the result was the same. Thorfinn enjoyed the support of a powerful Scottish mentor, and both he and Macbeth moved in the same circles of Scottish royalty and nobility.[7]

As for Macbeth, his father was Finlay, the same *mormaer* of Moray whom Thorfinn's father, Earl Sigurd 'the Stout', defeated in battle in Caithness with the help of his raven banner. Finlay survived the battle, though, and ruled Moray until 1020. Around the time that Thorfinn's problems were simplified by Thorkell's murder of Einar 'Crooked-mouth', a similar scene was being enacted in Moray. The *Annals of Ulster* claim that Finlay was killed by his own people. This suggested a rising rather than an assassination. But it could have been both. It seems the rising was orchestrated by the brothers Malcolm and Gille, sons of a Moray nobleman Máil Brigt.[8]

After Finlay's death in 1020, Malcolm mac Máil Brigt became the new *mormaer* of Moray. This was an incredibly powerful position. Essentially, he was a semi-independent sub-king – the equivalent of an Orkney earl. Officially, Malcolm of Moray still owed fealty to King Malcolm II of Scotland. In practice, though, he was Scotland's 'king in the north', responsible for protecting the country's northern borders and coasts. So, cultivating an alliance with the young Thorfinn made excellent diplomatic sense. This rise to power took place after Thorfinn had begun ruling Caithness. So when Thorfinn first sought refuge in Scotland, Malcolm was simply a powerful noble and kinsman of the Scottish monarch. Now, with both in positions of power in the north, Malcolm and Thorfinn could benefit greatly from their mutual support.

Unfortunately for Malcolm, the *mormaer* Finlay had a son. The boy, Macbethad mac Findláech (anglicised as Macbeth) was born around 1005, which made him four years older than Thorfinn. Little is known about Macbeth's early life, but it is likely he was the grandson of King Malcolm II of Scotland, whose daughter Donada married the *mormaer* Finlay. When Finlay died and his killers gained control of Moray, Donada and the now teenage Macbeth would have fled south and placed themselves under the protection of King Malcolm. The *mormaer* Malcolm, though, only ruled Moray for nine years. In 1029 he died, seemingly of natural causes, and was succeeded by his brother Gille.[9]

In the entry for 1032, the *Annals of Ulster* report that Gille, the *mormaer* of Moray, was brutally murdered. He'd been burned to death in his own hall, together with 50 of his men. Who was responsible for this wasn't clear, but the person who benefited the most was Macbeth, who by then was a seasoned 27-year-old warrior. After the murder, he claimed the title of *mormaer* of Moray for himself. This must have involved the approval of King Malcolm, who accepted this *fait accompli* by his grandson. This of course meant that any alliance Earl Thorfinn might have had with the *mormaers* of Moray was now over. Macbeth had inherited Gille's military muscle, and now had a Scots army at his back. Also, as King Malcolm's 'Steward of the Sea' – a post created for the Moray earls to protect Scotland's eastern coast from Viking raiders – Macbeth also inherited a fleet of longships.[10]

To strengthen his position, after Gille was burned to death, Macbeth then married his grieving teenage widow Gruoch. She was the daughter of Bouite, the son of either King Kenneth II or Kenneth III of Scotland – the records aren't clear. This means she'd been raised in the Scottish royal court and was of royal blood. This made Gruoch a useful spouse for a Scottish nobleman on the rise. Later she would become the inspiration for Shakespeare's Lady Macbeth. There's no evidence, though, that she shared the manipulative, murderous nature of her Shakespearian *alter ego*.[11]

For Earl Thorfinn, Macbeth now posed a threat to the Norse earldom. Since the victory of Earl Sigurd over the *mormaer* Finlay, the Orkney earldom hadn't been seriously bothered by the Scots. That was now about to change. Sure enough, as the *Earls' Saga* put it, 'The king of the Scots died when the brothers Brúsi and Þorfinnr were reconciled. Then Karl Hundasson took control of Scotland; he also considered he owned Caithness like previous kings of the Scots.'[12]

This wasn't quite correct. At the time King Malcolm II died in 1034, the saga's 'Karl Hundason' – the *mormaer* Macbeth, son of Finlay – had only seized control of Moray. When King Malcolm II died he was succeeded by his grandson Duncan. It was only later, in 1040, that Macbeth would murder Duncan and so gain the Scottish throne. It seems then that Shakespeare's 'Scottish play' followed the historical script more closely than the *Earls' Saga* did.

Macbeth's demand in 1041 that Thorfinn pay him tax for the Norse-held lands in Caithness and Sutherland was nothing short of a declaration of war. The Scots had largely abandoned any direct claim to the Orkney earldom's lands south of the Pentland Firth, save for token fealty to the Scottish king. Now, Macbeth was re-opening the old territorial dispute as an excuse to wage war against Earl Thorfinn.[13]

Earl Thorfinn, though, had cultivated strong ties with the Norse landowners in Caithness, which he saw as a key part of the earldom. As the senior partner and the brother responsible for the earldom's defence, Thorfinn's response was predictable: 'He wanted to have the taxes from that territory as elsewhere, but Earl Þorfinnr did not consider he had a large inheritance from his mother's father, even if he had Caithness. He claimed he had been given that territory and he did not wish to pay any taxes on it.' In other words, Thorfinn was throwing down the gauntlet to Macbeth. War between the two men was now inevitable.[14]

Macbeth's first move was to appoint a steward in Caithness. As the saga describes it, 'King Karl [Earl Macbeth] wanted to place the chieftain whose name was Mumtan or Muddan in Caithness; he was his sister's son, and he gave him the title of Earl. Muddan then rode down to Caithness and mobilised a troop in Sutherland.' Thorfinn, though, was having none of it. He was waiting in Caithness, where he'd gathered troops of his own. When Muddan realised this, he turned back. Afterwards, 'Earl Þorfinnr then went after them and subjugated Sutherland and Ross and raided widely around Scotland'. This might have been an exaggeration, as he already held Sutherland and Ross, and so this was just a cleaning up operation followed by a limited harrying of Macbeth's lands south of the Moray Firth.[15]

In around 1033 hostilities broke out in earnest. Earl Thorfinn remained in Caithness at his hall at Duncansby, the headland at the north-eastern tip of mainland Britain. The site of the hall was probably a mile east of John o'Groats, where the modern signpost reads 'Land's End 874 miles'. It was a good location, as from Duncansby Head you could spot anyone approaching by sea from the south, and a fire beacon lit there could be easily seen by watchers in South Ronaldsay, the southern end of the Orkney archipelago.

Thorfinn also kept a few longships there, beached in the little bay close by, to maintain communications with Orkney. He was there when Macbeth responded to Thorfinn's expulsion of Muddan. The Scots launched a two-pronged attack, with Muddan leading a sizeable Scots army north from Sutherland towards Caithness. For his part, Macbeth sailed north with 11 well-manned longships and put ashore a little to the south of Duncansby Head, possibly in Sinclair Bay.

Outnumbered, Thorfinn boarded one of the five longships kept on the headland's north side and set sail across the Pentland Firth to Orkney. Macbeth's force returned to their longships and gave chase. As they rounded Duncansby Head, 'then there was so little distance between them that Karl and his company saw Þorfinnr's sails as he sailed east into the firth, and straightaway they sailed after them.'[16]

Abandoning his plans for a two-pronged attack, Macbeth gave chase. Thorfinn rounded the eastern side of South Ronaldsay and headed north, up the West Sea coast of Orkney. Macbeth followed and saw his Norse rival put ashore in Deerness, the north-eastern corner of the Orkney mainland. This was probably at Skaill, where Thorkell 'Fosterer' had his hall. By now it was night, and Macbeth stayed his hand, waiting offshore to make a dawn assault.

Thorfinn and Thorkell, though, had a busy evening. Although Brúsi was out of reach in Orkney's North Isles, Thorfinn was able to gather warriors from the East Mainland. He found more longships too, probably ones Thorkell had in readiness nearby, possibly in the sheltered Pool of Ayre which led to the open sea. When dawn broke, Macbeth ordered his 11 longships to head towards the shore. No doubt Thorfinn had warriors there, waiting for him. It was only then that Macbeth spotted Thorfinn's five longships appearing from the north. So what was to be an amphibious landing now turned into a naval battle, fought off the eastern coast of Deerness.[17]

The Scots fleet turned to face the Norsemen, and minutes later the two sides clashed. The *Earls' Saga* describes what followed: 'The battle was both hard and long, and for a long time it was not possible to see which way it would go.' The two warrior earls were well-matched, but Thorfinn had the advantage of surprise. Gradually, in the hand-to-hand fight across the grappled ships, the Orcadians began to overpower their foes. As ever, the earl's *skald* Árnor Thordarsson described the Battle of Deerness in verse.

I believe the prince once gave Karl an extraordinary mail-coat
   verdict east of Deerness; the ruler's son's land was not to be taken.
The angry, flight-shunning man of magnificence steered five ships
   forward, with loyal heart, to the leader's eleven longships.

Men drove ships firmly to attack; troops fell on the deck-planks;
   rage-hard iron weapons swam in the dark blood of the Scots.
The prince's heart did not stop beating; bow-strings yelled, steel bit;
   barb flew; bright weapon-points quivered.[18]

As the *skald* Árnor suggested, Thorfinn emerged victorious after a hard-fought melee. Thorfinn had encouraged his men as they singled out Macbeth's longship. The Scots tried to cut the Norsemen's grappling hooks, but Thorfinn's men managed to swarm aboard. They then fought their way towards the stern, where Macbeth and his bodyguard were standing. At that, Macbeth and the last remaining knot of Scots warriors jumped overboard. They were quickly rescued by the other Scottish ships. Then the remainder of the Scottish fleet fled, the bedraggled Macbeth with them. Thorfinn and his battle-weary men gave chase, but eventually the Scots pulled clear.

Macbeth went to Moray to lick his wounds while Thorfinn collected more warriors and sailed for Caithness, where he prepared to deal with Muddan's landward thrust. Macbeth's deputy had reached Thurso, overlooking the Pentland Firth, and was waiting there for the Irish reinforcements he was expecting. It was the Norsemen, though, who struck first. Thorfinn remained with his fleet, harrying Moray, but he sent Thorkell ashore in Caithness with a few trusted men. They were very much on home territory, and the Norse farmers there helped them approach Thurso without being seen.

On reaching Thurso, Thorkell found out which house Muddan was in. He moved in at night, surrounding the house and setting fire to it before the Scots troops knew what was happening. Here's what the saga says of the incident: 'Muddan slept in a loft; and as soon as he leapt out and down over the gallery Þorkell struck at him and hit his neck and took his head off'. The surprise night attack took the Scots completely by surprise, and the bulk of them either surrendered or fled. Still, the saga claims that 'A lot of men were killed there but a large number were given leave to go.' That very effectively ended any Scots threat to Caithness.[19]

Meanwhile, some 50 miles to the south, Thorfinn's fleet had reached the Dornoch Firth, and Earl Thorfinn paused there, waiting for reinforcements before taking the fight into Moray. However, Macbeth was gathering much-needed reinforcements too. The Irish troops earmarked to reinforce Muddan arrived to join Macbeth, as did other troops raised in Scotland. That, though, took time, and winter effectively brought an end to the campaigning season. In the early summer of 1034, Macbeth led his army north into Sutherland to face Thorfinn on the Dornoch Firth. He was gambling everything on one final battle with the Orkney earl.

Although he was clearly outnumbered, Thorfinn willingly took up the challenge. Using his ships as ferries he landed his men at Tarbat

Ness, the headland marking the southern entrance to the Dornoch Firth. Macbeth advanced his army to meet Thorfinn there, hoping to pin the Norsemen with their backs to the sea. The two sides clashed about eight miles east of the modern town of Tain.

In the fight that followed, the Battle of Tarbat Ness, Thorfinn formed his shieldwall and then shouted encouragement to his men. The earl then took his place a little ahead of his shieldwall. He was easy enough for the enemy to spot. As the saga puts it: 'Earl Þorfinnr was in the front of his contingent; he had a gold-plated helmet on his head, a sword on his belt, he carried a large spear and he struck with it with both hands.' He'd left his linden-board shield behind, relying on his spear to keep his Scottish foes at bay. At that moment, Thorfinn was every inch the Norse hero.[20]

Despite being outnumbered, Thorfinn wasn't going to surrender the initiative. So, he attacked on the flank where the column of Macbeth's Irish mercenaries was standing. No doubt the attackers charged in a swine's snout, and the wedge dug deep into the Irish ranks. 'At first he attacked where the contingent of the Irish was; he was so vigorous with his troop that the Irish fell back at once and never again got redress'.[21]

At that point Macbeth counter-attacked. Both leaders fought under a banner, much as Thorfinn's father Earl Sigurd had done at Clontarf. Spotting the Norse standard of Thorfinn, Macbeth launched his main body of warriors towards it. A furious hand-to-hand fight followed, but gradually the Orcadians gained the upper hand: 'it was a hard fight and it ended with Karl being put to flight'.[22] Thorfinn had won a great victory, and as ever, Árnor 'Earl's-skald' wrote a victory poem.

> Bright blades reddened on wolf's munch, at a place called Tarbat Ness;
> the young ruler caused that; it was a Monday.
> Slim swords sang there south of the Oykel, as the prince,
> quick into conflicts, fought with Scotland's lord.
> The lord of the Shetlanders carried his helmet high in front of his host
> in spears' clanging; the rage-increaser reddened its point on the Irish.
> My generous lord used his strength beneath a British shield;
> Hlǫðvir's kinsman captured soldiers and began burning.[23]

For Macbeth, though, it was a disaster. The remnants of his army fled south to Moray, and his dreams of conquering Caithness and Sutherland lay in ruins. After the battle Thorfinn was joined by Thorkell with reinforcements from Caithness. Then Thorfinn crossed the Moray Firth and put Moray to the sword, his men burning and pillaging as they went. With no organised Scottish resistance he pressed on, columns of his men looting and burning their way through the fertile lands of Moray, and then on through the rich heartland of Scotland itself.

The *Earls' Saga* claims that 'Earl Þorfinnr chased those fleeing a long way up into Scotland and after that he went far and wide in the country. He then went all the way south into Fife and subjugated the land; people submitted to him wherever he went.' This is a little difficult to believe, as Earl Thorfinn had no intention of conquering anything that far south. It has been suggested that by this stage Thorfinn was operating as an ally of King Duncan. Instead, his victorious army had in effect become a large column of Viking raiders.[24]

With nobody opposing them they ran riot through much of the Scottish regions of Moray, Mar, Atholl, Buchan, Angus and then Fife, which was the usual home of King Duncan of Scotland. The likelihood is that the king withdrew before the Norsemen arrived. In all, it was claimed that Thorfinn had 'acquired nine earldoms in Scotland, and all the Hebrides and a great territory in Ireland.' This adds up if you included his own territories of Caithness, Sutherland and Ross.[25]

The saga claimed that a Scots army finally gathered to block Thorfinn's Norsemen, but it fled when the invaders deployed into formation and advanced towards them. What underlined the point that this was no campaign of conquest, even though much of Scotland lay open to him, was Thorfinn's decision to send Thorkell and his men home to Caithness. This, no doubt, was so that the *bændr* or yeoman farmers from his lands south of the Pentland Firth could return home and take in the harvest. A little later Thorfinn headed north too and spent the winter in Caithness. It was a time of feasting and celebration, and the division of the plunder. Árnor 'Earl's-skald' had the final word on Thorfinn's greatest campaign:

> Dwellings were destroyed, as he burned the realm of the Scots;
> red fire kindled in the smoking thatch; danger did not change that day.
> The death-dealer repaid men for injuries;
> in a single summer they three times got a worse deal from their ruler.[26]

Thorfinn Sigurdsson, Earl of Orkney, had surpassed the achievements of his father Sigurd 'the Stout'. He had held his father's sprawling northern earldom together in the face of sibling rivalry and royal interference. Then he'd conquered so much of Scotland that by late summer he could stand on the shore of Fife and look over the Firth of Forth. The fact that he didn't exploit this incredible achievement reveals a lot about Thorfinn.

He'd achieved his goal – the defeat of Macbeth and the securing of the earldom's southern borders. Macbeth would go on to greater things, and in 1040 Shakespeare's anti-hero would become king of Scotland. However, he wouldn't risk attacking the Norse earldom again. Macbeth had learned his lesson. As for Thorfinn, he'd really proved himself one of the greatest warriors of his age. It was then that he won the well-deserved epithet of Thorfinn 'the Mighty'.

PART FOUR
THE GREAT FEUDS

THIRTEEN

Thorfinn and Rognvald

F OR A WHILE, Earl Thorfinn 'the Mighty' was left in peace to savour the fruits of his victory. Despite the recent war with the Scots, trade continued to flow between the earldom and its neighbours. The farms thrived, boosted by the return of the plunder-laden menfolk, and the earl's coffers had been filled with the trophies of war. The only cloud was the death of Thorfinn's elder brother and joint earl, Brúsi Sigurdsson. The exact date of this is unknown, but it probably took place around 1033 or 1034. This meant that by 1035 at the latest, Earl Thorfinn was the sole earl of Orkney, and the master of all he surveyed.[1]

With his southern border secure, and no other threats on the horizon, Thorfinn was free to turn his attention to other matters. One of these was the earldom's holdings on Scotland's west coast. From 1035 on, it seems war returned to the area. This was partly triggered by the peaceful death of King Knut in November 1035. In England he was succeeded by his son Harold 'Hare-foot', who was fully occupied facing threats of invasion from Anglo-Saxon exiles as well as from his brother Harthaknut, the new king of Denmark. In Dublin, Knut's ally the elderly King Sigtrygg 'Silkbeard' was forced into exile in 1036 by Echmarcach mac Ragnaill who held lands in the Hebrides – possibly those vacated by the earls of Lade six years before.[2]

Earl Thorfinn saw opportunity there and renewed his plans to strengthen his hold over the Sudreyjar. This included the conquest of the lands in Lewis formerly held by the earls of Lade. The *Earls' Saga* claims that by the time of his death, Thorfinn controlled 'all the Hebrides and a great territory in Ireland'.[3] Thorfinn probably did campaign in part of Ireland, as the saga also claims he controlled 'a large realm' there. This may have been related to the large Irish contingent which had reinforced Macbeth before the Battle of Tarbat

Ness in *c.* 1034. Irish sources, though, are worryingly silent on this Irish venture, so perhaps the *Earls' Saga* is wrong, or confuses this with later events in the region.[4]

Then, in early 1038, everything changed. Rognvald Brúsason arrived back in Orkney. After the Battle of Sticklestad eight years before, the son of the late Earl Brúsi had quite the adventure. He and Harald 'Hardrada' escaped to Novgorod, where King Yaroslav looked after them. When Harald went on to Byzantium, Rognvald stayed in Novgorod, and campaigned with King Yaroslav, where he proved a skilled warrior. At Ladoga, near present-day St Petersburg, he encountered Kálf Árnason, who'd killed King Ólaf. Kálf apologised and said he wanted to make amends to Ólaf's young son Magnus. Then, in 1035, Kálf persuaded Yaroslav to back a rising in Norway, on behalf of Magnus. By the end of the year the 11-year-old Magnus was the new king of Norway, set on the throne by an army supplied by the Swedish crown. The following year, a peace deal was arranged with King Knut's successor in Denmark, King Harthaknut, which ensured a needless war was avoided.[5]

It was in Nidaros that Rognvald learned that his father had died and that his uncle Thorfinn was now the sole Orkney earl. As the *Earls' Saga* puts it, 'Rognvald wanted badly to visit his inherited lands, and asked King Magnus for leave to go there.' Magnus 'the Good' did better than that. He made him an earl of Orkney, so he could take up his late father's share of the earldom. Magnus also gave Earl Rognvald three longships and an offer of royal support and friendship, whenever he needed it. This was probably all necessary, given the earldom was held by Thorfinn.[6]

So, in mid-1038, Earl Rognvald appeared in Orkney. He sent a letter to his uncle, claiming his share of the earldom. His timing was perfect. As the saga says, 'And at that time Earl Þorfinnr was having great conflicts with the Hebrideans and the Irish; he thought he had great need of people's help.' In Rognvald and his men he'd found them. So he agreed to restore Brúsi's third of the earldom to his nephew Rognvald, After all, Thorfinn admitted it was Rognvald's by right. He still, though, had the third of the earldom which King Ólaf had kept, and which it seemed that his son King Magnus hadn't heard about.[7]

So Thorfinn encouraged his nephew to keep quiet about the unclaimed royal share. 'And if Rǫgnvaldr wants to be my loyal kinsman and supporter, as would be appropriate because of our relationship, then it seems to me to be a good thing for my territory if he has it for his amusement and for the support of both of us.'[8]

Rognvald swallowed the bait, and by agreeing, he found himself siding with his uncle Thorfinn rather than his friend King Magnus. The two earls got on well, and each continued ruling their share of the earldom – two-thirds in Rognvald's hands, and one-third with Thorfinn, plus Thorfinn's lands on the Scottish mainland held in the name of the Scottish king.

For a while, the two earls even worked together. Starting in the spring of 1039, the two fought side by side in the first of a series of campaigns off Scotland's west coast. The *Earls' Saga* claims, 'Þorfinnr subjugated wherever they went. They fought a sea battle at Vatzfjord' ('Loch Vatten') on the western coast of Skye, but who the opponents of the Orkney earls were wasn't recorded. The likelihood was that their opponents were Irish raiders or Hebridean rebels. Each winter, the earls returned to Orkney. These annual expeditions continued for eight years until the autumn of 1047.[9]

This meant that by 1042, Thorfinn had recovered all the lands in the Sudreyjar once controlled by his father Earl Sigurd. He then appointed Kálf Árnason, the 'King-killer', to act as his steward in the region. This was probably a very similar arrangement to the one between Thorfinn's father Earl Sigurd and the Hebridean Earl Gille. The saga also told of a raid into England, with the earls leading a combined force of Norsemen, Hebrideans, Scots and Irish warriors. This wasn't a conquest, though, just a glorified Viking raid. Still, the saga claims that 'a large and hard battle took place there, and the earls won the victory'.[10]

That autumn the two earls returned to Orkney for the winter. It was then during the winter of 1042–43 that Thorfinn and Rognvald fell out. Inevitably, the dispute was over the third of the earldom which had once belonged to King Ólaf. When they disagreed over what to do with it, the younger earl argued that King Magnus should be consulted. The two earls were embarking on a disagreement which could lead to civil war. If it came to it, this would be an unequal fight. Rognvald could draw on the resources of one-third of Orkney and Shetland, and while Thorfinn controlled two-thirds of the islands, as well as all of the earldom's lands in the Sudreyjar and the mainland of Scotland.

So when Rognvald learned that Thorfinn had been raising troops in Ireland and the Sudreyjar, he sailed to Norway to ask for help from King Magnus. That certainly helped even the odds. The Norwegian king willingly provided money, troops and longships, and in late 1045 Rognvald returned, prepared for a fight. First, though, Rognvald made landfall in Shetland to recruit more men. Then he continued to Orkney, where he did the same. Thorfinn was in Caithness, recruiting his own warriors. A clash between the two earls was now all but inevitable.

Rognvald, though, had a trick up his sleeve. He sent a message to his old enemy from Stiklestad, Kálf Árnason, who'd fled Norway to escape the vengeance of Magnus 'the Good'. Although Kálf had been an adviser to the young king, the two fell out over Kálf's leading part in the killing of Magnus' father, King Ólaf II. The message offered a royal pardon if Kálf didn't back Thorfinn in the coming fight. By then Rognvald had assembled 30 large longships, which he'd probably based in Kirkwall Bay. So he set off, sailing down Orkney's east coast to the Pentland Firth. There he must have found a place he could wait for Thorfinn to appear. This was possibly one of the anchorages off Hoxa Sound on the Orkney side of the Firth, or Sinclair Bay or Dunnet Bay on the Caithness shore.[11]

When Earl Thorfinn appeared, he was leading a fleet of 60 longships – twice the number Earl Rognvald had. There's some debate about where the two fleets met in battle. The *Earls' Saga* says, 'Their meeting took place off Roeberry and they went straight into battle.' The name 'Roeberry' comes from an Old Norse word which means 'red rock', a reference to the iron-stained rocks found on parts of the coastline on both sides of the Pentland Firth. Although there are a few contenders for the site of the sea battle, the likelihood is that the sea battle was fought off the southern coast of Hoy, near Cantick Head which overlooks the Pentland Firth and guards the entrance to Hoxa Sound.[12]

According to the saga, the 30 longships of Earl Rognvald were significantly larger than Earl Thorfinn's 60 longships, and so despite this numerical superiority in Thorfinn's favour, the odds were roughly even. 'And now an exceedingly tough battle began; each earl egged on his troop.' However, Kálf Árnason was there too with his own six large longships, probably brought over from the Sudreyjar. He, though, kept out of the battle and watched the fight from a distance. Clearly Árnason wanted to see how the battle would go before he committed himself to one side or the other.[13]

The battle was fiercely fought, with longships grappling together as warriors hewed and cut their way aboard the enemy ships. The larger longships were better fighting platforms and were better manned, so their crew could easily overpower Thorfinn's smaller vessels. Thorfinn, however, had a larger longship as his flagship, probably a *drakkar*, and inevitably as his smaller ships were overpowered the fight concentrated around Thorfinn's ship. Eventually, his flagship had enemy longships on either beam. As well as having to fight boarders on either side of the ship, undoubtedly Thorfinn's men were also being whittled down by arrows, shot by bowmen on the enemy ships. 'Rǫgnvaldr then egged on his men to board. But when Þorfinnr saw what a bad situation he was in, he had his ship cut off from its ropes and rowed to land.' Warrior prince or not, Thorfinn knew when to cut and run.[14]

As the battle raged on, Thorfinn's flagship backed water, then headed towards the nearby shore, which was probably South Walls. There he put ashore the bodies of 70 slain warriors from his flagship and ordered any others who were too badly injured to fight to go ashore too. At this stage he also landed Árnor 'Earl's-skald' to spare him from the coming fight. Thorfinn may have re-crewed his longship from men waiting ashore, then he headed back out to sea. Rather than head straight back into the melee, he had his men row to Kálf Árnason's longships. Thorfinn convinced Kálf that his interests lay with him rather than Earl Rognvald and King Magnus, both of whom would never forgive him for killing Magnus' father, King Ólaf.

So, bolstered by these reinforcements, Thorfinn returned to the fray. By then Thorfinn's remaining force was in a bad way. Casualties had been high, and some longships were beginning to turn away from the fight. Thorfinn's return with fresh ships and fighters put heart into his men. For his part, Thorfinn ordered his crew to force his longship alongside Rognvald's flagship. From the shore, Árnor put the scene into words.

> The lad's not keen to go against the son of Brúsi;
> it's good to follow a lord; I'll never conceal that from folk.
> We have a hard choice on our hands,
> if these battle-swift earls attack each other;
> there will be a harsh test of friendship.[15]

While Thorfinn took the fight directly to Rognvald, Kálf attacked the smaller longships in the enemy fleet, lurking on the fringes of Rognvald's force. Kálf's men began cutting their way through the smaller ships. 'And when the levy troop that had come from Norway saw ships cleared beside them, they cut their own ships loose from the ropes and fled, so that few ships were left with the earl's ship'.[16]

The situation had now been completely reversed. Now it was Rognvald who was on the back foot and found himself outnumbered and under ferocious attack. When Kálf finally came up to support Thorfinn's assault, it was clear the battle was over for Rognvald: 'And when Earl Rǫgnvaldr saw what a bad situation he was in, and that he would not be able to win against both Þorfinnr and Kálfr, then he had the ropes cut and fled.'[17]

By this stage it was almost dark. Rognvald headed for the open sea, and his men rowed east towards Norway. The remnants of his battered fleet followed suit. For Thorfinn and Kálf they savoured their victory, although any joy was matched by the knowledge that so many good men had been killed or wounded. So Earl Thorfinn now had complete control of the earldom of Orkney, with no jumped-up nephew sharing it with him.[18]

Earl Rognvald, though, wasn't going to give up so easily. In Norway he met King Magnus and the two decided what to do next. Rognvald realised that he'd no chance of wresting the earldom from Thorfinn by force. However, he might be able to kill Thorfinn in a surprise attack. 'Now I intend', he said, 'to go west with one ship and man it as best I can'. He continued to explain his plan to the king. Rognvald intended to sail to Orkney, and then launch a surprise attack and kill Thorfinn before the alarm could be raised. To add to the surprise, he decided to cross the West Sea in winter, a risky undertaking given the likelihood

The *Sea Stallion*, a Danish-built replica longship of the mid-11th century, pictured while visiting Orkney in 2007. (© Charles Tait)

Duncansby Head marked the north-east corner of Caithness. Beyond the lighthouse is the treacherous Pentland Firth, with the southern coast of Orkney visible just over six miles to the north. (© Charles Tait)

The Dornoch Firth and the River Oykel marked the southern border of the earldom. This viewpoint on Struie Hill, looking west, is on what was the Scottish side of the firth. (© Charles Tait)

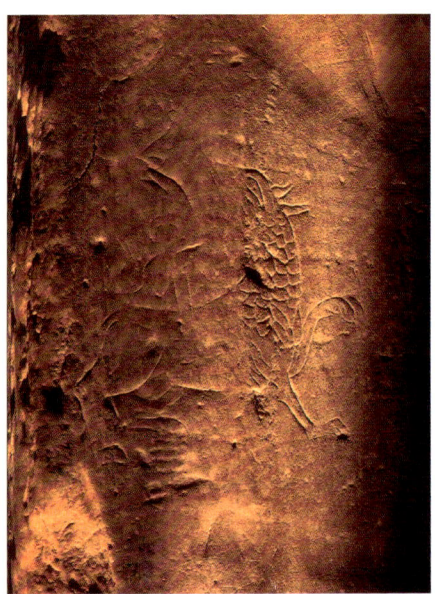

This dragon was carved by Norsemen into the interior wall of the Neolithic chambered tomb of Maeshowe in Orkney. (© Charles Tait)

This whalebone 'dragon plaque' dates from the early years of the Orkney earldom. (© Charles Tait)

The small tidal island of the Brough of Birsay was where the earls maintained their residence, and where Earl Thorfinn built his Christ Church. (© Charles Tait)

The excavation of the Norse settlement at Quoygrew in Westray, in the North Isles of Orkney, which was in use from the 10th to the 13th century. (© Charles Tait)

In 1136, Earl Paul Hákonsson was hunting otters on the island of Rousay when he was attacked and kidnapped by Svein Ásleifarson. The hall of his host, Sigurd of Westness, lay just behind these trees, overlooking Rousay's southern shore. (© Charles Tait)

These Norse runes are graffiti, carved inside the Neolithic tomb of Maeshowe, in Orkney, likely by 'mound-breakers' in early 1153. (© Charles Tait)

The Brough of Birsay was once a Pictish fortress. Later it became a prestigious Norse settlement, the ruins of which can be seen here. (© Charles Tait)

From the 12th century, the earls based themselves in Kirkwall, the main town of Orkney. It was an ideal location for administration, seaborne trade and communications. (© Charles Tait)

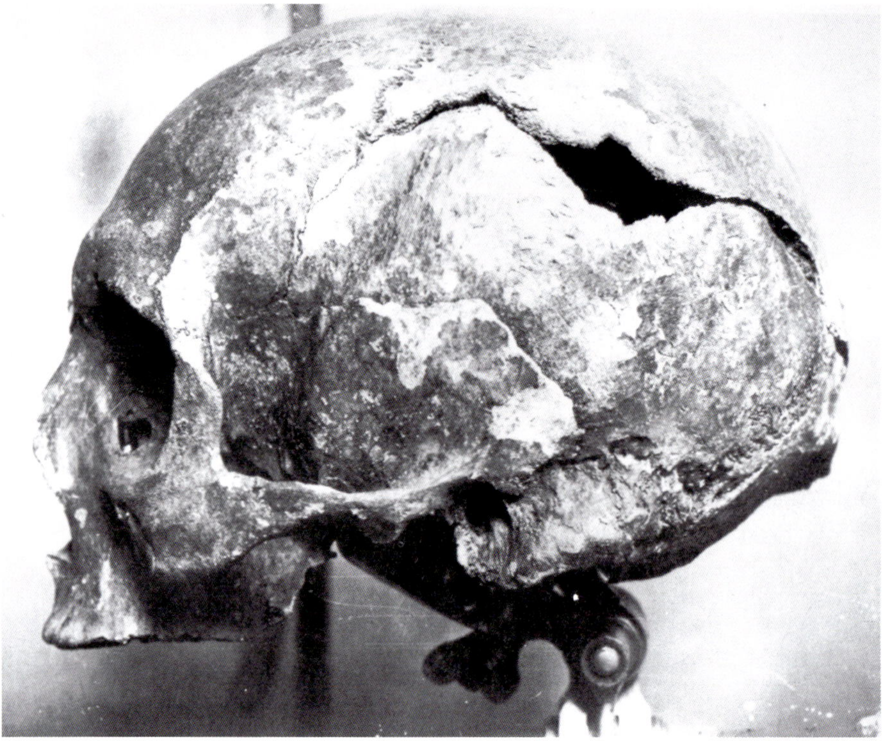

In 1919, workmen in St Magnus Cathedral unearthed a wooden box containing human remains. Analysis suggests this skull is that of St Magnus, which bears the axe blows that killed him in 1117. (© Charles Tait)

This ruined 12th-century church of St Magnus on Egilsay was reputedly built on the spot where Earl Magnus Erlendsson was murdered by Earl Hákon in 1117. (© Charles Tait)

St Magnus Cathedral in Kirkwall was built to serve as the resting place of the remains of Earl Magnus. Work on the cathedral began in 1137, during the reign of Earl Rognvald Kali. (© Charles Tait)

The creators of St Magnus Cathedral: Kol Kalason, his son Earl Rognvald and Bishop William 'the Old'. (© Charles Tait)

Every January, the Shetlanders celebrate 'Up Helly Aa', a fire festival which in theory celebrates the islands' Norse heritage, and burn a replica Norse longship. (© Charles Tait)

In the 12th century, the small island of Gairsay in Orkney was the home of the Viking adventurer Svein Ásleifarson. (© Charles Tait)

of winter gales. Then again, Earl Thorfinn wouldn't expect an attack
at that time of year.[19]

So, in early 1046, Earl Rognvald and his hand-picked crew of
veterans sailed to Shetland to gather intelligence. They soon learned
that Thorfinn was in his hall on the Orkney mainland, and had very
few men with him. Rognvald sailed south and beached his longship in
a quiet bay, close to Thorfinn's hall. Later that night Rognvald's men
surrounded the place. Inside, most of the earl's bodyguard had gone to
sleep, but Thorfinn was still up, sitting drinking by the hearth. Outside,
Rognvald ordered his men to set fire to the house. When Thorfinn saw
the flames, he woke his men and sent someone to the door to find out
who dared attack him. He was told it was Earl Rognvald.

Thorfinn and his men were now fully armed, but there was no way
out. To try to escape by the door would invite being cut down by
arrows or pounced on by the ring of waiting warriors. Still, Rognvald
showed some mercy, and agreed that the women and slaves could leave.
Only Thorfinn and his warriors would have to stay and face the flames.
By then the fire had really taken hold, and smoke and flames billowed
all around the hall. In the darkness and smoke, however, Thorfinn
managed to kick his way through a wooden partition wall in the side
of the hall 'and ran out there; he had his wife Ingibjǫrg in his arms.'
Nobody saw him go. Once outside, he found a small boat, and after
bundling Ingibiorg aboard it he set out for Caithness, rowing his way
across the Pentland Firth. Only someone who really knew these waters
could have made it safely across in midwinter, and in the dead of night.[20]

Meanwhile, Earl Rognvald, who knew nothing of his uncle's escape,
claimed all the earldom for himself. To make sure of his grip, he had
Thorfinn's remaining followers swear oaths of allegiance to him. The
winter gales were approaching by now, and so he left the subduing of
the earldom's lands across the Pentland Firth, as well as the Sudreyjar,
until the spring. Instead, he sent out envoys proclaiming that he was
now the sole ruler of the earldom. Meanwhile Thorfinn and Ingibiorg
were hidden by their many friends in Caithness, and Rognvald remained
blissfully unaware that his rival was still alive. Thorfinn bided his time
and plotted his revenge.

In the winter of 1046, Earl Rognvald intended to spend Christmas in
his feasting hall in Kirkwall. The saga claims: 'Earl Rǫgnvaldr resided
in Kirkwall and brought there all the provisions he would need for his

winter residence; he had many people there and it was magnificent.' As the Yule celebrations approached, Rognvald left for Papa Stronsay, one of the smaller of Orkney's North Isles. The earl kept a farm there, where the land was given over to the growing of malted barley for the making of ale. Unknown to Rognvald, spies passed news of the excursion to Thorfinn. It was exactly what he'd been waiting for.[21]

Rognvald arrived in Papa Stronsay with a small party of followers, and after loading the malt in their ship, they spent the night in the farmhouse. As they sat around the fire, Rognvald made a slip of the tongue. When someone said they were running out of firewood, the earl said: 'We will be fully old when these fires have burned out.' What he'd meant to say was they'd have been warmed up enough. This was a bad omen. When his foster-father King Ólaf had made a slip of the tongue like that, he was killed in battle the next day. A shocked Rognvald said to his followers, 'It might be that my kinsman Þorfinnr is alive'.[22]

Sure enough, a little while later there were sounds outside. It was Thorfinn. Learning that Rognvald was making this trip, he'd set off from Caithness in a well-manned longship, and reached Papa Stronsay that evening, his approach cloaked by the long, dark winter night. The sounds Rognvald and his men heard were Thorfinn's men piling Rognvald's own stack of firewood up against the door. Then Thorfinn called out, saying anyone apart from Rognvald and his warriors could leave. The servants and the farmers filed out, accompanied by a man dressed in what looked like a long, hooded robe. Thorfinn's men thought it was a deacon or priest and were about to help him. Suddenly, the man leaped over the wood pile and fled into the darkness. Thorfinn knew it was Rognvald, saying, 'Only he and nobody else can do that.' So he ordered his men to give chase.[23]

While the farm burned and guards covered the door, the rest of Thorfinn's men split into groups to scour the island. It was less than a mile long and just over half a mile across, so it was almost impossible for Rognvald to escape. In the end, he was betrayed by the barking of a dog. The earl had been hiding among the rocks on the shore, but his small dog had joined him, and it was his barks of joy that alerted the searchers. They ringed the earl, but Thorfinn's men were reluctant to strike him down. It was left to Thorkell 'Fosterer' to do it. After all, he'd killed an earl before. So Rognvald was hacked to death on the beach.[24]

The next morning, after making sure all Rognvald's followers were dead, Thorfinn took Rognvald's body into his late nephew's cargo boat, loaded it with the malt, and set off back to Kirkwall. As they entered the bay, Earl Rognvald's men came down to the shore, now a pool called the Peerie Sea, to help unload the malt. After all, it was the earl's own longship, and the shields of the earl's men were ranged along its sides. When Thorfinn and his warriors jumped out, it was too late to run. 'Earl Þorfinnr had nearly thirty men taken there and killed. They were mostly courtiers and friends of King Magnús'. However, he spared one of Magnus' men to take the news of Rognvald's death back to the king in Norway. With that brutal counter-stroke, in late 1046 Earl Thorfinn 'the Mighty' won back his earldom and could now rule it unchallenged.[25]

Earl Rognvald was eventually buried on Papa Westray in the North Isles, where a Celtic Christian church stood. A century later, St Boniface's Kirk was built on the spot, beside a Norse hog-back gravestone which, although dated to the 12th century, might have once marked the last resting place of Earl Rognvald Brúsason.[26]

In Norway, King Magnus 'the Good' didn't take the news particularly well. After all, Rognvald had been his loyal foster-brother. Indeed, Magnus might well have avenged Rognvald, but at the time he was fully occupied in a war with King Sveinn (also Svein or Sweyn) II of Denmark. He also had to share his kingdom. In 1046 his uncle Harald Sigurdsson had returned from Byzantium and threatened to reclaim his brother Ólaf's kingdom by force. So Magnus settled on a compromise and shared the kingdom with Harald. A year later, in 1047, Magnus died when falling off his horse and Harald 'Hardráði' (or 'Hardrada', meaning 'hard ruler') became the sole king of Norway.[27]

This was good news for Thorfinn. He knew King Magnus would never forgive him for killing Rognvald. Harald, though, was another matter. He immediately offered his loyalty to the new Norwegian king. Then, in 1048, Thorfinn crossed the West Sea and visited Harald in the region of Hordaland in the south-east of Norway. They exchanged warm words and presents before Thorfinn continued his voyage to Denmark. This was the start of a great journey for the Orkney earl.

He was on a pilgrimage to Rome. On the way he visited King Sweyn of Denmark at Aalborg and the Holy Roman Emperor, Henry III, who was in Saxony. In both meetings yet more kind words and gifts were exchanged.[28]

In Rome, Thorfinn was granted an audience with Pope Leo IX and was absolved of all his numerous sins. This was probably the main reason for the trip. Thorfinn 'the Mighty', after years of fighting, conquest and violence, seems to have turned over a new leaf. He was now a man of peace, and a man of God. On Earl Thorfinn's return to Orkney around 1051, he threw himself into furthering his new-found faith.[29]

Thorfinn had been raised as a Christian, but until this point religion seems to have played little part in his life. Although some of the people in his earldom still worshipped the Old Norse gods, Christianity was now the dominant religion throughout his lands. During his visit to Germany, the possibility of establishing a bishop in Orkney was discussed with Archbishop Adalbert of Hamburg. After his pilgrimage, Bishop Thorolf was appointed to the newly created Orkney see, by order of Pope Leo. His diocese was based in 'Blascona', a Latin corruption of Birsay in Orkney's West Mainland.[30]

It was probably there that Thorfinn built a church. He had a residence in Birsay, and so it was probably beside it that his 'Christ Church' was situated. It no longer exists, but despite some controversy over its location, the likelihood is that it was built where the present Birsay church stands today. Later, a bishop's hall was built, close to the earl's residence there. The other less likely candidate is on the nearby tidal island of the Brough of Birsay, which was both a Norse settlement and the site of a later, 12th-century Norse church. It seems Thorfinn spent most of his last years in Birsay, and devoted himself to governing his earldom, making laws, sitting in judgement and doing all the administrative duties that he'd spent much of his earlier years avoiding.[31]

Earl Thorfinn Sigurdsson 'the Mighty' died peacefully at some point in the early 1060s. He was the most powerful of all the earls of Orkney, and in his military heyday it was said that 'He won for himself nine Scottish earldoms, along with the whole of the Hebrides and a considerable part of Ireland.'[32]

Árnor 'Earl's-skald' gave his master this epitaph:

The army had to heed the Raven-feeder
from 'Troll's Skerries' to Dublin; I tell the nation
Truly how Þorfinnr was regarded.[33]

His last years of rule were peaceful, despite a claim that he took part in a raid on England in 1056, which isn't borne out in English chronicles. Still, Árnor 'Earl's-skald' composed eulogies which celebrated the extent of Thorfinn's rule, from Dublin to the northernmost skerries of Shetland. It was a shame that after his death his sons weren't up to the task of holding their father's 'empire' together.[34]

FOURTEEN

A Game of Thrones

T HE EXACT DATE OF Thorfinn's death remains a mystery. Most translations of the *Earls' Saga* say he was an earl for 70 years and place his death in the last years of the reign of King Harald Sigurdsson. As King Harald 'Hardrada' reigned as king of Norway from 1042 to 1066, then this would place it around 1060, give or take. Other factors, though, suggest that a date range between *c.* 1058 and *c.* 1064 would be the most probable. *The Saga of the Earls of Orkney* adds that, 'He was buried at Christ Church in Birsay, which he had had built'.[1]

It's equally frustrating that we have no clear age for Thorfinn's sons, Páll (or Paul) and Erlendr (or Erlend) when their father died. Still, there are clues. Their mother, Earl Thorfinn's wife Ingibjǫrg (or Ingibiorg) Finnsdóttir, who earned the epithet 'Mother-of-earls' probably married Thorfinn around *c.* 1040. That would suggest they might well be teenagers around 1058.

That year a major Viking raiding expedition left Norway. In theory it was led by Magnus Haraldsson, the son of the Norwegian king Harald 'Hardrada'. However, he was only about ten at the time, so for him this was more of a young boy's adventure. Although his name wasn't recorded, the real commander of the expedition was probably one of King Harald's lieutenants. The official aim of the expedition was to help Harald's allies, the Welsh king Gruffudd and Earl Ælfgar of Mercia, in their campaign against Harold Godwinson, the earl of Wessex. For King Harald, though, it was just as important that the expedition made sure the earldom of Orkney was still loyal to the crown.[2]

The venture isn't mentioned in the *Earls' Saga*, but it's amply covered in other chronicles. There's no record this expedition visited Orkney, but as Orcadians are mentioned in Irish annals, then we can be sure they stopped in the islands on their way west. The *Annals of Tigernach* record that 'A fleet led by the son of the king of Norway, with the foreigners of the Orkneys and Hebrides, and Dublin [tried] to seize the kingdom of England, but to this God didn't consent.' This was over-egging it. The expedition was there to support the kings of Wales and Mercia in a war against Wessex. The Norwegians had no intention of toppling the English king Edward 'the Confessor'.[3]

This illustrates another important point. Much as had happened in AD 954 with Eirík 'Bloodaxe', in 1014 with Sigtrygg 'Silkbeard' of Dublin, and now again in 1058 with the young Magnus Haraldsson, the earldom of Orkney was the place to go for Norse adventurers who needed a fleet of longships and a force of veteran Norse warriors. The earldom was an ideal recruiting ground for both Norse raiders or military leaders.[4]

After Earl Thorfinn died, this royal expedition would have visited Orkney to make sure that Ingibiorg and her two infant sons remained loyal, and to report back to King Harald on the earl's succession. Ingibiorg's sons would be as young as six or eight years old at the time, and so the security of the regency during their minority was of prime importance to the Norwegian crown. By 1066, when King Harald 'Hardrada' made his bid for the English throne, Erlend and Paul Thorfinnsson would probably have been in their mid-twenties.[5]

When Thorfinn died, Erlend and Paul both became joint earls of Orkney, ruling the earldom between them. They were still minors, though, and their mother Ingibiorg or a close relative would have acted as regent. As for Ingibiorg herself, she would have been in her thirties when Thorfinn died, although her exact age is unknown. She was the daughter of Finn Arnason, a *lendmann*, the Norse equivalent of a feudal baron, from Trøndelag. Through her mother she had royal blood and was a niece of Harald 'Hardrada'. She was also a niece of Kálf Árnason, the repentant killer of King Ólaf II. As her uncle, Kálf was well-placed to coach the young earls in their duties.[6]

The diplomatic value of the earldom of Orkney to the Scottish crown was underlined when Ingibiorg married again. This union with King Malcolm III of Scotland took place a few years after Thorfinn's death, in the early 1060s. This made sound political sense. Malcolm had gained the throne in 1058 after killing King Lulach, the stepson of

Macbeth. Lulach was born before his mother Gruoch married Macbeth, and so was the son of Gille, the *mormaer* of Moray who Macbeth had burned to death. Afterwards, Macbeth married Gruoch and adopted Lulach, raising him as his own son.

Macbeth himself had died the previous summer in a skirmish fought at Lumphanan, 20 miles west of Aberdeen. His opponents had been rebels fighting for Malcolm Canmore, the future Malcolm III. Lulach was crowned at Scone near Perth in September 1057, but six months later he was murdered on Malcolm's orders. Lulach was a weak, short-lived king, but Malcolm was the opposite and so was able to end the long-running feud between the house of Moray and the house of Dunkeld, founded by his father King Duncan. After Malcolm, his royal lineage would continue to hold the crown until the death of Alexander III in 1286. That accidental death when the king was out riding sparked the English occupation of Scotland and the long-running Wars of Independence which followed.

After marrying Malcolm, Ingibiorg produced two more children – the boys Duncan and Donald. Queen Ingibiorg died in the Scottish court around 1069. About 180 miles to the north, though, in Orkney, her two sons Erlend and Paul were still jointly ruling their powerful earldom. While Ingibiorg might have moved away and married into the Scottish royal family, to the Norse she was always Ingibiorg 'Mother-of-earls'.

Erlend and Paul Thorfinnsson gained full control of the earldom when they came of age, around 1065. The *Earls' Saga* describes the rule of the Thorfinnson brothers. 'Páll was the elder of them; he was also the one who took the decisions. They did not divide the lands between them and nevertheless for a very long time they were agreed on this arrangement.' Almost immediately after their coming of age, the two earls married. Paul's wife was the daughter of the Norwegian earl Hákon Ivarsson, and the couple had a son, Hákon, as well as two daughters, Ingrid and Herbiorg.[7]

As for Paul's younger brother, 'Earl Erlendr Þorfinnsson was married to a woman who had the name Þóra and was the daughter of Sumarliði Óspaksson'. She was from a leading Icelandic family. Erlend and Þóra (or Thora) had two sons, Erlingr (or Erling) and Magnus, and two daughters, Gunnhild and Cecilia. Both of Thorfinn's sons were following what was clearly their mother's advice to strengthen their links with Norway. These marriages, and the union of Ingibiorg to the

Scottish crown, were used to create a web of alliances across Norway and Scotland, which strengthened the influence of the Orkney earldom and gained it potentially useful alliances in time of war. Unfortunately for the two young earls, war would come looking for them before this web was spun.[8]

We have already heard how in July 1030, the teenage Harald Sigurdsson was badly wounded at the Battle of Sticklestad and was helped from the field by Rognvald Brúsason, son of the earl of Orkney. The two teenagers fled Norway, and eventually Rognvald returned to Orkney, while Harald, after serving the Byzantine Emperor for several years, headed back to Norway in 1042.

His sense of timing was impeccable. King Knut had died, and by 1046 the Norwegian throne was held by Magnus 'the Good', the illegitimate son of the late King Ólaf. Magnus quickly decided that fighting the battle-scarred Harald would be a mistake, so he agreed to share the Norwegian throne with his warrior uncle. Magnus died in late 1047, though, and afterwards Harald became the sole ruler of Norway. King Harald soon gained the epithet 'Hardrada', or 'hard ruler'.

For the next decade and a half, King Harald of Norway and King Sweyn of Denmark waged war against each other, but although Harald was more successful, he never managed to win the Danish throne. Meanwhile, Harald also plotted another war, this time against England. It all stemmed from a decade-old claim to the English throne. In 1038, Knut's son Harthaknut who ruled Denmark and England agreed with King Magnus that whoever died first would gain the other ruler's lands. In 1042, though, when Harthaknut died, the English chose his Anglo-Saxon half-brother Edward 'the Confessor' as their king.

So when Magnus died five years later, Harald also inherited this legal claim to the English throne. At first, he didn't do anything about it save for sending that expedition of 1058 led by his young son, which was probably Harald testing the waters, while weakening his main rival to Edward's throne, Harold Godwinson, Earl of Wessex. During his 24-year reign, Edward 'the Confessor' had hinted that several potential claimants might possibly succeed him. These included Harald 'Hardrada' as well as King Sweyn of Denmark and the strongest candidate, Duke William of Normandy. Still, Harald remained uninvolved until 1065. That was when Tostig Godwinson, the brother of Harold Godwinson, was ejected from his earldom in Northumbria during a revolt.

Tostig sought help to regain his earldom in Flanders, Normandy and Denmark, but never gained the support he needed. Meanwhile, in January 1066, Edward 'the Confessor' died. Despite his hints to other foreign rulers, Edward's crown was passed to Harold Godwinson. So, when Tostig's deputy Copsi arrived in Norway in the early spring, Harald 'Hardrada' was willing to listen. Copsi eventually persuaded Harald to invade England and claim the crown. Once in power, the plan was to return Tostig's earldom to him.[9]

As a result, in the late spring of 1066 Harald 'Hardrada' began gathering an invasion fleet in the Sognefjord, in western Norway. Meanwhile, far to the south, a similar fleet was being readied on the coast of Duke William's Normandy. The Norwegian expedition, though, would take several months to gather, and it would be August before it was ready. Any further delay was risky for Harald, as by mid-September autumnal gales would keep his fleet in port. Before sailing, as insurance in case he didn't return, Harald named his son Magnus Haraldsson king of Norway. The young man would be left to rule, guided by his mother Þóra (or Thora), while his father sailed off on his invasion accompanied by Tostig and Copsi as well as his first wife, Elisaveta of Kiev, his youngest son Ólaf, and two daughters.[10]

This is where the *Earls' Saga* picks up the story. 'King Haraldr Sigurðarson came west from Norway with a big army. He came first to Shetland; from there he went to the Orkneys.' Earls Erlend and Paul were forewarned that this invasion fleet was coming, and they'd decided on their course of action even before Harald's sails appeared in the offing. On arriving in Orkney, 'He had a large troop from the Orkneys; both the earls decided to accompany the king on his expedition'. In other words, not only did Harald recruit in the islands, but the earls willingly joined his army. Still, it must have been an awkward first meeting, between Harald and the sons of the earl who'd killed his good friend Rognvald Brúsason. In *Heimskringla*, Harald's fleet is numbered at around 200 ships when it left Norway, but English sources suggest a higher total of up to 300 ships. The difference could reflect the reinforcements provided by the two Orkney earls from throughout the earldom – Orkney, Shetland, Caithness and the Sudreyjar.[11]

So the two earls had time to assemble a sizeable fleet of their own. It would have been waiting in Orkney, ready for King Harald to arrive. By the time the invasion force left Orkney it was said to number about 7,500 men. As many as 2,000 of these could have been supplied by the two Orkney earls. For the earldom, a lot was riding on the success of Harald's invasion. Harald left Elisaveta and his daughters in Orkney, then pressed on south. The expedition sailed down the eastern coast of Scotland, and by early September it had reached the coast of Northumbria. There the Norsemen raided the coast and burned Scarborough. On 18 September it entered the River Humber, near Hull.[12]

Harald then continued up the River Ouse to the village of Riccall, 30 miles from Hull and a little way south of York. After making camp there, he marched on the city. Just outside it, at Gate Fulford, a local militia army, the *fyrd*, came out to meet him under the command of Earl Morcar of Northumbria and Earl Edwin of Mercia. The two armies were matched in numbers, as up to a third of the Norse army, including the Orkney earls, had been left in the camp at Riccall to guard the fleet. On 20 September the armies fought a bloody battle at Fulford, with Harald's men defending a waterlogged ditch between the Ouse and a marsh. According to *Heimskringla*, Harald feigned a withdrawal on his right, then caught the English in the flank and slaughtered them. It was said that afterwards the Norse could cross the marsh dry-shod on the bodies of the slain.[13]

York – formerly Jórvik – was now almost in King Harald's hands. All he needed was the capitulation of the garrison in the city, commanded by the defeated Earl Edwin. However, four days later, scouts reported that a fresh English army was advancing on York from the south. It was King Harold of England, who'd been on the south coast, awaiting a landing by William of Normandy. On hearing of the Norse invasion, he'd force-marched his men north to York. At the time, Harald's army was camped along the small River Derwent, six miles to the east of the city, at Stamford Bridge. Harald was expecting a capitulation from York, along with hostages. Instead, on Monday 24 September, Harold and his Anglo-Saxon army arrived.

It was a hot day, and many of the Norsemen had taken off their mailshirts. The arrival of King Harold's army took them by surprise.

The Norsemen on the west bank of the Derwent were overrun, but Harald's men rallied on the opposite bank where the bridge was held against all-comers. Then the English found an unguarded ford, and Harald was forced to pull back and form a circular shieldwall. There, the Norsemen were ground down by arrows, one of which struck Harald 'Hardrada' in the throat, killing him outright. In *Harald's Saga*, with a sense of irony, Harald's *skald* Thiodolf Arnorsson composed this:

> The army stands in hushed dismay, stilled in the clamour of the fray,
> Harald is dead, and with him goes, the spirit to withstand our foes,
> A bloody scat (tax) the folk must pay, for the king's folly on this day,
> He fell, and now without disguise, we say this business was not wise.[14]

That was something of an understatement. After being summoned to help, the third of the army left behind at Riccall arrived too late. The survivors of the slaughter at Stamford Bridge fled towards their boats. The *Earls' Saga* relates that 'After he [King Harald] fell, Eystein Heathcock and the earls of Orkney came ashore and launched a fierce attack, in which Eystein Heathcock perished, along with almost the whole Norwegian contingent.' Eystein was Eystein Orri, a kinsman of the Norwegian king who was betrothed to Harald's daughter Maria. He died, as did Tostig, but somehow the two young earls survived the carnage.[15]

Once the dust had settled, King Harold of England allowed Earl Erlend and Earl Paul of Orkney to return home, accompanied by the young Ólaf Haraldsson, whose father had just been killed. Accompanying them on their journey down the Ouse to the Humber and the open sea was a bishop – possibly Bishop Thorolf of Orkney. It was said that of the once-great fleet only two dozen boats returned. Meanwhile, on 28 September Duke William of Normandy landed at Pevensey on England's south coast and King Harold raced south to confront him. Just over two weeks later, on 14 October, Harold was killed at the Battle of Hastings, ironically by an arrow in the face just like Harald 'Hardrada', and the Anglo-Saxon army was defeated. On Christmas Day in 1066, William became the new king of England.[16]

Afterwards, Ólaf, the future king of Norway, spent the winter in Orkney, together with his mother and remaining sisters, as guests of the two Orkney earls. In the spring the guests would return to Norway, parting on excellent terms with the earls. Back in Norway, Harald's son Magnus Haraldsson had become King Magnus II on the death of his father, but from 1067 on he ruled jointly with his younger brother Ólaf, who became King Ólaf III 'the Peaceful'. Now, finally, after so much carnage, the earldom needed time to recover after its third foreign debacle in a century and a half.[17]

Despite this disastrous venture, during the years that followed the earldom recovered under the joint rule of earls Erlend and Paul. Of course this doesn't mean there weren't challenges. The two earls became embroiled in a few minor campaigns further south, where their father's sprawling territories were being eroded. The Isle of Man had already been lost around 1052, when Echmarcach mac Ragnaill, after being evicted from Dublin, set himself up as the new Manx ruler. While Thorfinn had been distracted by his feud with his nephew Rognvald, Echmarcach consolidated his position. On his death in c. 1065, he was succeeded by Godred, who was possibly the son of Sigtrygg 'Silkbeard', the former king of Dublin.[18]

Effectively, then, this southernmost cornerstone of the Orkney earldom was lost before the earls Erlend and Paul could reclaim it. With it was Orkney's influence around the basin of the Irish Sea. Perhaps their experience in 1066 had put them off ambitious ventures, and so their earldom's border now lay at Kintyre, on the southern tip of Argyll. After that, the earls seemed content with simply holding on to their remaining lands in the Sudreyjar.

The *Earls' Saga* tells us:

And when the brothers ruled the Orkneys, they were in thorough and good agreement for a long time. But when their sons began to grow into men, then Hákon and Erlingr became overbearing. Magnús was the quietest of them. All were tall and strong and very accomplished in everything. Hákon Pálsson wanted to be the leader of the brothers; he thought he was of better birth than Erlendr's sons because he was the son of the daughter of Earl Hákon Ívarsson by Ragnhildr the daughter of King Magnús the Good.

This claim to royal blood came through his mother Thora's side. Hákon felt it set him apart from his cousins.[19]

This lay behind the rivalry which would eventually spread between the offspring of the two earls, and which would eventually sour the relationship between Erlend and Paul. The eldest sons of the two earls had been born around 1080, and so it was the early 1090s when this tension between Hákon and his Erlendsson cousins began to come to the surface. The saga added that 'Then their fathers got involved; they were going to settle the matter.' Naturally, though, they favoured their own children, and bad feeling between the families continued to grow. Eventually, things had deteriorated so much that a *Thing* was held in Orkney in around 1092, and it was decided to split the earldom in two.[20]

Despite this, tensions continued, and so in 1093 Earl Paul decided it would be better if his son Hákon left Orkney for a while. Hákon Paulsson was no stranger to travelling, as he'd already taken part in Viking raids. So what followed was the equivalent of a Nordic gap year, as Hákon was sent to visit his kinsmen in Scandinavia. He began in Norway, visiting King Ólaf II 'the Peaceful', the son of Harald 'Hardrada'. Then Hákon set off to Sweden to meet King Inge 'the Elder'. While there, Hákon met a soothsayer who claimed he could predict the future. When asked, the reluctant wise man told Hákon that he'd rule Orkney, but it would take longer to gain the whole earldom than he'd expect. He also warned the young man that 'You will also in your time have that crime committed which you will either manage to atone for or not before the god in whom you believe'. That, though, didn't worry Hákon. His destiny of becoming the sole earl was all that mattered.[21]

By the time Hákon returned to Norway, King Ólaf had died, and his son Magnus III 'Bare-legged' (sometimes called 'Barefoot') was now the ruler of Norway. Unlike his more peaceable father, the 20-year-old King Magnus was a man of action, and as the *Earls' Saga* put it: 'Hákon was a wise man and he thought he understood from King Magnús' talk when they spoke, the king would be ambitious and covetous of other chieftains' territories.' This suited Hákon perfectly. By this time, around the spring of 1094, he'd learned that his father Paul had ceded day-to-day control of the earldom to his younger brother Erlend.[22]

This didn't sit well with Hákon, so he urged Magnus 'Bare-legged' to lead a force to Orkney and install him as the sole earl. Then, once Magnus reclaimed the Sudreys, he could use the earldom for further raids into the Irish Sea. King Magnus liked the idea but warned Hákon: 'But you must remember, Hákon, that if, because of your recommendation and encouragement, I go west across the sea with an army, it will not be unexpected for you when I make a substantial claim on those territories which lie there in the west, and in that I will make no distinction between people.' Clearly King Magnus would include the earldom of Orkney in his planned list of conquests, which wasn't what Hákon wanted at all. In raising the issue of the earldom, Hákon Paulsson had single-handedly placed the earldom in great danger.[23]

FIFTEEN

Hákon and Magnus

B EFORE KING MAGNUS 'BARE-LEGGED' could cross the West
Sea, he had to pacify Norway. He'd been at his father Ólaf's bedside
in south-east Norway when he died in September 1093. Then, Magnus
was quickly proclaimed king at a *Thing* held just a few days later. He still
had a rival, but his cousin Hákon Magnusson mysteriously died while
hunting, and a thorough campaign to deal with Hákon's supporters
left Magnus' realm secure. That meant that by 1096, Magnus was free
to plan his expedition to the west. This was largely about recovering
lands which had once been in Norse hands, and re-establishing royal
authority on the far side of the West Sea. While this mainly meant
Orkney, Shetland and the Sudreyjar, Magnus also planned to venture
further south into the basin of the Irish Sea. At its south-eastern side,
he even hoped to re-establish Norse rule in Wales.[1]

According to *Magnus Barefoot's Saga*, 'King Magnus undertook
an expedition out of the country, with many fine men and a good
assortment of shipping. With this armament he sailed out into the
West Sea, and first came to the Orkney islands.' The naïve Hákon
Paulsson had been hoping the new Norwegian king would name him
earl of Orkney. In fact, he'd pinned all his hopes on it. Instead, King
Magnus did away with the troublesome earldom altogether. When he
arrived in the islands in the spring of 1098 the king's first act was to
take the two earls Erlend and Paul prisoner. It was nothing short of a
regime change. It also left Hákon out in the cold, together with Earl
Erlend's two sons Erling and Magnus.[2]

As a deliberate insult to the earls and their sons, Magnus 'Bare-legged'
installed his eight-year-old son Sigurðr (or Sigurd) in Orkney as a
sub-king, supported by a council of Norwegian advisers. The deposed
Earls Erlend and Paul were then transported back to Norway as royal
prisoners. Their crime had been nothing other than overseeing the

earldom at a time when a rapacious new Norwegian king had arrived with a fleet at his back. At some point during that winter, both Orkney earls died in captivity, Erlend in Trondheim and Paul in Bergen. As for their three sons, Magnus and Erling Erlendsson and Hákon Paulsson, Magnus 'Bare-legged' took them with him when his great expedition left Orkney and set a course for the Sudreyjar.[3]

Magnus 'Bare-legged' then went on to wrest control of the Sudreyjar from its local rulers before sailing on to the Isle of Man to ensure Norse control was secure there too. This aim of this was to make sure that the patchwork of Norse, Norse-Gael and Hiberno-Norse rulers off Scotland's western coast owed their allegiance directly to him rather than to any other potential rival, foreign or domestic. That included any resurgent Orkney earldom. From the Isle of Man, Magnus then led his fleet across the Irish Sea to the island of Anglesey, in the north-west corner of Wales.[4]

Once again, his objective was regime change. A decade before, the Welsh kingdom of Gwynedd had been encroached on by two Anglo-Norman adventurers, Hugh d'Avranches, Earl of Chester, and Hugh of Montgomery, Earl of Shrewsbury. More entertainingly, the saga calls them 'Hugi the Fat' and 'Hugi the Proud' respectively.[5] The Norse-Welsh king of Gwynedd, Gruffudd ap Cynan, agreed to meet the two English nobles to discuss peace, but instead he was unchivalrously taken prisoner. After imprisoning Gruffudd in Chester, the two earls conquered all of Gwynedd.

By 1094, though, four years before King Magnus' expedition, Gruffudd managed to escape to Ireland. From there he led raids on English-occupied Wales. One of his targets was the Castell Aberlleiniog, a Norman timber-clad motte and bailey castle dominating the northern end of the Menai Strait. It was the key to the island, which he planned to use as a base for his eventual reconquest of his lost Welsh kingdom. Four years later, Magnus 'Bare-legged' vowed to help King Gruffudd regain his throne, and at the same time install a ruler in Wales who'd owe allegiance to the Norwegian crown.[6]

King Magnus' fleet arrived off Anglesey in mid-summer. According to one source, he only had six longships with him, but this sounds very unlikely given his objective of reclaiming a Welsh kingdom. When he arrived off the Menai Strait, Magnus had a red shield hoisted at the masthead of his *drakkar*, which signalled that he came in peace. Wisely, though, the two English earls didn't believe the Norse king and refused to let him land. Soon, both sides were exchanging flights of arrows, while English mounted knights guarded the shore in front of the castle and rode into the shallows, taunting the Norsemen lying offshore. At this point, as the battle was growing in ferocity, the 18-year-old Magnus Erlendsson declared that he refused to fight. He added that he didn't have a quarrel with anyone there.[7]

A disgusted King Magnus branded him a coward and ordered him away, saying, 'Go down below the decking, and don't lie about here under people's feet if you don't dare to fight, because I don't believe your faith is the reason for this'. The young man refused, though, and instead he spent the duration of the battle on the open deck of the *drakkar*, chanting psalms from a psalter. It was a precocious display of piety, and it guaranteed the enmity of the Norwegian king. Later, in the eyes of Magnus' Christian biographers, it was a sign that he was destined for sainthood. It mightn't have been religious resolve which drove him to rebel in this unusual way. It was more likely that Magnus simply refused to lift a finger for the man who'd imprisoned his father and seized his family's earldom.[8]

The battle raged on, with the Norse ships and the Norman troops on the shore exchanging volleys of arrows. The saga describes it as follows: 'The battle was both hard and long, and there was both shooting and striking; for a long time it was not possible to tell how it would all turn out.' Then it was claimed that King Magnus himself changed the course of the battle. 'King Magnus shot with his handbow and a Hågolander beside him'. Hagoland was a Norwegian province north of Trøndelag, known for its skilled archers. The saga continued, 'Hugi the Proud fought very vigorously; he was armed with chain mail in such a way that nothing showed of him except his eyes'. The king suggested that they should both shoot at the earl at the same time. 'One arrow landed on his nose-guard and the other in his eye and flew back through his head, and the latter was credited to the king'. Hugh 'the Proud', Earl of Shrewsbury fell from his horse, killed outright as he taunted the Norsemen from the shallows. Naturally the king took credit for the killing shot.[9]

This proved to be the turning point of the battle. It caused just enough confusion in the English ranks for the Norsemen to jump from their longships and wade ashore. Any attempt by the Anglo-Normans to launch a counter-attack was thwarted by the loss of the earl, which paralysed his retainers. The fight continued, but eventually the heart went out of the defenders, and they fled the field and withdrew from Anglesey. Soon, all the island including the castle at Aberlleiniog was in Magnus 'Bare-legged's' hands. It had been a hard-fought battle but worth it, at least for King Gruffudd. After swearing loyalty to the Norwegian king, he was handed control of Anglesey. By 1101, he had regained control of all of Gwynedd.

———

As for the Norse expedition, it turned back to the Isle of Man before eventually making its way back towards Orkney. Magnus Erlendsson remained in disgrace and was stripped of his job as the king's cup bearer. On the way home, the fleet put in to the Firth of Clyde and King Magnus went ashore, probably near Ayr, to meet King Edgar of Scotland. He'd gained the crown four years earlier after the imprisonment of his uncle King Donald. The meeting was to agree to the Norse control of the Sudreyjar. The treaty that came from this ceded Argyll and the Hebrides to Magnus, which avoided an unnecessary war for both kings. Edgar needed this to bring stability to a country ravaged by dynastic disputes and English invasion.[10]

However, the teenage Magnus seized the opportunity to escape. Under cover of darkness, he slipped overboard in his underclothes and swam to the shore. When dawn broke the king sent men and dogs to pursue Magnus, but the young man hid in a tree, drove off a hunting dog by throwing a stick at it, and so managed to evade his hunters. He then walked inland, found King Edgar, and begged for his protection. Magnus Erlendsson was welcomed at the Scottish court. In the end he spent several years there, waiting for his chance to regain his share of the earldom. For Edgar, Magnus was a useful pawn if he ever needed to stir up trouble against the Norwegian crown or wrest back control of his western coastline. Magnus benefited too, gaining connections in Scotland which should serve him well when he made his move.[11]

In 1101, King Magnus 'Bare-legged' led another expedition across the West Sea. In *Magnus Barefoot's Saga*, it claims that he stopped in Orkney on his way to Ireland, and brought Magnus and Erling Erlendsson with him. Here, the saga confuses the two expeditions. He might have visited Orkney in 1101 to recruit men and to visit his son Sigurd, who was now an 11-year-old. Magnus Erlendsson, though, was still in Scotland. King Magnus then pressed on to the Isle of Man to assure himself it was still safely under his control, before sailing over to Dublin.

Three years before, in 1098, King Magnus had formed an alliance with Muirchertach Ua Briain, the High King of Ireland. To cement it, the five-year-old Irish princess Blathmuine was married to the Norse king's young son Sigurd, the temporary ruler of the Orkney earldom. Magnus 'Bare-legged' hoped to renew this potentially useful alliance during this second expedition of his to Ireland. However, Muirchertach was suspicious that Magnus aspired to rule Ireland himself. Then, in August 1103, King Magnus was slain during a skirmish in Ulster, one which had probably been orchestrated by Muirchertach. After the king's death the expedition returned home. In the *Magnus 'Barefoot's' Saga*, it is claimed that Erling Erlendsson, the brother of Magnus, was also killed in Ireland that summer, fighting alongside the Norwegian king on his second and final expedition to the west.[12]

Meanwhile, in Orkney, Sigurd Magnusson, son of the late King Magnus, left the islands and also set sail for Norway, taking his child bride with him. He needed to make sure he shared the joint succession to his father's throne with his brothers Eystein and Ólaf. He left his island kingdom in the hands of a steward, who ruled the earldom for two more years. Then, in 1105, Hákon Paulsson petitioned the three Norwegian kings to become the new earl of Orkney. The plea was granted, and so Hákon gained 'such of the realm as was his birthright'. Half of it, though, was retained by the crown, on the grounds that it was the share which rightly belonged to Magnus Erlendsson, and they were holding it in trust for him.[13]

During all this, Magnus Erlendsson had been waiting for a chance to reclaim the earldom too. Before King Edgar died in 1107, he named Magnus as the new *mormaer* of Caithness. This gave Magnus a share of the earldom, albeit one which demanded his fealty to the Scottish crown. He also married, in *c.* 1105, 'when he asked for a hand of a girl from the most noble family there in Scotland'. If this is the case, her name Ingigerð (or Ingigerth) is surprising, although not impossible given the inter-marriage between Norse and Scottish nobility.

Again, the term 'girl' is interesting. In the *Longer Magnus Saga*, much is made that Magnus was chaste, and 'when he felt temptations coming to him ... then he bathed in cold water.' Despite the subsequent praise of the devout man who favoured his sanctity, there's a strong possibility Ingigerth was a child bride, which explains both this alleged 'cold water' chastity and the lack of offspring. The lack of any marital coupling was also no bar to extra-marital liaisons, which were perfectly acceptable among the Norse nobility. The *Longer Magnus Saga*, after all, was written after the event, with the view to promoting the earl's suitability for sainthood.[14]

After his marriage, in 1105 or 1106, Magnus, now the *mormaer* of Caithness, learned that his cousin Hákon had murdered the royal stewards who were entrusted with managing his share of the earldom. So, with the blessing of King Edgar, Magnus crossed the Pentland Firth to Orkney and laid a legal claim for his half of the earldom. The saga claims that 'The farmers were pleased, as Magnus was well-liked'.[15] Clearly this was a risk, given the animosity Earl Hákon felt for Magnus, and the earl had already begun raising a force to oppose Magnus if it came to it.

Magnus played it well, relying on due legal process rather than brute force. The arbitration of the Orkney elders at a *Thing* tipped the legal resolution in his favour. Still, the landowners advised Magnus to sail to Norway and seek approval from the three Magnusson kings for this legal solution. There, the joint Norwegian kings Eystein, Sigurd and Ólaf duly approved. When Magnus returned to Orkney, his cousin Hákon took the kings' verdict with surprising grace. From then on, each earl ruled half of the earldom.

For several years, from around 1106 to 1114, Earl Hákon and Earl Magnus 'rubbed along' reasonably well, and each ruled their half of the earldom. By now, though, thanks to Magnus 'Bare-legged', it had been stripped down to just Orkney and Shetland, as well as Magnus' lands in Caithness and Sutherland. The arrangement over Magnus' rule of Caithness survived the death of King Edgar of Scotland in 1107. Edgar's brother Alexander succeeded him to the Scottish throne, while the youngest brother David was merely given land in south-west Scotland.

He would eventually succeed Alexander in 1124, becoming King David I. However, while Edgar had been peaceful and devout, and encouraged his guest Magnus to be the same, King Alexander earned the nickname 'the Fierce'. Later, the earldom would understand how he suited it.[16]

The two Orkney earls also campaigned together in both Shetland, where there was a minor rebellion, and in the Hebrides. The Sudreyjar had been lost to the Norwegian crown, as had the earldom's lands in Argyll. Hákon and Magnus, though, reclaimed some of these lost territories for the earldom. Meanwhile their lands prospered from this lengthy period of peace. In 1114, Magnus answered a summons from King Alexander of Scotland to campaign with him in Wales. It was claimed that Magnus left with two well-manned longships and spent a year away from Orkney, serving both Alexander I and King Henry I of England, both of whom paid Earl Magnus for his services.[17]

This time the target of this joint military action by the English and Scots was none other than Gruffudd ap Cynan, King of Gwynedd. It goes against the later, sanctified portrayal of Magnus Erlendsson that the youth who'd chanted psalms amid a battle could also be a warrior. It seems that Earl Magnus was no saintly pacifist. In fact, just as his cousin Hákon had done, Magnus had taken part in Viking raids in his youth, and he knew how to hold his place in a shieldwall. He'd been trained in the martial arts and in hunting, much as any other offspring of the Norse nobility would have been. As a Norse ruler of the Orkney earldom, he'd also learned how to command warriors. Now, as part of his feudal commitment to the Scottish crown as earl of Caithness, Magnus led a small contingent of troops on the expedition. Welsh chronicles claimed that the Scottish force contained troops 'from the furthest corners of Pictland.' Caithness would undoubtedly qualify for that description.[18]

Earl Magnus must have met the Welsh king a few times before. King Gruffud had visited Orkney when Magnus' father and uncle were earls. Then, the Welsh ruler arrived with a fleet of two dozen longships, soliciting help in a campaign against the Anglo-Norman conquerors of Glywysing in South Wales – now Glamorgan. Magnus undoubtedly met him too during the expedition of King Magnus 'Bare-legged' in 1098, which led to the Battle of the Menai Strait. After the Anglo-Scots expedition to Gwynedd in 1114, Magnus spent several months in Wales, after the two kings leading the expedition had forced terms on King Gruffud. So, for a third time at least, Magnus Erlendsson had met the Welsh ruler of Gwynedd and used his time there to further his religious studies.[19]

A historian once summed up the problem facing Earl Magnus perfectly when he said that 'It was never advisable for earls of Orkney to be absent for too long.' While Earl Magnus was taking a year or more away from the earldom, he left things in the hands of his cousin Earl Hákon, aided no doubt by Magnus' own stewards. During this absence, Hákon seized the opportunity and took over Magnus' half of the earldom – or at least the half in Orkney.[20]

It seems that under the two rival earls there was an east-west split of Orkney, just as it had been in the time of their fathers, Earl Erlend and Earl Paul. So, although the way Orkney was divided isn't recorded, it was possible that one inherited his father's western side of the Orkney mainland while the other controlled the East Mainland, including the growing settlement at Kirkwall. The North and South Isles were similarly split, while Hákon might possibly have controlled Shetland to counter Magnus' holdings across the Pentland Firth.[21]

So to say it was a tense homecoming for Magnus in early 1117 was an understatement. The *Earls' Saga* claims that supporters of the two earls skirmished with each other during the weeks that followed. A single spark could ignite civil war, and *agent provocateurs* working for Hákon were busily trying to ignite it. So, in Lent, which in 1117 was in March, a *Thing* or assembly was held, probably at Tingwall in the West Mainland where a ferry now runs to the nearby islands of Rousay, Egilsay and Wyre. It lay neatly on the border of the two halves of the earldom. Attending it were the elders of the community, led by the *gödingar*, the upper strata of Orkney's landed gentry, who owned a large part of the islands.[22]

It was an extremely dangerous situation. Both Hákon and Magnus had arrived with their own sizeable and well-armed *hird*, or hearthguard of warriors, and as the saga tells, 'And when they arrived there, then each of the two mustered his troop and prepared for battle'. Somehow, though, both Hákon and Magnus kept their men in check, and the *Thing* went ahead. The saga continues, 'The earls were there and all the men of rank and there were many who were friends of both of them and had a part in reconciling them; many mediated between them with courage and goodwill'. It worked. Despite the volatile situation, the *göding* who led the *Thing* helped mediate between the rivals, and they reached a solution. As a result, the two earls were encouraged to take oaths of friendship, and civil war was averted.[23]

By the end of the assembly, a partition of the earldom had been agreed, probably along the old east-west lines that existed since their father's division of the earldom. Both earls agreed to hold a further meeting to put the finishing touches to the settlement. It would be held shortly after Easter, which in 1117 fell on 1 April. This meeting of the two earls would be held on the nearby island of Egilsay, which could be seen five miles away to the north. It was a small, flat, teardrop-shaped island, just three miles long and a mile across at its widest part. Like Tingwall, the island lay on the boundary of the two halves of the earldom and was probably owned by the church. Later, Bishop Vilhjálmr (or William) maintained a church and a small residence there. So it seemed ideal neutral ground for the meeting.[24]

The meeting on Egilsay was set for 16 April, two weeks after Easter. Magnus was the first to arrive the day before, presumably after sailing there from Kirkwall, just over ten miles away to the south. The arrangement made at the *Thing* was that each earl would bring two longships with him containing their close bodyguard, advisers, clerics, administrators and servants. As the saga puts it, 'Earl Magnus called in all those men whom he knew to be most well-intentioned and most likely to improve things between the kinsmen'. On the short voyage, though, which took place on a calm day, the crew of Magnus' ship were amazed when a rogue wave broke over the ship. The saga continues: 'Then the earl said, "It is not strange that you are astonished by this, but it's my suspicion that this is a portent of my death."' Still, he ordered his men to continue to Egilsay. Now though, Magnus had a feeling that Hákon was planning him harm.[25]

He was right. Late that afternoon, Hákon was sighted approaching Egilsay from the west, the direction of his hall in Birsay. He appeared around the bowl-shaped island of Hrólfsey (now Rousay), where high hills screened his approach through Eynhallow Sound ('Efjusund' in Norse) until he was close to Egilsay. When the fast-approaching longships were sighted, Magnus knew immediately that Hákon had treacherously broken his word. Instead of two ships carrying the earl's personal retinue, Hákon had brought eight longships, filled with his warriors. It was too late to flee, as by the time Magnus and his men had reached their ships Hákon would be upon them and would stop them from sailing. Magnus and his followers were trapped.

That night, Hákon and his men remained aboard their ships, anchored off the island's landing place at Skaill. Magnus ordered his men not to resist, as it would be a waste of their lives. Instead, he reputedly went to the island's small church and spent the night there in prayer, and had his clerics, possibly including Bishop Radulph, hold mass for him, and he received the sacraments.[26]

The next day, Hákon and his men landed on Egilsay. There are differing accounts of what happened. One had Hákon's men drag Magnus out of the small church and bring him to the waiting Hákon. Another version had Magnus hiding in the rocks on the island's shore. The first version, from the *Longer Magnus Saga*, was almost certainly included to stir outrage by suggesting Hákon violated the sanctity of a holy church. The real version might well be more akin to the account in the *Earls' Saga* and was more in keeping with Magnus' new-found mood of predestination. He was waiting for Hákon when he landed, calling out to his cousin's men so they knew where he was.[27]

In these sagas, Hákon then convened a *Thing*, presumably made up from the leading supporters of both earls, but with Hákon's followers overwhelmingly in the majority. This suggests it was included in the sagas to demonstrate due judicial process was being followed. The attitude of the assembly was notably different from the one held a few weeks before. This time there was no attempt at mediation, and little appeal in showing clemency. This turnaround of attitudes suggests the *Thing* was a fictional cover-up. Instead, Magnus was on trial for his life, and the judge and jury were made up exclusively of Hákon and his leading followers. The *Earls' Saga* claims that Magnus gave Hákon and the assembly three options. He'd leave the earldom with two ships and go on a pilgrimage to Rome and the Holy Land. He promised never to return. The second option was to go into exile in

Scotland, where he could be kept under guard if needs be. Both options were turned down by Hákon and the assembly.

Magnus' third option was for Hákon to 'Let me be dismembered as you like, or take my eyes, and place me in a prison'. According to the saga this option appealed to Hákon, but the assembly rejected it. Instead, they declared, 'We must kill one or the other of you now, and you shall not both rule the lands from this day forth.'[28] This was meant to be an expression of exasperation at the seemingly irreconcilable situation they were in. Only the death of Magnus would do. This declaration, however, might also have been another fabrication by the saga's author to give Earl Hákon a legitimate excuse for murdering his cousin. So, it was decided. Earl Magnus must die.

At first, Hákon ordered his standard bearer Ófeigr (or Ofeig) to kill Magnus, but he adamantly refused to do the deed. So it was Hákon's cook Lífólfr (or Lífólf) who was delegated to strike the killing blow. Presumably he had more experience with an axe than the crowd of warriors who were watching this macabre scene unfold. Magnus took off his tunic, and in his underclothes he kneeled with head bowed as the reluctant Lífólf prepared himself, while dozens watched. Just before Lífólf raised his axe, Magnus begged him to let him die like a Norse warrior. 'Stand in front of me, and strike a great wound on my head, because it is not fitting to cut down chieftains like thieves.' With that, Lífólf struck the blow, smashing a great gash into the left side of Earl Magnus' head. Magnus was killed outright. At that grisly moment, Hákon became the sole remaining earl of Orkney.[29]

SIXTEEN

Murder and Miracles

H AVING ORDERED THE KILLING of his cousin, Earl Hákon Paulsson now had to live with the consequences. The first problem was Magnus' mother Þóra (or Thora), the widow of Earl Erlend Thorfinnsson. She had already lost one son, Erling, who'd been killed in King Magnus 'Bare-legged's' last raid in 1103. Around the same time her eldest daughter Gunnhild had been married to Kol Kalason, the son of Kali Sæbjarnarsson, a Norse chieftain who'd been a close adviser to Magnus 'Bare-legged'. Her youngest daughter Cecilia had also been married off. Kol Kalason and Gunnhild Erlendsdóttir would return to play a leading part in the story of the earldom, but for now the widow Thora still had to be told her remaining son had just been slaughtered.

A feast had been arranged by her to celebrate the peace settlement between the two rival cousins. Callously, Earl Hákon and his men turned up at the feast, but there was no sign of Magnus and his men. The dreadful realisation quickly dawned on Thora. Still, she calmly served up ale and food, and waited for her moment, once Hákon was mellowed by drink.

Then, with tears in her eyes, she begged permission to take the body of her son and bury him. With that, 'The earl falls silent and thinks over the matter and felt guilty of his misdeeds…' A guilty Earl Hákon 'looked at her and shed a tear and spoke to her, "Bury your son where you like."' So, after the doomed feast, Thora and her household sailed to Egilsay, collected the body, and took it to Birsay in Orkney's west mainland. There, Magnus was buried in Christ Church, which his grandfather Earl Thorfinn 'the Mighty' had built.[1]

After the drama of Egilsay, the earldom returned to something resembling an even keel. As the *Earls' Saga* puts it, 'After the killing of Magnus, Hákon took over the whole of Orkney, and made all those who had previously served Magnus swear oaths of allegiance to himself.'

This, though, wasn't just about healing open wounds. Thanks largely to Hákon, the earldom had almost been plunged into civil war. Magnus had been well-liked, and the swearing of allegiance to his killer wouldn't have endeared Hákon to a larger swathe of the earldom's landowners. Hákon dealt with the threat posed by this potentially rebellious group head on. 'He then became a great chieftain and oppressed greatly those friends of Earl Magnus whom he thought had been most against him in their dealings.' Eventually, whatever people felt in private, they kept any dislike of Hákon to themselves.[2]

Despite everything he did, Earl Hákon couldn't avoid the remorse he felt for killing his cousin. So, around 1119, Earl Hákon set off on a pilgrimage to Rome, a journey which undoubtedly had been organised by Bishop William of Orkney. After crossing the West Sea and probably making landfall near the River Weser, he might have visited Frederick, Archbishop of Bremen, in whose archdiocese Orkney now lay. The earl then continued southwards across Europe until he reached Rome. There he would have had an audience with Pope Callixtus II. Either encouraged by him or on his own initiative, Earl Hákon then exceeded the pilgrimage made by his grandfather Earl Thorfinn 'the Mighty' and took passage from Italy to the Holy Land. There, as the saga puts it, 'In that journey he went out to Jerusalem, visited the holy relics there, and bathed in the River Jordan, as is the custom with pilgrims'.[3]

On Earl Hákon's return to Orkney around 1120, he returned to what was still a peaceful realm. He then continued to rule his earldom without any notable interference from Norway, Scotland or elsewhere. It was said, 'He then became a good ruler and brought peace to his territory. He then made new laws in the Orkneys which the householders liked much better than those which had been before. With this his popularity began to grow; in the end, the Orcadians wanted nothing more than to have Hákon as their ruler.'

All this time – in fact from well before his feud with his cousin Magnus – Hákon had a mistress, Helga Moddansdóttir. Her father Moddan was a wealthy Norse *göding* or landowner from the Dale area of Caithness, which was probably the valley of the River Helmsdale, which reaches the West Sea at the small cliff-fringed fishing haven of Helmsdale. Helga was the eldest of three daughters, all of whom married into the earldom's landowning society in Caithness and Orkney.[4]

Earl Hákon and his Caithness mistress had a son called Haraldr (or Harald) Hákonsson, who earned the epithet 'Smooth-talking'. There was an elder brother too, Páll (or Paul) 'the Speechless' from an earlier mistress of Earl Hákon. In addition, Helga bore the earl two daughters, Ingibjorg (or Ingibiorg) and Margaret. Ingibiorg, who was the eldest, married Ólaf Morsel, king of the both the Isle of Man and the Hebrides. This established a useful link to the Sudreyjar, which had been lost to the earldom ever since the campaigns of King Magnus 'Bare-legged'. This, though, didn't mean that it couldn't be won back, and so a marital union with the most powerful ruler in the region was useful.[5]

Earl Hákon ruled the earldom for several years after his return from his pilgrimage. Then, the *Earls' Saga* says that 'Earl Hákon Pálsson was struck down by a disease there in the islands. People thought that was a great shame, because it was very peaceful in his latter days.' It seems that his feelings of guilt were assuaged by his pilgrimage, and he then made up for his divisive and troublesome early reign by becoming a model ruler, who eventually came to be liked by most of the people.[6]

Undoubtedly, there were some who never forgave him for the murder of his cousin. Still, for the most part the subsequent years of peace went some way towards atoning for his brutality on Egilsay. The problem, though, for many was what came next. Hákon was succeeded to the earldom by his two sons, who despite their illegitimacy were destined to divide the earldom between them. However, as the saga puts it, 'the householders were doubtful of any cooperation between the brothers Páll and Haraldr'.[7]

So, in *c.* 1123 Earl Hákon's two sons Earl Harald 'Smooth-talking' and Earl Paul 'the Silent' duly inherited their father's earldom. Although both Harald and Paul were illegitimate – the offspring of two of Hákon's mistresses – this didn't get in the way of them succeeding their father. They were probably in their twenties at the time and had been raised as befitted their status as the heirs of an earl. The arrangement Hákon had decided was that the earldom would be split in two again, with each brother governing half of the earldom. This was done along the same lines as it had been in the past, under their grandfathers, Earls Erlend and Paul, and their father and uncle, Earls Hákon and Magnus. Earl Harald got the West Mainland of Orkney as well as the South Isles bordering Scapa Flow, while Paul ruled the East Mainland and most of the North Isles as well as Shetland.

In addition, 'Earl Haraldr held Caithness for the king of Scots and was there frequently, and sometimes up in Scotland because he had many relatives and friends there'. At the time, that would have been Alexander I, the king whom Harald's uncle Magnus had fought alongside in Wales.[8] Harald spent most of his time in Caithness, leaving stewards to look after his other lands. Sometimes, according to the saga, he would go south into the kingdom of Scotland, 'Where he had a good many kinsmen and friends.'

For his part Paul largely remained in Orkney, basing himself in his father's hall in Kirkwall. The temperament of the brothers was very different. Harald was sociable and even gregarious, while his half-brother Paul was quiet and reserved. While the two were children they got on well enough, but this gradually changed as they grew older. By the time their father died there was little love lost between them.[9]

In Sutherland, Earl Harald 'Smooth-talking' encountered Sigurd 'the Fake', also known as the 'Fake Deacon'. Sigurd had gained his strange epithet because he'd once trained to be a priest but never took his vows. He was reputedly the son of a priest too, called Aðalbriktr. This meeting probably took place at the estate of Earl Harald's uncle-in-law Ljót 'the Scoundrel', who was married to Helga's sister Frakǫkk Moddansdóttir. Sigurd 'the Fake' had recently been at the court of the new Scottish king David I, which shows he was fairly well-connected. King David had succeeded his brother Alexander several years before in 1124.

When he met Earl Harald, Sigurd 'the Fake' was on his way to Orkney. He stayed with Harald for a while and befriended both Helga and Frakǫkk. Soon, the saga claims with candour, 'They all had great affection for Sigurðr the Fake'. This happy group then decided to accompany Sigurd 'the Fake' to Orkney. This proved to be a disastrous decision, as Harald's arrival rekindled the barely-hidden animosity between the two earls.[10]

Factions soon began to form, and with that came the risk of violence erupting. Sure enough, it did, thanks to Sigurd 'the Fake'. At the time, one of Earl Paul's closest advisers was Þorkell Sumarlaðason (or Thorkell Sumarlidason). He was also known as Thorkell 'the Fosterer'. This of course, wasn't the Thorkell 'Fosterer' who raised Earl Thorfinn over a century before. This Thorkell had been loyal to Earl Magnus and had suffered during Earl Hákon's persecution of the murdered earl's supporters. However, he now provided counsel to Hákon's son Earl Paul. Earl Harald, though, didn't trust Thorkell, and 'This ended with Earl Haraldr and Sigurðr the Fake attacking and killing Þorkell the Fosterer'. Sigurd 'the Fake' had probably helped Harald in the killing to please his new-found patron. Instead, this murder made the rift between the two brothers all but irrevocable.

Earl Paul was rightly outraged by this murder and began gearing up for a fratricidal war. So too did Earl Harald. What prevented it was the intervention of the friends of both parties. These were probably the same *gödingar* and other leading Orkney landowners who'd played the same role in the feud between the earls Hákon and Magnus several years before. This time, though, Paul refused any form of reconciliation, but in the end, for the sake of peace, a settlement of sorts was reached. 'It thus came about that Sigurðr was expelled from the islands and those others whom Earl Páll thought were most guilty of the deed'. This didn't include Earl Harald, who clearly had blood on his hands. He was forced, however, to pay compensation for the murder to Thorkell's family.[11]

The mediators also came up with a plan to encourage the half-brothers to improve their relationship with each other. 'It was also stipulated in the agreement that the relationship between the brothers Páll and Haraldr should be improved, and they should be both together at Christmas and all the major festivals'. Nobody could have realised it at the time, but this would be a recipe for disaster. An attempt to do what the *gödingar* had requested led to the two earls coming together in late 1131 for the Christmas celebrations. These were held in Hákon's feasting hall at Orphir, on the western side of Scapa Flow. Both earls would have brought their entourage, which included Earl Harald's mother Helga and her sister Frakǫkk. The pair of them decided to make this a Christmas to remember.[12]

When Harald 'Smooth-talking' entered their chambers, he found his mother and aunt sitting sewing something. 'The sisters Frakǫkk and Helga, the earl's mother, were there and sat at their sewing in the smaller room. Earl Haraldr then went into the room and the sisters were sitting on the cross-wise platform and a newly-sewn linen garment lay between them, white as a snowdrift. The earl took the garment and saw that it was extensively stitched with gold'.[13]

When Harald asked who it was for, he was told it was to be a present for his brother Paul. Harald was overcome by jealousy. This snow-white shirt or tunic was better made than anything his mother had ever made for him. So the earl decided to try the beautiful garment on. After pulling off his own shirt he began unfolding this new one. Agitated, his mother sprang up and grabbed it from him, while telling her son that he'd no reason to feel envious. Harald, though, was determined to try it on.

'The earl snatched it back and was about to put it on when the sisters pulled off their bonnets, tore their hair, and told him that if he put on the garment, his life would be at risk.' Nothing was stopping Harald though, who ignored the wailing and hair-pulling and slipped the shirt on. 'No sooner was the garment upon his back than his flesh started to quiver, and he began to suffer terrible agony. He had to go to bed, and not long after that he died.'[14]

It was soon discovered that the inside of the shirt had been coated in some kind of fast-acting poison. Earl Paul realised immediately that the poisoned shirt had been meant for him. So he wisely banished both the poisoners Helga and Frakǫkk from Orkney. The pair of murderesses moved back to the Sutherland estate of Frakǫkk's husband Ljót 'the Scoundrel'. He'd died not long before and his lands had been left to Frakǫkk. There, the sisters raised Erlendr (or Erlend) Haraldsson, the son of Harald 'Smooth-talking', as well as Erlend's sister Margaret Hákonsdóttir. Other high-born youngsters in the household were also raised alongside Harald's children, and all of them were told that they had a claim to the earldom, which had once belonged to their kinsman Earl Harald 'Smooth-talking'. Some of them would later attempt to reclaim part of that stake.[15]

So from the end of 1131 on, Earl Paul 'the Speechless' ruled the earldom alone. He proved to be a popular leader, and following the end of the rivalry between him and his half-brother the earldom prospered. He seemed unaware that across the Pentland Firth, Helga and Frakǫkk, supported by their powerful Moddan relatives, were planning to steal the earldom from him. Also unknown to Earl Paul, another threat would appear from the far side of the Salt Road. In Norway, a powerful rival was preparing to make his bid to take over the Orkney earldom. For the moment, though, life in the earldom continued, although increasingly Paul was plagued by reports of strange happenings. All of these were tied to his murdered uncle Earl Magnus, whom his father had ordered to be killed. However much Paul tried to suppress these reports, more of them kept taking place. It was almost as if the murdered earl was talking to his descendants from beyond the grave.

Earl Hákon had been prevailed upon by Magnus' mother Thora to let her bury her son wherever she wished. When the earl agreed, Magnus was interred at Christ Church in Birsay, in the West Mainland of Orkney, a stone's throw from the Atlantic Ocean. Since the death of Earl Magnus in April 1117, though, strange and unexplained events began to happen. The *Earls' Saga* claims that the first 'miracle' took place in Egilsay itself, where the spot where Earl Magnus had been killed had been rocky and overgrown with moss. Afterwards, the saga claims that the spot miraculously turned into a luscious field of green grass. This unlikely event was only the start. Soon heavenly lights were seen dancing over Magnus' grave in Birsay, and a strange, perfumed fragrance hung over it.[16]

Bishop William 'the Old' was as loyal to Earl Paul as he had been to his father Earl Hákon, and he refused to believe these tales. In fact he saw them as being akin to heresy. This, though, didn't stop more reports of other strange events reaching him – some of which were nothing short of miraculous. The blind farmer Bergfinn Skatisson from Shetland recovered his sight after visiting Magnus' grave, and two cripples with him were able to walk again. Word spread, and at the Easter of 1118, on the first anniversary of Magnus' murder, two dozen worshippers maintained a graveside vigil. In the morning, they claimed that their various ailments had miraculously been healed. Still, the bishop was having none of it.[17]

It was clear that a populist religious cult was forming, centred around the murdered earl. First Hákon and then his sons were rigidly opposed to this, as ultimately it would show Hákon in a bad light. Eventually, as secular pressure mounted, and some 20 years after Magnus' burial, the bishop finally agreed to exhume Magnus' body.

By then Hákon had died, and his son Paul reigned as the sole earl. The impetus for this change of heart, according to the saga, came soon after Bishop William was suddenly struck by blindness. Then, after praying at the graveside, his sight was restored.

So, in front of witnesses, including the island's leading *gödingar* or landowners, the body was exhumed. Not only had the coffin almost risen to the surface of the grave, but a knuckle bone inside was tested using fire, and it refused to burn. Instead, it supposedly turned a golden colour. This, it seems, was enough for William, who was now a thoroughgoing convert to the 'Magnus cult'. He decided that the body was sanctified.[18]

So Magnus' remains were moved into the Christ Church and held in a shrine above the altar. After that the 'Magnus cult' grew apace, and more miracles were reported. The two Magnus sagas – the long and the regular version – contain a lengthy catalogue of these so-called miracles. In truth, they very much resemble similar miraculous occurrences ascribed to other medieval saints and so were probably invented. This long list of the cures of lepers, the blind, the crippled and the mad was, if nothing else, an interesting selection of 12th-century afflictions.[19]

What set the 'Magnus cult' apart as a populist religious movement was its steadfast official opposition by the earldom. This continued even after Bishop William came to accept the sanctity of Earl Magnus' remains. Then Gunni, a farmer from Westray in Orkney's North Isles, claimed in the Christ Church that Magnus had appeared in a dream. He announced that the murdered earl had told him that his remains should be moved from Birsay to Kirkwall. Earl Paul who was at the service was clearly not impressed by this, but even he was unable to prevent the gathering momentum.[20]

It was little wonder. It was clear the 'Magnus cult' was evolving. It was now a borderline political movement as much as a religious one, with Earl Hákon and his son Earl Paul cast as the 'bad guys'. To those who subscribed to the cult, the two earls had angered God by murdering such a holy man, or by denying his obvious claim to sainthood. As described in the saga, this suggested that if someone could harness this cult, then they could use it to gain power within the earldom. They might even be able to overthrow Earl Paul. Unbeknown to the earl, somebody was already waiting in the wings preparing to do exactly that.[21]

PART FIVE
THE EARLDOM'S RENAISSANCE

SEVENTEEN

Kali Kolsson

FOR FIVE YEARS BETWEEN 1098 and 1103 the earldom of
Orkney didn't exist. This interregnum – the first in the earldom's
history – began when King Magnus 'Bare-legged' captured earls Erlend
and Paul. He then shipped them off to Norway, where they didn't even
last through the winter before dying in captivity. In their place the
Norwegian king made his young son Sigurd Magnusson as ruler of
the earldom. The child ruler governed the island while his father
carried out his expedition into the Hebrides and the Irish Sea – the one
that ended up in the Battle of the Menai Strait. There, Earl Erlend's
son Magnus preferred to chant psalms rather than to fight for the man
who'd imprisoned his father.[1]

During this five-year interregnum, a Norwegian couple gave birth
to a son. The father was Kolr (or Kol) Kalason, whose own father
Kali Sæbjarnarsson was a warrior and *skald*. He'd sailed with Magnus
'Bare-legged' on his great expedition, and was well respected: 'Kali was
a great sage, and dear to the king and skilled at poetry.' Kali, though,
had been mortally wounded while fighting at the king's side in the
Battle of the Menai Strait. He died the following winter. Afterwards,
King Magnus compensated Kali's family by offering the hand of
Gunnhildr (or Gunnhild) Erlendsdóttir to the fallen warrior's son Kol.
Gunnhild was the daughter of Earl Erlend of Orkney, and the elder
sister of his sons Erling and Magnus. After the two Orkney earls had
mysteriously died in captivity, King Magnus 'Bare-legged' assumed
the guardianship of the earl's offspring. So, the king was within his
rights to marry off his captive's daughter. Some lands in Orkney were
also given to Kol as part of the dowry.[2]

This was a step down for Gunnhild – the daughter of an earl
marrying a *lendmann* (the Norse equivalent of a 'baron'). Still, she
moved to Kol's estates in Agder, near the southern tip of Norway, and

around 1100, while young Sigurd was still presiding over her father's earldom, she had a son, who was named Kali after his grandfather, and then she also gave birth to a daughter called Ingriðr (or Ingirid).[3]

Kali grew up to be very intelligent – a trait shared by his father and grandfather – and was described as 'the most promising person, of medium height and well-formed, with strong limbs and light-brown hair; he was a very popular person, and more skilful than most other people.' He was popular and a real all-rounder – a Renaissance man before his time, if you will. That, at least, is what Kali later bragged. He was – it was claimed – equally skilled at chess, music and poetry as at skiing, rowing or archery. Although the grandson of an earl, his chances of inheriting any part of the earldom of Orkney seemed hopelessly remote. His mother, though, must have kept something of that dream alive in him.[4]

This remoteness was especially true as while he grew up in southern Norway, Hákon and then Paul maintained a tight hold over the Orkney earldom. So the boy put his claim to the earldom out of his mind. As a teenager, Kali Kolsson took part in trading voyages between Norway and England. While in port in Grimsby around 1115, he met a young man who went by the name of Gillekristr (or Gilchrist) from either Ireland or the Hebrides. It turned out his real name was Haraldr (or Harald) Gille, the illegitimate son of the late King Magnus 'Bare-legged'. Then, on a drinking spree in Bergen, he met the son of a *lendmann*, Jón Pétrsson from Sogn in western Norway. In both cases Kali got on very well with these other adventurous young men, forming bonds of friendship which would play a major part in his life.[5]

However, a lethal tavern brawl between their followers soured the relationship between Kali and Jón, and in 1129, the whole problem was set before King Sigurd 'Jerusalem-farer' for judgement. Sigurd was none other than the boy-earl his father Magnus 'Bare-legged' had placed in charge of Orkney and Shetland all those years before. He was the last remaining Magnusson prince, who'd ruled Norway since the death of their father in 1103. His nickname was earned when as a young man, Sigurd led a Norwegian contingent on a crusade to the Holy Land. Now in 1129, the 40-year-old Sigurd was showing signs of the mental degeneration which would contribute to his early death the following year. Still, Sigurd 'Jerusalem-farer' agreed to judge the case.[6]

After ruling that both sides had suffered equally, and so the effects cancelled each other out, Sigurd ordered that Jon should marry Kali's sister Ingirid to strengthen the links between the two sides. This way, the families were encouraged to support rather than feud with each other. Then, somewhat surprisingly, King Sigurd expressed an interest in Kali Kolsson's claim to a share of the earldom of Orkney. After some debate, Sigurd ruled that Kali should be given a half share of the earldom – the part that had once belonged to his grandfather Earl Erlend, and then his uncle Earl Magnus. However, Sigurd decided that Kali wasn't a suitable name for this new earl. Following the advice of Kali's mother Gunnhild, the king decreed that the new earl should henceforth be known as 'Rognvald Kali', after Rognvald Brúsason, 'because his mother Gunnhildr said that he had been the most effective of all the earls of the Orcadians.' Clearly King Sigurd agreed with her.[7]

Unfortunately for the new earl, King Sigurd died the following year, and so Rognvald Kali lost the backer he needed to claim his share of the earldom. The king's death was also followed by a period of war and turmoil in Norway. Three years before, Harald Gille – Kali's old friend from Grimsby – arrived in Sigurd's court. There, he convinced the king that he was his half-brother after submitting to an ordeal by fire – walking over red-hot ploughshares. Sigurd then agreed that Harald could succeed, but only after both Sigurd and his illegitimate son Magnus Sigurdsson had ruled first. After Sigurd's death in 1130, though, Harald reneged on the deal and pressed his own claim. As a result, at a *Thing* assembled to decide the issue, both Harald and Magnus received half of the kingdom. Almost inevitably, the two rulers fell out, and civil war known as the *Borgarkrigstida* broke out. It would continue intermittently for more than a century.[8]

In January 1135, King Magnus was captured by King Harald in Bergen, after Harald unexpectedly advanced on the city and stormed it. The 20-year-old Magnus was blinded, then castrated. Harald Gille seized the throne but was assassinated the following year by Sigurd 'Slembe', another royal contender, and almost certainly the same Sigurd 'the Fake' who'd been exiled from Orkney by Earl Harald a decade before. Sigurd, though, was outlawed after the murder, and when he returned to Norway in 1139 he was accused of regicide by the supporters of the infant Norwegian ruler King Inge Haraldsson. Sigurd 'the Fake' was then brutally tortured to death – a bad end for a bad troublemaker.

All this conflict did little to help Rognvald claim his share of the earldom. Harald Gille had renewed his friend Kali's claim in early 1134, and so envoys were sent to Earl Paul in Orkney requesting that he give up half of his earldom. However, Earl Paul was having none of it. So, Rognvald decided he had no other option. He had to seize the earldom for himself.[9]

Rognvald planned a two-pronged campaign. First, he approached Margaret, the daughter of Earl Hákon, and the sister of Earl Harald and Earl Paul. She and her Scottish husband the *mormaer* Maddaðr (or Maddad) of Atholl were willing to support Rognvald in return for a share of the earldom in the name of their son Erlendr (or Erlend) 'the Young'. Rognvald also approached Frakǫkk in Sutherland, who with her sister Helga had made the infamous poisoned shirt. There, Rognvald's envoys promised a share of the earldom to her grandson Ǫlvir 'Brawl' ('the Brawler') if he led a diversionary attack on Earl Paul. Once that was done, Rognvald, helped by his father, his friend Jón Pétrsson and his kinsman Sǫlmundr (or Solmund) Sigurdarsson, planned his own attack, launched across the West Sea.[10]

In the mid-summer of 1135, while Norway descended into turmoil, Rognvald sailed across the West Sea to Shetland. He had five or six longships, filled with his armed followers. It was a small enough force to take on the might of a whole earldom. Still, he was counting on Ǫlvir's diversion. Still, no word had been heard of it when he dropped anchor in Yell Sound in the north of Shetland. About 115 miles to the south-east, Earl Paul was at Westness in the Orkney island of Rousay, attending a feast. There, word reached him that Ǫlvir had been gathering troops in the Hebrides and planned to attack him. He also heard of Rognvald's arrival in Shetland. So he returned to Kirkwall and began gathering his men and longships.[11]

He planned to strike at Rognvald first, but when a dozen longships were reported passing through the Pentland Firth, he knew Ǫlvir 'Brawl' was the greater threat. So Paul led his longships to sea and waited for the enemy off Tankerness, a little to the east of Kirkwall. When Ǫlvir's fleet appeared off Mull Head on the coast of Deerness – the north-east corner of the Orkney mainland – Paul had his longships roped together to form a fighting platform.

In the bruising clash that followed, Qlvir's smaller Hebridean longships were at a disadvantage. This helped Earl Paul gradually to win the upper hand. However, Qlvir wasn't done. In the hand-to-hand fight on board Paul's fighting platform, Qlvir was close enough to throw a spear at Paul, which the earl skilfully deflected with his shield. Then, one of Paul's leading warriors Sveinn (or Svein) 'Breast-rope' threw a large rock at Qlvir, which was carried on the platform for just that purpose. The boulder struck Qlvir squarely in the chest and pitched him overboard.[12]

When Qlvir's men hauled him from the sea, they saw he'd been knocked unconscious. So, losing heart, they cut their grappling hooks and broke off the battle. When Qlvir came to, he begged his followers to return to the fight, but it was too late. What remained of his fleet was in full retreat, and there was no going back. After chasing them off towards Caithness, Paul returned to claim the five of Qlvir's longships which he'd captured off Mull Head. Then, barely pausing to reinforce his crews, Earl Paul set off north to deal with Rognvald.[13]

It was night, a day and a half after the sea battle, when Earl Paul entered Yell Sound with 12 well-manned longships. He quickly spotted Rognvald's ships there, but found them only lightly guarded. It seems Rognvald and most of his men were ashore. So Earl Paul quickly captured the longships, stranding his cursing rival on the beach. Rognvald challenged him to come ashore and fight, but Paul wisely didn't rise to the bait. Instead, he returned to Orkney with Rognvald's ships in tow. No doubt his men were laughing about it all the way home. So Rognvald's attempt at leading an invasion was left in tatters. To add insult to injury, that autumn Rognvald and his would-be invaders had to take a passage home to Norway in a menial merchant ship.[14]

The *Earls' Saga* neatly sums up his situation when it declares that 'their journey was thought rather shameful'. When Rognvald's father asked him how his attempt had fared, 'He says he thinks his journey did not achieve much and was rather unworthy'. His father Kol, though, argued that he'd made friends in Shetland, which was a useful start. Impressed by his father's sagacity, Rognvald asked for more words of wisdom. However, when Kol recommended trying again in the spring, using men supplied by Harald Gille, Rognvald said he didn't plan to make another attempt.[15]

That winter, Earl Paul felt reasonably content with his position. He'd seen off both threats to the earldom, and though both Rognvald and Qlvir might try again, he was confident he could deal with them. Just in case, though, he had a network of beacons built, starting on Fair Isle – midway between Orkney and Shetland – and then through Orkney's North Isles, so they could be seen in Kirkwall. It wasn't recorded, but undoubtedly similar beacons on South Ronaldsay, Hoy and the Orkney mainland covered the approaches from the south by way of the Pentland Firth.

Next time Rognvald appeared, Earl Paul would be ready. Then, fate intervened on behalf of Rognvald. That December, Earl Paul held a Yuletide feat in his estate in Orphir overlooking Scapa Flow, where 'there was a large drinking-hall.' Invited to it, as was the custom, were both his leading supporters and officials, and the earldom's leading *gödingar*, or landowners.[16]

At the gathering, an unexpected visitor arrived from Caithness. He was Sveinn (or Svein) Oláfsson, the son of Óláfr (or Ólaf) Hrolfsson, whom Paul had appointed as his steward in his estates at Duncansby. That was where his great-grandfather Thorfinn 'the Mighty' had maintained his Caithness Hall. A heartbroken Svein reported to Earl Paul that his father had been killed, burned alive in his hall, together with six of his men. The culprit was Qlvir 'Brawl', who'd been busily strengthening his position in Caithness following his defeat that summer off Deerness. Shortly afterwards, news reached Orphir that Svein's brother ValÞjófr (or Valthjof) had just drowned while on his way to the feast from the North Isles. So, while sparing the youngster this extra piece of devastating news, Earl Paul invited a distraught Svein Oláfsson to stay and spend Yule with him.

This quickly led to trouble. Svein Oláfsson was drinking at a table opposite Svein 'Breast-rope', who'd thrown the rock which ended the sea battle off Deerness that summer. They were playing a drinking game, and 'Breast-rope' accused the younger man of cheating by using a smaller drinking horn. This sort of thing was taken seriously by

Norse warriors, and it wasn't helped when the older man muttered a threat: 'Sveinn will be the death of Sveinn, and Sveinn shall be the death of Sveinn.' Later, when Earl Paul attended mass, Svein Ólafsson lay in wait for Svein 'Breast-rope' behind the ale barrels stored outside the drinking hall. Svein hid behind a large upright stone slab by the barrels, and swung his axe at 'Breast-rope's' forehead as he passed.

The earl's warrior staggered but didn't fall. Then, when he recovered his senses, he spotted a shadowy figure standing in the doorway of the drinking hall. Although gravely wounded, as Svein 'Breast-rope' fell, he threw his own axe at the man, then followed this up by pulling out his sword and cutting him down, the blow slicing through the man's head and shoulder. Svein thought the man was his assailant. It wasn't. In fact it was Jón, one of his own kinsman, who died instantly. Svein 'Breast-rope' was mortally wounded himself, though, and he died later that evening.[17]

By then Svein Ólafsson was long gone. Fearing retribution, he rode a horse cross-country over the Orphir hills, then took a boat across to the small island of Damsay in the Bay of Firth. He then found refuge with Bishop William on the island of Egilsay. Meanwhile, Earl Paul had quickly figured out that Svein was responsible for the death of his warrior but felt that there must have been a reason for the killing. Still, when Svein didn't return to explain himself, the earl branded Svein Ólafsson an outlaw. However, Svein sailed off to Tiree in the Hebrides, and so evaded justice. He changed his surname too, adopting his mother Asleif's first name, and becoming the son of Asleif. From that point on he became known as Svein Ásleifarson. The *Earls' Saga* would follow Svein's often tempestuous career, and he would become a sort of anti-hero – a true Viking – who would eventually help Rognvald win his earldom.[18]

In the following spring, 1136, Rognvald decided to make another attempt at capturing the earldom. By then, thanks to his father, he'd come up with a ploy designed to tip the scales in his favour. Kol Kalason advised his son that in the face of last year's invasion attempts most of Orkney had rallied behind Earl Paul. He proposed that the way to undermine this was to use the 'Magnus cult'. Rognvald was, after all, the nephew of the murdered earl. He needed to convince people he was the worthy successor to Earl Magnus. Kol knew that the bones of

Magnus had been moved from Christ Church in Birsay to the smaller St Ólaf's Church in Kirkwall.[19]

So he suggested Rognvald make a vow: 'I want you to promise that if he grants you his patrimony and his legacy, you will have a stone minster built in Kirkwall in the Orkneys, if you get that territory, than which there will be no more splendid one in the land, and dedicate it to the old Earl Magnús, your mother's brother.' It was a brilliant gambit. He would, in effect, make the 'Magnus cult' his own. By promising to build a great cathedral in his name, then not only would Magnus' route to sainthood be mapped out, but it would rally the people of Orkney behind the one man able to make this happen – Magnus' kinsman Rognvald. Then, Rognvald promised to provide the funds to make this 'stone minster' a reality. He also promised to move the episcopal seat there too to help ensure the bishop of Orkney would also back Rognvald's bid for the earldom.[20]

Rognvald now had a political campaign to win the peoples' 'hearts and minds'. Now all he needed was a military one. By the early summer of 1136, Rognvald had gathered 12 longships, one of which was supplied by King Harald Gille, as well as three supply *knorrs*, the archetypal Scandinavian trading vessel. Once again, Rognvald sailed across the West Sea to Shetland, which he used as his forward base. While there he recruited more men from his Shetland supporters and planned his invasion of Orkney. He was told about Earl Paul's warning beacons, so he asked his father to figure out a way to counter them.[21]

Eventually, they came up with a ruse. The first link in Earl Paul's beacon chain was the small island of Fair Isle, the midway point in the 50-mile gap between the southernmost tip of Shetland and the northernmost island in Orkney. If the attackers could neutralise the warning beacon there, they'd have a good chance of reaching Orkney before the alarm was raised.

Kol's ruse to trick Dagfinnr (or Dagfinn), the beacon-keeper on Fair Isle, was simple. He took several ships and sailed south until they were visible from the island. Their sails had only been raised to half-mast, so by keeping their position but gradually raising their sails, they'd create the illusion that the ships were drawing closer to Fair Isle. It worked a treat. Dagfinn lit the beacon fire, and soon the next one in the chain was lit in response, on the Orkney island of Rinansey (or North Ronaldsay), where 'Turf' Einar had once 'blood-eagled' a Norwegian prince. From there, the chain went on to Kirkwall to warn Earl Paul that Rognvald was coming. Instead, though, Kol's ships returned to Shetland. This venture was staged to decrease the readiness of Earl Paul's men – just like 'the boy who cried wolf' in the fables.[22]

In fact it all worked so well that Dagfinn and the North Ronaldsay beacon-keeper Þorsteinn (or Thorstein) came to blows when they met just outside Kirkwall during a meeting with Earl Paul. Each beacon-keeper accused the other of incompetence, and inevitably axes were drawn. Moments later Dagfinn was killed, and a fight erupted between Thorstein's kinsmen and those who sought justice for Dagfinn. Eventually, cooler heads prevailed and the men returned home until Earl Paul could adjudicate between the two sides.[23]

This false alarm and the death which resulted from it undermined the morale of Earl Paul's men. Presumably some of the *bøndr* or yeoman farmers who'd answered the summons to serve under Earl Paul's banner returned home to their farms. This made Rognvald's work easier. This, though, was only the first part in Kol's plan. His old friend Uni from Sogn in Norway rowed over from Shetland to Fair Isle with three young men. When he landed there he told the new beacon-keeper Eirík that they were fishermen who'd been robbed by Rognvald and his men. The youngsters, who Uni said were his sons, returned to their fishing, but the older man stayed behind in Fair Isle, using the excuse that he was looking after their catch.[24]

Over the next few weeks Uni gained Eirík's trust and eventually offered to keep watch for him during the day, when Uni had nothing else to do. Eirík readily agreed and never realised that Uni quietly soaked the warning beacon with sea water until it was saturated. Meanwhile Rognvald had been biding his time, waiting for a combination of favourable wind and tide. When Rognvald sailed past Fair Isle, Eirík the beacon-keeper couldn't get his warning beacon to light. By then, Uni had already made his escape, rowing out to join Rognvald's ships as they passed. Thanks to this, Rognvald's force reached Orkney without Earl Paul knowing about it. Rognvald established himself in Pierowall in Westray, one of Orkney's North Isles, and after some discussion the islanders agreed to support him. It seems that 'the vow' was working to sway public opinion in Rognvald's favour.[25]

When word of Rognvald's arrival reached Paul, it was too late to prevent his rival from establishing a foothold in Orkney. At that point the 'Magnus cult' stratagem bore even richer fruit. Bishop William – with one eye on the promised cathedral – proposed a short truce to allow him to mediate between the two sides. Both Paul and Rognvald agreed to this, each thinking they could use the time to strengthen their position and recruit more men. Rognvald's supporters used the time to spread the word about Rognvald's vow. Leaving these tasks to others, though, Earl Paul decided to take a few days off and go otter hunting with his good friend and kinsman Sigurd of Westness.[26]

Taking time off to go hunting might have relieved stress, but it also took Earl Paul away from his waiting army, which had gathered at Kirkwall. Still, he sailed to Sigurd's farm on the south side of the island of Hrólfsey (Rousay), close to the shore. Rousay lay ten miles to the north of Earl Paul's hall, midway between Kirkwall and Rognvald's base at Pierowall. As there was a truce, Paul didn't expect any trouble from Rognvald and his men, so he only took a small bodyguard with him, just enough for his own personal protection. When trouble came, though, it appeared from a completely unexpected direction.

While hiding out in the Hebrides, the outlaw Svein Ásleifarson – formerly Svein Ólafsson – had heard of the power struggle being waged in Orkney. He clearly saw an opportunity there and set about working on his own plan to take advantage of the situation. That spring, Svein sailed to the Scottish mainland and visited Earl Maddad and his wife Margaret in Atholl, in the Highlands. He then made his way to Caithness.[27]

There he talked with the *mormaer* Ottar of Thurso in Caithness. He was the brother of Frakǫkk, whose grandson Ólvir had murdered Svein's father at Duncansby on the north-eastern tip of Caithness. Ottar paid Svein reparations for the murder, and then agreed to support him in the scheme the outlaw was forming. In essence, it centred around the feelers Rognvald had put out two years before, when he'd sent envoys to Caithness and Atholl. In return for supporting the aspirations of Margaret's son Harald Maddadarson and Frakǫkk's nephew Erlend Haraldsson to a share of the earldom, Svein would 'deal' with Earl Paul, who'd ruffled so many family feathers.[28]

By keeping abreast of events in Orkney, Svein Ásleifarson was able to judge his moment. When it came, he left Caithness in a small trading ship, a *knorr*, with 30 men aboard and headed north. After crossing the Pentland Firth, he hugged the western coast of Orkney before rounding the top of the mainland and steering towards Rousay. It was early morning. Off the south side of the island, they spotted a group of men hunting along the shore of a headland. Svein had most of his men hide themselves in their sleeping sacks, so it looked as if the *knorr* only had a small crew of ten unarmed sailors. He hid too, in case he might be recognised. Drawing close, Svein's crewmen hailed the men, who were hunting otters, and learned that Earl Paul was part of the hunting party. The hunters encouraged the traders to anchor off Westness and sell their cargo to the earl's men. The earl himself was about to return there 'for the morning drink'.[29]

So, Svein did what they said – with a slight difference. Once out of sight he had his men drop anchor. Then he and his followers armed themselves and jumped ashore. The saga explains what happened:

> Sveinn then told them to anchor there where they could not be seen from the headland. Then Sveinn said that they should arm themselves and attack those earls' men they could find straightaway; and they did so. They killed nineteen men there, and six were felled by Sveinn. They captured Earl Páll with force and led him to the ship.[30]

This is exactly what they did, after secretly rowing ashore. In the short, sharp and brutal hacking match which followed they ended up 'killing nineteen men there, though six of Svein's men were killed too. They took Earl Paul by force and led him back to the boat.' With that, Svein and his men beat a hasty retreat with their noble captive as their prisoner. When a search party set out looking for the missing hunters, they came across the bodies but found no sign of Earl Paul. By then he was already on his way south, passing through Scapa Flow to reach the Pentland Firth, and then on down the eastern coast of Scotland towards their destination.[31]

Earl Paul was taken to his sister Margaret in Atholl. When Svein and his men arrived Paul was treated well – almost as a house guest. The two siblings discussed what should happen next. Earl Paul seemingly gave up his earldom and offered to join a monastery. Exactly what followed the discussion is unclear: 'But it was said by some, which is less fitting, that Margarét had advised Sveinn Ásleifarson to blind her brother Earl Páll and put him in prison, and afterwards she arranged for another man to cause his death there.' Svein denied it, but the saga says of Earl Paul, 'It is generally known that he never again came to the Orkneys'.[32]

With Earl Paul's mysterious disappearance, support for him crumbled away. Bishop William investigated the scene in Rousay and discovered the *knorr* had been seen heading south through Scapa Flow rather than north to Rognvald in Westray. So he felt Rognvald hadn't necessarily been involved in the abduction. It was only when Svein Ásleifarson returned to Orkney that the bishop learned what had happened to the missing earl.

Meanwhile, an increasing number of Orkney landowners swore allegiance to Rognvald. So, at a *Thing* held in Kirkwall, and encouraged by the bishop, Rognvald Kali was duly proclaimed as Orkney's new earl. It had been a hard and bloody road, but now, thanks to a little heavenly aid and the support of a growing religious movement, Rognvald had won his earldom. Now all he had to do was to make good on his vow. He had to make sure that the people of Orkney got the cathedral they'd been promised.[33]

EIGHTEEN

The Light in the North

I T WAS LATE 1136 when Rognvald Kali Kolsson became the earl of Orkney. Since Earl Paul was abducted that summer, he'd been touring the islands, meeting the *gödingar* of Orkney as well as the smaller farmers and landowners, and pressing his case. He realised he'd been a troublemaker, as Paul's reign as earl had largely been a time of peace and plenty, with a string of good harvests. His two invasions had ended all that, as had the supporting one by Qlvir of Caithness. As his father Kol had said, 'They won't soon give up that enmity which they have taken up against you, kinsman'. However, Rognvald and his leading followers had also been spreading his political message and his vow.[1]

Unlike him, the late Earl Magnus had been widely popular across Orkney and Shetland. So Rognvald stressed the point that he was the nephew of the saintly Earl Magnus, and as he shared his uncle's beliefs, he claimed that Magnus would have wanted Rognvald to succeed him. As his father had stressed: 'Seek support where there is plenty of it, that he should grant you the territory who owns it by right, namely the holy Earl Magnús, your mother's brother'. Essentially, Rognvald needed to win over the people who'd admired Magnus both for his honesty and his religious beliefs. Rognvald needed to show that he shared these traits. Certainly, the shadow of Earl Paul's disappearance still loomed over Rognvald, as many thought he'd been responsible. Rognvald needed to prove his innocence, as well as display his uncle's forbearance.[2]

Above all, Rognvald needed to harness the 'Magnus cult'. The head of the Church in Orkney, Bishop William, who was now referred to as 'the Old', had become convinced of the validity of the 'cult', and so Rognvald's support of it might buy him an extremely useful ally. Bishop William had been extremely sceptical of the movement. The turning point had come when he regained his lost sight, after which he 'promised that he would translate the holy relics of Earl Magnús whether Earl Páll liked it or not'.[3]

The bishop then convinced the ecclesiastical court of Archbishop Unwan of Bremen by his test of burning one of Magnus' knucklebones in consecrated fire, which was undamaged by the flames. The repeating of the test suggests Bishop William wanted to gather unequivocal scientific proof – or rather its medieval equivalent. After that, both Bishop William and Archbishop Unwan were convinced that Magnus was a worthy candidate for sainthood.[4]

Earl Magnus' bones were moved from the grave and carefully enshrined in a casket. This was then placed reverently above the altar in Christ Church in Birsay. Their next move was largely due to another intervention of the 'Magnus cult', when Bishop William decided to support the move of the 'holy relics' from Orphir to Kirkwall. 'After this, Bishop Vilhjálmr went east to Kirkwall with a renowned retinue and moved the holy relics of Earl Magnús there, and placed a casket over the high altar of the church that was there then.' Today, there's a pilgrimage path, the St Magnus Way, which follows part of this procession's supposed route.[5]

This was done before Rognvald undertook his invasion of Orkney, but dating errors in the saga make it hard to determine exactly when it happened. In Kirkwall, the remains of Earl Magnus were housed in St Ólaf's Church. It had been built during the reign of Earl Rognvald Brúsason around 1040 and was dedicated to his foster-father King Ólaf Haraldsson, who'd died at the Battle of Stiklestad ten years before. Ólaf was beatified by Bishop Grimketel in Nidaros in Norway in 1031, and so, at least for the people of the Nordic world, he became a saint. It was only in the 12th century that the Church imposed the more formal requirement of canonisation by the pope. St Ólaf's Church hasn't survived, save for an archway, but in the 11th and early 12th centuries it formed the religious heart of Kirkwall.[6]

Bishop William 'the Old' had been loyal to his secular patron Earl Paul, but during the weeks after the earl's abduction he appears to have switched his allegiance to Rognvald. He then became a key player in the drive to have Rognvald chosen as the new earl. It is more than likely the vow made by Rognvald to build a new cathedral in Kirkwall in honour of Magnus lay behind this political *volte-face*.

He might also have been influenced by the unexpected appearance of Svein Ásleifarson, who revealed that Rognvald had played no part in Earl Paul's disappearance. Svein and the bishop knew each other of old, and undoubtedly Svein was able to convince Bishop William that Earl Paul's half-sister Margaret, rather than Rognvald, had hired the outlawed Viking to abduct the earl. Surprisingly, Svein suffered no official censure for his actions.[7]

A final influencing factor was Rognvald's firm promise to move the holy seat of the bishopric to a purpose-built new residence in Kirkwall. That must have appealed to William, although the vow to build a new and impressive cathedral would have been the biggest draw, as it would greatly boost the importance of the bishopric. By then, Bishop William was an ardent advocate of the 'Magnus cult' and had endorsed the long and often bizarre list of miracles attributed to the 'martyred' earl.

So, in late 1136, in a mass which was almost certainly held in St Ólaf's Church, Magnus Erlendsson was 'beatified' – declared in a status of being blessed by God. This, together with the official approval of the list of miracles, was enough. Before the assembly, which no doubt included Earl Rognvald, Bishop William 'the Old' then officially sanctified the blessed Magnus. In that instant, the slain earl became Saint Magnus. The diocese of Orkney as well as the Orkney earldom now had its own saint. That done, it was time for Earl Rognvald to complete his part of the bargain. Now he had to build a magnificent cathedral, dedicated to the new saint, so his remains could be given a suitably impressive home.[8]

The *Earls' Saga* declares that towards the end of 1136, just weeks after Rognvald became the new earl, this great undertaking was begun. 'And not so much later the foundations of St Magnús' Church were laid and craftsmen were recruited and the work progressed well for three seasons, but less so four or five seasons from then'.[9] The site for this enormous building was chosen with care, and a view to the future. At the time, Kirkwall consisted of a dog-legged main thoroughfare, about 400 yards long, running from north to south.[10]

On its western side, an inlet of Kirkwall Bay called the Oyce (now the Peerie Sea) ran parallel to this street. This formed the town's harbour, which was all but cut off from Kirkwall Bay by a spit of land called the Ayre. Off the thoroughfare, small closes (or alleys) ran between the buildings to the shore, allowing fishermen or traders to unload anywhere along the town's waterfront. Most probably wooden wharves and piers lined the medieval harbour front – traces of some of these have been found.[11]

The main part of the town lay at the street's northern end (now called Bridge Street), near where it ended by the seashore to the east of the harbour. There, the buildings were clustered around the town's jewel, St Ólaf's Church, where St Magnus' remains were interred. To the street's southern end, past the end of the long shoreline which formed the harbour, the town's thoroughfare opened out onto communal pasture. In essence, the town hugged the harbour. This was appropriate, as it was maritime trade which had formed Kirkwall, and upon which it relied for its prosperity.[12]

It was here in December 1046, on the medieval harbour-front, that Earl Thorfinn and his men had leapt out of Earl Rognvald Brúsason's captured longship and cut down Rognvald's supporters, clustered on the waterfront to celebrate his return. Today, the town's quaint main thoroughfare – made up of Bridge Street and Albert Street – follows the course of this medieval one. The only major difference to the layout of the town is that the Oyce has retreated 100 yards or so to the west as the town expanded and land was reclaimed. Also, Kirkwall's busy harbour now sits at the main street's northern end, a little to the north of the spot where St Ólaf's Church once stood.[13]

Today, Orcadians stop and chat to friends in 'the street' while out shopping – a scene that almost certainly mirrors what happened in the same spot nine centuries before. Kirkwall has been described as 'Norway's best-preserved medieval town', and there's probably some truth in that Nordic link. Orkney, after all, celebrates Norwegian Constitution Day with a parade down 'the street', and it boasts a small Norwegian consulate. Even the name, Kirkwall, is a derivation of the Norse *Kirkjuvágr*, meaning 'a bay with a church on it'. The church this referred to, though, was St Ólaf's, rather than St Magnus'.[14]

Kirkwall lies at the southern end of a sheltered bay, where it is partly protected from cold winter northerlies by Orkney's scattering of northern isles. The closest of these, Hjálpandisey (or Shapinsay), is less than four miles away. Kirkwall is extremely well-placed for a voyage north to Shetland or eastwards across the West Sea to Norway. A little over a mile and a half to the south, across this narrow neck of land, Scapa Bay marked the northernmost part of Skalpaflói (now called Scapa Flow), which offered easy sea links to all of Orkney's southern isles. The isthmus there was also meant to serve as a portage point, allowing ships to be hauled between the Oyce and Scapa. Effectively, then, Kirkwall lay at the centre of Orkney, with good sea communications to the north and the south. By the 11th century, Kirkwall had become Orkney's largest trading port, bigger than Hafnarvágr (now Stromness) on the West Mainland. Still, this smaller settlement offered better sea links with Caithness.

By the 12th century the Orkney earls had already realised the strategic importance of Kirkwall, which effectively lay at the centre of the whole archipelago. The period of jointly ruled earldoms under the three sons of 'Turf' Einar, the sons of Sigurd 'the Stout', Thorfinn and Rognvald Brúsason, Paul and Erlend, and then Magnus and Hákon, delayed the centralisation of the earldom's centre of power. For much of this time, the seat of the earls varied between one part of the Orkney mainland to another. Occasionally, it was even sited on Caithness. From the time of Earl Rognvald Kali, though, and encouraged by his building of a cathedral, Kirkwall became the capital, not just of Orkney but of both the bishopric and the whole sprawling Orkney earldom.

The problem facing Earl Rognvald in late 1136 was exactly where in Kirkwall to build this great church. There was a lot to consider. The weight of such a building would be colossal, and so it needed a firm footing. It wasn't just the cathedral itself to consider, as if the diocese was going to be moved from Birsay to Kirkwall, then space needed to be set aside for the bishop's residence. The same applied to the earl's own residence as well as the attendant storehouses and other buildings the earldom needed to function, holding records, storing provisions and *skatt* payments in kind, and of course arms and armour.

By the end of the year, Rognvald had settled on the spot for his new church. It would be on a 'green field site' on the southern edge of town, just beyond the end of its main thoroughfare. As ecclesiastical tradition demanded, the building would face west, looking towards the harbour just a few score yards away. Behind it, and on its southern side, there was plenty of good and level land for any ecclesiastical buildings

Bishop William and his successors would require. Wherever it was, though, the new cathedral, once it was finished, would tower over the smaller buildings of the medieval town. It would be visible for miles to anyone approaching the town by either land or sea. In other words, if the cathedral was as impressive as Earl Rognvald wanted, it would be a real statement to the power and the piety of the earl and his earldom.[15]

Work began in earnest in 1137. Bishop William had been impressed by descriptions of the cathedral which had recently been completed at Durham. He'd also heard good reports of the abbey newly built in Dunfermline, which was earmarked to become the new burial place of the Scottish kings. So, accompanied by Kol Kalason, the bishop sailed south to the Firth of Forth so they could see Dunfermline Abbey for themselves. There, they succeeded in poaching the project's master mason, an artisan called Master Stephen. He was also able to supply a team of both Scottish and English craftsmen skilled in the numerous trades needed to turn Earl Rognvald's vision into reality.[16]

Rognvald left the design of the cathedral to his father, Kol, and Bishop William. It would be built in a cruciform and would be roughly half the size of Durham Cathedral, which had taken 40 years to complete and was much taller and grander than the building Kol and William envisaged. While Durham was unusually tall, the two-man 'project managers' in Orkney favoured a lower building, more in keeping with the abbey in Dunfermline. Both Durham and Dunfermline had been built in the Romanesque style introduced to Britain by the Normans just over half a century before. It drew inspiration from classical Roman and Greek architecture, and emphasised symmetry, simplicity, sturdiness and elegance. This style suited Kol and William perfectly. Equally important to Kol was the fact that it represented the height of architectural fashion. He wanted nothing but the best for his cathedral.

Their cathedral, with its cruciform shape, would obviously have four limbs, representing a Christian cross. These limbs came together beneath the cathedral's single tower. Inside, its chapel and nave were flanked by Romanesque arches and aisles.[17]

Above these were galleries and smaller arches, and windows to let in the light. So, the simple lines of the building were broken by these graceful arches. At their end, behind the high altar and the space for the choir, a semi-circular chapel and shrine housed the remains of St Magnus.

The whole structure would be covered with a simple wooden roof overlaid with flagstones. For the most part, the cathedral was built using warm yellow sandstone blocks. Interspersed among them, though, were blocks of red or white sandstone, to pick out features such as pillars and mouldings. The result was a pleasing and restrained three-tone effect. The building work progressed well, given the scale of the project, and the problems caused by the Orkney weather. In winter this could be extremely challenging and necessitated the temporary downing of tools during a season marked by Atlantic gales sweeping in over the islands.[18]

After eight years, the chapel had almost been completed to roof level, while the transepts were only slightly further behind. The nave was the last element to be built, and so by 1145 it was less advanced than the rest of the building. Today, this nave is twice the size of the original one. The more modest design approved by William and Kol only extended for three arches to the west of the crossing. This was later doubled to six. The nave, as well as the chapel and transepts, would be covered by elegant, vaulted ceilings. Work then began on the chapel roof, using triangular wooden trusses. Boarding was placed over these and then came the attachment of the sandstone flagstones.[19]

So, on 13 December 1146 – the tenth anniversary of the beatification of St Magnus – his remains were carried from St Ólaf's Church to the chapel of the new cathedral, the casket containing them the centrepiece of a grand procession. This was followed by the consecration of the cathedral and its dedication to St Magnus. Of course, there was a lot still to do. Kol retired in 1148 and returned to Norway, where he died four years later. Master Stephen left too, to work on a new abbey in England. Inevitably, work on the cathedral slowed. In fact, its building would outlast Earl Rognvald, his father Kol Kalason and Bishop William 'the Old'.[20]

In the end, St Magnus Cathedral would take over a century to be fully complete. It was also expanded, the nave was enlarged and beautiful circular windows were added, while the doorway was given an ornate front, decorated with statues of Magnus and Rognvald, among others. Finally, on 19 August 1255, St Magnus Cathedral was declared complete – or almost so – 118 years after the work began.

In fact, it took another five years to finish the work on the cathedral's single elegant tower.

Three years later, in late November 1263, King Hákon IV of Norway attended a mass in the newly completed St Magnus Cathedral. Just a few weeks before, Hákon and his sizeable Norse expeditionary force had suffered a reverse at the hands of the Scots at Largs, on the Firth of Clyde. So he returned to Orkney to regroup over the winter. Then, soon after the mass, his health began to deteriorate. It would be the last mass King Hákon ever attended. Despite visiting the remains of St Magnus in the cathedral, his condition steadily worsened. His death in the Bishop's Palace on 16 December, a mere stone's throw from the cathedral, marked the end of an era.[21]

It also marked the start of the closing chapters of the Norse earldom in Orkney. For those willing to see it, the decline began following the death of Earl Rognvald. Gradually, thanks to the inroads made by royal power in both Norway and Scotland, the influence and prestige of the earldom of Orkney began to decline. It was not without irony that as the beautiful cathedral slowly grew above the rooftops of Kirkwall, the status of the earldom shrank at a corresponding rate.

Still, visitors then and now are captivated by the building, and it has been called the 'Light in the North', still standing proudly on the spot chosen by Earl Rognvald almost nine centuries ago. Despite all that history could throw at it, this 'Light in the North' remains as a lasting reminder of the earldom of Orkney, and the islands' remarkable Norse past.

NINETEEN

Earl Rognvald the Crusader

E ARL ROGNVALD'S FIRST YEARS as earl weren't just dominated by the building of his great cathedral. He also attempted to strengthen his control over Orkney and Shetland, as well as Caithness and Sutherland. The cathedral, though, loomed large in his thoughts, as it was a hugely expensive project, and he was fast running out of money. He needed to raise funds, either through plunder or taxation. Wary of his reputation as an outsider in the aristocratic sphere he now moved in, he was keen to boost his own reputation in Norway and Scotland as well as his own lands. So he concentrated on being a just ruler, rather than an ambitious one.

This partly explains his reaction in early December 1139 when an unexpected visitor arrived to see him. At the time, Rognvald was at his farm estate at Knarston. It was situated above the west end of Scapa Beach, less than two miles from Kirkwall, with fine views over Scapa Flow. It also overlooked the portage point used to transport ships between Kirkwall Bay and Scapa Flow. The vessel anchored there, and the visitor – 'a very odd-looking man' – was rowed ashore, accompanied by more than a dozen retainers. He turned out to be Bishop Jon 'of Atholl', which probably meant he was John Scotus, the Bishop of St Andrews and Dunkeld, who held the episcopal seat encompassing part of the Highlands, a little north of Perth. The *Earls' Saga* describes him as wearing a blue cloak, with his hair tucked into a cap, and a full beard which was oddly shaved around the chin but flanked by a long, drooping moustache.[1]

The next day, Bishop Jon left to meet Bishop William in Egilsay, and a few days later they reappeared. Surprisingly, they were accompanied by Svein Ásleifarson. The Viking adventurer lived on the island of Gairsay, a few miles from the bishop's retreat on the neighbouring island of Egilsay. Then, in Rognvald's farm or hunting lodge in

Knarston, the trio laid out the reason for this mission. They revealed Svein's promise to Maddad and Margaret, that their young son would get half of the earldom in return for their support in dealing with Earl Paul. Faced with documentary proof, no doubt Rognvald couldn't really say no to the arrangement. So he agreed to the division of the earldom pending a meeting in Caithness in Lent to arrange the details.

This duly took place, and so, in *c.* 1139, the boy-earl Harald Maddadarson arrived in Orkney, accompanied by his new foster-father Þorbjǫrn (or Thorbjorn) 'Cleric'. Thorbjorn is described in the saga as brave, shrewd and forceful, and 'in general a great bully'.[2] Thorbjorn was also the grandson of Frakǫkk, one of the two accidental poisoners of her nephew Earl Harald about 13 years before. The arrangement reached with the bishops was that Earl Rognvald would rule the earldom as before, and even once Harald came of age, he'd continue to be the dominant partner in the joint earldom. Surprisingly, given Thorbjorn's kin Qlvir 'the Unruly' had killed Svein Ásleifarson's father, the two men got on well, and Thorbjorn ended up marrying Svein's sister Ingigerðr (or Ingigerd).[3]

By this time the building of the cathedral was coming on apace, but this was a hugely expensive project. There was a real risk the work might have to be halted, as by 1140 Rognvald was running out of money. His only sensible option – apart from going plundering somewhere – was to raise taxes. That, though, would have a huge impact on Rognvald's popularity within the earldom. Fortunately, his father Kol came up with an idea. He suggested a revision of the land tax system linked to the odal rights of the earldom's landowners. Careful negotiations with these landowners led to public support for an extra tax, levied specifically to pay for the building of St Magnus Cathedral. So work on it continued, but from that point on it wasn't just the earl who paid for the new church, but the people of Orkney contributed their share too. Rather than making this a burden and a potential source of discontent, Kol managed to portray this as a matter of pride within the Orkney community.[4]

As the cathedral was beginning to grow, Earl Rognvald's court was also becoming a centre for *skald*s and musicians, visiting nobles, clerics and other important visitors. Rognvald, who was an accomplished poet himself, was a wholehearted supporter and patron of the arts. It was said that his court in Orkney 'was a culture centre of some importance, where ecclesiastical and secular music and music-making had its natural share and place, and where the influences of the Celtic area and the south, especially England and France, blended with the Norse heritage'. As a result, the earldom of Orkney became the heart of a cultural Renaissance that both absorbed and influenced the rest of the Norse world, fusing its culture with that of the rest of Northern Europe.[5]

Life in the earldom, though, wasn't all about poetry and music. Earl Rognvald still ruled over a community which included violent men, including a number of active Viking raiders. One of these was the former outlaw and earl-abductor Svein Ásleifarson, who'd inherited his late father's estates on the small island of Gairsay, six miles north of Kirkwall. He also held lands in Caithness, near Duncansby, where his father had been a steward of the earldom's estates. As well as looking after his lands, Svein also made regular trading voyages and occasionally led Viking raids.

Svein still held a grudge against Qlvir 'the Unruly' who'd killed his father Ólaf Hrolfsson by burning him inside his hall in Caithness. He wanted vengeance both on Qlvir and his grandmother Frakǫkk, who'd incited her grandson's actions in the first place. So Svein approached Earl Rognvald and asked for his blessing to pursue his vendetta. Rognvald tried to argue that they weren't worth it, but Svein replied that 'There will always be harm from them as long as they live'. Rognvald was indebted to Svein for his help in winning his earldom, and so he duly lent Svein two well-manned ships, and, in the early summer of c. 1138, the vigilante set off to seek his revenge.[6]

He knew Qlvir's men were watching the roads in Caithness, while his target lay further south, near Helmsdale in Sutherland. So he headed south, keeping out of sight of the Caithness coast, and made landfall in Moray. He then travelled to Atholl, where he secured local guides from his friends the *mormaer* and his wife. He then led his raiders north, back across Moray and into the earldom's lands in Sutherland. The plan worked. As he avoided Qlvir's lookouts, he reached Helmsdale without the alarm being raised. On finding Frakǫkk's hall and farm, the attackers prepared for battle, as 'Sveinn and his men arrived on a certain slope behind Frakǫkk's farmstead'. They took Ǫlvir and his 60 followers completely by surprise: 'it straightaway turned into a fight and there was little resistance'.[7]

Ǫlvir and his men retreated into Frakǫkk's farmhouse, which was quickly surrounded by Svein's men. There was brutal slaughter there, as Svein's warriors stormed the building, and no quarter was given. Somehow, though, Ǫlvir managed to slip away and, after running down to the Helmsdale River, he followed it upstream into the mountains and escaped. Eventually, according to the saga, he would land up in the Hebrides and was never heard of again. No doubt Svein was hugely disappointed his father's killer had escaped, but he still had Frakǫkk to deal with. First, Svein's raiders looted the farm buildings. 'And after that they burned the farmsteads and all those people who were inside there'. That included Frakǫkk, much as her grandson had done to Svein Ásleifarson's father. Justice of sorts was finally done.[8]

Someone who wasn't in the house, though, was the earl's son Erlend Haraldsson, who remained a contender for a share of the earldom. In theory he'd as much a right to rule part of the earldom as Earl Rognvald did, or even as much as the boy-earl Harald Maddadarson. Before Svein returned to Orkney, he plundered in Sutherland – probably the lands owned by Frakǫkk's family. He then spent the summer raiding in Scotland before returning to Orkney in time for the autumn harvest. Then, after returning the two ships to Earl Rognvald, Svein spent the winter in his estate in Caithness.

The next year, in the spring of 1144, Svein and his followers led five longships in a Viking raid down Britain's west coast, venturing as far as Lundy Island in the Bristol Channel, some 700 miles away from Orkney. Svein even wrote a verse about it:

> Six farmsteads have been burned this morning, and the farmers robbed;
> Sveinn has arranged this. He did plenty for each one of them;
> he rents out charcoal there to the one who rents.[9]

Anyone who suggests Viking raids miraculously ceased in 1066 clearly hasn't heard of Svein Ásleifarson.

On his return, he learned that while he was away, Thorbjorn 'Cleric' had executed two of Svein's men who'd taken part in the burning of Frakǫkk's farmstead. This enraged Svein, but Thorbjorn was after all acting as Earl Rognvald's law enforcer in Caithness, and so there was little he could do. The following year, Svein and Thorbjorn went on a Viking raid together on the Hebrides, with five ships. They fell out over the division of the plunder, and as a result Thorbjorn divorced his wife Ingigerd, which achieved its purpose of insulting her brother Svein.[10]

The two men were now enemies, and so when Svein raided Thorbjorn's family lands in Caithness, the earl and his retainers arrived there to deal with the growing feud. Encouraged by Thorbjorn, and to stop the local pillaging, Rognvald laid siege to Svein's clifftop stronghold at Lambaborg, a few miles south of Duncansby. When supplies ran low, Svein made his escape down the cliffs and into a boat, then sailed off to seek sanctuary with King David of Scotland.[11]

Although Orkney was peaceful, across the West Sea in Norway the war-ravaged country was still in turmoil. The civil war which had followed the death of King Sigurd I 'the Crusader' in 1130 cost the life of Rognvald's good friend King Harald Gille in 1136, slain by the hand of the slimy assassin Sigurd 'the False' (or 'Slembe'). He'd been exiled from Orkney following the murder of Earl Paul's adviser Thorkell 'the Fosterer' seven years before. Now he claimed to be another long-lost son of King Magnus 'Bare-legged', but his own attempt to gain the throne ended in disaster. Sigurd died horribly in 1139, while being crushed, flayed and decapitated. You get the impression that Norway would have been a much more stable place if the country's kings had been a little more monogamous. Harald Gille was succeeded by a group of Norway's leading nobility, who ruled the country on behalf of the murdered king's two infant boys Sigurd 'Munn' and Magnus, until they came of age.[12]

In 1148 the 15-year-old Sigurd 'Munn' reached his majority and was crowned King Sigurd II of Norway. His brother Magnus died before he became old enough to rule. However, in 1148, Sigurd 'Munn' shared his crown with his half-brother Eystein, an older son of Harald Gille who'd arrived in Norway to claim his father's kingdom six years earlier. One of Sigurd's first acts as Norway's new ruler was to order Earl Rognvald of Orkney to visit him in Bergen.[13]

So Rognvald crossed the West Sea, accompanied by Earl Harald Maddadarson, now aged 14 and so old enough to assume his duties as an earl. While at court, they were joined by the Norwegian *lendman* Eindriði (or Eindridi) 'the Young', a kinsman of Rognvald who'd just returned from the Holy Land. He told tales of his service in the Byzantine 'Varangian Guard' – the elite corps established by Harald 'Hardrada' – and of his campaigning in Outremer, the Crusader States.[14]

While in court, he urged Earl Rognvald to consider going on a crusade himself, as it would bring him considerable glory, honour and renown. Others offered their support, and Eindridi said he'd be the earl's guide. So, it was agreed; they'd all go on crusade after two winters had passed. This great adventure would begin in Orkney. Before leaving court, Rognvald ordered a *drakkar* to be built, a longship worthy of such a great venture. Despite being shipwrecked in Shetland on his return voyage, Rognvald survived the experience, and made it safely home. Back in Orkney, Rognvald revealed his plans and, despite his age, Bishop William offered to come along as a diplomat and interpreter. So it was that in the spring of 1150, Earl Rognvald entrusted the earldom to the 16-year-old Earl Harald Maddadarson and then crossed over to Bergen to take charge of his new flagship.

Built there by the port's leading shipwright, the earl's new *drakkar* or dragon ship was breathtaking. 'The ship that Jón had made for the earl was also there by the quayside; it had thirty-five rowing spaces and was meticulously fashioned and fully decorated and all the stems and weathervanes were covered in gold, and it was widely decorated elsewhere; the ship was the greatest treasure of its kind'. Earl Rognvald named his new flagship the *Sea Elk*. Their departure for Orkney and the start of the crusade was delayed for a few weeks by Eindridi, whose own new ship was still being completed. Eventually he joined them in a *drakkar* every bit as magnificent as Rognvald's one, only more gaudily painted. This demonstration of hubris did little to endear Eindridi to the earl.[15]

The crusaders' longships became separated during the voyage to Orkney, as Eindridi sped ahead of the rest. When Rognvald arrived there was no sign of their crusading guide. It then turned out that his elegant dragon ship had been wrecked in Shetland. Eindridi promised to join Rognvald the next spring and returned home to commission a replacement. So the would-be crusaders overwintered in Orkney, where they entertained themselves with brawling and falling out 'about trade and about women, and many things happened'. In the spring of 1151, when Eindridi rejoined them with a much less ostentatious longship, Rognvald finally gave the order to set sail. The great crusading adventure was finally under way.[16]

They sailed down the east coast of the British Isles before passing through the English Channel and then on to Frankia (now France). They then hugged the Atlantic coast of France and Spain, putting in for supplies whenever they needed. So far it had been a leisurely but uneventful cruise. One of these port visits was in Galicia in north-east Spain, which (although the saga doesn't say) was possibly La Coruña or Ferrol. The Norse fleet arrived in early December 1151, and so Rognvald decided to remain there for the Christmas festivities. The locals, though, were reluctant to trade as they were short of supplies because of pillaging raids by local bandits. These brigands were led by a foreigner called Guðifreyr (or Godfrey), who'd taken over a nearby castle. The bandits now used it as their base to terrorise the region. On hearing the story, Earl Rognvald offered to help the locals in exchange for the supplies he needed.[17]

He sent his Norwegian kinsman Erlingr (or Erling) 'Skakke' (or 'the Lopsided') to spy out the place, and this skilled and intelligent Norse chieftain returned to report that he'd found a weakness in the defences. The mortar used in the walls looked weak and crumbly, and Erling thought that if they burned it the walls might collapse. This would cause a breach which they could then storm. Bishop William, though, stopped them from attacking the castle until after the impending Christmas celebration. When it was over, Rognvald's Norsemen appeared under cover of darkness and piled wood against sections of the castle walls. These were then set alight. It worked perfectly, and soon large breaches appeared in the castle walls. The Norsemen stormed the castle, and Rognvald, supported by a young Norse warrior called Sigmundr (Sigmund) 'Hook', the stepson of Svein Ásleifarson, spearheaded the assault.[18]

A good many of the bandits were killed in the storming, and many others surrendered, but there was no sign of the bandit leader Godfrey. The *Earls' Saga* points the finger at Eindridi, who it claims received a substantial bribe and so let the bandit leader escape. Still, they'd achieved their goal, and on their return to port they were given all the provisions they needed. No doubt they were also cheered by the locals as they left. The voyage continued, passing down the coast of the kingdom of Portugal, which at this time only extended as far south as Lisbon. Everything beyond that was the territory of the Muslim Almoravid Empire, which meant that for the crusaders, the locals were fair game. So as the saga puts it, 'They raided widely in heathen Spain and got a lot of wealth there'.[19]

So far, the crusade was little more than an exotic Viking raid. Rognvald's fleet of 15 Norse longships then turned towards the southeast to enter the Strait of Gibraltar. Whilst there the fleet was split up in a storm. After it passed, Rognvald discovered that Eindridi had gone, having sailed on towards the southern coast of France with six longships, without waiting for Rognvald and the others. The problem of deciding what to do with their perfidious young crusading guide could wait for the moment, and so in the spring of 1152 Rognvald led his remaining ships up the Spanish coast, looting the Moorish Amoravid lands as they went. Eventually, they reached the Christian kingdom of Aragon, and then, past it, they arrived off the French coast.

There, they turned into the mouth of the River Aude, and rowing a few miles upstream, Rognvald and his men reached the city of Narbonne. There they learned that the Viscount Aimery of Narbonne, the largely independent ruler of the city state, had died fighting the Moors almost 20 years before. His lands and title had then passed to his infant daughter Ermengard. By the time Rognvald arrived, Ermengard, Viscountess of Narbonne was in her early twenties, and although she'd been forcibly married a decade before, her husband Bernard of Anduze seems to have been more occupied fighting the Moors than living with his younger wife.[20]

The Norsemen were welcomed by Ermengard, and a great banquet was held in their honour. During it, Ermengard served Rognvald's wine herself, pouring it into a golden goblet. Rognvald was smitten. He spent a lot of time with her and even composed love poems celebrating her charms. The saga claims that the locals even encouraged Rognvald to settle down with Ermengard and help her rule the city. No doubt Bishop William was on hand, though, to remind him that he had other commitments. He also probably noted that the viscountess was already married. So, after a pleasant stay, this holiday romance came to an end. The Norse crusaders left Narbonne and continued their journey, although Rognvald promised to visit her on his way back from the Holy Land. However, he never did.

After leaving Narbonne, Rognvald abandoned any notion of finding the slippery Eindridi, who it was said had reached Marseilles. Instead, Rognvald cut across the Western Mediterranean, skirting Sardinia to reach the Sicilian Channel. It lay between the Norman kingdom of Sicily and the North African shore, which was in Muslim hands. It now formed part of the Almohad Caliphate, a new Muslim dynasty which was busily taking over the lands ruled by their predecessors, the Almoravids. While close to this shore of Serkland (Africa), they ran into a thick sea mist. When it lifted the Norsemen sighted two ships. Given where they were, the chance was these were Arab vessels – therefore legitimate prey for Viking crusaders.[21]

The ships they spotted were Muslim *shalandiyyat*, the Arabic version of the Byzantine *dromōns* – powerful war galleys which were equally efficient under oars or sail. With nine longships, these should be easy prey, so Rognvald decided to attack them. The Arab ships seemed to be becalmed, but a light breeze sprang up and one of them raised sail and headed away from the approaching longships. The remaining *shalandī* was large, much higher-sided than the Norse longships, so attacking it wouldn't be easy. Erling 'the Lopsided' suggested that by coming close alongside, 'it might be, I think, that most of their projectiles would go beyond our ships if we lie side-by-side with it'. That decided, the earl briefed his captains and then gave the order to attack.[22]

Then 'Earl Rǫgnvaldr laid his ship alongside the dromond at the back on the starboard side, and Erlingr did the same on the port side, Jón and Áslákar at the front on each side, and the others amidships on both sides, and they surrounded it with all the ships'. The Norsemen grappled their enemy, and the Arabs countered by pouring boiling pitch over the sides of their ship. As Erling had anticipated, though, most of this fell outboard of the Norsemen huddling under the Arab ship's overhang. The sides of the *shalandī* were too high to board, so Rognvald ordered his men to use their axes to hack their way into the enemy's hull. They boarded through the lower deck and fought their way upwards through the *shalandī*. Once Rognvald and Erling's men joined forces the Arabs fell back, retreating towards the bow.[23]

The Arab crew were no match for the Viking-trained warriors, and eventually most of them were cut down, save for a distinctive, well-dressed nobleman, who became Rognvald's prisoner. Inevitably, Rognvald composed a poem to celebrate the victory:

> Erlingr, the renowned spear-tree, went, threateningly strong,
> towards the dromond with success and victory,
> where our standards were reddened.
> We piled up the heroes of the black men,
> and blood was widely taken from the people;
> valiant men reddened sharp swords.[24]

Rognvald was hoping the news would impress the Viscountess Ermengard. They plundered the *shalandī*, then set it on fire. This appalled their prisoner and surprised the Norsemen, until they saw 'what looked like a flaming wave running into the sea.' It seems Rognvald's men hadn't searched the Arab ship thoroughly enough for hidden caches of gold. Afterwards, the somewhat deflated Norsemen put into a small North African port. This was probably somewhere close to Tripoli, where they bought supplies and set their prisoner ashore. He confessed as they parted that he'd indeed been carrying gold and silver, and that, as a local ruler, he'd spare the Norsemen, but in return he never wanted to see them again.[25]

After that, Rognvald's crusaders passed into the Eastern Mediterranean. Then, after pausing in Crete to take on supplies and no doubt spruce up their longships, they sailed the final leg to their destination – the Holy Land. They disembarked in Acre, which at the time formed part of the crusading kingdom of Jerusalem, the leading state in Outremer. There, though, they were affected by the disease ravaging the city, and some of the Norse contingent died. So Rognvald led the rest of his men inland to escape the disease, and of course to tick all the key pilgrim boxes.[26]

Still, this comes over as more of a sightseeing tour than a real pilgrimage. It included a visit to Jerusalem, where no doubt Earl Rognvald had an audience with King Baldwin, and where the Christian ruler was busily planning a fresh campaign against the Saracens. Rognvald and his men then bathed in the holy waters of the River Jordan. His brief pilgrimage complete, Rognvald returned to Acre, and then in mid-summer he set sail for Constantinople (now Istanbul), the capital of the Byzantine Empire. For Rognvald, it seems, crusading and pilgrimage were more about the journey than the destination. No doubt Outremer in mid-summer was a little too hot for Norse warriors used to a cooler, more northern climate.

They reached Constantinople in the autumn of 1152, where Rognvald was welcomed by the Byzantine Emperor Manuel I 'the Great'. There, some of Rognvald's 'crusaders' left the expedition to join the emperor's Varangian Guard. They might have been bartered to the emperor by Rognvald, along with some of his longships including the earl's *drakkar*, to raise funds for the return leg of the pilgrimage, which Rognvald now planned to make overland rather than by sea. They also encountered Eindridi 'the Younger' there, but Rognvald had little time for him, particularly as it appeared he'd been disparaging the Orkney earl in the Byzantine court. Still, Rognvald and his men remained in Constantinople until the spring, when they sailed on around Greece to the Adriatic Sea.[27]

There, at the Italian port of Bari or Brindisi in Apulia they went ashore, and Rognvald exchanged his last remaining longships for horses. From there they rode north to Rome, where Rognvald completed his pilgrimage by being granted an audience with Pope Eugenius III. Then it was off across the Alps on horseback, across the Germanic Holy Roman Empire and so on to Denmark. Rognvald and his remaining men reached Norway by the summer of 1153, where no doubt the 'crusaders' celebrated their safe return. Then they went their separate ways. A few weeks later, Earl Rognvald, Bishop William and their companions arrived back in Orkney. There, these crusading exploits quickly became the stuff of legend. They'd displayed their devoutness while combining their crusade with some old-fashioned Viking raiding. As the saga writer puts it, 'This was a famous journey, and everyone was considered the better who had done it.' That, for a Norse earl of Orkney, was what it was all about.[28]

PART SIX
THE CRUMBLING EARLDOM

TWENTY

The War of the Three Earls

D URING THE TWO YEARS Earl Rognvald was away, the earldom had been left in the hands of the young Earl Harald Maddadarson. However, when Rognvald returned there was no sign of his young kinsman. Instead, the rumours he'd heard in Norway were correct, and the entire earldom was now ruled by another earl altogether. It seemed that Earl Rognvald had returned in the middle of a power struggle, one that had been raging ever since he'd left. Clearly Rognvald wasn't going to put up with this and wished to restore the *status quo*. What had started as a two-sided civil war was about to evolve into 'the War of the Three Earls'.[1]

The trouble began in the early summer of 1151, just weeks after Rognvald's departure. It was instigated by Erlendr (or Erlend) Haraldsson, the son of the late Earl Harald 'Smooth-talking'. Erlend's father had died 23 years before when he'd worn the poison-smeared shirt made by his mother – his father's mistress Helga, and her sister Frakǫkk. After this accidental murder, Harald's brother Earl Paul banished the poisoners from Orkney. His punishment could have been more draconian, but frankly they'd done him a service, as the relationship between the two brothers had been at breaking point.[2]

The two women had gone to Caithness, accompanied by Earl Harald 'Smooth-talking's' four-year-old son Erlend. Two decades later, Erlend planned to return to Orkney and claim what he saw as his birthright. Arguably, he had a better claim to the earldom than either Earl Rognvald or the young Earl Harald Maddadarson. After all, his father had been an Orkney earl, which neither of the two current rulers could claim. Still, he bided his time until Earl Rognvald sailed off to the Holy Land.

His first move was to claim half of Caithness from the Scottish king David I. Again, his grounds were that his father Earl Harald had held half the *mormaership* of Caithness before him, a Scottish title he'd shared with his brother Earl Paul. King David, no doubt influenced by the principle that a divided enemy was better than a united one, was happy to oblige. So, Erlend would share Caithness and Sutherland with Earl Harald Maddadarson. That allowed Erlend to turn Caithness into his powerbase, drawing on his family's strong connections there. Then, heeding the advice of his foster-father and chief adviser, the Hebridean warlord Anakol, Erlend began raising troops. To him, Caithness was just a springboard for his bid for the Orkney earldom.[3]

Meanwhile, Earl Harald Maddadarson had been having a tough time. His father Mormaer Maddad had died and was succeeded to the Atholl title by Harald's younger brother Malcolm. Unwelcome at home, as she didn't get on with her younger son, the new *mormaer* Malcolm, Harald's widowed mother Margaret travelled north to move in with her eldest son. Margaret, the daughter of the saint-killer Earl Hákon, was a beautiful and vivacious woman for her age. Soon, Harald learned that his widowed mother Margaret had taken a lover, Gunni Óláfsson, the brother of her old accomplice Svein Ásleifarson. Harald wasn't impressed, especially when he learned his mother was now pregnant. So he declared Gunni an outlaw and had him banished from the earldom. This of course didn't please either his mother or Svein Ásleifarson. Still, at the time, Harald had a bigger problem to worry about.[4]

In the summer of 1151, not long after Earl Rognvald had left, King Eystein II arrived in Orkney on his way to lead a Viking raid down the east coast of Scotland. He ruled Norway jointly but not always peaceably with his half-brothers Sigurd 'Munn' and Inge 'the Hunchback'. Learning that Earl Harald Maddadarson was in Caithness, Eystein surprised the earl there in the town of Thurso, where the earls maintained a hall. He took Earl Harald captive and only agreed to release him if Harald swore an oath of fealty and paid the king a ransom of three gold marks.[5]

As if that wasn't enough, on his return to Norway King Eystein decided to grant Erlend Haraldsson half of the Orkney earldom. Unwilling to take Rognvald's portion, Eystein stripped Harald of his half and gave it to Erlend. Naturally Harald had no intention of complying. If Erlend wanted the earldom, he'd have to fight for it.[6]

Meanwhile, the banishment of his brother Gunni encouraged Svein Ásleifarson to ally himself with Erlend Haraldsson. This alliance was quite a *volte-face*, as it had been Svein who'd been responsible for burning Erlend's great-aunt Frakǫkk to death. From his base in eastern Caithness, Svein began launching Viking raids on Harald's lands in Orkney. The aim was to sow unrest among Harald's followers and prepare the way for Earl Erlend's invasion. Sure enough, in late September 1152, Earl Erlend Haraldsson led a small fleet of ships to Orkney and anchored them off Cairston, near where the small, picturesque town of Stromness now stands.[7]

Earl Harald was aboard a ship there, and when he saw the longships approach he rowed ashore, and he and his men took refuge by running 'into a castle which was there then'. This might have been the ruins of an Iron Age broch near Cairston, or possibly at the nearby farm of Howe. These old ruins soon became a battleground. 'Earl Erlendr and Sveinn ran from their ships after Earl Haraldr and his men went to the castle and attacked them during the day with both fire and weapons. They defended themselves valiantly and the dark of night intervened. Many men on both sides were wounded there, and Earl Haraldr would have had to submit if the attack had lasted any longer.'[8]

In the morning, local *gödingar* placed themselves between the two factions and encouraged the earls to make peace. As a result, Harald bowed to the inevitable and surrendered his half of the earldom to Erlend. He then sailed south to Scotland, promising not to return. Meanwhile, at an assembly, the leading people of Orkney swore oaths of loyalty to Earl Erlend, on the agreement that Earl Rognvald would return to ratify the arrangement and to reassume control of his half of the earldom.[9]

Harald, though, had no intention of keeping his promise. In January 1153 he sailed to Stromness and went ashore with 20 men. Their destination was Firth, midway between Kirkwall and Stromness, where Earl Erlend was visiting friends. It was only seven miles away, but halfway there Harald and his raiders were caught in a blizzard. Orkney isn't prone to snow – something to do with the sea salt-laden air – so blizzards are rare, but not unknown. They were forced to seek shelter in Orkahaugr, the large earth-clad Neolithic tomb now called Maeshowe.[10]

Somehow they found a way inside, then hunkered down to wait for the blizzard to pass. It was a long wait, as they had to spend the night in the dark, cavern-like tomb, huddling there beside the spirits of the dead. It can't have been pleasant, as two of the raiders lost their sanity that night. When the blizzard passed and they finally got moving again, the demented pair delayed their slow and stumbling progress. Still, they eventually reached the farmstead before dawn the following morning. After surrounding it they launched their surprise attack while it was still dark. Two of Earl Erlend's men were killed in the raid and four more were captured, but the earl himself wasn't there. It turned out he'd spent the night aboard his longship, anchored just offshore.[11]

Afterwards, Harald and his men returned to Caithness for the winter, and there was a lull in the feuding. As a precaution, though, Earl Erlend took to sleeping aboard his longship at night surrounded by his bodyguard. In February, Anakol, the Hebridean foster-father of Erlend, led a raid on Lambaborg, the old coastal stronghold where the prisoners captured in the raid on Firth were held. One of them was Anakol's brother Arnfinn, and while Anakol couldn't rescue him, he took Eirík, one of Earl Harald's men, and a prisoner exchange was arranged. The conflict between Earl Erlend and Earl Harald, however, was clearly far from over.[12]

In the spring, Harald Maddadarson bypassed Orkney and sailed up to Shetland to find his mother. The widow Margaret had now eloped with Erlend 'the Younger', a Shetlander, who'd then had the temerity to ask Harald for permission to marry the young earl's mother. Not only had Harald refused, but he set off north to kill Erlend and bring his troublesome mother back home. When he arrived, Harald found the pair had taken refuge in the old broch at Mousa, on a little island 11 miles south of the island's main town of Lerwick. Together with some supporters they'd barricaded themselves inside the Iron Age broch, whose high circular stone walls were nigh-on impregnable. So negotiations began, and by the end of it Harald had given his approval of the marriage in return for Erlend's help in recovering the earldom.[13]

After that, Harald sailed to Norway to solicit support from the three Haraldsson kings, Eystein, Inge and Sigurd. Eystein of course would be a challenge, as he had already stripped Harald of his share of the earldom. Harald was still there when Earl Rognvald arrived in

Orkney. He'd heard rumours of the coup by Erlend Haraldsson and of the subsequent war between him and Earl Harald Maddadarson. So at least the returning crusader was forewarned. Rognvald realised that his own half of the earldom was secure. That at least would save him fighting for it. Beyond that, he decided to see how things played out. Rognvald arrived back in Orkney that December, and after the Christmas festivities he met Erlend, and the two earls seemingly hatched a deal.

Both Earl Rognvald and Earl Erlend would continue to rule their halves of the earldom. They would also cooperate for mutual defence and oppose Harald Maddadarson if he returned. Pragmatically, Rognvald was accepting the current situation, or at least he appeared to be. Earl Erlend thought that Earl Harald Maddadarson would begin any invasion across the West Sea by landing in Shetland, much as Rognvald had 18 years before. So he and Svein Ásleifarson went north to defend the archipelago. For his part Rognvald went to Caithness in case Harald tried to use his contacts to raise an army there.

In the summer of 1154, Harald sailed from Norway with seven longships. A storm dispersed his fleet and three of them were driven into Shetland, where they were captured. Harald reached Orkney with the rest, where he discovered that Rognvald was in Caithness. So Harald sailed there in the hope that he could strike his own deal. When word reached him that Harald had landed in Caithness, Rognvald set off to intercept him. When Rognvald and Harald met, though, they decided to join forces and turn against Erlend instead.[14]

Svein Ásleifarson's spies soon learned of this new deal, and so in winter, when the two earls crossed the Pentland Firth to invade Orkney, Earl Erlend and Svein kept out of their way. However, when Svein learned that Rognvald and Harald's fleet of 14 longships was anchored in Scapa Bay, off Rognvald's farm or hunting lodge at Knarston, they decided to launch a surprise attack. Rognvald was ashore when Erlend and Svein attacked, their approach through Scapa Flow masked by icy rain and sleet. Harald was aboard his longship, though, and his men, taken unawares, had the worst of the fight. In the end Harald had to swim for the shore just as his opponents captured the last of his longships.[15]

When the victors came knocking on the door of Knarston, the quick-thinking steward claimed his master was off hunting wildfowl and the men withdrew, leaving Rognvald free to escape. Eventually he and Harald made it to safety in Caithness. Just before Christmas, though, they were back. Earl Erlend was on Damsay, the little island in the Bay of Firth which Svein Ásleifarson had fled to years before after murdering Svein 'Breast-rope'. Rognvald learned of this, and on 21 December they carried out a surprise attack on Erlend's longship, where the earl was sleeping off a drunken night's revelry.[16]

He didn't even stir when the ship was boarded, the crew taken prisoner, and the still-groggy earl bundled over the side and quietly spirited away in a small boat. After the abduction, the earl's men launched a large-scale search. Two days later, a spear shaft was spotted sticking out of a mound of seaweed on the shore of the Bay of Firth. Beneath the seaweed pile was the body of Earl Erlend Haraldsson, his chest transfixed by the spear.[17]

Days later, Earl Rognvald offered Svein Ásleifarson a Yuletide gift of forgiveness. In return, Svein was pardoned for his part in the war after paying a token reparation of a gold mark to each of the remaining earls, as well as giving up half his land and his best longship. After Christmas, Earl Erlend Haraldsson was buried in the unfinished St Magnus Cathedral, and peace seemed to have been restored. However, enmity still lurked beneath the surface. Earl Harald Maddadarson and Svein soon argued, and Earl Harald then raided Svein's hall in Gairsay when Svein was away hunting hares. As a result, Svein fled in a longship, taking his wives and daughters with him. Harald gave chase, and the two longships raced northwards through Orkney's North Isles.[18]

Svein hid his longship in a 'sea cave' until the pursuers had sailed past. It has been suggested that this cave was possibly on the small islet of Muckle Green Holm, a few miles to the north, which still has places big enough to hide a sizeable vessel in. When he heard of this latest incident, Rognvald insisted on a truce and a patching up of the quarrel. So, regardless of how fraught the meeting was, in May 1155 the three men met, and after a lengthy and no doubt voluble discussion their differences were patched up. Earl Harald Maddadarson and Svein Ásleifarson shook hands, and everything was resolved. After so much violence and death, 'The War of the Three Earls' was finally over.[19]

However, in the Norse earldom danger was never far away. Three years later, in the summer of 1158, tragedy would strike once more. It all stemmed from an incident almost five years earlier in late 1153, when Rognvald and Harald met in Caithness and formed their alliance during the celebrations surrounding the wedding of Rognvald's daughter. While the two earls were talking together in Thurso, Thorbjorn 'Cleric' arrived at the earl's hall with a large group of armed men. Thorbjorn was loyal to his foster-son Earl Harald. Still, like anything in the earldom's politics, it was a complicated relationship, as Thorbjorn also loathed Harald's ally Svein Ásleifarson, who'd burned his kinswoman Frakǫkk to death. This evening, Thorbjorn thought that Harald had been captured by Rognvald, and acted accordingly.[20]

In the skirmish that followed, Thorbjorn and his men killed 13 of Rognvald's bodyguard, and the earl himself, who joined in the fight, took a cut to the face before the attackers were repulsed. In the end the mistake was recognised, everything was smoothed over and peace was restored. Later, though, over the winter, a brawl in a Kirkwall alehouse between Thorbjorn and one of Rognvald's followers Thorarin 'Bag-nose' led to the death of the Earl's retainer. As a result, Thorbjorn was branded an outlaw and was banished from the earldom. He fled to Scotland, but he still maintained his strong contacts in Caithness, and he used their help to plot his revenge.[21]

In August 1158, as was their new-found custom since the end of the civil war, Earl Rognvald and Earl Harald Maddadarson crossed over to Caithness to hunt the red deer which were found in the region's wilder hinterland. When they arrived in their hall in Thurso, they were warned that Thorbjorn 'Cleric' had returned to Caithness and was gathering supporters there. His intention, it seemed, was to ambush the earls' hunting party and to kill Earl Rognvald. The earl wasn't too worried, though, and instead of hunting deer the next day, the two earls left Thurso with a hundred warriors with them, plus another 20 armed horsemen to act as scouts. The nature of the hunt had changed. Instead of red deer, the earls were now hunting rebels.[22]

The first day this armed posse found nothing, and they probably spent the night somewhere near Reay, on the coast. The next day, 20 August, they moved down the valley of the Forss Water, a stream between Reay and Thurso, which ran south towards the boggy flow country. Presumably – although the saga doesn't say – this was an area where either Thorbjorn had been spotted, or it was an area owned by his Caithness kinsmen. Then as now, the land there was flat, with a few scattered farms. Five miles south-east of Thurso, they reached the farmstead of Forsie, which was owned by a farmer called Hallvard. When they approached, Hallvard and his farmhands were busy building a haystack. The farmer immediately began acting suspiciously, calling out to the posse, loudly greeting the earls by name in a voice designed to carry. It was almost as if he was warning someone.

Sure enough, Thorbjorn 'Cleric' and his men had been hiding in the farmhouse. Thanks to Hallvard they had time to grab their armour and weapons and prepare themselves. A slab of stone covering a hidden back door to the farmhouse was slid aside, and Thorbjorn and his gang crept outside. They then hid themselves behind the walled lane leading to the farmstead's door. While Harald questioned the farmer, Rognvald and about eight horsemen rode up the lane towards the farmhouse. The *Earls' Saga* described what happened next. 'The earl and his men had then reached the door. Then Þorbjǫrn struck at the earl and Ásólfr [a young warrior] moved his hand and the hand came off. Then the sword caught the earl's chin and that was a bad wound'.[23]

Asolf was only 18 and he'd just joined the earl's retinue, but he took the blow like an experienced warrior, and even taunted Thorbjorn as his severed forearm pumped out blood. The earl was caught in the middle of the ambush. 'Earl Rǫgnvaldr wanted to jump off his horse when he saw Þorbjǫrn but his foot became caught in the stirrup. At that moment [the rebel] Stefánn came up and thrust a spear into the earl. Þorbjǫrn then gave the earl a second wound.' It was looking bad for Earl Rognvald, and due to the constricting walls of the lane by the farmhouse door, most of his mounted retainers couldn't help him. One, though, had dismounted and had taken the place of the wounded Asolf. 'And at that moment [the retainer] Jómarr thrust a spear into Þorbjǫrn's thigh and the lunge continued into his intestines.'[24]

By now the rest of Rognvald's men had managed to dismount and protect the death-wounded earl. Although badly injured himself, Thorbjorn ordered his men to withdraw. They headed towards the boggy ground between the farm and Loch Calder, just over a mile away, and there they stood their ground behind a belt of mossy bogland. Thorbjorn had about 50 rebels with him and so was outnumbered once Earl Harald and his pursuers arrived. The two sides threw spears at each other without achieving much, and then Thorbjorn tried to parley. Harald almost agreed to spare the rebels after Thorbjorn claimed he'd acted for Harald's benefit. However, a kinsman of Earl Rognvald, Magnus Hávardsson, warned the earl that 'If Þorbjǫrn is given a truce after this deed and also that he dares to tell you to your face in every word that he has done this evil deed for you or to honour you, it will bring everlasting shame and dishonour to you and all the earl's kinsmen, if he is not avenged.'[25]

That helped firm up Earl Harald Maddadarson's resolve, and he led his men into the bog and attacked the rebels. At that point most of them fled, leaving the wounded Thorbjorn and about eight others to face the earl's men. Thorbjorn dropped to his knees and pleaded for mercy, which after some discussion Earl Harald eventually gave. This didn't sit well with Magnus and others loyal to Earl Rognvald, so they broke ranks and gave chase. There, by a deserted hut beyond the loch, Thorbjorn and his remaining men were all cut down. Afterwards, examining Thorbjorn's body, it appears that the spear thrust by Rognvald's bodyguard Jomar had pierced his stomach and half of his intestines had fallen out. It was a grisly end for the assassin, but at least Earl Rognvald's seemingly mortal injury had been avenged.

Afterwards, when Earl Harald returned to the farmhouse, they found that Earl Rognvald had died of his wounds. His body was carried back to Thurso and from there the earl was taken to Kirkwall, where a tomb was made for him in his half-built cathedral. He was interred there in a funeral mass officiated by Bishop William 'the Old'. Burying his fellow crusader was an act of friendship the bishop wouldn't have missed. The bishop died ten years later in 1168, when he was about 66 years old, and was succeeded by another bishop of the same name. The saga says that 'Earl Rǫgnvaldr's death was much lamented, because he was very popular there in the isles, and widely elsewhere.'[26]

By then, the arguments of whether the Orkney bishopric formed part of the archdiocese of York, Durham or Nidaros had been resolved. By order of Pope Adrian IV, Orkney formed part of the archbishopric of Nidaros, strengthening the strong bond between the Orkney earldom and Norway. This was a bond which would be tested in the years that followed, as Orkney became involved in a feudal power struggle between Norway on one side and Scotland on the other.[27]

As for Earl Rognvald, several miracles were attributed to him in the years that followed, linked both to his tomb in the cathedral, which became a place of pilgrimage, and to the Caithness farmstead where he'd died. The new Bishop William 'the Younger' as well as his Norwegian successor Bjarni pressed for the earl's beatification. Eventually, in 1192, Earl Rognvald was canonised by Pope Celestine III, and so became Saint Rognvald. In terms of local saints, both the earldom and the diocese of Orkney were punching well above their weight. Above all, Rognvald was remembered as the last of his kind: a warrior, a Viking, a poet, a patron of culture, and a good ruler. He was also the last truly Norse earl of Orkney.[28]

TWENTY-ONE

Declining Fortunes

To FULLY UNDERSTAND Harald Maddadarson, we need to go back a little. Until 1139, all the earls of Orkney had been the sons of Norsemen. That chain stretching back almost 300 years was broken when the Scottish-born Harald Maddadarson became the joint earl, ruling alongside Norwegian-born Earl Rognvald. Three years before, Rognvald's rival Earl Paul had been abducted by Svein Ásleifarson, who'd handed him over to Harald's mother Margaret. To complete the bizarre circle, Earl Paul was the half-brother of Margaret, and their father was Earl Hákon Paulsson, the man responsible for the murder of St Magnus. Margaret was also the first cousin once removed of St Magnus, and the second cousin of Kali Kolsson, who became Earl Rognvald. Family life in the Norse earldom was rarely simple.

In c. 1133, Margaret married Matad, the *mormaer* of Atholl, who'd just inherited the title following the death of his father. Matad, or 'Maddad' in Norse, was a man with Scottish royal connections. His father was supposedly the son of King Duncan, and the brother of King Malcolm 'Canmore'. His marriage to a scion of the Orkney earldom could only be advantageous, as it was still a power to be reckoned with in northern Scotland. In 1134, Margaret gave birth to Harald. In the 12th century, nationalism was a largely unknown concept, and ties of blood and family meant more than regional identity. Thanks to his mother the infant Harald had both a Norse name and Norse blood, and as the grandson of an earl and the nephew of another, he had a valid claim to the Orkney earldom.[1]

That explained why Harald's mother arranged the abduction of her half-brother Paul. Put simply, that cleared the way for her son gaining a share of the earldom. This was the deal hatched between Margaret and Svein Ásleifarson, which committed Earl Rognvald to share the earldom with her infant son. So in 1139 that's exactly what happened, and the child earl was taken north to Orkney to take up his inheritance. Under Rognvald's guardianship the arrangement worked out well for the boy. Then, in 1151 Earl Rognvald went on his crusade. Harald, then aged 18, was left to rule both halves of the earldom in Rognvald's absence. That's when King Eystein of Norway arrived and took Harald prisoner. The teenage earl was only freed once he'd sworn fealty to Eystein and paid the Norwegian king a ransom for his release. Unfortunately, this wasn't the worst of it. The king then stripped Harald of his share of the earldom. Next, Eystein gave it to Harald's first cousin Erlend Haraldsson. That plunged the earldom into a civil war that raged until Erlend's death in 1154. Then both peace and the old status quo was restored, and Harald and Rognvald jointly ruled the earldom together until Rognvald's assassination four years later. From that point on, the Scottish-born Harald Maddadarson became the sole earl of Orkney.[2]

In 1158, when Harald became the sole earl, he'd been ruling Orkney alongside Rognvald for two decades. Despite that, he was still just 25 years old. It's clear he was a gifted and intelligent ruler, and he'd learned his role well. The *Earls' Saga* views him kindly, saying, 'Earl Haraldr was a great leader, a very tall and strong man'. It also lists him among the greatest of the earls of Orkney, alongside the first earl, Sigurd 'the Powerful' and Earl Thorfinn 'the Mighty'. This, though, didn't reflect the major setbacks of the last years of his reign, the greatest of which was the loss of Shetland. For almost five decades Earl Harald was forced to walk a diplomatic and political tightrope. For the most part he didn't fall off. When he did take a tumble, though, the results were disastrous.[3]

The problem was, Harald became the sole earl at a particularly challenging time. In both Norway and Scotland, royal authority had been undermined by a series of feuds and wars. This was then followed by a royal pushback. By the mid-12th century, royal power in both countries was strengthening. By the time Harald became the sole earl, formidable kings were sitting on the two thrones. Before, monarchs hadn't the time or resources to deal with the semi-independent rulers of the Orkney earldom – a place with a feudal foot in both kingdoms. It was Harald's misfortune to eventually be caught between two powerful kings who made it their job to bring his earldom to heel.[4]

To be fair, Harald's problems with the Norwegian and Scottish kings didn't emerge until the last decade of his reign. In Scotland, Harald had a good relationship with King Malcolm IV. Unfortunately, on his death in 1165, Malcolm was succeeded by his headstrong younger brother King William. As a result Harald's the cosy diplomatic relationship with Scotland came to an abrupt end.[5] In Norway, though, King Eystein died in 1157, and so any further interference in the Orkney earldom seemed much less likely. Harald then enjoyed a good relationship with King Magnus V, who ruled Norway for more than two decades.[6]

Part of Earl Harald Maddadarson's warm relationship with King Magnus stemmed from his own association with Earl Rognvald. Magnus was the son of Erling Skakke, or Erling 'the Lopsided', who'd been Earl Rognvald's heroic deputy during his crusade to the Holy Land. As Magnus was only five years old at the time of his coronation in 1161, his father Erling 'the Lopsided', who was now an earl, ruled Norway on his son's behalf. So Earl Harald was loyal to King Magnus. However, following the appearance of another royal contender, Sverrir (or Sverre) Sigurdsson, that loyalty to King Magnus would draw the earldom of Orkney into a major crisis which would end in disaster.[7]

Sverre claimed to be the illegitimate son of King Sigurd 'Munn', who'd been killed in Bergen in mid-1155 on the orders of his half-brother King Eystein. This claim was almost certainly an invention, as he was more probably the son of a humble comb-maker from the Faeroes. Sverre, though, was an astute politician, and by 1174 he'd gained control of the Birkebeinar party, one of what had become the two main factions in the 'Borgarkrigstida', the intermittent civil war era in Norway which began in 1130 and smouldered for more than a century. It was really a struggle between royal claimants, but by the later 12th century it came to be dominated by two factions – the Birkebeinar and Bagler parties.[8]

The Birkebeinar faction opposed King Magnus, but until the appearance of Sverre they hadn't achieved very much. Sverre reorganised the rebel party, and he also increased its military effectiveness by hiring Swedish mercenaries. In 1177, the Birkebeinar proclaimed Sverre king. However, his realm didn't extend beyond the borders of the rebels' power base in rural Trøndelag. Two years later, though, Sverre attacked Nidaros, and Erling 'the Lopsided' was killed there. After that, Sverre's supporters began working their way south towards Bergen. In June 1184

King Magnus led a fleet to confront Sverre and the rival fleets clashed on the Sognefjord. There, at the Battle of Fimreite, Magnus was defeated and the king drowned in the cold waters of the fjord. As a result, Sverre became the sole ruler of Norway.[9]

On the far side of the West Sea, King Sverre's rise to power didn't sit well with Earl Harald Maddadarson or indeed most of his people. However, from 1184 on, despite resistance to Sverre, there was only one real attempt to overthrow the new king. A rising in Bergen and Nidaros was orchestrated by Jon Kuvlung, a monk from Oslo who claimed to be the son of the late King Inge. This rising, though, was stamped out in 1188. The following year Sverre married Margaret, the sister of the Swedish ruler King Knut, which safeguarded his eastern borders. Sverre also worked hard to consolidate his grip on power throughout Norway itself.

For a few years, peace of sorts returned to Norway, although this was still a period of the *Borgarkrigstida*, the near-constant civil war, driven by a succession of claimants to the Norwegian throne. When the next claimant appeared, it would begin again in earnest. This time, the would-be king of Norway was based much closer to Kirkwall than Oslo. In early 1193, egged on by his relatives, the teenager Sigurðr (or Sigurd) Magnusson from Orkney announced his claim to the Norwegian throne. He was, it seems, the illegitimate son of King Magnus, who'd been killed in battle nine years earlier. The man who seized Magnus' throne, Sverre Sigurdsson, now ruled Norway. So thanks to this local contender for the throne, both Earl Harald Maddadarson and the earldom became embroiled in the next bloody phase of Norway's civil war.[10]

As the *Earls' Saga* records, it was in the last few years of Earl Harald Maddadarson's rule that, 'Ólafr, his in-law, and Jón Hallkelsson took a division from the Orkneys east to Norway against King Sverrir. They took Sigurður, the son of King Magnús Erlingsson, as king. In that army were many men of noble family from the Orkneys; that was the strongest division.'[11] Of the two rebel leaders the saga mentions, Ólaf Sveinsson 'Earl's Kin' was one of the sons of adventurer Svein Ásleifarson, who'd married Elín Eiríksdóttir, the granddaughter of Earl Rognvald. The second leader was Jón Hallkelsson, a leading Orkney *göding*, who was married to Ragnhild Eiríksdóttir, the sister of Sverre's old rival King Magnus, and the aunt of this new contender for the Norwegian throne. This rebel band duly became the ardent followers of the teenage Sigurd, who was also Ólaf and Ragnhild's foster-son.[12]

Earl Harald now had a decision to make. He could either support King Sverre and suppress this rebel army gathering in Orkney and Shetland, or he could throw in his lot with them. By then, though, the rebel army mustering in Orkney was probably too large for him to disperse, so he became a possibly reluctant recruit to their cause. His support would markedly boost the rebels' strength by adding the earl's own followers and ships to their force. *Sverre's Saga* records the moment: 'The earl supported the boy's cause [Sigurd] heartily, and gave him a good longship, for King Magnus had been an excellent friend of Earl Harald. The Earl also gave leave to all who wished to join the expedition of Hallkel and Ólaf, and their companions.'[13]

By now these rebels had a name. They called themselves the Eyjarskeggjar (or simply the Eyskeggs), which meant 'islanders' – a nod to their origins in Orkney and Shetland. By the summer of 1193 they were ready, and the Eyskeggs set off across the West Sea to topple King Sverre from his throne. Once this was achieved, they'd install King Magnus' teenage son Sigurd Magnusson as the new ruler of Norway. The Eyjarskeggjar venture began in the late summer when they crossed the West Sea, probably making landfall off Bergen. They then sailed south, following the Norwegian coast into the Skagerrak, and on to Tunsberg (now Tønsberg), where King Sverre maintained his royal court.[14]

Tunsberg was on an inlet of the Oslofjord, some 45 miles south of Oslo. This attack was a bold stroke, but it proved to be a wasted one as the king wasn't there. Their consolation prize was King Sverri's nephew Jon, whom they killed. The Eyskeggs then raised the royal standard and proclaimed the teenager Sigurd Magnusson the new king of Norway. More accurately, he was a claimant, as King Sverre was still very much in power. The Eyskeggs then went to Oslo, where they recruited followers before heading west again to Bergen, and seized the city in the name of the young King Sigurd. Around this time they also tried to rebrand themselves along more Norwegian lines, preferring to be known as the Gullbeiner ('gold-legs') to taunt Sverre's supporters, the Birkebeiner ('birch-legs').[15]

Whatever they called themselves, the Eyskeggs spent the winter in Bergen, but while they held the city, they couldn't eject the garrison of 300 Birkebeiners from the Sverresborg. That was the castle built by King Sverre overlooking Bergen harbour. Over the winter, King Sverre in Nidaros and the rebels in Bergen both prepared for the spring. So in early 1194, Sverre sailed south at the head of a royal fleet. The Eyskeggs' longships gathered in Bergen harbour, which opened onto the Byfjorden, the last of a network of linked fjords which led to the open sea.[16]

On 2 April, Sverre's fleet came into view. The Eyskeggs' fleet deployed across the three-mile-wide fjord to the south of the fishing harbour of Florvåg on the island of Askøy, which formed the north shore of the fjord. King Sverre's fleet then deployed a little to the west of the rebel fleet. Sverre had 20 small, fast longships with him, but as it was evening when he arrived, he decided to wait until morning to begin the battle. He sent spies ashore, though, and they brought back the news that the Eyskeggs planned to attack him at dawn. So Sverre decided to strike first, in the pre-dawn darkness. To help his men identify friend from foe, he had them tie white linen tapes around the prows of their longships.[17]

The longships of the Eyskeggs' fleet included 14 longships from Orkney and Shetland, which were generally larger than those in the royal fleet. The rebel leaders discussed avoiding battle and linking up with a naval detachment in Stavanger, but eventually they decided to stay and fight. So, early on 3 April the Battle of Florvåg began, but not in the way Sverre had planned. It was the Eyskeggs who made the first move well before dawn, roping their longships together to make a fighting platform and then gliding forward towards Sverre's fleet. *Sverre's Saga* described how the battle began: 'The Eyskeggs made a fierce onset, and the Birkibeiners held their shields over their heads, so close together that they were nowhere uncovered.'[18]

Sverre's men rode out the arrow storm and waited for the enemy to tire. Then Sverre ordered them to attack. A fierce hand-to-hand melee began, where the undoubted skill of the Norwegian king's warriors was countered by the height advantage enjoyed by the defenders of the larger rebel ships. The Eyskeggs singled out Sverre's *drakkar* and boarded it, clearing the defenders from its forecastle and capturing 'Sigrfluga', the king's standard. That, though, is when the battle turned. Sverre ordered his men to cut the enemy's grappling ropes, and as his flagship drifted off several of the Eyskeggs' longships broke away from their fighting platform and set off after Sverre. This disrupted the rebels' strong position, and their longships drifted apart on the ebbing tide.

King Sverre ordered his men to concentrate on a handful of enemy longships, swarming them with two or three royal ships at a time. One of these was the Eyjarskeggjar flagship whose crew had captured the Sigrfluga. 'Then they [Sverre's warriors] boarded the ship and stripped it from stem to stern.' That was a polite way of saying they slaughtered everyone on board. Sigurd 'King's-son' jumped overboard but was killed as he swam away. Ólaf 'Earl's Kin' did the same and made it to land, only to be killed by troops from the Sverresborg. By this stage the battle was as good as won. All King Sverre's men had to do was to mop up.[19]

Hallkell Jonsson was slain aboard his ship, along with his men. At that point King Sverre offered quarter to the tiny handful of the rebels who remained alive. The Eyskeggs' rebellion had been comprehensively crushed, and King Sverre's throne was safe. The body of the teenage Sigurd 'King's-son' was buried in Mariakyrkja (or St Mary's Church) in Bergen, while King Sverre and his commanders held a victory mass. The rest of the rebels from Orkney and Shetland were buried in a mass grave outside Bergen, with the body of King Sigurd's foster-father Ólaf 'Earl's Kin' thrown on top of them.

Then it was time for revenge. The following summer, in 1195, an assembly was held in Bergen. Earl Harald Maddadarson was ordered to attend, accompanied by the new head of the Orkney diocese, Bishop Bjarni and other leading men of the earldom. Earl Harald was well aware that the king planned to punish him for his part in the rebellion. He'd also learned that King Sverre was threatening to lead a punitive expedition across the West Sea to wreak vengeance on the islanders. As the *Earls' Saga* phrased it, 'After that King Sverrir had great hatred for Earl Haraldr and blamed him for what the division had done.' Essentially, Harald was there to surrender himself to the king and await whatever justice King Sverre chose to dispense. When the judgement came, though, it wasn't a death sentence for the earl. It was much worse than that. 'Then King Sverrir took all of Shetland off Earl Haraldr with taxes and dues.'[20]

It was a mortal blow to the earldom. At a stroke, the earldom was ripped in two. While Harald could keep Orkney and his Scottish lands south of the Pentland Firth, Shetland was now to be governed directly by the Norwegian crown, with royal stewards doing the job the earl's men had done for more than three centuries. As the saga said of the stripping of Shetland from the earldom, 'The earls of the Orkneys have not had it since'. The loss of revenue was bad enough for Earl Harald, but the loss of prestige to the earldom was immense. At a stroke, it had been turned from a regional powerhouse into little more than a small island earldom, with some additional land on the Scottish mainland.[21]

The loss of Shetland in 1195 was certainly a grievous blow to Earl Harald Maddadarson, but at the time he had an even more serious problem to deal with – one which threatened the very survival of what remained of his earldom. It all stemmed from the appearance of another contender. This one, though, wasn't trying to gain the Norwegian kingdom. His aim was to win the earldom of Orkney.

This was a problem which had been some 15 years in the making. Shortly before his death in 1179, Erling 'the Lopsided' was approached by a young man from Orkney called Haraldr (or Harald) Eiríksson. He was the son of Ingirid, the daughter of Earl Rognvald Kali, the builder of St Magnus Cathedral. His father, Eirík 'Stay-Brailer', was a member of the troublesome but powerful Moddan family of Caithness, and had been brought up by his grand-aunt Frakokk. At the time Erling 'the Lopsided', who'd gone on crusade with Earl Rognvald, was the chief adviser to his 23-year-old son, the Norwegian king Magnus Erlingsson. With Erling's help Harald was granted an audience with the king. There, he pressed his claim for the Orkney earldom, or at least a share of it, based on his right as the grandson of Earl Rognvald. King Magnus thought this was fair, and so he duly granted Harald a half share of the earldom. Of course at the time it was firmly in the hands of Earl Harald Maddadarson. The teenage earl-contender's two brothers Magnus and Rognvald stayed in Norway. Not long afterwards they were killed in battle outside Nidaros, fighting for King Magnus alongside Erling 'the Lopsided'. The old crusader Earl Erling also died in the fight.

Of course, Harald still had to lay hands on his claim. Then, after the death of King Magnus in the summer of 1184, his royal rival Sverre Sigurdsson seized the Norwegian throne. The young Harald bided his time before approaching the new king. After all, Norway was a country which was still riven by civil war. However, the quashing of the Eyjarsker rebellion in 1194 gave Harald the opportunity he'd been waiting for. So he travelled to Norway, and begged an audience with King Sverre. There, he pressed his claim again, and swore his allegiance to the powerful Norwegian king. King Sverre duly confirmed the arrangement made by King Magnus. Harald's right to half of the Orkney earldom was reconfirmed.[22]

As King Sverre knew that Earl Harald Maddadarson had supported the Eyjarskeggjar rebellion, this arrangement suited both the Norwegian king and the new Orkney earl. Earl Harald Eiríksson, though, whom the *Earls' Saga* now called Harald 'the Young', still needed troops. So he used a route to win the earldom that had proved successful before – the soliciting of Scottish support. There was no reason to think it couldn't work again. The saga explains how Harald achieved it: 'They arrived first in Shetland and from there to Caithness and so up into Scotland to meet Vilkjámr [William], king of the Scots.'[23]

In return for his pledge of fealty, in mid-1195 King William 'the Lion' granted Harald 'the Young' half of the *mormaership* of Caithness and Sutherland to rule, as his grandfather had before him. This, though, wasn't what he really wanted, which was a share of the whole of the earldom. So, Harald's next move was to head north to Caithness to raise an army. After all, his family had strong connections in the region. He then sent a message to Earl Harald Maddadarson, whom the saga calls Harald 'the Old' from this point, to differentiate between the two rivals. Harald 'the Young's' request was that the older earl give up half of his earldom. Inevitably, Earl Harald Maddadarson refused outright, and began raising forces of his own. It looked like another internal civil war was about to begin.

As winter approached, the two earls prepared for war. Harald 'the Young' sent his brother-in-law and deputy Lífólfr (or Lífólf) 'Bald-head' and a few men over to Rognvaldsey (South Ronaldsay), to spy out the lie of the land. They'd heard this was where Earl Harald Maddadarson 'the Old' was gathering his ships and men. Lífólf landed on the east side of the island and climbed a hill, 'and there he found three of Earl Haraldr the Old's watchmen and killed two of them and had the third with him for information. Lífófr then also saw the earl's army and he had many ships and most were big'. He raced back to Harald with the news.[24]

Harald 'the Young' now knew he was outnumbered. Still, when Harald 'the Old's' fleet appeared in the Pentland Firth, the younger contender decided to stand and fight. The saga describes the battle that followed. 'Earl Haraldr [the Old] went ashore and arranged his troop; he had a much bigger army. Sigurðr Sprat and Lífólfr arranged the troop of the young earl.'[25] Fighting was a vainglorious gesture by the younger earl, as he had no real chance of victory. Still, he'd made his decision and had to see it through. 'And when they had arranged the troop, the battle got going, and was very tough. In Earl Haraldr the Old's troop there were many of the toughest men, who were overbearing and exceedingly well-equipped'. In other words, one army was made up of the earl's veteran retainers, while the other contained a smattering of regulars, with their numbers made up by Caithness farmers.[26]

The outcome was a foregone conclusion. All Harald 'the Young's' men could do was to die well or to flee. 'After a while, the young Norwegian warrior Sigurd 'Sprat' was killed, fighting bravely like a true champion. Among the others, Lífólf fought best, and the Caithness people say that he cut his way three times through the enemy ranks before he was killed and died a hero's death.' With that the rest of Harald 'the Young's' army broke and ran. As for the army's leader, 'Earl Haraldr the Young fell by some peat workings'. The earl's grave was unmarked, but the saga claimed that, 'there is now a church where he fell', and 'he is buried there on the headland'. As no church survived, these clues remain our only hint to the location of the battlefield.[27]

Then, Earl Harald 'the Old' toured Caithness to ensure the region's loyalty before returning to Orkney. Harald Maddadarson was also dealing with the fallout resulting from the rising against King Sverre, so the loyalty of his Caithness subjects was key to the financial and political future of his earldom. Still, by vanquishing this dynastic threat, Harald Maddadarson kept his hold over his much-reduced territories. The killing of Harald 'the Young', though, angered King William 'the Lion' of Scotland, who decided to teach his troublesome northern neighbour a lesson.[28]

King William responded by leading a large Scottish army north through the Highlands to Caithness. He was joined there by another contingent raised from the Hebrides and Ireland. When King William arrived in Caithness in the late summer of 1196, Earl Harald wisely kept out of his way and remained in Orkney. So William captured Caithness without a fight. However, the Scots withdrew the following year, although William left a small garrison behind, as well as three stewards who were to rule Caithness in the king's name. Harald wasn't having this, and he eventually sent an assassin over, who killed one of the three stewards, Hlífófr (or Hlifolf) 'the Old'. In 1201 Harald sailed to Caithness, and landed a large army there at Scrabster, near Thurso.[29]

This time the only real opposition came from Bishop Jón of Caithness, who took refuge in the Scottish-held castle overlooking Scrabster. The bishop then approached Earl Harald Maddadarson and tried to reason with him, to avoid further bloodshed. It wasn't his wisest move. Harald had the cleric taken prisoner, and then ordered his tongue to be cut out and a knife to be driven into his eyes. The mutilated bishop was then set free, but according to the saga he was met by a woman who took him 'to the place where St Trǫllhœna rests. There the bishop was cured of both his speech and his sight.' After that, Earl Harald captured Scrabster castle without a fight. He then drove off the two remaining Scottish stewards, and the Scottish garrisons, and reconquered the rest of Caithness and Sutherland. He then he required the people there to renew allegiance to him.[30]

In December 1201 the surviving stewards arrived at the Scottish court in Edinburgh and gave King William a detailed account of what had happened. William flew into a rage and began raising an even larger army than before. In the spring of 1202, he led it north towards Sutherland. There, according to the saga, at Ausdale (now Ousdale, north of Helmsdale) near the border of Caithness and Sutherland, his army pitched camp, where their encampment was so large it filled the moorland valley from end to end. For his part, Harald Maddadarson had done well to raise an army of 6,000 men. Clearly, he was badly outnumbered. Worse, King William had a reputation as an excellent military commander. So Earl Harald wisely sent envoys south to see if they could salvage some form of peace deal.[31]

King William was reluctant to agree to a negotiated peace, but by then he had another insurrection to deal with in Moray. Also, William and the new English ruler King John had clashed over ownership of Northumbria on the Anglo-Scottish border. So, the risk of a major war there was never too far away. So King William reluctantly offered Earl Harald a deal. In return for a quarter of all the earl's revenues from Caithness and Sutherland, Harald could keep his lands there, and William would lead his army south again. Harald, of course, would still owe fealty to the Scottish king for his tenure of his earldom on the Scottish mainland. Given the circumstances, it was a deal Earl Harald couldn't refuse.[32]

So, in 1202, when faced with annihilation, Earl Harald managed – by the skin of his teeth – to keep hold of his lands south of the Pentland Firth. If they'd been lost, it would have reduced his earldom to just Orkney itself. He was already suffering from the loss of Shetland to the Norwegian crown. Having Caithness and Sutherland stripped from him would have been an unmitigated financial and political disaster.

This, though, meant many of the people of Orkney had to scrimp and save to pay the reparations demanded by King Sverre. Earl Harald 'the Old' did too, and as a result it was an impoverished rump of an earldom that remained. Somehow, this seems to have been repaid before the three-year deadline imposed by Sverre. Failure would have resulted in forfeiture, and in that case Harald could well have lost Orkney too. In the end, King Sverre barely lived beyond this, as he died in March 1202. In that same year, Pope Innocent absolved Harald of the maiming of Bishop Jón of Caithness, but he ordered Bishop Bjarni 'Poet' of Orkney to prosecute one of Harald's followers, a scapegoat who was duly named as the real culprit.

Earl Harald Maddadarson died of natural causes in 1206, at the impressively old age of 72. By then he'd ruled Orkney for over six decades, and for 48 of these years he'd been the sole earl. A lot was thrown at Harald; first the War of the Three Earls, and then the challenges posed by Norway and Scotland. Harald proved to be a real survivor, a trait that was never more in evidence than during his final tumultuous decade. Earl Harald Maddadarson might well have been listed as one of Orkney's three greatest earls, but compared to the others – Earl Sigurd 'the Mighty' and Earl Thorfinn 'the Mighty' – Harald hadn't conquered anything and ended up losing a significant portion of the earldom. Somehow, Earl Harald 'the Survivor' doesn't quite have the same ring to it.

TWENTY-TWO

The Last Earl and the Great Sea King

E ARL HARALD MADDADARSON WAS married twice in his long life. For some reason, he always chose Scottish partners rather than Norse ones. Perhaps it was a way of rebelling against his spirited Norse mother Margaret Hákonsdóttir, the widow of the *mormaer* of Atholl. His first wife was called Afreka, the daughter of Duncan, the *mormaer* of Fife. They had two sons, Heinrekr (or Henry) and Hákon, as well as two daughters called Helena and Margaret. Hákon was fostered by Svein Ásleifarson and went on raids with him, but little is known about his three siblings.

Then, around 1168 when Earl Harald was in his forties, he divorced Afreka, supposedly for political reasons. At the time Earl Harald was supporting a rising in the Highlands, which Mormaer Duncan opposed. It could, though, have been nothing other than some form of mid-life crisis. The earl then married Hvarflǫð (or Hvarflod), the daughter of Malcolm mac Alexander, a Moray nobleman of royal blood. This second union produced six children, three boys called Þorfinnr (or Thorfinn), Davið (or David) and Jón, and three girls, Gunnhildr (or Gunnhild), Herborga and Langlíf.[1]

When Earl Harald died, his sons David and Jón succeeded him. It had already been agreed that they'd share the much-reduced earldom between them. Their elder brother Thorfinn, though, was left out of the division. During his invasion of Caithness in 1202, King William 'the Lion' had captured Thorfinn, and held him as a hostage. Then, possibly in retaliation for the mutilation of Bishop Jón, the Scottish king ordered Thorfinn to be blinded and sent back to his father. The blinded Thorfinn was deemed incapable of ruling the earldom and spent his days being cared for by his kin.[2]

It is at this point that the *Earls' Saga* comes to an end. In fact the original version of the manuscript didn't include Earl Harald or his sons. These were added in a later addendum to the original saga. After mentioning the death of Earl Harald in 1206 and the beginning of the joint rule by David and Jón, this magnificent sweeping story comes to an abrupt close.[3]

Certainly, the joint rule of David and Jón Haraldsson appeared to be a tranquil one, and the earldom slowly recovered from the traumas of the past decade. There was nothing of the great drama of their father's time, or of the sibling rivalry, the civil war and the murders that ran like a bloody trail through the tales of their Norse predecessors. In Kirkwall, now a booming town, the cathedral was slowly rising above the buildings, and the harbour was filled by trading ships from Norway, Scotland and further afield.

This wasn't to say the two earls didn't face some potentially dangerous external threats. In Norway, King Sverre had made it clear that the earls now owed allegiance to the Norwegian crown for their title. Defeat in the Battle of Florvåg ended the earldom's pretentions to being a regional power, while King Sverre had also brought the earldom's autonomy to a close. From that point on, the earldom was an adjunct of Norway. The exception, of course, was Caithness and Sutherland. There, as King William 'the Lion' made clear, these lands formed part of the kingdom of Scotland. The Orkney earls could rule them, but only by leave of the Scottish king. If the two earls or their successors stepped out of line, they could lose everything.

The earls had other problems too. These included the continued dynastic claims by the descendants of Earl Erlend Haraldsson. There was also a growing animosity between Bishop Bjarni 'Poet' of Orkney, whose Norwegian diocese was part of the archdiocese of Nidaros, and Bishop Adam of Melrose, who was part of the archdiocese of York.

In addition, there was unrest in Sutherland, the most southerly part of the earldom. This followed a serious rebellion further south in the Highlands, incited by the MacWilliams clan. In the mid-12th century this low-key rising began in the western part of Moray and spread into neighbouring Ross, Argyll and then Sutherland.

Harald's support of the rebels was probably offered to limit the advance of Scottish power into the north of Scotland. Still, it did little to endear him to the Scottish crown, and it left King William 'the Lion' wary of further unrest in the north. It also led to him building castles on the Cromarty Firth and the Moray Firth to safeguard his hold on Moray.[4]

The first real test of the two earls, though, was a Norwegian one. Before King Sverre died in March 1202, he named his 18-year-old illegitimate son Hákon as his heir. The youth was elected king in Nidaros that spring, and conditions in Norway improved, largely because of Sverre's death. The Church had excommunicated King Sverre eight years before, and now relations between church and state were restored. Bagler opposition also faded in the wake of Sverre's death. However, a rift developed between Hákon and his father's Swedish-born wife Margaret, as he refused to let her and her daughter leave the Norwegian court. Then, in December 1203 Hákon fell ill, and he died on 1 January 1204. Margaret was suspected of poisoning him, and so she wisely fled the country, and returned to her native Sweden.[5]

In January 1204 Sverre's four-year-old grandson Guttorm was proclaimed king, which provoked a backlash from the Bagler party. A renewed armed conflict seemed inevitable, but that August the boy fell ill and died. It seemed there were no more suitable descendants of Sverre to crown. At that point Archbishop Eirík of Nidaros proposed Inge Bårdsson as a royal candidate. The 19-year-old was the son of Bård Guttormsson, a leading Birkebeiner who was also the son-in-law of Sverre. So, Inge was elected king, albeit he ruled in the shadow of a resurgent civil war and the presence of the ambitious and volatile Earl Hákon 'the Crazy', leader of the Birkebeiner army.[6]

The joint earls thought this created a diplomatic opportunity for them. So in 1208, they sent Bishop Bjarni 'Poet' over to lay the ground for improved relations with the Norwegian crown. Two years later they rather reluctantly visited King Inge in Bergen to offer their fealty and obtain official royal approval of their succession to the earldom. Unfortunately for them, this visit led to increased taxation, the taking of hostages and the imposition of a royal *sysselman* or sheriff in Orkney to oversee Norwegian royal interests. This was another stitch-up by the Norwegian crown, designed to ensure both the earls and the islanders knew their place.[7]

It was a similar situation in Scotland. In the summer of 1212, the MacWilliam revolt resurfaced in Ross, supported by the local nobility. This possibly meant the earls' half-brother Henry was involved, as he lived on his estates there. This rising alarmed the aged King William 'the Lion', who sent Flemish crossbowmen to the region borrowed from King John of England. The following year the now ailing William journeyed north to meet Earl Jón Haraldsson in Caithness to extract an oath of fealty.[8] It seems King William didn't completely trust the new Orkney earls any more than King Inge did. So to safeguard the arrangement, the Scottish king took the earl's daughter as a hostage.[9]

In 1214 Earl David Haraldsson died of an unidentified sickness, and so his brother Jón became the sole earl of Orkney. King William also died late that December, aged 72. He was succeeded by his 16-year-old-son Alexander II, who was cast in a similar aggressive mould. The Scottish king was heavily involved in events over his southern border following the death of King John of England in late 1216. However, relations between the earldom and the new Scottish kings were fairly amicable, but this ended abruptly when the bishop of Caithness was murdered by a baying mob.

In 1201 Bishop Adam succeeded Bishop Jón, who'd been mutilated by Earl Harald's men a decade before. Adam, the former abbot of Melrose, was over-zealous in collecting tithes, his tax of a tenth of the income or produce of the people in his diocese. The tipping point came over a tub of butter. The greedy bishop had doubled the butter tithe from one tub for every 20 cows to one per ten. This was a step too far for many Caithness farmers, and in September 1222 they rose up in revolt. They marched on the bishop's residence in Hawick, five miles south of Thurso, and demanded the butter tithe be reduced.[10]

When the bishop and a dean called Serlo stepped outside to confront the farmers, the situation became heated, and the mob attacked the clerics. Dean Serlo was killed, and the mob bundled Bishop Adam into his outside kitchen. Then, when Bishop Adam still refused to acquiesce, the mob set the building on fire. The bishop suffocated to death before his own guards could come to his aid.[11] Earl Jón Haraldsson wasn't involved in all this, but he was nearby in Thurso at the time, and a messenger had arrived from the bishop, begging for help. The earl ignored him, and afterwards it was claimed he'd said, 'The devil take the bishop and his butter; you may roast him if you please!'[12]

By the time Alexander II heard the news, the tale had changed, and it was claimed that Earl Jón had murdered the bishop and his dean. Alexander led a small army north, and on reaching Caithness he rounded up the perpetrators and cut off the hands and feet of 80 of them. The king's men then castrated the farmers' sons and banished the farmers' wives from their homes. Presumably they set fire to the farmsteads for good measure. When Pope Honorius III learned of this, he called the Scottish king a 'Champion of God'.[13]

Earl Jón wisely kept out of the king's way, but in the following year, 1223, he travelled south to Fife to meet Alexander. There he insisted he had played no part in the bishop's death. Nevertheless, Jón was forced to give up half of his lands in Caithness and Sutherland as surety until he could prove he wasn't involved. The following year Earl Jón made the trip again after his innocence was proved, and his forfeited lands were returned to him.[14]

The next crisis arose in 1229, when a new claimant to the earldom emerged. Snaekoll Gunnisson was a nephew of Harald 'the Young', and as well as a share of the earldom he also demanded the return of his family's confiscated estates. Snaekoll's supporters in Orkney began provoking fights with the earl's men, and the situation soon became tense. Snaekoll also found an ally in the royal *sysselmann* in Orkney, Hanef Ungi. He was an Orcadian himself and the nephew of Bishop Bjarni 'Poet', who'd died in 1223. Matters came to a head in the autumn of 1230 and ended with the brutal killing of Earl Jón.[15]

He was in Caithness at the time, in his hall in Thurso, which had been used as a hunting lodge since the days of Earl Rognvald. This suggests Jón was there for a deer hunt. Whatever the cause, Snaekoll Gunnisson was in Thurso too, staying in lodgings he shared with his supporters, including Hanef Ungi. They'd all been drinking heavily, but suddenly someone burst in and warned them that Earl Jón intended to attack them that evening. So Snaekoll and Hanef decided to strike first. As *Hákon's Saga* puts it, 'They were all so drunk they thought what they intended was a good plan.' They poured themselves out onto the street, and on reaching the earl's lodge they took his guards by surprise and burst into the building.[16]

It seems Earl Jón was asleep when the intruders appeared, and he didn't have time to arm himself. Instead, he and a few retainers hid in a cellar behind the stacks of barrels. The attackers found them, though, and with no way out the earl was trapped. Snaekoll stabbed and killed the earl, along with the earl's retainers. It was said Earl Jón was stabbed a total of nine times, in the front and the back. The murderers then fled into the night and took a boat to Orkney before heading for the small island of Wyre, beside Egilsay and Rousay, off the north-western side of the Orkney mainland.[17]

The murderers and their followers took refuge in the small stone-built keep there, built a century before by the Viking Kolbein Hruga. Today, the place is called 'Cubbie Roo's Castle'. When Earl Jón's men arrived, they found it almost impossible to attack the place, and so a truce was called. It was agreed that both parties would sail to Norway and let the king settle the matter. In Norway, though, most of the murderers fled into the countryside, and all the earl's supporters could do was to execute the few who remained before returning home to Orkney.[18]

On the way back, in late 1232, their ship foundered in the West Sea, and everybody was drowned. The lost vessel became known as the *göding*'s ship, as most of Orkney's leading men were on board. It was a sad footnote to a dismal tale, just as the squalid murder of Earl Jón Haraldsson in a Caithness cellar was a sordid finale for a ruler who would become the last earl of Orkney with any claim to having any Norse blood in his veins. After the foundering of the *göding*'s ship, there were no viable successors to the earldom. So the title passed to the descendants of Earl Jón's grandparents, the Scottish earls of Atholl. In the future, there would be no more Norse earls of Orkney – only Scottish ones. Not only did this mark the end of an era, but it ended a chain of succession that stretched back five centuries to Earl Rognvald of Møre, the descendant of giants and mythical sea kings.[19]

Still, the Norse earldom of Orkney had one great drama left before the curtain finally dropped. In the previous chapter, we said that 'It seemed there were no more suitable descendants of Sverre to crown'. This, though, wasn't strictly true. There was one which the Norwegian court didn't know about. In the spring of 1204, a few months after King Hákon Sverresson died, Inga of Varteig gave birth to a baby boy. This took place in the Østfold, a Norwegian region lying between the Oslofjord and the Swedish border. King Hákon had been campaigning there the previous autumn, and Inga had briefly been his mistress. The baby was named Hákon after his father, but from birth his life was in deadly danger. The Østfold was hostile Bagler territory, and when they heard of this baby, death squads were sent to hunt down and kill the infant.[20]

However, the tiny Hákon was spirited away by the Birkenbeiner, and at one point, when a blizzard struck, he was taken across the mountains by a pair of Birkenbeiner skiers. Eventually Hákon reached safety in Nidaros, the Birkenbeiner capital. Hákon grew up there, and in 1217, following a peace deal between the two rival parties, the 13-year-old Hákon was proclaimed the new king of Norway.

Still, Bagler-inspired unrest continued for another decade, despite Hákon's marriage in 1225 to Margaret, the daughter of Earl Skule Bårdsson, a rebel leader and rival claimant to the throne. Despite this appeasement the rebellion continued until 1227, when Hákon subdued the rebels in south-eastern Norway. Then, after a ten-year lull, Earl Skule instigated another rising and was proclaimed king in 1239. Hákon reacted vigorously, defeating the rebels in 1240 and killing his father-in-law. This effectively ended the civil war that had ravaged Norway for more than a century. As a result, Hákon emerged as the undisputed ruler of all of Norway.[21]

King Hákon Hákonsson proved to be a good ruler and greatly expanded the prestige of Norway, both at home and elsewhere. His royal court at Bergen became a centre for learning and culture, as well as one for legislation and diplomacy. Hákon also pursued an aggressive foreign policy, clashing with the rulers of Novgorod, the Hanseatic League in the Baltic, and the Danes. All these led to peace treaties, and the Hanseatic League, who were then allowed access to Bergen, which helped turn it into a booming trading port.[22]

One of Hákon's concerns was extending Norwegian sovereignty over Norse overseas territories from Greenland and Iceland to the Isle of Man. By 1262 Iceland and Greenland joined the Faeroes and Shetland by being formally incorporated into the Norwegian kingdom. At that point King Hákon turned his attention to the cluster of island territories around the Scottish coast. The earldom of Orkney was securely linked to Norway, but to the west the Norse Kingdom of the Isles and the Isle of Man had been neglected by Norway during the civil war and so had become autonomous.

In the 12th century the Sudreyjar was ruled by the Norse-Gaelic warlord Somerled. In theory Somerled ruled his Kingdom of the Isles on behalf of the Norwegian crown. In practice, he barely paid lip service to this. On Somerled's death in 1164 his kingdom was divided between his sons Dougal, Angus and Ranald. The brothers feuded and fought, and so these petty kingdoms remained divided at a time when the Scottish kings were attempting to expand their influence beyond their western shores.[23]

In the mid-1230s King Alexander II of Scotland tried to buy the Hebrides from Norway, but King Hákon rejected the offer. In 1249, Alexander even led a fleet from the Clyde into these western seas, but took ill and died while anchored in the Sound of Kerrera, off the coast of what is now the town of Oban. So, his planned conquest came to nothing. His son Alexander III redoubled his father's efforts, though, and in 1262 he formally laid claim to the Hebrides. If Hákon didn't sell them to him, the young Scottish king said he'd take them by force. This was, in effect, a declaration of war, and King Hákon IV responded accordingly.

No Norwegian king had visited the Sudreyjar since Magnus 'Bare-legged' 160 years earlier. Hákon vowed he would end that oversight. So at Christmas 1262 he issued a call to arms, and by May a 'great host' had assembled in Bergen of 120 longships and storeships, and at least 10,000 men were embarked. Hákon's magnificent *drakkar* with its distinctive dragon's prow was described as a ship with no equal in Europe. It would also be one of the last ships of its kind. Before he sailed, Hákon sent ships ahead of him to Orkney, Shetland and the Sudreyjar to rally the islanders, and requested volunteers to join the royal expedition. This great Norse armada sailed from Bergen on 8 July, accompanied by Magnus Gilbertsson, Earl of Orkney, who'd inherited the earldom on the death of his father Earl Gilbert in 1256. This fleet made the crossing to Shetland amid 'excellent wind and fair weather.'[24]

They spent two weeks there before sailing on to Orkney and anchoring off the island of Shapinsay, three miles to the north of Kirkwall. Harald then sailed down to Widewall Bay in South Rognvaldsay. Finally, on 10 August King Hákon led his fleet out into the Pentland Firth and rounded Cape Wrath to reach Scotland's west coast. From there Hákon cruised through the Sudreyjar, where the fleet's presence was enough to encourage the islanders to remember their Nordic allegiance. Off Skye Hákon was joined by King Magnus of Man and Dougal, King of the Isles. So far, Hákon's expedition had been a resounding success. Once again, the whole of the Sudreyjar was back in Norse hands.[25]

In September Hákon reached the Firth of Clyde and anchored in the lee of the tiny island of Great Cumrae. At that point Hákon was approached by a Scottish delegation, who seemed eager to negotiate a peaceful settlement. Eventually, though, it became clear that the Scots were stringing Hákon along, hoping to delay the Norwegian fleet until the coming of the winter storms. The scheme worked, as a few days later a heavy westerly gale arrived and lashed Hákon's fleet.

Michaelmas was a Saturday, and on the night of the Monday following [30 September/1 October] a storm came in with fury. A merchant ship and longships were driven ashore. On the Monday the storm was so violent that some hewed down their masts, and some drifted ... A merchant ship drifted down on the king's ship, and took off the dragon's nostrils, and its anchor caught in the anchor cable of the king's ship ... Hákon bade them cut the cable of the merchant ship, which drifted ashore.[26]

The autumnal storms had arrived. When they passed it was clear that several Norse ships had run aground on the Scottish mainland, near the Ayrshire village of Largs. King Alexander III's Scottish army was encamped several miles to the south, so on 2 October Hákon ordered men ashore, to salvage what they could. This work was still going on under Hákon's supervision when the Scottish vanguard was seen approaching from the south. The Norsemen were taken by surprise. Hákon's lightly armed group of salvors was no more than a thousand men strong at most. The advancing Scots force led by Sir Robert Boyd probably wasn't much larger, but crucially it included a body of mounted men-at-arms.

What the Scots grandly called the Battle of Largs was little more than a skirmish. On sighting the cavalry, Norse lookouts on a small hill a little further inland withdrew towards the beach, which alarmed the salvors, especially when they saw the Scottish cavalry appear behind the retreating Norsemen. It descended into an unseemly rout as men scrambled into their boats, while the Scottish horsemen hacked at men floundering in the shallows. Eventually, the Norse salvagers withdrew to their ships, while the Scots army waited inland as reinforcements hurried to join them. The whole thing was probably over in less than half an hour.[27]

Afterwards, King Hákon sized up the situation. Although he'd been forced to abandon the stranded ships, he still had a mighty fleet and an army eager for revenge. Still, the storm had been a harbinger of more winter weather to come. He'd achieved much of what he'd wanted by re-establishing Norwegian control over the Sudreyjar and the Isle of Man. So he decided to return to Orkney for the winter. Then, with fresh men and supplies, he could return and force the Scots to the negotiating table. So Hákon's fleet headed north, passing through the Sound of Islay in mid-October. In the open water beyond they were hit by another westerly gale, 'so great a storm that few ships kept their sails'.[28] They ran for shelter in the Sound of Kerrera and rode out the rest of the gale there. Then, when it had passed, they resumed their voyage.

That showed the wisdom of Hákon's decision to break off the campaign. If that storm had hit Hákon off Largs, then half of his fleet could have been driven ashore. The weather remained foul, but by 29 October they reached Orkney. There the fleet was dispersed into winter havens around Scapa Flow, while the king journeyed on to Kirkwall. By then, though, Hákon had taken ill.[29]

Still, he attended mass and saw to the billeting and payment of his army and the laying up of his ships. He lodged in the Bishop's Palace in Kirkwall, beside St Magnus Cathedral. For a few days his illness abated, so he seized the opportunity to visit the cathedral to see the remains of St Magnus. No doubt the bishop was there, although Hákon was probably unable to attend a mass. The next day his sickness returned, and this time there was no respite. He withdrew to his chambers in the top floor of the palace, and there he lay in bed, having the Bible read to him, followed by Norse sagas.

By now King Hákon knew he was dying. So he also dictated his last letter to his heir Magnus Hákonsson, with advice on how to rule the kingdom. His condition deteriorated, and Hákon finally died a little after midnight on 16 December 1263. Two days later, King Hákon's coffin was taken to St Magnus Cathedral, where a funeral mass was held. His body was interred there until it was taken to Bergen in the spring for final burial in the cathedral there.[30]

So ended the life of King Hákon IV of Norway, the last of the great Norse Sea Kings, a leader in the mould of Harald 'Finehair', Harald 'Hardrada' and Magnus 'Bare-legged'. These were the kings who'd crossed the Salt Road to Orkney before leading expeditions of conquest and glory worthy of the sagas. King Hákon Hákonsson was the last of that breed of Norse heroes. With his passing the Norse world moved on to embrace a new and less turbulent age, but one that lacked the colour and drama of the past.

In Orkney that change had already happened. After the death of Earl Jón Haraldsson in 1231 a succession of Scottish-born earls followed him. By then Earl Jón's successors were known as the 'Earl of Orkney and Caithness'. As Jón had no successor he was followed by Magnus, the son of Gille Crist, Earl of Angus. At least Earl Magnus had a Norse mother, the granddaughter of Earl Rognvald. On his death eight years later, though, his son Gilbert who succeeded him had no real claim to Norse heritage. His roots were firmly planted in the Scottish heartland.

The Angus earls still owed fealty to the Norwegian crown for one part of their title and the Scottish crown for the other, which generally led to a lack of enthusiasm to 'rock the boat'. Inheritance by succession also ended, so now they acquired their title through their appointment by the Norwegian king. The dynastic succession that had lasted for centuries was no more.

Still, when Gilbert's son Magnus succeeded him in 1256, he answered the call of King Hákon. Scottish-born or not, he supported him in his last great expedition of 1263. Even so, Magnus stayed behind when the king sailed for the Sudreyjar. Probably his dual loyalties would be stretched too far if he went to war against the Scottish king.

Earl Magnus paid a price for it too, as in 1264 a Scottish army plundered its way through Caithness in retribution, although they were harried by Dougal, King of the Isles as they returned home with their plunder. The likelihood is that Earl Magnus had little choice but to support King Hákon, and afterwards he lay low, probably as the Scottish crown had taken hostages from his Scottish family. In doing so, he rode out the storm.

Soon, the earldom of Orkney would be the last Norse outpost in the British Isles. After Hákon's death, King Alexander of Scotland received the fealty of Magnus, king of Man, while the Scots quickly subdued much of the Hebrides. In 1266, when a peace between Scotland and Norway was agreed and the Treaty of Perth was signed, this was little more than a rubber-stamping acceptance of the situation. The

Sudreyjar – now the Hebrides – was sold to the Scots, as was the Isle of Man. Only Orkney and Shetland remained part of Norway. It was a strange, wasting half-life for an earldom that had achieved so much, and which had so often been the epicentre of 'headline-grabbing' events.[31]

The earldom continued to exist, in a fashion, ruled by a succession of Scottish nobles, until the mid-15th century. These are the ones which 'Willie' Thomson aptly called 'the shadow earls'. Then, in 1468, Orkney and Shetland were pawned to Scottish ownership in lieu of a marriage dowry. It had been arranged between King James III of Scotland and Margaret of Denmark, whose father Christian I ruled all of Scandinavia. Four years later, when the dowry wasn't paid, the archipelagos of Orkney and Shetland were transferred to Scottish ownership, in forfeit of the unpaid dowry. They have remained in Scottish and then British hands ever since.[32]

Even today, many native inhabitants of the so-called 'Northern Isles' of Orkney and Shetland have a strong attachment to their Norse heritage. Many also think of themselves as different from the Scots or the British from the mainland. They would argue that the islands are not really part of these lands to the 'sooth' at all, but are a special place, quite separate from them. After all that happened when the islands formed the crossroads of the Salt Road, these Orcadians and Shetlanders might well have a point.

Today, the islands are a haven for tourists, and throughout the summer enormous cruise ships and ferry-loads of cars, RVs and tour buses bring visitors eager to see these somewhat magical islands for themselves. Few, though, even when they're being shepherded around the many world-class archaeological sites, are fully aware of the richness of the islands' Norse heritage. Few, for instance, when visiting the broch at Mousa or the burial mound at Maeshowe know that these played a part in the story of the Norse earls.

In winter, as temperatures drop and the gales sweep in from the Atlantic, the islanders are largely left to themselves. Sometimes, when the ferries and planes are disrupted by the weather, the islanders are completely cut off from the rest of the world – or would be if it weren't for phones, television and the internet. Then, a sort of strange mood of complacency can descend. For many, especially the more introverted, this time of short days and week-long gales is perfectly suited to settling down by the fire with a 'dram' and a good book.

Other, more extroverted types draw on the islanders' strong sense of community. They use the time to entertain friends and neighbours – play music, drink and eat, swap tales and enjoy good company. This is a way of passing the winter which has been practised in Orkney and Shetland for centuries. To some, it might even seem to mirror an earlier time when, in a packed feasting hall after a communal feast, *skald*s read aloud tales from the sagas – just as it was done back in the days when the Norse earls of Orkney truly were the Lords of the Salt Road.

EPILOGUE

Throughout the last half of this book the name Svein Ásleifarson appears a lot, like a human strand running through these pages. So, I couldn't finish this book without rounding off his side of the story. When he was 20, he'd murdered a man and been branded an outlaw. Two years later he returned to kidnap Earl Paul and handed him over to the earl's scheming half-sister. Afterwards, Svein orchestrated the killing of the poisoner Frakǫkk, and then briefly fell out with Rognvald over Svein's plundering in Caithness. Then, in the War of the Three Earls, Svein sided with Erlend, but after the earl's death Svein swore allegiance to Earl Rognvald. Then, in 1155, Earl Harald Maddadarson agreed to make peace with Svein too.

Svein Ásleifarson owned the island of Gairsay, six miles north of Kirkwall, as well as an estate in Caithness. In theory he lived his life as a wealthy farmer and landowner. In fact, most of his riches came from plunder. Since he was a teenager, Svein had gone on Viking raids, and he continued to lead them throughout his life. This of course was when he wasn't acting as a kidnapper, an adventurer, a sword for hire and a gentleman farmer. Here's what the *Earls' Saga* has to say about his activities:

> It was Sveinn's custom at that time that he resided at home in Gairsay in the winter and always had eighty men staying with him. He had such a big drinking-hall that there was no other as large in the Orkneys. Sveinn had much work in the spring and sowed a large amount of seed and did much of it himself. And when the work was done, he went every spring on a viking expedition and raided around the Hebrides and Ireland, and came home after the middle of the summer; he called that 'spring-viking'. Then he was at home until the fields were harvested and the grain was processed. Then he went on a viking expedition and did not come home until a month had gone of winter, and he called that 'autumn-viking'.[1]

In other words, Svein Ásleifarson was a Viking chief, but he timed his raids around the farming season. After his two raids and the crops were in, he'd spend winter with his warriors, feasting in what the saga described as the largest drinking hall in Orkney. This pattern of seasonal Viking raiding to coincide with the farming calendar was what had probably gone on in the earldom since it was first created. This, though, is the first detailed description of the practice. Svein just did it on a much grander scale than most. He also probably continued it long after the others, into a time when most rulers would describe Vikings like Svein as pirates. If they caught him, they'd deal with him accordingly.

In the spring of 1171, Svein led a particularly successful raid with five longships. He ranged as far as the Isle of Man in search of plunder. Then, in the middle of the Irish Sea, he captured two English merchant ships, their holds filled with English broadcloth. As the saga says, 'The Englishmen gave little resistance and they robbed every penny from the ships, except the Englishmen had the clothes they were wearing and some provisions'. On the way home, Svein had his men stitch bolts of this colourful cloth into the sails of his longships. 'They sewed the cloth on the front part of the sail so that it looked from that direction as if the sail was made only of fine cloth. This they called "fine-cloth viking."' It made for a very showy homecoming to Gairsay.[2]

On his return, Svein invited Earl Harald Maddadarson out to Gairsay for a feast. During it, after drinking captured English mead, the earl advised Svein to retire, saying that he was pushing his luck. He added, 'But it often happens to men of iniquity that they die on a raid, if they do not remove themselves from that.' Svein agreed with Harald and promised that his autumn cruise would be his last. Svein, who was now pushing 60, vowed to make it a good one.[3]

In the autumn of 1171, Svein Ásleifarson sailed with seven longships, and was accompanied by his foster-son Hákon Haraldsson, the son of the earl from his first marriage. Presumably the 'autumn cruise' had some form of financial backing from Earl Harald. This time, Svein headed south to Dublin. They took the city by surprise, and the city elders surrendered to the raiders. After plundering Dublin, rather surprisingly the elders asked Svein to govern the city in return for his protection. Svein agreed to return the next morning to finalise the arrangement, collect a payment and take hostages.

In the morning, Svein and his Vikings arrived in front of the city gates, which were open. People even lined the road, welcoming them into Dublin. Svein and his men must have been delighted by their reception. Then, disaster struck. As they walked through the gates a pit opened beneath them, and Svein and many of his men fell in. Others, trying to escape, fell into other pits, or were killed by Irish warriors hiding behind the buildings.

It seems that during the night, the Dubliners had come up with a plan. 'They dug deep pits, some inside the city gates, and others here and there between the houses … then covered the pits with branches.' These were then camouflaged by a layer of straw to blend in with the road. As Svein and his men stepped onto these traps, they fell headlong into the hidden pits. Then, armed with long spears, the Dubliners killed the defenceless Vikings. The saga concludes, 'Sveinn died there in the ditch and all those who had gone into the town.' It added that Svein Ásleifarson's last words were, 'All men should know, whether I die today or not, that I am a courtier to the old Earl Rǫgnvaldr, and I think it is a comfort that he is with God.'[4]

Svein Ásleifarson, one of the greatest Viking adventurers of the Norse world, was dead. In his time he'd been a larger-than-life character, an adventurer, freebooter, landowner, warrior and pirate. He was also, almost certainly, the last true Viking to sail the Salt Road in search of plunder. With his death, the era known as 'The Viking Age' truly ended. Svein Ásleifarson was truly the last of his breed.[5]

NOTES

CHAPTER 1

1 *The Saga of the Earls of Orkney*, trans. Judith Jesch (Edinburgh: John Donald, 2025), Chapter 4, p.53. This is the most modern translation of what has often been called the *Jarla Saga* (Saga of the Earls), or more commonly the *Orkneyinga Saga* (Saga of the Orkney Islanders). As Prof Jesch points out (ibid., pp.18–28), each translation is slightly different, as it draws on different parts of the saga's fragmentary elements. This new version is not only the most encompassing, but it is also the most accurate at reflecting the saga writer's original words.

2 Snorri Sturlasson, *Heimskringla: The Chronicle of the Kings of Norway*, Project Gutenberg e-book edition (2009). Unless otherwise noted, all subsequent extracts from *Heimskringla* are drawn from this source. This is a compilation of several sagas describing the lives of Norwegian kings. This extract is drawn from Harald Finehair's (or Harald Harfager's) Saga, Chapter 22.

3 This later raid is described in *Chronicles of the Kings of Alba*, in Alan Orr Anderson, *Early Sources in Scottish History, AD 500–1286*, Vol. 1 (Edinburgh: Oliver and Boyd, 1922; repr. 1990), pp.395–96.

4 W. P. L. Thomson, *A History of Orkney* (Edinburgh: Mercat Press, 1987), p.16. Also see Sawyer, 'Harald "Finehair" in the British Isles', in R. Boyer (ed.), *Les Vikings et leur Civilisation* (Paris: Mouton Histoire, 1976), pp.124–39.

5 Tom Muir, *Orkney in the Sagas: The Story of the Earldom of Orkney as told in the Icelandic Sagas* (Kirkwall: The Orcadian, 2005), p.6. Also see W. P. L. Thomson, *A New History of Orkney* (Edinburgh: Mercat Press, 2001), pp.25–39.

6 *Heimskringla*, Harald Finehair's Saga, Chapter 22.

7 *Chronicles of the Kings of Alba*, in Anderson, *Early Sources in Scottish History*, p.390.

8 Alfred P. Smyth, *Warlords and Holy Men: Scotland, AD 80-1000* (Edinburgh: Edinburgh University Press, 1984), pp.44–52. Also see S. T. Driscoll, *Alba: The Gaelic Kingdom of Scotland, AD 800–1124* (Edinburgh: Birlinn

with Historic Scotland, 2002), pp.9–20 and Sally Foster, *Picts, Gaels and Scots: Early Historic Scotland* (London: Batsford, 1999), pp.120–36.

9   *Heimskringla*, Harald Finehair's Saga, Chapter 22.

10   *Eyrbyggja Saga*, trans. Hermann Pálsson and Paul Edwards (London: Penguin, 1989), p.15.

11   Claus Krag, 'Norge som odel i Harald Hårfagres ætt. et møte med en gjenganger' in *Historisk Tidskrift*, No. 3 (1989), pp.288–302; Barbara E. Crawford, *The Northern Kingdoms: Orkney and Caithness from AD 870 to 1470* (Edinburgh: John Donald, 2013), p.85.

12   *Heimskringla*, Harald Finehair's Saga, Chapter 1. Vestfold lay on the western side of the Oslofjord, to the east of what would be considered the Vestlandet.

13   Ibid., Chapters 5–11.

14   Ibid., Chapter 15. The feud and battle are also recounted in *Fagrskinna Saga*, trans. Peter Andreas Munsh (Dublin: Legare Street Press, 2022), pp.41–48, and *Egil's Saga*, trans. Bernard Scudder (London: Penguin Books, 1997), pp.12–13.

15   Torbjørn 'Hornklove', *Hrafnsmál* (Raven Song) or *Haraldskvæthi* (Harald's Lay] in Diana Whaley (ed.), *Poetry from the King's Sagas 1* (Turnhout: Brepols, 2012), p.91.

16   *Heimskringla*, Harald Finehair's Saga, Chapter 19.

17   *Heimskringla*, Harald Finehair's Saga, Chapters 20–21.

CHAPTER 2

1   Thomson, *History of Orkney*. The book launch, sponsored by James Thin of the Mercat Press, was held in the Papdale Halls of Residence, Kirkwall in July 1987.

2   Thomson later expanded on this in an essay, 'Harald Finehair, Turf Einar and Saga of the Earls of Orkney', published in Olwen Owen (ed.), *The World of the Saga of the Earls of Orkney* (Kirkwall: The Orcadian, 2005), pp.1–10.

3   *Saga of the Earls of Orkney*, trans. Jesch, Chapter 1, p.49.

4   For a detailed analysis of this origin story, see Preben Sørensen, 'The Sea, the Flame and the Wind' in Colleen E. Batley, Judith Jesch and Christopher Morris (eds), *The Viking Age in Caithness, Orkney and the North Atlantic* (Edinburgh: Edinburgh University Press, 1995), pp.212–21. Also see Sturlasson, *The Prose Edda: Tales From Norse Mythology*, trans. Jesse Byock (London: Pengiun, 2005), p.34.

5   *Flateyjarbók*, trans. Carl Unger and Guobrandur Vigfusson (New York: Nabu Press, 2014), Chapter 39; 'Hversu Noregr byggðist' ('How Norway was Built'), Appendix A in *The Orkneyingers Saga: Icelandic Sagas, and*

other historical documents relating to the settlements and descents of the Northmen on the British Isles, trans. Geroge W. Dasent, Vol. III (London: Eyre and Spottiswood, 1894), pp.142–157.

6   Ibid. For a further development of this theme see Muir, *Orkney in the Sagas,* pp.1–2.

7   *Saga of the Earls of Orkney,* trans. Jesch, Chapters 1 and 2, pp.50–51.

8   Ibid., Chapter 2, p.51.

9   Ibid., Chapter 3, p.52.

10 Ibid., Chapter 2, p.51.

11 Ibid., Chapter 3, p.52.

12 *Heimskringla,* Preface by Snorri Sturlasson.

13 The *Skjöldungs* (or *Scyldings* in Anglo-Saxon English) were a semi-legendary Danish ruling dynasty, who were mentioned in *Beowulf.*

14 Although the *Skjöldunga Saga* hasn't survived in its entirety, some of these fragments are incorporated in other works. See Ben Waggoner (trans.), *The Sagas of Ragnar Lodbrok* (Philadelphia, PA: Troth Publications, 2009), p. xxv and Margaret Clunies Ross (ed.), *Old Icelandic Literature and Society* (Cambridge: Cambridge University Press, 2000), pp.221–24.

15 Sørensen, 'The Sea, the Flame and the Wind', pp.218–19.

CHAPTER 3

1   This argument is put forward very convincingly by an Orcadian schoolfriend of mine, Prof Peter Marshall, in his excellent study of early modern Orkney history, *Storm's Edge: Life, Death and Magic in the Islands of Orkney* (London: William Collins, 2024), Chapters 1–2.

2   *Historia Norvegiae,* quoted in Anderson, *Early Sources in Scottish History,* I, pp.330–31. Also see F. T. Wainwright, *The Problem of the Picts* (Edinburgh: Thomas Nelson & Sons, 1962), p.35; Thomson, *History of Orkney,* p.1.

3   This first appeared in a Latin poem in AD 297, and was probably a nickname used by Roman soldiers garrisoning the northern frontier of Roman Britain. See Anna Ritchie, *Picts* (Edinburgh: HMSO, 1989), p.5.

4   Foster, *Picts, Gaels and Scots,* pp.1–4.

5   Tacitus, *Agricola & Germania,* trans. Harold Mattingly (London: Penguin Books, 2010), p.10; Thomson, *History of Orkney,* pp.2–3.

6   Ibid., p.3.

7   Adomnan, *Life of St Columba,* trans. Richard Sharpe (London: Penguin Books, 1995), pp.56–57. See also *Annals of Tigernach,* trans. Whitely Stokes (Dublin: Legare Street Press, 2022), p.190

8   Thomson, *History of Orkney,* p.6.

9 Ibid., p.6. Also see William of Malmesbury, *Gesta Regum Anglorum* (The History of the English Kings), trans. R. A. B. Mynors and R. M. Thomson, Vol. 1 (Oxford: Clarendon Press, 1998), p.172.

10 The most celebrated example is Svein Asleifarson, whose activities are described in *Saga of the Earls of Orkney*, trans. Jesch, Chapter 56, p.101.

11 *The Anglo-Saxon Chronicle*, trans. James Ingram (London: J.M. Dent & Sons, 1823) – entry for AD 793, p.55.

12 Alcuin of York's poem *De clade Lindisfarnensis monasterii*, quoted in Kevin Crossley-Holland, *The Anglo-Saxon World: An Anthology* (Oxford: Oxford University Press, 1999), p.186.

13 Thomson, *History of Orkney*, pp.16–17.

14 For details of the Buckquoy excavation see Hunter, Bond and Smith, 'Some Aspects of Early Viking Settlement in Orkney', in Batley, Jesch and Morris (eds.), *Viking Age*, pp.272–85, and Anna Ritchie, 'Orkney in the Pictish Kingdom', in Colin Renfrew (ed.), *The Prehistory of Orkney BC 4000–1000 AD* (Edinburgh: Edinburgh University Press, 1985), pp.183–204.

CHAPTER 4

1 *Saga of the Earls of Orkney*, trans. Jesch, Chapter 4, p.53. The term 'forecastle-man' or 'focscleman' could refer to someone from among the ranks of the crew, but in this case it is singular, which suggests Sigurd was a leader of these men. In a longship this would have almost certainly have been a warrior of notable prowess.

2 For a discussion of this, see Crawford, *Northern Kingdoms*, pp.89–90. Evidence for the south-western Norwegian connection is found in the hidden caches or hoards of plunder found there, which was brought back from these early Viking raids.

3 Christopher Morris, 'Viking Orkney: A Survey', in Renfrew (ed.), *Prehistory of Orkney*, pp.213–42.

4 *Historia Norvegiae* in Anderson, *Early Sources in Scottish History*, I, pp.330–31.

5 For a discussion of this and its ramifications, see Crawford, *Northern Kingdoms*, pp.90–91.

6 *Fragmentary Annals of Ulster*, trans. Joan S. Radnor (Cork: Corpus of Electronic Texts, 1999), pp.322–23.

7 Thomson, *History of Orkney*, p.12.

8 Crawford, *Northern Kingdoms*, pp.83–84. Also see Frederic Amory, 'The Historical Worth of Rígsmál', *Alvíssmál* magazine, No. 10 (2001), pp.3–16.

9 *Heimskringla*, Harald Harfagr's Saga, Ch. 6. Also Crawford, *Northern Kingdoms*, p. 84.

10   Peter Foote and David Wilson, *The Viking Achievement: The Society and Culture of Early Medieval Scandinavia* (London: Sidgwick and Jackson, 1990), p.136. Also Crawford, *Northern Kingdoms*, p.84.

11   Crawford, *Northern Kingdoms*, pp.84–85.

12   Ibid., p.120.

13   J. Storer Clouston (ed.), *Records of the Earldom of Orkney 1299–1614* (Edinburgh: Scottish History Society, 1914) provides an excellent historical overview of the earldom's administration during both the Norse and post-Norse eras.

14   Crawford, *Northern Kingdoms*, pp.122–23.

15   *Saga of the Earls of Orkney*, trans. Jesch, chapters 107–08; The *Irish Annals of the Four Masters* (Cork: Corpus of Electronic Texts, 2013) contains a useful outline of these events in Dublin.

16   Crawford, *Northern Kingdoms*, p.122. 'Hack silver' refers to objects or coins which had been cut into pieces, or even nicked with shears, so they weighed an exact amount.

17   There seems to be many ways to spell the first name of this Viking adventurer; Svein, Sveinn, Sweyn or even Swein can be found in various accounts. His surname too – Ásleifarson – has often been Anglicised to Asleifsson. Here though, I prefer to use the version given in the saga: Svein Ásleifarson.

CHAPTER 5

1   *Saga of the Earls of Orkney*, trans. Jesch, Chapter 5. For a scholarly account of Sigurd's achievements and the estimation of the date of his death, see Crawford, *Northern Kingdoms*, pp.92–99. Any dates are little more than 'educated guesses', however, based on sources that are often vague and contradictory.

2   *Saga of the Earls of Orkney*, trans. Jesch, Chapter 5, p.54.

3   Foster, *Picts, Gaels and Scots*, pp.36–38; Wainwright, *Problem of the Picts*, pp.46–47; Peter McNeill and Ranald Nicholson, *An Historical Atlas of Scotland, c.400-c.1600* (St Andrews: Conference of Scottish Medievalists, 1976), pp.11–13.

4   *Eyrbyggja Saga*, trans. Pálsson and Edwards, Chapter 1.

5   *The Laxdæla Saga*, trans. Muriel Press (London: J.M. Dent, 1964), Chapter 1.

6   Ibid., Chapter 4.

7   *The Book of Settlements – Landnámabók*, trans. Hermann Pálsson and Paul Edwards (Winnipeg: University of Manitoba, 1972), Book 2, Chapter 4. Also see Alex Woolf, *From Pictland to Alba: 789–1070* (Edinburgh: Edinburgh University Press, 2001), p.297.

8 *Annals of Ulster*, trans. Radnor, p.853. The identification of Ólaf as Amláib has its sceptics. See Gwyn Jones, *A History of the Vikings* (London: Oxford University Press, 1984) for an example.

9 *Annals of Ulster*, trans. Radnor, p.871. Also see *Annals of Ireland: Three Fragments*, trans. John O'Donovan (Dublin: Dublin University Press, 1860), p.195.

10 William Skene, *Chronicles of the Picts, Chronicles of the Scots and Other Memorials of Early Scottish History* (Edinburgh: T. Constable, 1867), p.xxiv. Also see Smyth, *Warlords and Holy Men*, pp.159–60.

11 *Laxdæla Saga*, trans. Press, Chapter 4.

12 Crawford, *Northern Kingdoms*, p.95.

13 *Life of St Columba*, trans. Sharpe, p.176. Adomnán was an abbot of Iona, biographer of St. Columba and later a saint in his own right.

14 Crawford, *Northern Kingdoms*, pp.94–95.

15 Ibid. See also Martin Carver, *Portmahomack: Monastery of the Picts* (Edinburgh: Edinburgh University Press, 2008), pp.135–44.

16 Skene, *Chronicles of the Picts*, Chronicle of the Kings of Alba, p.83.

17 Ibid., *Chronicles*, p.9.

18 Ibid., *Chronicles*, pp.15–30. See also Tim Clarkson, *Strathclyde and the Anglo-Saxons in the Viking Age* (Edinburgh: John Donald, 2014), Chapter 3, p.26; S. T. Driscoll, 'Discourse on the Frontiers of History: Material Culture and Social Reproduction in Early Scotland', *Historical Archaeology*, Vol. 26.3 (1992), pp.12–25.

19 Skene, *Chronicles of the Picts*, p.9; Anderson, *Early Sources in Scottish History*, I, p.358.

20 Anderson, *Early Sources in Scottish History*, I, pp.395–97.

21 *Mormaer* was a Scots Gaelic term for a provincial ruler, the equivalent of an earl.

22 *Saga of the Earls of Orkney*, trans. Jesch, Chapter 5, p.54.

23 Crawford, *Northern Kingdoms*, p.95.

24 Ibid., p.95 and p.108. The possibility is also explored in James Graham-Campbell and Colleen Batley, *Vikings in Scotland: An Archaeological Survey* (Edinburgh: Edinburgh University Press, 1998). Also see Foster, *Picts, Gaels and Scots*, pp.46–52 for a discussion of the importance of Burghead as a regional powerbase.

25 For a discussion of this portage route, see Crawford, *Northern Kingdoms*, p.22–24.

CHAPTER 6

1 *Saga of the Earls of Orkney*, trans. Jesch, Chapter 5, p.54.

2 Ibid.

3   Ibid.

4   Crawford, *Northern Kingdoms*, p.93; Muir, *Orkney in the Sagas.*, p.9. Also see Bo Almqvist, 'What's in a Word? Folklore Contacts between Norsemen and Gaels as Reflected in the *Saga of the Earls of Orkney*', in Owen (ed.), *World of the Saga of the Earls of Orkney*, pp.25–38.

5   *Lœxdala Saga*, trans. Press, Chapter 4.

6   Ibid., Chapter 4.

7   A discussion of the siting of Sigurd's Howe can be found in Barbara E. Crawford, *Scandinavian Scotland* (Leicester: Leicester University Press, 1987), pp.38–39, and Crawford, *Northern Kingdoms*, pp.97–98. Modern Ordnance Survey Maps mark the location of both the wood and the farm. Also see P. Anderson, 'Introduction' in *The Orkneyinga Saga*, trans. Jon Hjaltalin and Gilbert Goudie (Edinburgh: James Thin, 1873; repr. 1973), pp.ix–cxiii.

8   *Saga of the Earls of Orkney*, trans. Jesch, Chapter 5, pp.54–55.

9   Ibid., Chapter 4, p.53. In *Heimskringla*, Ragnhildr is called 'Hild', an abbreviation of her full name.

10   *Heimskringla*, Harald Finehair's Saga, Chapter 24; *Saga of the Earls of Orkney*, trans. Jesch, Chapter 6, p.56.

11   Dudo of St Quentin, *History of the Normans*, trans. Eric Christianssen (London: Boydell, 1998), Chapters 4–5. Although this 10th century source may be considered unreliable in places, it generally supports the claim that Rolf Rognvaldsson became Rollo, Count of Normandy. See Davis Bates, *Normandy Before 1066* (London: Longman, 1982), pp.8–16 for a discussion of the role played by Rollo in the foundation of Normandy.

12   *Saga of the Earls of Orkney*, trans. Jesch, Chapter 5, pp.54–55.

13   Ibid., p.55. However, there's another possibility, which reflects better on Earl Hallad. In the north of Caithness there is a glen called Strath Halladale, where the small River Halladale flows northwards into the sea at Melvich Bay to the west of the Pentland Firth. According to early 19th-century writer John Pinkerton, local tradition has it that Hallad Rognvaldsson returned to Caithness a few years later, and was slain there, while resisting a Viking raid. He was buried in a circular grave in Strath Halladale, which was named in his honour. No trace of a Norse grave has ever been found, though, and the story isn't supported by any other evidence. It would be nice to think that Hallad had tried to redeem himself. See John Pinkerton, *A General Collection of the Best and Most Interesting Voyages and Travels in All Parts of the World*, Vol. 3 (London: Longman, Hurst, Reeve and Orme, 1809), p.152. He claimed that the burial site was at Dalhalvaig, which is just over six miles from the coast.

14   *Saga of the Earls of Orkney*, trans. Jesch, Chapter 6, p.56.

15 Ibid., Chapters 6 and 7, pp.56–57, and Muir, *Orkney in the Sagas*, p.16. Also see *Heimskringla*, Chapter 27.

16 *Saga of the Earls of Orkney*, trans. Jesch, Chapter 6, p.56.

17 Ibid., Chapter 7, p.57.

18 *Heimskringla*, Chapter 27; *Saga of the Earls of Orkney*, trans. Jesch, Chapter 7, p.57. However, there is archaeological evidence that peat was being cut, dried and burned in Orkney and Shetland since neolithic times.

19 *Heimskringla*, Chapter 30.

20 *Saga of the Earls of Orkney*, trans. Jesch, Chapter 8, pp.58–59.

CHAPTER 7

1 *Saga of the Earls of Orkney*, trans. Jesch, Chapter 8, p.58.

2 Ibid. Also *Heimskringla*, Chapter 31; Muir, *Orkney in the Sagas*, p.18; and Thomson, *History of Orkney*, p.11.

3 *Heimskringla*, Chapter 31.

4 *Saga of the Earls of Orkney*, trans. Jesch, Chapter 8, p.58.

5 Ibid.

6 Ibid.

7 *Heimskringla*, Harald Finehair's Saga, Chapter 31.

8 See The Tale of Ragnar's Sons, Chapter 3 in Waggoner, *Sagas of Ragnar Lodbrok*.

9 See Roberta Frank, 'The Blood Eagle Again', *The Saga Book*, Vol. XXII (1998), pp.287–314. See also Luke John Murphy, Heidi R. Fuller, Peter L. T. Willan, and Monte A. Gates, 'An Anatomy of the Blood Eagle: The Practicalities of Medieval Torture' in *Speculum*, Vol. 97:1 (2002), pp.1–39. In Muir, *Orkney in the Sagas*, p.118, the link between 'Turf' Einar and Odin is clearly and convincingly made.

10 *Saga of the Earls of Orkney*, trans. Jesch, Chapter 8, p.59.

11 Ibid., pp.59–60.

12 Ibid., p.60.

13 Ibid.

14 *Heimskringla*, King Harald Finehair's Saga, Chapter 32.

15 *Saga of the Earls of Orkney*, trans. Jesch, Chapter 8, p.60.

16 The 'sixty marks of gold' were therefore rare, expensive and difficult to find. The most prestigious of these coins was the Byzantine gold *solidus*, just under an inch across, and weighing a sixth of an ounce. In late 9th century Europe, one of these gold coins, commonly called a *bezant*, could probably buy a pair of good horses. This was the *mark* mentioned in the saga. In today's currency, a single coin of this type would be the equivalent of a marker for £6,000 (or $8,000). See Michael F. Hendy, *Studies in the Byzantine Monetary Economy c.300–1450* (Cambridge: Cambridge

University Press, 1985), pp.124–76; Philip Grierson, *Byzantine Coinage* (Washington DC: Dumbarton Oaks, 1999), pp.6–9.

17 *Saga of the Earls of Orkney*, trans. Jesch, Chapter 8, p.60.

18 Ibid, p.60.

19 For a discussion of Einar's poetry, see Else Mundal, 'The Orkney Earl and Skald Turf-Einarr and his Poetry', in Batley, Jesch and Morris (eds), *Viking Age*, pp.248–59.

20 Muir, *Orkney in the Sagas*, p.19.

21 Crawford, *Northern Kingdoms*, pp.104–07.

22 Angelo Forte, Richard Oram and Frederik Pedersen, *Viking Empires* (Cambridge: Cambridge University Press, 2005), pp.86–90.

23 Ibid., pp.83, 92–93, 101–03.

24 Ibid., pp.103–05. Also Marc Morris, *The Anglo-Saxons: A History of the Beginnings of England* (London: Hutchinson, 2021), pp.255–89.

25 Jones, *A History of the Vikings*, pp.94–95.

26 *Heimskringla*, Chapter 45. See Jones, *A History of the Vikings*, p.89, for a discussion of the possible dates of Harald's reign and its aftermath, including the accession of his son Hákon to the throne.

27 *Heimskringla*, Hákon the Good's Saga, Chapters 1–3. Also Jones, *A History of the Vikings*, pp.94–95.

CHAPTER 8

1 *Saga of the Earls of Orkney*, trans. Jesch, Chapter 8, p.32; *Heimskringla*, Hákon the Good's Saga, Chapter 3. For a discussion of the timeline, see Jones, *A History of the Vikings*, p.89.

2 *Heimskringla*, Hákon the Good's Saga, Chapter 3.

3 Ibid., Chapter 3.

4 Peter Sawyer, 'The Last Scandinavian Kings of York', *Northern History*, Vol. 31 (1995), pp.39–44; Claire Downham, 'The Chronology of the Last Scandinavian Kings of York', *Northern History*, Vol. IV (2003), pp.27–51.

5 Ibid. Also *Anglo-Saxon Chronicle*, trans. Ingram, entries for AD 944–46, p.89.

6 Ibid. Also *Saga of the Earls of Orkney*, trans. Jesch, p.32.

7 Ibid. Also see Forte, Oram and Pedersen, *Viking Empires*, pp.109–13; Jones, *A History of the Vikings*, pp.138–40.

8 *Saga of the Earls of Orkney*, trans. Jesch, Chapter 8, p.61.

9 Ibid.

10 Ibid. Also see John Cannon (ed.), *The Oxford Companion to English History* (Oxford: Oxford University Press, 1997), p.147; Sir Frank Stenton, *Anglo-Saxon England* (Oxford: Oxford University Press, 1971), p.362. Also see 'Bloodaxe's Final Stand' in *BBC History Magazine*, No. 34 (September 2017).

11 *Heimskringla*, Harald Finehair's Saga, Chapter 46.

12 *Heimskringla*, Saga of Ólaf Haraldsson, Chapter 99.

13 Ibid. Also *Saga of the Earls of Orkney*, trans. Jesch, Chapter 8, p.61. Also see Muir, *Orkney in the Sagas*, p.20. However, there is an element of doubt if this usurpation of Earl Thorfinn's rule ever happened. Crawford, *Northern Kingdoms*, p. 61 and Forte, Oram and Pedersen, *Viking Empires*, pp.114–15 suggest that the Orkney earls acknowledged Eirík as their ruler and so Queen Gunnhild's seizing of power in Orkney was merely an extension of this authority.

14 Quoted in *Heimskringla*, Saga of Ólaf Haraldsson, Chapter 99.

15 Jones, *A History of the Vikings*, pp.118–20.

16 *Saga of the Earls of Orkney*, trans. Jesch, Chapter 8, pp.61–62. Also Muir, *Orkney in the Sagas*, p.20; Jones, *A History of the Vikings*, pp.121–22.

17 *Heimskringla*, Harald the Good's Saga, Chapter 20.

18 Ibid., Chapters 24–26.

19 Ibid., Chapter 29. Also see Jones, *A History of the Vikings*, p.122.

20 *Heimskringla*, Harald the Good's Saga, Chapters 30–32.

21 Ibid., Chapter 32.

22 Jones, *A History of the Vikings*, pp.122–23.

23 Harald 'Greycloak' was lured to Denmark by Harald 'Bluetooth's promise of greater power. Instead, when he landed at Hals on the Limfjord in northern Jutland, he and his followers were attacked and killed by Earl Hákon of Lade, an ally of Bluetooth. *Heimskringla*, Saga of Ólaf Trygvason, Chapter 13.

24 Jones, *A History of the Vikings*, pp.123–25.

25 *Saga of the Earls of Orkney*, trans. Jesch, Chapter 9, p.63.

26 Ibid., pp.33–35. Linklater, *The Ultimate Viking* (London: Macmillan, 1955), p.38.

CHAPTER 9

1 Muir, *Orkney in the Sagas*, p.20, *Saga of the Earls of Orkney*, trans. Jesch, Chapter 9, p.63. Regrettably, the saga is silent on the motive behind this alleged murder.

2 *Saga of the Earls of Orkney*, trans. Jesch, Chapter 9, pp.63–64.

3 In earlier translations of the saga 'Butty' was translated as 'Butter-mouth', but 'Butty', a term still used to refer to a buttered bread roll, is much closer to the original meaning.

4 Ibid., pp. 63–64. What follows is entirely drawn from *The Saga of the Earls of Orkney*. While the saga's account lacks corroboration elsewhere, it's so vital to the development of the earldom that it would be impossible

to omit it from the story. See Thomson, *History of Orkney*, pp.35–36 for a discussion of Ragnhild's activities.

5   *Saga of the Earls of Orkney*, trans. Jesch, Chapter 9, p.64.

6   Archibald A. M. Duncan, *The Kingship of the Scots, 842–1292: Succession and Independence* (Edinburgh: Edinburgh University Press, 2001), pp.24–25.

7   Sutherland was literally the southern land of the earldom, and still part of Caithness. However, during the late 10th century there appears to have been a southern migration of Norse settlers, the extent of which can still be traced through placenames. By the reign of Earl Thorfinn 'the Mighty' in the early 11th century 'Sutherland' was given its own identity, and following the earl's conquests in the region, it seems it no longer was a frontier zone. Sutherland had become an established Norse community, and under Thorfinn the border region was moved some 25 miles south from the Dornoch Firth to the Moray Firth. This new 'southern land' encompassed the old Scottish province of Ross, which never officially became part of the earldom's territory. See Crawford, *Northern Kingdoms*, p.100–19.

8   *Saga of the Earls of Orkney*, trans. Jesch, Chapter 10, p.65. Also J. S. Clouston, 'Two Features of the Orkney Earldom', *Scottish Historical Review*, XVI (1918), p.26. The reference to the 'Ness' most probably means Tarbat Ness, the headland at the southern side of the Dornoch Firth, just beyond the borders of the earldom.

9   *Saga of the Earls of Orkney*, trans. Jesch, Chapter 10, p.65.

10 Ibid., pp.65–66. Highland Historic Environment Record MHG2005 – Battle Site – Skitten.

11 *Saga of the Earls of Orkney*, trans. Jesch, pp.65–66.

12 Ibid.

13 Ibid., Chapter 11, p.66; Thomson, *History of Orkney*, pp.36–37.

14 *Saga of the Earls of Orkney* is clear that Earl Sigurd's mother was Eithne. However, a dalliance between Earl Hlodfer and Ragnhild is raised as a possibility in Thomson, *History of Orkney*, p.58 and discussed in Crawford, *Northern Kingdoms*, pp.112-13. The likelihood, though, if for no other reason than the tale of Sigurd's magical raven banner, is that Earl Sigud's mother was Eithnie.

15 John B. Mowat, *The Placenames of Canisbay, Caithness* (London: Viking Society for Northern Research, 1931), p.27. *Saga of the Earls of Orkney* says 'Ham', but research on Caithness placenames shows no such place. However, local tradition claimed the burial place was at Huna.

16 *Saga of the Earls of Orkney*, trans. Jesch, Chapter 11, p.66. The bulk of what we know of Earl Sigurd's achievements comes from other contemporary Norse Scots and Irish sources. The most significant of these are *Njal's Saga*, *Eybryggia Saga* and the *Saga of Gunnlaug Serpent-Tongue*.

17 Ibid., Chapter 11, p.66. *Heimskringla*, Saga of Ólaf Haraldsson (St Ólaf), Chapter 99. The point about the peaceable accession is made succinctly by Thomson, *History of Orkney*, p.27.

18 *Njal's Saga*, trans. Robert Cook (London: Penguin Books, 1981), Chapter 86, p.139. In earlier translations, Argyll was translated as 'the Dales', which may stem from 'Dalr' (the Norse term for Scottish Dál Riáta), or, as Thomson suggested, they might just as possibly refer to the straths or glens of north-western Caithness (see Thomson, *History of Orkney*, p.37).

19 Crawford, *Northern Kingdoms*, pp.114–16.

20 *Njal's Saga*, trans. Cook, Chapters 88–89, pp.138–53. Peter Andreas Munch (ed. & trans.), *The Chronicle of Man and the Sudreys 'Chronica Regnum Manniae et Insularem'* (Douglas, Isle of Man: The Manx Society, 1874) provides an interesting account of activities in the region during this period from the perspective of the Isle of Man.

21 The first outcome is recorded in *Annals of Ulster*, in Anderson, *Early Sources in Scottish History*, I, ff489. While the Norse version appears in *Njal's Saga*, trans. Cook, Chapter 89, p.152.

22 Anderson, *Early Sources in Scottish History*, I, p.494; *Annals of Tigernach*, trans. Stokes, entries for 1002–1014; *Njal's Saga*, trans. Cook, Chapter 86, p.140.

23 *Saga of the Earls of Orkney*, trans. Jesch, Chapter 11, p.66.

24 Ibid., Chapter 11, pp.36–37.

25 Ibid.

26 Ibid. Also see Crawford, *Northern Kingdoms*, p. 46, Muir, *Orkney in the Sagas*, p.27 and Thomson, *History of Orkney*, p.42 for a discussion of the significance of Sigurd's magic raven banner.

27 Thomson, *History of Orkney*, p.66.

28 *Annals of Ulster*, entry for 1020. Also see Woolf, *From Pictland to Alba*, pp.134–36.

29 Thomson, *History of Orkney*, p.39.

30 *Heimskringla*, Ólaf Tryggvason's Saga, Chapters 31 and 33.

31 Ibid.

32 *Anglo-Saxon Chronicle*, trans. Ingram, entry for AD 994, p.102.

33 Ibid. Also *Heimskringla*, Ólaf Tryggvason's Saga, Chapter 32.

34 Ibid., Ólaf Tryggvason's Saga, Chapters 50–52.

CHAPTER 10

1 *Saga of the Earls of Orkney*, trans. Jesch, Chapter 12, p.67. Today, Osmundswall is called South Walls. To the Norse, though, it was Ásmundarvágr. Near Longhope in South Walls, a modern plaque marks the event.

2   *Heimskringla*, Ólaf Tryggvason's Saga, Chapters 52–55.

3   Ibid., Chapters 55–56.

4   *Saga of the Earls of Orkney*, trans. Jesch, Chapter 12, p.67. There is no mention of Earl Sigurd being married before his union with the daughter of Máel Coluim (Malcom II), King of Scots in *c.* AD1006. The likelihood is he had been married before, as Hundi was regarded as his heir, which suggests his legitimacy. Hundi was also called 'Hvelpr', which means 'dog' or 'puppy' in Norse. These were probably nicknames, and the name Hlǫðvir (or Hlodvir), which the saga claims was a baptismal one given by Ólaf, was actually the youth's real name. This makes sense, as Sigurd would have named his son after his own father, Earl Hlǫðvir (or Hlodvir).

5   Ibid. For a discussion of this spread of Christianity, see Thomson, *History of Orkney*, pp.8, 39–40.

6   Ibid., pp.39–40.

7   George M. Brundsen, *Thorfinn the Mighty: The Ultimate Viking* (Stroud: The History Press, 2009), p.19 argues that Ólaf wasn't a devout Christian but used the religion as a pragmatic means of portraying himself as a moral ruler to increase his standing in Norway and elsewhere.

8   *Saga of the Earls of Orkney*, trans. Jesch, Chapter 12, p.67.

9   Benjamin T. Hudson, *Kings of Celtic Scotland* (London: Praeger, 1994), pp.131–34. The name 'Plantula' is suggested in Thomson, *History of Orkney*, p.39. The 'late source' he cited was George Barry, *History of the Orkney Islands* (London: Longman, Hurst, Rees and Orme, 1808), p.137. However, as there is no indication of Barry's own source, its accuracy cannot be affirmed.

10   Hudson, *Kings of Celtic Scotland*, pp.134–35; Crawford, *Northen Kingdoms*, p.113.

11   *Thorstein Sidu-Hallsson's Saga*, quoted in Muir, *Orkney in the Sagas*, p.28.

12   *Saga of Gunnlaug 'Serpent-Tongue*, paraphrased from Muir, *Orkney in the Sagas*, p.28. In his book, Tom Muir draws on his extensive knowledge of Icelandic sagas to create the first in-depth study of Earl Sigurd.

13   Crawford, *Northern Kingdoms*, pp.114–20.

14   Forte, Oram and Pedersen, *Viking Empires*, pp.81–82; Seán Duffy, *Brian Boru and the Battle of Clontarf* (Dublin: Gill and Macmillan, 2013), pp.123–35.

15   Forte, Oram & Pedersen, *Viking Empires*, pp.224–26; Darren McGettican, *The Battle of Clontarf: Good Friday 1014* (Dublin: Four Courts Press, 2013), pp.61–63.

16   Duffy, *Brian Boru*, pp.211–13.

17   *Njal's Saga*, trans. Cook, Chapter 156, pp.300–01. Also see Muir, *Orkney in the Sagas*, pp.34–35.

18 *Njal's Saga*, trans. Cook, Chapters 155–57, pp.298–308; *The Annals of Ulster*, trans. Seán Mac Airt and Gearóid Mac Niocaill (Dublin: Institute for Advanced Studies, 1983), pp.446–49; *Annals of Inisfallen*, trans. Seán Mac Airt (Dublin: Institute for Advanced Studies, 1951), pp.184–85; *The Annals of Loch Cé*, trans. W. M. Hennessy (London: Longman, 1871), pp.2–15; *War of the Gaedhil with the Gaill*, trans. James Henthorn Todd (London: Longman, 1867), pp.151–205.

19 *Njal's Saga*, trans. Cook, Chapter 157, p.302; Duffy, *Brian Boru*, p.210, citing *War of the Gaedhil with the Gaill*, trans. Todd, pp.174–75.

20 *Njal's Saga*, trans. Cook, Chapter 157, p.302. Although the Irish warrior Kerthjalfad was identified by Robert Cook, the translator of Njal's Saga, as King Brian Boru's foster-son, comparison with the Irish annals suggest this it is more likely he was Murchad mac Briain, Brian Boru's biological son.

21 Ibid.

22 Ibid., Chapters 156–57, pp.303–07. Also see Muir, *Orkney in the Sagas*, for an evocative retelling of these supernatural events.

CHAPTER 11

1 Kormlod, or Gormflaith in the name's Irish version, was a widow who'd previously been married to Ólaf Kvaran, the son of Sigtrygg 'Silkbeard'.

2 *Saga of the Earls of Orkney*, trans. Jesch, Chapter 13, p.69; Muir, *Orkney in the Sagas*, pp.43–44; Crawford, *Northern Kingdoms*, p.129; Brundsen, *Thorfinn the Mighty*, pp.27–28.

3 Crawford, *Northern Kingdoms*, p.129; Hudson, *Kings of Celtic Scotland*, p.135. Prof Crawford's discussion of the earldom makes it clear that by this stage Caithness and Sutherland were viewed separately from Orkney and Shetland, as the lands on the Scottish mainland were officially the lands of the King of Scots, rather than the King of Norway. So, as Thorfinn was made an earl there by the Scottish king, these lands were usually omitted from any division of the earldom.

4 *Saga of the Earls of Orkney*, trans. Jesch, Chapter 13, p.69.

5 Crawford, *Northern Kingdoms*, pp.129–30.

6 Ibid., pp.134–36; Hudson, *Kings of Celtic Scotland*, p.83.

7 *Saga of the Earls of Orkney*, trans. Jesch, Chapter 13, p.69.

8 Ibid., Chapter 15, p.72.

9 Ibid. Also see Muir, *Orkney in the Sagas*, p.45.

10 *Saga of the Earls of Orkney*, trans. Jesch, Chapter 14, p.70. Today, the site of this howe and the importance of the area as a *Thing* location is noted and explained on information panels, sited next to one of the nicest beaches in Orkney.

11 Ibid.

12 Ibid.

13 Ibid.

14 Ibid. The Irish ruler was possibly Niall mac Eochada, king of Ulster, although *The Saga of the Earls of Orkney* calls him 'King Konufogur'. Also see Muir, *Orkney in the Sagas*, p.45, who dates the battle to the summer of 1017, three years after Einar gained his share of the earldom.

15 Muir, *Orkney in the Sagas*, p.46.

16 *Saga of the Earls of Orkney*, trans. Jesch, Chapter 16, p. 74. Although the saga claims Thorkell's hall was in Sandwick, in the West Mainland of Orkney, it has been identified as Hlaipandanes, his family estate in Deerness. It has been proposed that this is at Skaill. See Muir, *Orkney in the Sagas*, pp.45–46.

17 *Saga of the Earls of Orkney*, trans. Jesch, Chapter 16, p.74.

18 Ibid., pp.74–75.

19 *Saga of the Earls of Orkney*, trans. Jesch, Chapter 17, p.76.

20 Ibid, pp.76–77.

21 This account of the negotiations with King Ólaf is based on *The Saga of the Earls of Orkney*, trans. Jesch, Chapters 17–19, pp.76–82.

22 This version of Óttar 'the Black's' poetry is quoted in T. O. Clancy (ed.), *The Triumph Tree: Scotland's Earliest Poetry, AD 550–1350* (Edinburgh: Canongate Press, 1998), p.168. *The Saga of the Earls of Orkney* provides a slightly different version of the verse; see *Saga of the Earls of Orkney*, trans. Jesch, Chapter 19, p.81.

23 *Saga of the Earls of Orkney*, trans. Jesch, Chapters 17–19, p.49.

24 Ibid., Chapter 19, p.80.

25 Forte, Oram and Pedersen, *Viking Empires*, pp.184–92.

26 *Saga of the Earls of Orkney*, trans. Jesch, Chapter 19, p.82.

27 Ibid.

28 Ibid.

CHAPTER 12

1 Jones, *A History of the Vikings*, pp.379–82.

2 *Saga of the Earls of Orkney*, trans. Jesch, Chapter 20, p.83.

3 Jones, *A History of the Vikings*, pp.383–84 In old Norse, the battlefield is called Stiklastaðr.

4 *Heimskringla*, St Ólaf's Saga, Chapter 238. The account of the Battle of Stiklestad (1030) which follows is largely based on Snorri Sturlasson's account from the saga, Chapters 238–41. Also see Kim Hjardar and Vegard Vike, *Vikings at War* (Oxford: Casemate Publishing, 2016) for a detailed discussion of Norse troop types and tactics.

5   *Heimskringla*, St Ólaf's Saga, Chapter 241.

6   Ibid., Chapter 245. Also Muir, *Orkney in the Sagas*, p.49; Brunsden, *Thorfinn the Mighty*, pp.69–70; Don Hollway, *The Last Viking: The True Story of King Harald Hardrada* (Oxford: Osprey Publishing, 2021), pp.50–52.

7   Skene, *Chronicles of the Picts*, pp.99–100; Anderson, *Early Sources*, I, pp.574–75. Also see Edward J. Cowan, 'The Historical Macbeth', in W. D. H. Sellar (ed.), *Moray: Province, Land and People* (Edinburgh: Scottish Society for Northern Studies, 1993), pp.117–42; Brundsen, *Thorfinn the Mighty*, pp.50–51; Smyth, *Warlords and Holy Men*, pp.225–27.

8   CELT, *Annals of Ulster*, p.454, f.56ra. Also see Woolf, *From Pictland to Alba*, pp.228–30.

9   Cowan, 'The Historical Macbeth', pp.119–21.

10 William Dickinson, *Scotland from Earliest Times to 1603* (Edinburgh: Thomas Nelson, 1961), p.61. Also Brundsen, *Thorfinn the Mighty*, p.52. Thomson, *History of Orkney*, p.48 suggests Karl Hundasson was actually the Earl Gille, but more recent research now strongly favours Macbeth.

11 CELT, *Annals of Ulster*, Vol 1, p.470, ff57rb, entry for 1032.

12 *Saga of the Earls of Orkney*, trans. Jesch, Chapter 20, p.83.

13 See Crawford, *Northern Kingdoms*, pp.134–36.

14 *The Saga of the Earls of Orkney*, trans. Jesch, Chapter 20, p.83.

15 Ibid., p.84. Also see Crawford, *Northern Kingdoms*, pp.136–37.

16 *Saga of the Earls of Orkney*, trans. Jesch, Chapter 20, p.84.

17 Ibid., pp.84–86. Also Brundsen, *Thorfinn the Mighty*, pp.56–58; Cowan, 'The Historical Macbeth', pp.126–27; Crawford, *Northern Kingdoms*, p.136.

18 *Saga of the Earls of Orkney*, trans. Jesch, p.85. This and the following account of the campaign between Earl Thorfinn and Mormaer Macbeth are largely drawn from the *Saga of the Earls of Orkney*, supported by Brundsen, Cowan and Crawford. Also see Muir, *Orkney in the Sagas*, p.47 for a useful précis of these events.

19 *Saga of the Earls of Orkney*, trans. Jesch, Chapter 20, p.86. Also see Crawford, *Northern Kingdoms*, p.137; Brundsen, *Thorfinn the Mighty*, p.59.

20 *Saga of the Earls of Orkney*, trans. Jesch, Chapter 20, p.86. Also Brundsen, *Thorfinn the Mighty*, pp.60–62.

21 *Saga of the Earls of Orkney*, trans. Jesch, Chapter 20, p.86.

22 Ibid., p.87.

23 Ibid.

24 Ibid.

25 Ibid., pp.87–88, Chapter 32, p.111. Also Crawford, *Northern Kingdoms*, pp.135–38. The theory that Thorfinn was an ally of Duncan is proposed in Thomson, *History of Orkney*, pp.49–50.

26 *Saga of the Earls of Orkney*, trans. Jesch, Chapter 20, p.88.

CHAPTER 13

1 Forte, Oram and Pedersen, *Viking Empires*, pp.227–28. Also Claire Downham, 'Scottish Affairs and the Political Context of Cogadh Gaedhel re Gallaibh', in Jamie Barnes et al. (eds.), *Traversing the Inner Seas* (Edinburgh: Scottish Society for Northern Studies, 2017), pp.86–106.

2 *Saga of the Earls of Orkney*, trans. Jesch, Chapter 32, p.111. Also Crawford, *Northern Kingdoms*, pp.138–39; Thomson, *History of Orkney*, pp.50–51.

3 *Saga of the Earls of Orkney*, trans. Jesch, Chapter 32, p.111.

4 *Heimskringla*, Saga of King Magnus the Good, Chapters 1 to 3.

5 *Saga of the Earls of Orkney*, trans. Jesch, Chapter 21, p.58.

6 Ibid., Chapter 22, p.59.

7 Ibid. Chapter 22, p.92.

8 Ibid.

9 Ibid.

10 Ibid., Chapter 24, p.95. Also see *Anglo-Saxon Chronicle*, trans. Ingham, entries for 1040–42. The *Anglo-Saxon Chronicle* contains no mention of this battle, so the likelihood was that if it did happen, it was merely a skirmish linked to raiding on the western coast of England and Wales.

11 *Saga of the Earls of Orkney*, trans. Jesch, Chapter 26, p.99.

12 Ibid. 'Roeberry' is an anglified version of 'Raudabiorg' or 'Rauðabjorg' meaning 'Red Cliff', a reference to the red-stained sandstone cliffs which fringe parts of the Pentland Firth. There are three possible sites for this battle. The first, 'Roeberry' in South Ronaldsay, overlooks Widewall Bay, which is too small to host a naval battle of that size. In the Hjaltalin & Goudie translation of *The Orkneyinga Saga* (1873), the editor Joseph Anderson favoured a site in Caithness just south of Duncansby Head, where a prominent and suitable red-stained rock stack called Brough of Ratter is a name derived from Raudabiorg. In 1872, six silver Norse amulets were found, near the site of an early Christian chapel. This, according to Anderson, makes it likely the battle was fought there, off nearby Duncansby Head. However, an area of cliff called 'The Berry' is found on the southern coast of South Walls. In *The Orkneyinga Saga*, trans. Hermann Pálsson and Paul Edwards (London: Penguin, 1981), the notes identify South Walls as the site of the battle, a view shared by Muir, *Orkney in the Sagas*, p.51; Linklater, *The Ultimate Viking*, p.64. Crawford, *Northern Kingdoms*, p.140 and Peter Berresford Ellis, *Macbeth: High King of Scotland, 1040–57* (London: Frederick Muller, 1980), p.69 opted for South Ronaldsay, while Thomson, *History of Orkney*, p.51 says the battle took place in 'an unknown location'. The weight of evidence together with the

tactical situation makes South Walls in Hoy off Cantick Head the most likely site for the battle.

13 *Saga of the Earls of Orkney*, trans. Jesch, Chapter 26, pp.99–101.

14 Ibid.

15 Ibid., pp.99–100.

16 Ibid.

17 Ibid.

18 Ibid., p.101.

19 Ibid., Chapter 27, p.102.

20 Ibid., Chapter 28, p.103.

21 Ibid., Chapter 29, p.104. Kirkwall comes from the Norse name Kirkjuvár (or Kirkjuvgar) meaning a bay with a church on it.

22 Ibid. Papa Stronsay was 'Papey in Litla' in Norse. The account of the farm-burning is based on the saga. It has been suggested, though, that due to the burial of Earl Rognvald in Papa Westray, the saga's author may have confused the two islands.

23 Ibid.

24 Ibid., pp.104–05.

25 Ibid., Chapter 29, p.105.

26 Ibid., Chapter 30, p.106. Papa Westray is 'Papey hin Meiri' in Norse. The presence of the 12th-century hogback gravestone has fuelled speculation that Earl Rognvald was killed on the island, rather than on Papa Stronsay. However, there is no proof it was ever used to mark the earl's burial place. The medieval gravestone itself was later moved and reused over the grave of a local landowner.

27 *Saga of the Earls of Orkney*, trans. Jesch, Chapter 30, p.71; Nic Fields, *God's Viking: Harald Hardrada: The Varangian Guard of the Byzantine Emperors AD 998 to 1204* (Barnsley: Pen & Sword, 2019), pp.191–92; Hollway, *The Last Viking*, pp.248–50.

28 *Saga of the Earls of Orkney*, trans. Jesch, Chapter 31, p.74. Also see *Orkneyinga Saga*, trans. Hjaltalin and Goudie, pp.42–43.

29 *Saga of the Earls of Orkney*, trans. Jesch, Chapter 31, p.109.

30 Thomson, *History of Orkney*, p.52.

31 Ibid. Also Crawford, *Northern Kingdoms*, pp.146–47.

32 *Saga of the Earls of Orkney*, trans. Jesch, Chapter 32, p.111.

33 Ibid., 'Troll's Skerries' probably refers to the Out Skerries in the north of Shetland.

34 Crawford, *Northern Kingdoms*, pp.162–63. Crawford lists Thorfinn's death as 'early 1060s'. See note 1 in Chapter 14 for a more detailed look at this problem of ascribing an accurate date to this.

CHAPTER 14

1   *Saga of the Earls of Orkney*, trans. Jesch, Chapter 32, p.111. Also see *Orkneyinga Saga*, trans. Pálsson and Edwards, Chapter 32, p.75 and *Orkneyinga Saga*, trans. Hjaltalin and Goudie, Chapter XXI, p.44. Crawford, *Northern Kingdoms*, p.130 proposes Thorfinn died in 'the early 1060s', while *Orkneyinga Saga*, trans. Hjaltalin and Goudie, contains notes by Joseph Anderson, which propose a date of 1064. Muir, *Orkney in the Sagas*, proposes an earlier date of *c.* 1058, while Duncan, *The Kingship of the Scots, 842–1292*, p.42 goes further back, suggesting Thorfinn died in the early 1050s. My estimate of *c.* 1058–64 is principally based on other dated events in Scandinavia and the British Isles. One of these relates to the age of Thorfinn's widow Ingibiorg (or Ingibjorg in its Norse form). Essentially, choosing a date for Earl Thorfinn's death is a little like the game of pinning the tail on the donkey.

2   Kelly de Vries, *The Norwegian Invasion of England in 1066* (Woodbridge: Boydell & Brewer, 1999), p.78; Duncan, *The Kingship of the Scots, 842–1292*, pp.42–48.

3   *Tigernach Chronicles*, in Anderson (ed.), *Early Sources in Scottish History*, Vol II, 1 (entry for 1058).

4   This point was first made in Crawford, *Northern Kingdoms*, pp.85–86.

5   This possibility is explored in Thomson, *History of Orkney*, p.52.

6   Ingieborg's family are described in *Heimskringla*, Saga of Ólaf Haraldsson (St Ólaf's Saga), Chapter 194 and Saga of Harold Sigurdsson, Chapter 46.

7   *Saga of the Earls of Orkney*, trans. Jesch, Chapter 33, p.113.

8   Ibid.

9   Stenton, *Anglo-Saxon England*, pp.586–88.

10 *Heimskringla*, Harald Sigurdsson's Saga, Chapter 80. Also Fields, *God's Viking*, p.222, and Hollway, *The Last Viking*, p.310.

11 *Saga of the Earls of Orkney*, trans. Jesch, Chapter 34, p.115; *Heimskringla*, Harald Sigurdsson's Saga, Chapter 87; *Gesta Regum Anglorum*, ed. and trans. Mynors and Thomson, Vol I, pp.420–21; *Anglo-Saxon Chronicle*, trans. Ingham, pp.146–51, entry for 1066.

12 Fields, *God's Viking*, p.222.

13 *Heimskringla*, Harald Sigurdsson's Saga, Chapter 88. Also Forte, Oram and Pederson, *Viking Empires*, p.210, and Fields, *God's Viking*, pp.223–24.

14 *Heimskringla*, Harald Sigurdsson's Saga, Chapter 96. It is thought that the Icelandic *skald* was killed at Stamford Bridge, shortly after his king. See also Fields, *God's Viking*, pp.231–34.

15 *Saga of the Earls of Orkney*, trans. Jesch, Chapter 34, pp.115–16. *The Saga of the Earls of Orkney* adds a peculiar rider to the story. It claims that

when Harald Hardrada was killed in battle, hundreds of miles away, at the same moment, his daughter Maria died too. It was claimed in the saga that some people thought the two shared a single life between them. Also see Fields, *God's Viking*, p.232; Hollway, *The Last Viking*, p.338.

16   *Anglo-Saxon Chronicle*, trans. Ingham, pp.146–51, entry for 1066. Also Forte, Oram and Pederson, *Viking Empires*, pp.210–11.

17   *Saga of the Earls of Orkney*, trans. Jesch, Chapter 34, p.78.

18   Forte, Oram and Pederson, *Viking Empires*, pp.230–32.

19   *Saga of the Earls of Orkney*, trans. Jesch, Chapter 34, pp.115–16.

20   Ibid, p.116.

21   Ibid., Chapter 36, p.120.

22   Ibid., Chapter 38, p.122.

23   Ibid.

CHAPTER 15

1   *Heimskringla*, Magnus Barefoot's Saga, Chapters 1–8. Also Jones, *A History of the Vikings*, p.392, and Rosemary Power, 'Magnus Barelegs' Expeditions to the West', *Scottish Historical Review*, Vol. 65 (1986), pp.107–32.

2   *Heimskringla*, Magnus Barefoot's Saga, Chapter 9; *Saga of the Earls of Orkney*, trans. Jesch, Chapter 38, p.122.

3   *Heimskringla*, Magnus Barefoot's Saga, Chapter 9; *Saga of the Earls of Orkney*, trans. Jesch, Chapter 39, p.123.

4   Power, 'Magnus Barelegs' Expeditions', pp.230–42, provides a detailed account of the expedition as well as Magnus' second one in the same region four years later.

5   *Saga of the Earls of Orkney*, trans. Jesch, Chapter 39, p.123.

6   Power, 'Magnus Barelegs' Expeditions', pp.233–34.

7   Orderic Vitalis, *Historia Ecclesiastica*, quoted in Power, 'Magnus Barelegs' Expeditions', p.119. Magnus' age is provided in *Historia de Antiquitate Regnum Norwegiensium*, in Anderson (ed.), *Early Sources in Scottish History*, Vol. II, pp.110–11.

8   *Saga of the Earls of Orkney*, trans. Jesch, Chapter 39, p.123. Also see Thomson, *History of Orkney*, p.55, who first suggested that Magnus wasn't necessarily displaying his faith when refusing to participate in the battle, doing so for his own more personal reasons. In the saga the episode was so described in order to portray Magnus as a future saint. In any case, it was clear from later in Magnus' career that he was no pacifist. He'd willingly fought – when he wasn't doing so on behalf of King Magnus.

9   *Saga of the Earls of Orkney*, trans. Jesch, Chapter 39, pp.123–24. Power, 'Magnus Barelegs' Expeditions', pp.124–29.

10 Richard Oram, *David I: The King Who Made Scotland* (Stroud: Tempus Publishing, 2004), p.48.

11 *Saga of the Earls of Orkney*, trans. Jesch, Chapter 40, p.125.

12 *Heimskringla*, Magnus Barefoot's Saga, Chapter 27.

13 *Heimskringla*, Saga of Sigurd the Crusader, and his brothers Eystein and Óláf, Chapter 2; *Saga of the Earls of Orkney*, trans. Jesch, Chapter 43, p.129.

14 Ibid., Chapter 45, p.90; *Longer Magnus Saga*, trans. Hermann Pálsson and Paul Edwards (Oxford: Perpetua Press, 1987; repr. St Magnus Cathedral, 1996), Chapter 14. Like most of this saga, its aim was to portray Magnus as a saintly figure. If his wife was indeed an unsuitable sexual partner, then among the Norse nobility it was perfectly acceptable to have a mistress or a concubine. There is no evidence to suggest Magnus was chaste and took cold baths – other than in this rewriting of events in a more favourably Christian light.

15 *Longer Magnus Saga*, trans. Pálsson and Edwards, Chapter 14.

16 *Saga of the Earls of Orkney*, trans. Jesch, Chapter 46, p.132; Oram, *David I*, pp.60–62.

17 *Longer Magnus Saga*, trans. Pálsson and Edwards, Chapter 19. Also Thomson, *History of Orkney*, p.58.

18 *Longer Magnus Saga*, trans. Pálsson and Edwards, Chapter 8. Also Anderson (ed.), *Brut y Tywyssogion, Early Sources in Scottish History*, Vol. II, pp.144–45; Archibald A. M. Duncan, *Scotland: The Making of a Kingdom* (Edinburgh: Oliver and Boyd, 1975), p.128.

19 Arthur Jones, *History of Gruffydd ap Cynan* (Manchester: Manchester University Press, 1910), pp.37–38. Thomson, *History of Orkney*, p.57 recounts a tale where during a raid, Vikings from Orkney landed at the mouth of the River Usk in south Wales, near modern-day Newport, and ransacked a church there dedicated to the Welsh St Gwynllyw (or 'St Woolos' in English). This is now Newport Cathedral, and the saint's burial place. According to legend the Welsh warrior saint appeared on horseback and raised a storm which scattered the Viking longships. Thomson surmises that the ruined medieval Twinly Kirk on the Orkney island of Swona in the Pentland Firth may well have been dedicated to the Welsh saint because of the effect this apparition had on the raiders. He suggests that the youthful Magnus might even have participated in this failed Viking raid. Also see A. W., *Vitae Sanctorum Britanniae et Genealogiae: Classic Texts in Medieval Welsh Studies, Vol 1 – The Lives and Genealogies of the Welsh Saints* (Cardiff: Welsh Academic Press, 1944, reprinted 2013), pp.172–73. Also see 'Canmore.org.uk' – Swona, Twinly Kirk for an archaeological appreciation of the chapel's ruins.

20 Thomson, *History of Orkney*, p.58.

21 Crawford, *Northern Kingdoms*, p.192; Thomson, *History of Orkney*, p.44.

22 *Saga of the Earls of Orkney*, trans. Jesch, Chapter 47, p.133. The term *göding* (or *gæðingr* in the original Norse) as well as their role in the earldom is discussed in Crawford, *Northern Kingdoms*, pp.173–74. The term equates to 'man of good family' or 'man of property'. These were the men who primarily held the fate of the two rival earls in their hands.

23 *Saga of the Earls of Orkney*, trans. Jesch, Chapter 47, p.133.

24 Ibid. Thomson, *History of Orkney*, p. 59 contains a description of the ecclesiastical arrangement in Orkney at the time. Bishop William 'the Old', appointed in 1102, was based at the episcopal see in Birsay, which formed part of the archbishopric of Hamburg-Bremen. Then, at some time between 1109 and 1114, Bishop Radulph was consecrated in York, as part of the Anglican archbishopric's bid to expand its influence further north. Letters from the archbishopric of York suggest Bishop Radulph resided in Orkney, possibly in Kirkwall, but after 1117 his presence there was contested. The reason suggested by Thomson was that William was loyal to Earl Hákon, while Radulph (or Ralph or Radulf Novell) was Magnus' supporter. Also see De Geer, *Earl, Saint, Bishop, Skald - and Music* (Uppsala: Uppsala Universistet, Institutionen för Musikvetenskap, 1985), pp.82–86.

25 *Saga of the Earls of Orkney*, trans. Jesch, Chapter 47, pp.133–34.

26 Ibid., Chapter 48, p.135.

27 Ibid., Chapter 49, pp.136–37. *Longer Magnus Saga*, trans. Pálsson and Edwards, Chapter 25, claims Magnus was captured in the church, while *Magnus Saga*, trans. Pálsson and Edwards, Chapter 18, has him taken from the shore. Also see Thomson, *History of Orkney*, p.59; Muir, *Orkney in the Sagas*, p.65. Tom Muir convincingly argues that the *Long Magnus* version was designed to stir Christian outrage and was a less plausible version of events than the other sources.

28 *Saga of the Earls of Orkney*, trans. Jesch, Chapter 49, pp.136–37.

29 Ibid., Chapter 50, p.138; *Longer Magnus Saga*, trans. Pálsson and Edwards, Chapters 26–27; *Magnus Saga*, trans. Pálsson and Edwards, Chapters 12–13. Also see Thomson, *History of Orkney*, p.59; Muir, *Orkney in the Sagas*, pp.65–66; Crawford, *Northern Kingdoms*, p.199. Each of the three sagas recounts the death of Earl Magnus slightly differently, as described in Muir. In 1919, the remains of Magnus were found in St Magnus Cathedral, and the skull clearly shows the death-wound inflicted by Lífólf's axe.

CHAPTER 16

1 *Saga of the Earls of Orkney*, trans. Jesch, Chapter 52, p.140.

2 Ibid., Chapter 52, pp.140–41.

3 Ibid., Chapter 52, p.141.

4   Ibid., Chapter 53, p.141. Also see Gareth Williams, 'These People Were High-Born and thought Well of Themselves: The Family of Moddan of Dale', in *West over Sea: Studies in Scandinavian Sea-borne Expansion and Settlement Before 1300*, ed. Simon Taylor, Beverley Ballinn Smith and Gareth Williams (Leiden: Brill, 2007), pp.136–39.

5   Richard Oram, *Domination and Lordship: Scotland 1070–1230* (Edinburgh: Edinburgh University Press, 2011), pp.66–75; Barbara E. Crawford, 'The Kingdom of Mann and the Earldom of Orkney – Some Comparisons', in *Celtic-Norse Relationships in the Irish Sea in the Middle Ages, 800–1200*, ed. Jon Sigurðsson and Timothy Bolton (Leiden: Brill, 2014), pp.65–66.

6   *Saga of the Earls of Orkney*, trans. Jesch, Chapter 53, p.142.

7   Ibid. Also see Williams, '"These People Were High-Born' pp.138–39 for a discussion of the relationship between the earl and his mistresses.

8   *Saga of the Earls of Orkney*, trans. Jesch, Chapter 54, p.143. Also see Thomson, *History of Orkney*, pp.44, 176–77; Muir, *Orkney in the Sagas*, p.66.

9   *Saga of the Earls of Orkney*, trans. Jesch, Chapters 53–54, pp.142–43.

10 Ibid., Chapter 54, p.143. Also Oram, *David I*, pp.70–72.

11 *Saga of the Earls of Orkney*, trans. Jesch, Chapter 54, pp.143–44. Sigurd 'the Fake', according to the saga, took refuge in the Scottish court before travelling on to the Holy Land. However, it is highly likely he reappeared in 1135 as Sigurðr 'Slembe' ('the Noisy') when the fake priest claimed to be the son of Magnus 'Bare-legged'. His bid for power though, ended badly four years later, when he was captured and then slowly and brutally executed. For details, see Sverre Bagge, *Society and Politics in Snorre Sturlasson's* Heimskringla (Berkeley, CA: University of California Press, 1991), pp.169–74; Muir, *Orkney in the Sagas*, p.66.

12 *Saga of the Earls of Orkney*, trans. Jesch, Chapter 54, p.144.

13 Ibid., Chapter 55, p.145.

14 Ibid. The poisoned shirt segment of the saga might well have been a literary invention to explain such a quick and unexpected death. It may also, at least to the medieval reader, have suggested that sorcery rather than poison had been used, with spells said over the shirt by its two makers, rather than a poisoned ointment applied.

15 Ibid., Chapter 51, p.139; Muir, *Orkney in the Sagas*, p.67.

16 *Saga of the Earls of Orkney*, trans. Jesch, Chapters 51–52, pp.139–41.

17 Ibid., Chapter 57, p.149. Also Muir, *Orkney in the Sagas*, p.71; Thomson, *History of Orkney*, p.60.

18 *Saga of the Earls of Orkney*, trans. Jesch, Chapter 57, pp.149–50; Thomson, *History of Orkney*, p.60.

19 Thomson, *History of Orkney*, p.60.

20   *Saga of the Earls of Orkney*, trans. Jesch, Chapter 57, p.150.

21   Ibid., Chapter 57, pp.150–53; Thomson, *History of Orkney*, p.60. Much of this populist anger is probably over-egged in the saga, so it was less widespread than the saga writer claims, especially as the chapter dealing with the 'miracles' and the rise of the religious cult was clearly written separately and inserted into the sagas later. It even ends with a religious paean, which ended with a heart 'AMEN'. As a result, it has been suggested that it was added to the saga from the 'miracle book' of St Magnus. Jesch's footnote on p.153 of *The Saga of the Earls of Orkney* outlines this argument.

CHAPTER 17

1   *Saga of the Earls of Orkney*, trans. Jesch, Chapters 38–39, pp.122–23.

2   Ibid., Chapter 33, p.113, and Chapter 42, p.128.

3   Ibid., Chapter 42, p.128.

4   Ibid., Chapter 58, p.154.

5   Ibid., Chapters 59–60, pp.155–56.

6   Ibid., Chapter 61, p.161. Also see Jones, *A History of the Vikings*, p.86; Christopher Crocker & Ármann Jakobsson, 'The Lion, the Dream and the Poet: Mental Illnesses in Norway's Medieval Royal Court', *Mirator*, Vol. 20.2 (2021), pp.91–102.

7   *Saga of the Earls of Orkney*, trans. Jesch, Chapter 61, p.161. Also Thomson, *History of Orkney*, p.61; Muir, *Orkney in the Sagas*, p.77.

8   *Heimskringla*, Saga of Magnus the Blind and of Harald Gille provides a narrative of the cause of this conflict, and the opening years of the Norwegian *Borgarkrigstida* (civil war era).

9   *Saga of the Earls of Orkney*, trans. Jesch, Chapters 62–63, pp.162–65. The *mormaer* Maddad had royal blood, being the nephew of the late King Malcolm, and the cousin of Malcolm's son King David, who was then sitting on the Scottish throne. To say the *mormaer* and his Orcadian wife had strong connections is something of an understatement. They were also willing to use these to advance the careers of their offspring.

10   Ibid., Chapter 53, p.142, Chapters 63–64, pp.164–66. Also Thomson, *History of Orkney*, p.61.

11   *Saga of the Earls of Orkney*, trans. Jesch, Chapter 64, p.166.

12   Ibid., Chapter 65, pp.167–68.

13   Ibid., Chapter 65. Also Muir, *Orkney in the Sagas*, pp.77–78.

14   *Saga of the Earls of Orkney*, trans. Jesch, Chapter 65, pp.168–69.

15   Ibid., Chapter 65, p.169.

16   Ibid. Chapter 66, pp.170–71.

17 Ibid., pp.172–73.

18 Ibid., Chapter 67, pp.174–75.

19 Ibid., pp.175–76.

20 Ibid., Chapter 68, p.177.

21 Ibid., Chapters 68 and 69, pp.177–78. Also see Thomson, *History of Orkney*, p.61.

22 *Saga of the Earls of Orkney*, trans. Jesch, Chapter 70, p.180.

23 Ibid.

24 Ibid.

25 Ibid., Chapters 70–71, pp.180–82.

26 Ibid., Chapter 72, p.183.

27 Ibid., Chapter 74, p.187.

28 Ibid.

29 Ibid., p.187.

30 Ibid., p.188.

31 Ibid.

32 Ibid., Chapter 75, p.139.

33 Ibid., Chapter 76, pp.190–91. Also see Thomson, *History of Orkney*, p.62; Crawford, *Northern Kingdoms*, p.183–84. Crawford also provides a detailed examination of the role played in all this by Frakǫkk and the rest of the Moddan family of Caithness.

CHAPTER 18

1 *Saga of the Earls of Orkney*, trans. Jesch, Chapter 68, p.177.

2 Ibid.

3 Ibid., Chapter 57, pp.149–50.

4 Ibid.

5 Ibid., Chapter 57, pp.149–50. The St Magnus Way was established in 2017, covering a 58-mile pilgrimage route across the Orkney mainland. Only 20 miles of it, though, from Birsay to Finstown – seven miles short of Kirkwall – mirror the probable route of Bishop William's procession. The remainder of the pilgrimage route visits important sites relevant to the life of St Magnus. For more information, visit www.stmagnusway.com.

6 John Lindow, 'St Ólaf and the Skalds', in Thomas DuBois, *Sanctity in the North: Saints, Lives, and Cults in Medieval Scandinavia*, ed. Thomas DuBois (Toronto: University of Toronto Press, 2017), p.106; National Record of the Historic Environment: Kirkwall, St. Olaf's Church and Burial Ground, Site 2480.

7 *Saga of the Earls of Orkney*, trans. Jesch, Chapter 76, pp.190–91.

8 Thomson, *History of Orkney*, pp.62–63; John Mooney, *The Cathedral and Royal Burgh of Kirkwall* (Kirkwall: W. H. Mackintosh, 1947), pp.83–84. It

was unusual for someone to be beatified and then canonised on the same day. This, though, was before the practice was firmly established by the Catholic church. In fact, the canonisation of St. Magnus only received cultus confirmation at the hands of Pope Leo XIII on 11 July 1898.

9   *Saga of the Earls of Orkney*, trans. Jesch, Chapter 76, p.192.

10   The extent of Kirkwall at this time is very clearly described in Spencer J. Rosie, *Kirkjuvgar to Kirkwall: The Early History of a Danish/Norwegian and Scottish Royal Burgh, and a Study of its Charters* (Kirkwall: self-published, 2023), pp.16–30.

11   *Saga of the Earls of Orkney*, trans. Jesch, Chapter 76, p.192. The description of 12th-century Kirkwall is primarily drawn from Crawford, *Northern Kingdoms*, pp.204–07; Rosie, *Kirkjuvgar to Kirkwall*, pp.16–20; Mooney, *Cathedral and Royal Burgh of Kirkwall*, pp.93–96; Julie Gibson, 'Kirkwall' in Muir, *Orkney in the Sagas*, pp.74–75; Thomson, *History of Orkney*, pp.63–65. Also see Buckham H. Hossack, *Kirkwall in the Orkneys* (Kirkwall: William Peace and Son, 1900). Incidentally, 'perrie' is a largely Shetland word, meaning 'small'. In Orkney the word 'peedie' is generally used instead.

12   Rosie, *Kirkjuvgar to Kirkwall*, pp.16–18; Mooney, *Cathedral and Royal Burgh of Kirkwall*, pp.94–95.

13   Thomson, *History of Orkney*, pp.63–64.

14   Ibid., p.64.

15   *Saga of the Earls of Orkney*, trans. Jesch, Chapter 76, p.192.

16   This entire section is drawn from five main sources: Hossack, *Kirkwall in the Orkneys*, and Mooney, *Cathedral and Royal Burgh of Kirkwall*, were used extensively, as was *St Magnus Cathedral and Orkney's Twelfth Century Renaissance*, ed. Barbara E. Crawford (Aberdeen: Aberdeen University Press, 1988). However, the most useful source of all, somewhat surprisingly, is the well-researched and delightfully-illustrated work designed primarily for younger readers, Ruairidh MacLeod, *Building St Magnus Cathedral, Kirkwall* (Hostwick: Halmac Publishing, 1994).

17   Crawford, *St Magnus Cathedral*, pp.81–92.

18   MacLeod, *Building St Magnus Cathedral*, pp.32–38.

19   Ibid. *Saga of the Earls of Orkney*, trans. Jesch, Chapter 76, p.192.

20   MacLeod, *Building St Magnus Cathedral*, p.42.

21   *Heimskringla*, King Hákon's Saga, Chapter 323.

CHAPTER 19

1   *Saga of the Earls of Orkney*, trans. Jesch, Chapter 77, p.193. Also see C. Richard Bates, Martin R. Bates, Barbara Crawford, Alexandra Sanmark and John Whittaker, 'The Norse Waterways of West Mainland Orkney, Scotland', in *Journal of Wetland Archaeology*, 20 (2020) pp.25–42; Barbara

Crawford, 'Huseby, Harray and Knarston: Toponymic Indicators of Administrative Authority?', in *Names through the Looking Glass: Festschrift in Honour of Gillian Fellows-Jensen*, ed. Peder Gammeltoft and Bent Jørgensen (Copenhagen: Hans Reitzels Forlag, 2006), pp.21–24; Hugh Marwick, *Orkney Farm-Names* (Kirkwall: W. H. Mackintosh, 1954), p.116.

2 *Saga of the Earls of Orkney*, trans. Jesch, Chapter 77, pp.193–94.

3 Ibid., p.194. Thomson, *History of Orkney*, pp.69–70 suggests this was tied in with the Orkney earl owing fealty to the Scottish king in return for their lands in Caithness and Sutherland. Thomson suggests that Rognvald's acceptance of the arrangement was linked to his continued holding of these lands south of the Pentland Firth.

4 Crawford, *Northern Kingdoms*, pp.217–18; Thomson, *History of Orkney*, p.63.

5 *The Northern and Western Isles in the Viking World: Survival, Continuity and Change*, ed. Alexander Fenton and Hermann Pálsson (Edinburgh: John Donald, 1984), pp.114–19. Also see Thomson, *History of Orkney*, p.65.

6 *Saga of the Earls of Orkney*, trans. Jesch, Chapter 78, p.195.

7 Ibid.

8 Ibid., Chapter 78, pp.144–45. Also see Muir, *Orkney in the Sagas*, pp.88–89. For a discussion of the excavation of 'Cairston Castle', see Storer Clouston, *Proceedings of the Society of Antiquaries of Scotland* (POAS), Vol. VII, p.57.

9 *Saga of the Earls of Orkney*, trans. Jesch, Chapter 78, p.197.

10 Ibid., Chapter 82, pp.202–03.

11 Ibid., Chapters 82–83, p.203–04; Crawford, *Northern Kingdoms*, p.176; Muir, *Orkney in the Sagas*, p.89. Crawford suggests Svein's stronghold at Lambaborg might well have been what is now known as Buchollie Castle on the Bay of Freswick, or possibly a nearby Iron Age broch, the Broch of Ness, although there is no evidence there that it was rebuilt as a stronghold in the medieval period.

12 Knut Helle, 'The Norwegian Kingdom: Succession Disputes and Consolidation, in *Cambridge History of Scandinavia, vol. 1: Prehistory to 1520* (Cambridge: Cambridge University Press, 2002), pp.369–91 unravels the often-tangled web of this long-running civil war in Norway.

13 Ibid. Also *Saga of the Earls of Orkney*, trans. Jesch, Chapter 85, p.209.

14 *Saga of the Earls of Orkney*, trans. Jesch, Chapter 85, pp.209–10.

15 Ibid., Chapter 85, p.215.

16 Ibid., pp.216–17.

17 Ibid., Chapter 87, p.223.

18 Ibid., Chapter 87, pp.223–24.

19 Ibid., Chapter 87, p.225.

20 Ibid., Chapter 86, pp.219–20. The saga confuses the geography of the voyage during its account of the 'Crusade', with this visit to Narbonne coming before the transit of the Strait of Gibraltar. For the Narbonne backstory, see Frederic L. Cheyette, *Ermengard of Narbonne and the World of the Troubadours* (New York: Cornell University Press, 2001), pp.16–22.

21 *Saga of the Earls of Orkney*, trans. Jesch, Chapter 87, p.227.

22 Ibid. For a discussion of the *dromōn* and *shalandī*, see Angus Konstam, *Byzantine Warship vs Arab Warship, 7th–11th Centuries*, Duel 64 (Oxford: Osprey Publishing, 2015), pp.18–26.

23 *Saga of the Earls of Orkney*, trans. Jesch, Chapter 88, p.229.

24 Ibid., Chapter 88, p.230.

25 Ibid. Also see Muir, *Orkney in the Sagas*, p.92.

26 *Saga of the Earls of Orkney*, trans. Jesch, Chapter 88, p.232.

27 Ibid., Chapter 89, pp.235–36.

28 Quoted in Barbara Crawford, 'Earl Rognvald's Pilgrimage', in Muir, *Orkney in the Sagas*, pp.84–85.

CHAPTER 20

1 *Saga of the Earls of Orkney*, trans. Jesch, Chapter 90, p.237. Also Muir, *Orkney in the Sagas*, p.97.

2 *Saga of the Earls of Orkney*, trans. Jesch, Chapter 90, p.237.

3 Crawford, *Northern Kingdoms*, p.186.

4 *Saga of the Earls of Orkney*, trans. Jesch, Chapter 92, p.239.

5 Ibid.

6 Ibid., pp.239–40.

7 *Saga of the Earls of Orkney*, trans. Jesch, Chapter 92, p.241. In the Norse era, Stromness, now Orkney's second-largest town, probably wasn't a settlement but a sheltered haven for mariners called 'Straumnes'.

8 Ibid., pp.241–42.

9 Ibid., p.242.

10 Ibid., Chapter 93, p.243. Maeshowe contains runic inscriptions and Norse carvings, which might have been done during this January blizzard. See Michael Males, 'Imagining the Holy Land in the Old Norse World' in Aavitsland & Bonde, *Tracing the Jerusalem Code Vol. 1, The Holy City: Christian Cultures in Medieval Scandinavia*, ed. Kristin B. Aavitsland & Line Bonde (Berlin: De Gruyter, 2021), pp.455–76 for a discussion of this.

11 *Saga of the Earls of Orkney*, trans. Jesch, Chapter 93, p.243.

12 Ibid., p.244. Lambaborg has been tentatively identified as an old broch or similar pre-Norse stronghold on the cliff-lined coast south of Freswick Bay in Caithness, a few miles south of Duncansby Head. Ness Broch

and Bucholie Castle have both been suggested as the possible site of Lambaborg. See Crawford, *Northern Kingdoms*, p.176.

13 Crawford, *Northern Kingdoms*, p.176.

14 *Saga of the Earls of Orkney*, trans. Jesch, Chapter 94, p.247.

15 Ibid., p.249–50.

16 Ibid., p.251.

17 Ibid., p.252.

18 Ibid., p.255.

19 Muir, *Orkney in the Sagas*, pp.100–01.

20 *Saga of the Earls of Orkney*, trans. Jesch, Chapter 94, p.248.

21 Ibid. Also see Linklater, *The Ultimate Viking*, p.137.

22 *Saga of the Earls of Orkney*, trans. Jesch, Chapter 103, pp.266–69 provides us with a detailed account of the ambush and everything that followed. Also see Crawford, *Northern Kingdoms*, pp.219–20; Linklater, *The Ultimate Viking*, pp.147–50; Muir, *Orkney in the Sagas*, pp.101–03; Thomson, *History of Orkney*, p.71. Of these, Eric Linklater's account, as you'd expect from a great writer, truly captures the dramatic moment. The following account is predominantly based on the saga version.

23 *Saga of the Earls of Orkney*, trans. Jesch, Chapter 103, p.266.

24 Ibid., pp.266–67.

25 Ibid., p.268.

26 Ibid., Chapter 104, p.270.

27 De Geer, *Earl, Saint, Bishop, Skald - and Music*, pp.85–88.

28 Muir, *Orkney in the Sagas*, p.103.

CHAPTER 21

1 Crawford, *Northern Kingdoms*, pp.177–78; Thomson, *History of Orkney*, pp.56–69.

2 *Heimskringla*, The Saga of Sigurd, Inge and Eystein, the Sons of Harald, Chapter 20; *Saga of The Earls of Orkney*, trans. Jesch, Chapter 91, p.238. Also Crawford, *Northern Kingdoms*, p.23.

3 *Saga of the Earls of Orkney*, trans. Jesch, Chapter 103, pp.266–69, Chapter 105, p.271 and Chapter 112, pp.282–83.

4 Crawford, *Northern Kingdoms*, pp.23–24.

5 Duncan, *Scotland: The Making of a Kingdom*, pp.521–27; Duncan, *The Kingship of the Scots*, pp.146–52; Alister Farquhar Matheson, *Scotland's North-West Frontier: A Forgotten British Borderland* (Harborough: Troubadour Publishing, 2014), pp.18–24.

6 Sverre Bagge, *Cross and Scepter: The Rise of the Scandinavian Kingdoms from the Vikings to the Reformation* (Princeton, NJ: Princeton University Press, 2014), pp.54–55; Geoffrey Malcolm Gathorne-Hardy, *A Royal*

Imposter: King Sverre of Norway (Oxford: Oxford University Press, 1956), pp.124–46 explores the claim of Sverre Sigurdsson to the Norwegian crown and his rise to power.

7   *Heimskringla*, The Saga of Hákon 'Herdebreid' (Broad-Shouldered'), Chapter 18, and Magnus Erlingsson's Saga, Chapter 1; *Saga of the Earls of Orkney*, trans. Jesch, Chapter 88, pp.228–32.

8   *Heimskringla, Magnus Erlingsson's Saga*, Chapter 43. Also Bagge, *Cross and Scepter*, pp.54–55. The *Borgarkrigstida* lasted from 1130 until 1240, but from the 1170s the two main factions – each backing their preferred claimants to the throne – were the Birkebeinar and the Bagler parties. In theory the latter represented the establishment – the nobles, clergy and merchants. *Birkebeinar* meant 'birch-bark legs', a reference to the bark shoes sometimes worn by the Norwegian poor. This wasn't really a conflict based on social status, but on royal succession, and the ability to gain power on the backs of successful royal claimants.

9   Gathorne-Hardy, *Royal Imposter*, pp.180–87; Wanner, 'Royal Legitimation in Magnus's saga *Erlingssonar*', *Saga Book*, Vol XX (2006).

10 *Saga of the Earls of Orkney*, trans. Jesch, Chapter 112, pp.282–83. Also see Gathorne-Hardy, *Royal Impostor*, pp.192–204.

11 *Saga of the Earls of Orkney*, trans. Jesch, Chapter 112, p.283; *Orkneyinga Saga*, trans. Pálsson and Edwards, Chapter 112, p.224.

12 Ibid. The saga is incorrect in suggesting that Ólaf was the brother-in-law of Harald Maddadarson. Instead, he was the brother-in-law of Harald Eiríksson 'the Younger', who became a joint earl of Orkney with Earl Harald Maddadarson.

13 Sverre's Saga, quoted in Muir, *Orkney in the Sagas*, p.116.

14 Crawford, *Northern Kingdoms*, p.243; Muir, *Orkney in the Sagas*, p.116.

15 *Sverrisaga (The Saga of King Sverri of Norway)*, trans. J. Sephton (London: David Nutt, 1899), Chapter 119. Also Crawford, *Northern Kingdoms*, pp.243–44.

16 *Sverrisaga*, trans. Sephton, Chapter 120. Also Muir, *Orkney in the Sagas*, p.116.

17 Ibid.

18 Ibid.

19 Ibid. Also see Muir, *Orkney in the Sagas*, pp.116–17.

20 *Saga of the Earls of Orkney*, trans. Jesch, Chapter 112, p.283.

21 Ibid.

22 *Scottish Annals from English Chroniclers, AD 500 to 1286*, ed. Alan Orr Anderson (London: David Nutt, 1908), pp.316–18; Thomson, *History of Orkney*, p.73.

23 *Saga of the Earls of Orkney*, trans. Jesch, Chapter 109, p.276.

24 *Saga of the Earls of Orkney*, trans. Jesch, Chapter 109, p.277. This outpost was probably on top of Ward Hill in South Ronaldsay, with Harald's fleet gathering in Widewall Bay three miles to the south-west. The dating of what follows is problematic, but the likelihood is that the final confrontation between the two Orkney earls took place either in late 1195 or early 1196. For chronological reasons based on King William 'the Lion's' response to the battle, the later timeframe is the more probable of the two.

25 Sigurd 'Sprat' was the son of Ivar Flaw, who was killed near Nidaros in 1179 while fighting for King Magnus of Norway. Sigurd was described as youthful, handsome, and something of a dandy. *Saga of the Earls of Orkney*, trans. Jesch, Chapter 109, p.276.

26 Ibid.

27 *Saga of the Earls of Orkney*, trans. Jesch, Chapter 109, p.278. According to Joseph Anderson's notes in *The Orkneyinga Saga*, trans. Hjaltalin and Goudie, the *Fagrskinna* mentioned that Harald fell at Wick, and this location was adopted by Crawford, *Northern Kingdoms*, p.243. However, Anderson added that local tradition places the battle at Clairdon Hill, a mile and a half east of Thurso. An old chapel there, supposedly erected on the spot where Harald 'the Young' fell, was demolished in the 19th century and replaced by a family tomb, known as 'Harold's Tower'.

28 Matheson, *Scotland's North-West Frontier*, p.19.

29 *Saga of the Earls of Orkney*, trans. Jesch, Chapter 110, p.279. Also see Geoffrey Barrow, *The Acts of William I, King of Scots, 1165–1214* (Edinburgh: Edinburgh University Press, 1971), p.11.

30 *Saga of the Earls of Orkney*, trans. Jesch, Chapter 111, p.280. St Trǫllhœna (also known as St Tredwell or Triduana) was a female saint of the early Christian Church in Scotland. The remains of a chapel to her can be found in the Orkney island of Papa Westray.

31 *Saga of the Earls of Orkney*, trans. Jesch, Chapter 112, pp.282–83.

32 Ibid. Also see Matheson, *Scotland's North-West Frontier*, p.19; Barrow, *Acts of William I*, pp.20–25.

CHAPTER 22

1 *Saga of the Earls of Orkney*, trans. Jesch, Chapter 105, p.271 and Chapter 109, p.276. The saga claims that Hvarflod was the daughter of Malcolm, Earl of Moray, but Richard Oram, the leading academic in this period of Scottish history, has identified the father as Malcolm mac Alexander. See Oram, *Domination and Lordship*, pp.101–02. Thomson, *History of Orkney*, p.72 states that Hákon was killed in Ireland fighting alongside Svein Ásleifarson, while after his father's death Henry inherited lands in Ross.

2   *Saga of the Earls of Orkney*, trans. Jesch, Chapter 112, pp.282–83.

3   Thomson, *History of Orkney*, p.79.

4   Ibid., p.72.

5   *Sverrisaga*, trans. Sephton, Chapters 181–82. Also see Knut Gjerset, *History of the Norwegian People* (New York: Macmillan, 1915), pp.407–10; Bagge, *Cross and Scepter*, pp.50–58, 74–86.

6   Gjerset, *History of the Norwegian People*, pp.410–11; Halvdan Koht, *The Scandinavian Kingdoms until the End of the 13th Century* (Cambridge: Cambridge University Press), pp.84–85.

7   This meeting is outlined in the fragmentary *Inga Saga* (or *Croziermens' Saga*) compiled in *The Orkneyingers' Saga*, trans. George Dasent (London: Eyre and Spottiswood, 1894), Part III. Also see Thomson, *History of Orkney*, p.80.

8   As there is no mention of Earl David, it is likely he was already incapacitated by the illness that resulted in his death two years later. See Crawford, *Northern Kingdoms*, p.261; Thomson, *History of Orkney*, p.80.

9   Thomson, *History of Orkney*, p.80, citing *John of Fordoun's Chronicle of the Scottish Nation*, ed. William Skene (Edinburgh: Edmonston & Douglas, 1872), p.218. Also see John Duncan, 'King of England and the King of Scots' in *King John: New Interpretations*, ed. Stephen Church (Woodbridge: Boydell Press, 2003), pp.253–325; Stephen Church, 'The Earliest English Muster Roll, 18-19 December 1215', in *Historical Research*, Vol. 67 (1994), pp.1–7.

10 Thomson, *History of Orkney*, pp.80–81.

11 Anderson, *Scottish Annals from English Chroniclers*, II, p.337, pp.449–50.

12 Ibid., pp.450–52. Also Crawford, *Scandinavian Scotland*, pp.28–29; Crawford, *Northern Kingdoms*, pp.268–69; Thomson, *History of Orkney*, pp.80–81.

13 Anderson, *Early Sources in Scottish History, Vol. II*, pp.451–52; Thomson, *History of Orkney*, p.81.

14 Earl John's innocence was proven through the testimony of 'good men' – presumably leading landowners in Caithness. Crawford, *Scandinavian Scotland*, pp.28–32; Crawford, *Northern Kingdoms*, p.274.

15 Crawford, *Northern Kingdoms*, p.275; Thomson, *History of Orkney*, p.81.

16 *Hákonar Saga (Hákon's Saga or Hacon's Saga)*, in *Icelandic Sagas and Other Historical Documents relating to the Settlements and Descents of the Northmen of the British Isles*, Vol. 2, ed. Gudbrand Vigfusson (Cambridge: Cambridge University Press, 2012), Chapters 169–70.

17 Ibid.

18 Ibid., Chapter 156. Also Crawford, *Northern Kingdoms*, p.276; Thomson, *History of Orkney*, p.82.

19 *Hákonar Saga*, ed. Vigfusson, Chapter 173. Also Crawford, *Northern Kingdoms*, p.277.

20 *Hákonar Saga*, ed. Vigfusson, Chapters 1–3.

21 Ibid., Chapters 5–24. Also Sverre Bagge, *From Gang Leader to the Lord's Anointed: Kingship in Sverris Saga and Hákon ar Saga Hákon arsone* (Odense: University Press of Southern Denmark, 1996), pp.108–30. The dramatic story of Hákon's rescue is told in the 2016 film *The Last King*, and is celebrated in an annual skiing event, the *Birkebeinerrennet.*

22 Bagge, *From Gang Leader to the Lord's Anointed*, pp.121–25.

23 Forte, Oram and Pederesen, *Viking Empires*, pp.241–57; Gordon Donaldson, *A Northern Commonwealth: Scotland and Norway* (Edinburgh: Saltire Society, 1990), pp.74–79; Thomson, *History of Orkney*, pp.86–87.

24 *Hákonar Saga*, ed. Vigfusson, Chapters 317–19.

25 Ibid., Chapter 318.

26 Ibid., Chapter 322.

27 Anderson, *Early Sources in Scottish History*, II, pp.626–28; *Hákonar Saga*, ed. Vigfusson, Chapters 319–24; Forte, Oram and Pedersen, *Viking Empires*, p.260; Derek Alexander, Tim Neighbour and Richard Oram, 'Glorious Victory? The Battle of Largs, 2 October 1263', *History Scotland*, Vol. 2 (2000), pp.17–22.

28 *Hákonar Saga*, ed. Vigfusson, Chapter 323.

29 Ibid., Chapters 323–26.

30 Ibid., Chapter 328.

31 Anderson, *Early Sources in Scottish History*, II, p.356. Also Donaldson, *Northern Commonwealth*, pp.92–97; Thomson, *History of Orkney*, p.88.

32 Donaldson, *Northern Commonwealth*, pp.118–27; Thomson, *History of Orkney*, pp.79–80.

EPILOGUE

1 *Saga of the Earls of Orkney*, trans. Jesch, Chapter 105, p.271.

2 Ibid., Chapter 106, p.272.

3 Ibid.

4 Ibid., Chapter 108, p.275.

5 In most histories, the end of the 'Viking Age' comes in 1066 with the death of Harald Hardrada. They forget that Viking raids still continued for another century, thanks to the likes of Svein Ásleifarson.

BIBLIOGRAPHY

PRIMARY SOURCES

Anderson, Alan Orr (ed.), *Scottish Annals from English Chroniclers, AD 500 to 1286* (London: David Nutt, 1908)

Anderson, Alan Orr (ed. & trans.), *Early Sources in Scottish History, AD 500–1286*, 2 vols. (Edinburgh: Oliver and Boyd, 1923; repr. 1990)

Munch, Peter Andreas (ed. & trans.), *The Chronicle of Man and the Sudreys 'Chronica Regnum Manniae et Insularem'* (Douglas, Isle of Man: The Manx Society, 1874)

Skene, William (ed.), *Chronicles of the Picts, Chronicles of the Scots and Other Memorials of Early Scottish History* (Edinburgh: T. Constable, 1867).

Skene, William (ed.), *John of Fordoun's Chronicle of the Scottish Nation* (Edinburgh: Edmonston & Douglas, 1872)

Tacitus, *Agricola and Germania*, trans. Harold Mattingly (London: Penguin, 2010)

The Anglo-Saxon Chronicle, trans. James Ingram (London: J. M. Dent, 1934)

Annals of Inisfallen, trans. Seán Mac Airt (Dublin: Institute for Advanced Studies, 1951)

Annals of Ireland: Three Fragments, trans. John O'Donovan (Dublin: University Press, 1860)

The Annals of Loch Cé, trans. W. M. Hennessy (London: Longman, 1871)

The Annals of Tigernach (being Annals of Ireland, 807 BC to AD 1178), trans. Whitley Stokes (Dublin: Legare Street Press, 2022)

The Annals of Ulster, trans. Seán Mac Airt and Gearóid Mac Niocaill (Dublin: Institute for Advanced Studies, 1983)

The Annals of Ulster (Dublin: CELT, 2008)

The Book of Settlements: Landnámabók, trans. Hermann Pálsson and Paul Edwards (Winnipeg: University of Manitoba, 1972)

Egil's Saga, trans. Bernard Scudder (London: Penguin, 1997)

Eyrbyggja Saga, trans. Hermann Pálsson and Paul Edwards (London: Penguin, 1979)

Fagrskinna Saga, trans. Peter Andreas Munch (Dublin: Legare Street Press, 2022)

Flateyjarbók, trans. Carl Unger and Gudbrand Vigfusson (New York: Nabu Press, 2014)

Fragmentary Annals of Ulster, trans. Joan S. Radnor (Dublin: CELT, 1999)

William of Malmesbury, *Gesta Regum Anglorum* (The History of the English Kings), trans. R. A. B. Mynors and R. M. Thomson, Vol. 1 (Oxford: Clarendon Press, 1998)

Hákonar Saga (*Hákon's Saga* or *Hacon's Saga*), in Gudbrand Vigfusson (ed)., *Icelandic Sagas and Other Historical Documents relating to the Settlements and Descents of the Northmen of the British Isles*, Vol. 2 (Cambridge: Cambridge University Press, 2012)

Sturlasson, Snorri, *Heimskringla: The Chronicle of the Kings of Norway* (Project Gutenberg, 2009)

Dudo of St Quentin, *History of the Normans*, trans. Eric Christianssen (London: Boydell, 1998)

Inga Saga (or Croziermens' Saga), trans. Peter Clauson Undal, in Gudbrand Vigfusson (ed)., *Icelandic Sagas and Other Historical Documents relating to the Settlements and Descents of the Northmen of the British Isles*, Vol. 3 (Cambridge: Cambridge University Press, 2012)

Irish Annals of the Four Masters (Cork: Corpus of Electronic Texts, 2013)

The Laxdale (or *Lœxdala*) *Saga*, trans. Muriel Press (London: J. M. Dent, 1964)

Adomnan of Iona, *Life of St Columba*, trans. Richard Sharpe (London: Penguin, 1995)

Longer Magnus Saga, trans. Hermann Pálsson and Paul Edwards (Oxford: Perpetua Press, 1987; repr. St Magnus Cathedral, 1996)

Magnus Saga, trans. Hermann Pálsson and Paul Edwards (Oxford: Perpetua Press, 1987; repr. St Magnus Cathedral, 1996)

Njal's Saga, trans. Robert Cook (London: Penguin Books, 1981)

The Orkneyinga Saga, trans. Jon Hjaltalin and Gilbert Goudie (Edinburgh: James Thin, 1873; repr. 1973)

The Orkneyinga Saga: The History of the Earls of Orkney, trans. Hermann Pálsson and Paul Edwards (London: Penguin, 1978)

The Orkneyingers' Saga, trans. George Dasent (London: Eyre and Spottiswood, 1894)

The Prose Edda: Tales From Norse Mythology, trans. Jesse Byock (London: Penguin, 2005)

The Saga of the Earls of Orkney, trans. Judith Jesch (Edinburgh: John Donald, 2025)

The Sagas of Ragnar Lodbrok, trans. Ben Waggoner (Philadelphia, PA: Troth Publications, 2009)

Sverrisaga (The Saga of King Sverri of Norway), trans. J. Sephton (London: David Nutt, 1899)

War of the Gaedhil with the Gaill, trans. James Henthorn Todd (London: Longman, 1867)

SECONDARY SOURCES

Aavitsland, Kristin B. and Bonde, Line M. (eds.), *Tracing the Jerusalem Code Vol 1: The Holy City: Christian Cultures in Medieval Scandinavia* (Berlin: De Gruyter, 2021)

Bagge, Sverre, *Society and Politics in Snorre Sturlasson's* Heimskringla (Berkeley, CA: University of California Press, 1991)

Bagge, Sverre (ed.), *From Gang Leader to the Lord's Anointed: Kingship in Sverris Saga and Hákon ar Saga Hákon arsone* (Odense: University Press of Southern Denmark, 1996)

Bagge, Sverre, *Cross and Scepter: The Rise of the Scandinavian Kingdoms from the Vikings to the Reformation* (Princeton, NJ: Princeton University Press, 2014)

Barnes, Jamie et al. (eds), *Traversing the Inner Seas* (Edinburgh: Scottish Society for Northern Studies, 2017)

Barrow, Geoffrey, *The Acts of William I, King of Scots, 1165–1214* (Edinburgh: Edinburgh University Press, 1971)

Barry, George, *History of the Orkney Islands* (London: Longman, Hurst, Rees and Orme, 1808)

Bates, Davis, *Normandy Before 1066* (London: Longman, 1982)

Batley, Colleen E., Jesch, Judith and Morris, Christopher D. (eds), *The Viking Age in Caithness, Orkney and the North Atlantic* (Edinburgh: Edinburgh University Press, 1995)

Boyer, Regis (ed.), *Les Vikings et leur Civilisation* (Paris: Mouton Histoire, 1976)

Brundsen, George M., *Thorfinn the Mighty: The Ultimate Viking* (Stroud: The History Press, 2009)

Cannon, John (ed.), *The Oxford Companion to English History* (Oxford: Oxford University Press, 1997)

Carver, Martin, *Portmahomack: Monastery of the Picts* (Edinburgh: Edinburgh University Press, 2008)

Cheyette, Frederic L., *Ermengard of Narbonne and the World of the Troubadours* (New York: Cornell University Press, 2001)

Church, Stephen (ed.), *King John: New Interpretations* (Woodbridge: Boydell Press, 2003)

Clancy, T. O. (ed.), *The Triumph Tree: Scotland's Earliest Poetry, AD 550–1350* (Edinburgh: Canongate Press, 1998)

Clarkson, Tim, *Strathclyde and the Anglo-Saxons in the Viking Age* (Edinburgh: John Donald, 2014)

Clouston, J. Storer (ed.), *Records of the Earldom of Orkney, 1299–1614* (Edinburgh: Scottish History Society, 1914)

Clunies Ross, Margaret (ed.), *Old Icelandic Literature and Society* (Cambridge: Cambridge University Press, 2000)

Crawford, Barbara E., *Scandinavian Scotland* (Leicester: Leicester University Press, 1987)

Crawford, Barbara E. (ed.), *St Magnus Cathedral and Orkney's Twelfth Century Renaissance* (Aberdeen: Aberdeen University Press, 1988)

Crawford, Barbara E., *The Northern Kingdoms: Orkney and Caithness from AD 870 to 1470* (Edinburgh: John Donald, 2013)

Crossley-Holland, Kevin, *The Anglo-Saxon World: An Anthology* (Oxford: Oxford University Press, 1999)

De Geer, Ingrid; *Earl, Saint, Bishop, Skald - and Music: The Orkney Earldom of the Twelth Century: A Musicological Study* (Uppsala: Uppsala Universistet, Institutionen för Musikvetenskap, 1985)

De Vries, Kelly, *The Norwegian Invasion of England in 1066* (Woodbridge: Boydell & Brewer, 1999)

Dickinson, William, *Scotland from Earliest Times to 1603* (Edinburgh: Thomas Nelson, 1961)

Donaldson, Gordon, *A Northern Commonwealth: Scotland and Norway* (Edinburgh: Saltire Society, 1990)

Driscoll, S. T, *Alba: The Gaelic Kingdom of Scotland, AD 800–1124* (Edinburgh: Birlinn, 2001)

DuBois, Thomas (ed.), *Sanctity in the North: Saints, Lives, and Cults in Medieval Scandinavia* (Toronto: University of Toronto Press, 2017)

Duffy, Seán, *Brian Boru and the Battle of Clontarf* (Dublin: Gill and Macmillan, 2013)

Duncan, Archibald A. M., *Scotland: The Making of a Kingdom* (Edinburgh: Oliver and Boyd, 1975)

Duncan, Archibald A. M., *The Kingship of the Scots, 842–1292: Succession and Independence* (Edinburgh: Edinburgh University Press, 2001)

Ellis, Peter Berresford, *Macbeth: High King of Scotland, 1040–57* (London: Frederick Muller, 1980)

Fenton, Alexander, and Pálsson, Hermann (eds), *The Northern and Western Isles in the Viking World: Survival, Continuity and Change* (Edinburgh: John Donald, 1984)

Fields, Nic, *God's Viking: Harald Hardrada: The Varangian Guard of the Byzantine Emperors AD 998 to 1204* (Barnsley: Pen & Sword, 2019)

Finlay, Alison (ed.), *Saga Book*, Vol. XX (London: Viking Society for Northern Research, 2006)

Foote, Peter, and Wilson, David, *The Viking Achievement: The Society and Culture of Early Medieval Scandinavia* (London: Sidgwick and Jackson, 1990)

Forte, Angelo, Oram, Richard, and Pedersen, Frederik, *Viking Empires* (Cambridge: Cambridge University Press, 2005)

Foster, Sally, *Picts, Gaels and Scots: Early Historic Scotland* (London: Batsford, 1996)

Gammeltoft, P., and Jørgensen, B. (eds), *Names Through the Looking Glass: Festschrift in Honour of Gillian Fellows-Jensen* (Copenhagen: Hans Reitzels Forlag, 2006)

Gathorne-Hardy, Geoffrey Malcolm, *A Royal Imposter: King Sverre of Norway* (Oxford: Oxford University Press, 1956)

Gjerset, Knut, *History of the Norwegian People* (New York: Macmillan, 1915)

Graham-Campbell, James, and Batley, Colleen, *Vikings in Scotland: An Archaeological Survey* (Edinburgh: Edinburgh University Press 1998)

Grierson, Philip, *Byzantine Coinage* (Washington DC: Dumbarton Oaks, 1999)

Helle, Knut (ed.), *The Cambridge History of Scandinavia Vol. 1: Prehistory to 1520* (Cambridge: Cambridge University Press, 2002)

Hendy, Michael F., *Studies in the Byzantine Monetary Economy, c.300–1450* (Cambridge: Cambridge University Press, 1985)

Hjardar, Kim and Vike, Vegard, *Vikings at War* (Oxford: Casemate Publishing, 2016)

Hossack, Buckham H., *Kirkwall in the Orkneys* (Kirkwall: William Peace and Son, 1900)

Hudson, Benjamin T., *Kings of Celtic Scotland* (London: Praeger, 1994)

Jones, Arthur, *The History of Gruffydd ap Cynan* (Manchester: Manchester University Press, 1910)

Jones, Gwyn, *A History of the Vikings* (London: Oxford University Press, 1984)

Koht, Halvdan, *The Scandinavian Kingdoms until the End of the 13th Century* (Cambridge: Cambridge University Press, 1929)

Konstam, Angus, *Byzantine Warship vs Arab Warship, 7th–11th Centuries*, Duel 64 (Oxford: Osprey Publishing, 2015)

Linklater, Eric, *The Ultimate Viking* (London: Macmillan, 1955)

MacLeod, Ruairidh, *Building St Magnus Cathedral Kirkwall* (Hostwick: Halmac Publishing, 1994)

Marshall, Peter, *Storm's Edge: Life, Death and Magic in the Islands of Orkney* (London: William Collins, 2024)

Marwick, Hugh, *Orkney Farm-Names* (Kirkwall: W. H. Mackintosh, 1954)

Matheson, Alister Farquhar, *Scotland's North-West Frontier: A Forgotten British Borderland* (Harborough: Troubadour Publishing, 2016)

McGettican, Darren, *The Battle of Clontarf: Good Friday 1014* (Dublin: Four Courts Press, 2013)

McNeill, Peter and Nicholson, Ranald, *An Historical Atlas of Scotland, c.400–c.1600* (St Andrews: Conference of Scottish Medievalists, 1976)

Mooney, John, *The Cathedral and Royal Burgh of Kirkwall* (Kirkwall: W. H. Mackintosh, 1947)

Morris, Marc, *The Anglo-Saxons: A History of the Beginnings of England* (London: Hutchinson, 2021)

Mowat, John B., *The Placenames of Canisbay, Caithness* (London: Viking Society for Northern Research, 1931)

Muir, Tom, *Orkney in the Sagas: The Story of the Earldom of Orkney as told in the Icelandic Sagas* (Kirkwall: The Orcadian, 2005)

Olwen, Owen (ed.), *The World of the Saga of the Earls of Orkney* (Kirkwall: The Orcadian, 2005)

Oram, Richard and Stell, Geoffrey (eds), *Galloway: Land and Lordship* (Edinburgh: Scottish Society for Northern Studies, 1991)

Oram, Richard, *David I: The King Who Made Scotland* (Stroud: Tempus Publishing, 2004)

Oram, Richard, *Domination and Lordship: Scotland 1070–1230* (Edinburgh: Edinburgh University Press, 2011)

Pinkerton, John, *A General Collection of the Best and Most Interesting Voyages and Travels in All Parts of the World*, Vol. 3 (London: Longman, Hurst, Reeve and Orme, 1809)

Renfrew, Colin, *The Prehistory of Orkney, BC 4000–1000 AD* (Edinburgh: University of Edinburgh Press, 1985)

Ritchie, Anna, *Picts* (Edinburgh: HMSO, 1989)

Ritchie, Anna, *Viking Scotland* (Edinburgh: Batsford, 1993)

Ritchie, Anna, *Prehistoric Orkney* (Edinburgh: Batsford, 1995)

Rosie, Spencer J., *Kirkjuvgar to Kirkwall: The Early History of a Danish/Norwegian and Scottish Royal Burgh, and a Study of its Charters* (Kirkwall: self-published, 2023)

Sellar, W. D. H. (ed.), *Moray: Province Land and People* (Edinburgh: Scottish Society for Northern Studies, 1993)

Sigurðsson, Jon and Bolton, Timothy (eds), *Celtic-Norse Relationships in the Irish Sea in the Middle Ages, 800–1200* (Leiden: Brill, 2014)

Smyth, Alfred P., *Warlords and Holy Men: Scotland, AD 80–1000* (Edinburgh: Edinburgh University Press, 1984)

Stenton, Sir Frank, *Anglo-Saxon England* (Oxford: Oxford University Press, 1971)

Svenungsen, Pål, 'Kings, Crusades and Competitions: The Danish-Norwegian Conflict in the 1160s', MLitt thesis (University of Aberdeen, 2013)

Taylor, Simon, Smith, Beverley Ballin and Williams, Gareth (eds), *West Over Sea: Studies in Scandinavian Sea-borne Expansion and Settlement before 1300* (Leiden: Brill, 2007)

Thomson, W. P. L., *A History of Orkney* (Edinburgh: Mercat Press, 1987)

Thomson, W. P. L., *A New History of Orkney* (Edinburgh: Mercat Press, 2001)

Venning, Timothy, *Lords of the Isles: from Viking Warlords to Clan Chiefs* (Stroud: Amberley Publishing, 2015)

Wade-Evans, A. W., *Vitae Sanctorum Britanniae et Genealogiae: Classic Texts in Medieval Welsh Studies, Vol 1 – The Lives and Genealogies of the Welsh Saints* (Cardiff: Welsh Academic Press, 1944, reprinted 2013)

Wainwright, F. T. (ed.), *The Problem of the Picts* (Edinburgh: Thomas Nelson & Sons, 1962)

Whaley, Diana (ed.), *Poetry from the King's Sagas, Vol. 1* (Turnhout: Brepols, 2012)

Woolf, Alex, *From Pictland to Alba, 789–1070* (Edinburgh: Edinburgh University Press, 2007)

INDEX

Note: All earls and kings are Orcadian or Norwegian respectively unless otherwise stated.